Horace William Wheelwright

Sporting Sketches

Home and Abroad

Horace William Wheelwright

Sporting Sketches
Home and Abroad

ISBN/EAN: 9783744678261

Printed in Europe, USA, Canada, Australia, Japan

Cover: Foto ©Thomas Meinert / pixelio.de

More available books at **www.hansebooks.com**

SPORTING SKETCHES.

Home and Abroad.

BY

THE OLD BUSHMAN,

AUTHOR OF
"BUSH WANDERINGS IN AUSTRALIA," "TEN YEARS IN SWEDEN," ETC.

WITH ORIGINAL ILLUSTRATIONS BY G. BOWERS.

Printed in Colours.

LONDON:
FREDERICK WARNE AND CO.
BEDFORD STREET, COVENT GARDEN.
NEW YORK: SCRIBNER, WELFORD AND CO.

PREFACE.

THE following Sketches have already for the most part appeared in the columns of *The Field* newspaper; the one entitled "Lost in the Bush," in the *Intellectual Observer*. By the kindness of the editors of that newspaper and journal, the author has now gathered them together into a volume, and presents them to his friends as old acquaintances. He thinks it right to observe, that every chapter in this book is strictly matter of fact, except the sketches entitled "My First Steeple Chaser," "The Trotter," "The Jibber," "The Best Fourteen Hander in England," and "The Poacher;" in which—(although events took place much as read, and in which every character is drawn from life)—the author has, for obvious reasons, deemed himself justified in mystifying names and localities, and colouring plain facts.

PUBLISHER'S PREFACE,

AND

MEMOIR OF THE "OLD BUSHMAN."

WE sincerely regret to inform our readers that during the time arrangements were being made for the publication of "Sporting Sketches," an accident fatal in its results deprived the Author of his life, and so prevented his anticipated pleasure of revising this work through the press. It fell, however, into sympathetic hands, and it is hoped that the public will kindly excuse under the circumstances any shortcomings. By the kind permission of the proprietors of the "Field" Newspaper, we insert a Memoir of the "Old Bushman."

HORACE WILLIAM WHEELWRIGHT, known as a constant contributor to the columns of this journal under the *nom de plume* of the "Old Bushman," was the second son of the Rev. C. A. Wheelwright, rector of Tansor, Northamptonshire, and of Castle and Little Bytham, in Lincolnshire, and prebend of Lincoln Cathedral. He was born at Tansor on January 5th, 1815, and died on November 16th, 1865, in the fiftieth year of his age. He was educated at the Reading Grammar School, under Dr. Valpy. He was brought up to the profession of the law, and practised as a solicitor at Thrapston, Northamptonshire, between 1843 and 1847. From a boy, however, he expressed a strong disinclination to "settle" in the quiet work of a profession. He was fond of all kinds of field sports, and had a yearning for a life of wild adventure; we therefore find him, in 1847, an exile from his native land and a wanderer among the wild mountains, woods, and lakes of Sweden and Norway. The details of this part of his life are entirely wanting. In 1851 he went to Australia, and lived some years on the banks of the Murray, as a wandering sportsman in the bush. After his return to Europe he wrote and published his first work—a small book entitled "Bush Wanderings of a Naturalist; or, Notes on the Field Sports and Fauna of Australia Felix, by an Old Bushman," a new edition of which is now issued.*

From the introduction of this interesting little book we copy the following:—

"Six years' rambling over the forests and fells of Northern Europe had totally unfitted me for any settled life. I had no luck in the diggings. The town was out of the question; and to keep the wolf from the door there were but two alternatives—to seek work in a situation, or face the bush on my own account. I chose the latter, and never regretted that choice. I luckily fell in with a mate in the same circumstances as myself. The gun had often brought both of us 'to grief' in the Old World, so we agreed that for once it should help us out in the New. Our tastes were similar. The sphere of life in which we had both moved at home had been the same, and therefore all those little disagreements and collisions which are the inevitable consequences when men of different education, training, and tastes are shut up together in the close companionship of a bush tent, were avoided. For nearly four years did we rough it under the same canvas, with scarcely a single dispute, and very rarely even 'a growl.' We had, it is true, hardships to contend with, but we never met troubles half way.

* London: Frederick Warne and Co.

We took the rough with the smooth, and whether game was plentiful or scarce, generally had a fair share of it. Many a happy day did we pass together in the forest. Many a good bag of game we brought home; and often, though thousands of miles now separate us, do my thoughts fly back to the old bush tent and the old comrades left behind me; and the chequered scenes of a wild forest life crowd upon my mind like the vision of yesterday."

This yearning after the wild bush life of Australia is characteristic of that love of adventure which formed a strong feature in the "Old Bushman's" character. Oftentimes during the last four years, in his letters to the writer of this notice, has he expressed a strong desire to go back again and "leave his bones" in the Australian bush.

To the details of his Australian life there are several references in one of his other works; but the "Bush Wanderings" is an interesting work, which all naturalists should possess.

In 1856 the "Old Bushman" returned to Sweden, and took up his residence at Gardsjo, near Carlstadt, where he devoted himself to the life of a working naturalist, and there is no doubt that by his perseverance and enterprise he has added some valuable facts to natural history.

In 1860 he commenced his connexion with *The Field*, and continued one of its most welcome contributors to the day of his death.

In 1862 he passed a spring and summer in Lapland for the purposes of natural history. Of the nature of this journey he writes: "Lulea, Lap., April 14, 1862.—We have safely reached this place after a cold, tedious, troublesome, and expensive journey of nearly three weeks, being about 1000 English miles, in open sledges. It certainly has been the most laborious trip I ever took in my life, but I hope it will lead to some good results, although I cannot expect it will pay me after poor Wolley. I am just off to Quickiock.

The country looks gloomy enough to make one shudder—gloomy pine woods and snow-covered plains; but I saw two swans yesterday, and as the reindeer are getting very restless, and the Laps are moving up to the fells, spring will soon break upon us."

The result of this visit was, on the whole, very satisfactory. "I have collected," he writes (Quickiock, Aug. 4, 1862), "550 birdskins, 800 eggs, 1000 lemmings, and above 1000 insects, and a lot of other odds and ends—not bad work for two of us in less than four months."

Among the scientific facts worked out during the journey, the same letter above quoted contains the following: "Contrary to all our naturalists' dicta, the lesser European sparrow owl (*Strix passerina*, Linn.) *does* breed here, and I have got the eggs. Moreover, I shot three flyers the other day, one of which I have saved for you."

The life of a working naturalist within the Arctic circle, is not, however, all pleasure—for a little further on he remarks: "I long to be back once more among my books, for my life now is that of a savage. I have never seen a book for four months—nothing but the slavery of, day after day, first shooting and then skinning." We in England do not sufficiently value specimens obtained by such personal sacrifice as this.

In 1864 the "Old Bushman" brought out his largest and most important work, entitled "Ten Years in Sweden," a thick octavo volume,* The first half of the work consists of a description of the habits and customs of the Swedes, their agriculture, universities, nobles, clergy, &c.; and also contains the fullest instructions to those who wish to enjoy the sports of the field, loch, and river in that country. The remainder of the work is a valuable compilation of the vertebrate fauna of Scandinavia, interspersed here and there with original remarks.

* London: Groombridge and Sons.

It is a very valuable list to those who do not read the Swedish language.

The letters received from Mr. Wheelwright during the past summer, express the pleasure he anticipated from an intended visit to England in the autumn. With the exception of one or two short and flying trips, he had not seen the land of his birth for nearly twenty years; and his heart, in his wild northern solitude, warmed with affection towards the good old country where his boyish and happiest days had been passed. How that visit terminated we all know too well. It is hardly necessary to dwell upon particulars. A little circumstance occurred, however, prior to his fatal accident, which illustrates forcibly the apparently trifling grounds upon which our life or death depends. Mr. Wheelwright was at *The Field* office on the afternoon of the 7th of November, and seemed anxious to get down that evening to his brother's at Crowhurst. One of the gentlemen connected with the office pointed out to him that he had three-quarters of an hour to spare, that he might jump into a cab, get round for his luggage, and still be in time for the train. The poor "Old Bushman" hesitated, and, thinking he should not be able to accomplish it, decided to pass the night in London. Next morning, hearing of the arrival of his natural history specimens from Sweden, he resolved to stay until they were unpacked. When on his way to see about this, he slipped down in the street, and a hernia, from which he had suffered for years, thereby became strangulated. In this condition he went to his brother's house, was obliged to submit to the operation for its relief, and sank three days afterwards.

It is needless to dwell upon the character and literary qualifications of our deceased friend; all who are familiar with his writings possess the same means of judging. He was less a scientific naturalist than one of those pioneers who, by their adventure and daring, clear up points which would otherwise remain doubtful. He was not an accomplished scholar, but he was an apt observer, and had powers of description possessed by very few. The sunrise in Lapland, the details of his being lost in the snow, and the lifelike descriptions contained in his "Sporting Sketches," can hardly, we will venture to say, be surpassed. Readers, we think, will be most amused by his "Bush Wanderings" and "Summer in Lapland," just as they will be most instructed by the perusal of his "Ten Years in Sweden;" but in none of his works will they find more originality—more, in fact, of those qualities which mark the man of genius—than in his "Sporting Sketches."

But the "Old Bushman" was more than we have described him. He was a kind-hearted, highly principled, honourable, manly fellow, beloved by all who knew him, and long to be held in cherished remembrance. Peace to his ashes! He is buried in Crowhurst Churchyard, beneath an ancient yew, one of the few that have become historical by their antiquity. Decandolle and others have reckoned it to be fourteen hundred years old; and under its venerable shadows we must feel that our departed friend, who loved nature so well, has found a worthy resting-place.

CONTENTS.

	Page
A BEAR HUNT IN NORDLAND. WITH A DESCRIPTION OF BEAR HUNTING	1
SWEDEN. A SHORT DESCRIPTION OF THE LANDSCAPE, FAUNA, AGRICULTURE, AND FIELD SPORTS OF THAT COUNTRY. WITH A FEW NOTES ON THE ICHTHYOLOGY OF THE GREAT LAKE WENERN, AND SOME REMARKS ON THE NORTHERN SALMON RIVERS	6
DUCK-SHOOTING IN WERMLAND, SWEDEN	56
MY FIRST STEEPLE-CHASER	71
THE TROTTER	115
THE FISHING DAY	176
THE BEST FOURTEEN-HANDER IN ENGLAND	185
THE KEEPER'S TREE	219
THE RABBIT BATTUE	230
MY LAST DAY IN THE FEN	243
DID YOU EVER DRIVE A JIBBER DOWN TO A FIGHT?	257
THE LEATHER PLATER	275
THE POACHER	334

Contents.

	Page
GUN ACCIDENTS	363
ON THE ENCOURAGEMENT OF MANLY AND ATHLETIC EXERCISES, SUCH AS SPARRING; AND A FEW WORDS IN DEFENCE OF THE MUCH-ABUSED CUSTOM OF BRITISH BOXING	377
THE WRECK	392
THE AUSTRALIAN BUSH	411

SPORTING SKETCHES.

A BEAR HUNT IN NORDLAND.

WITH A DESCRIPTION OF BEAR HUNTING.

THE following description of a bear hunt in Nordland, in the winter of 1864, extracted from the *Hernosand Post*, will show that the chase of the Swedish bear is not altogether unattended with danger. The writer says: Time after time has the *Hernosand Post* alluded to the damage which has been suffered by the cattle in the Shelleftea and the neighbouring parishes through the attacks of bears, and of the various bear hunts which have taken place in this district; and the following little history will prove what adventures the bear-hunter will occasionally suffer, especially when he goes out to attack the bear single-handed, or accompanied only by one or two comrades. The narrator, a good old bear-hunter himself, was wont to call this "a bear-dance," and a lively dance it must have been.

On the 17th Dec., 1863, six hunters, peasants in the neighbourhood (more daring than prudent, although tolerably well armed with guns and spears, and accompanied by two hounds coupled up), set off to attack a she-bear, which, after having been hunted from one fell to another, had eight days previously been "ringed in"* on Graininge Fell, not far from Shelleftea.

They seemed to have apprehended little danger, and having

---

* "Ringing" a bear is making a large circle round the place where the animal was last seen, and proving that it must be somewhere within the circle.—Ed.

separated, they wandered carelessly within the circle of the ring to endeavour to find out the bear's winter-quarters; but one of the peasants, who had unconsciously come within a gunshot of her "ide," woke the bear up, and she suddenly rushed out upon him, seized him, and inflicted three deep wounds on his body—one on the thigh, another on the arm, just above the wrist, and a third on the face, which completely scalped his forehead, the skin hanging down over his eyes. During the struggle one of the hunters ran up and shot at the bear; but his gun missed fire, which was probably lucky, for in the *mêlée* he was just as likely to have shot his comrade as the bear. She immediately left the wounded man, rushed upon the other hunter like lightning, gave him a deep gash on one thigh, and mangled his head so that the hair and skin were torn off for a width of four inches. This man was so injured, that he was obliged to be carried home on a sledge, before they got his wounds dressed. A third hunter, who had by this time come up, attacked the bear with his spear; but in the hurry and confusion of the moment he planted it so badly that the steel point glanced off the thick hide of the bear. Suddenly the head of the hunter dashed against that of the bear, and he immediately shoved one hand down her throat and seized fast hold of the roots of her tongue, and with the other belaboured her lustily about the nose and head. The bear, now more than ever irritated by the punishment she was receiving at this man's hands, rose upon her hind legs and challenged him to a wrestling bout. The peasant, who, like many others of these peasants, was a good and strong wrestler, closed in with the bear and gave her a very clean back fall. Astonished more than ever at such unlooked-for treatment, the bear became nearly mad with rage, and uttering a tremendous growl, she at once sprung up and rushed upon the fourth hunter. He was, however, an old hand, and planting the butt of his spear firmly on the ground, with the head slanting out towards the bear, he waited quietly for her attack. Blind with rage she came carelessly on, the sharp blade of the spear went right through her heart, and she fell dead without a groan. The two hounds, of whom the hunters thought a great deal, kept at a respectful distance till the bear fell dead.

The old bear was followed by three young cubs about a year old, which of course shared the fate of the mother, but without giving the hunters so much trouble. The old she-bear was a very large specimen, yielding not less than 100lb. of fat, and a skin about eight feet long.

It is not, however, that we often hear of an accident happening in a bear hunt, especially unless the bear is wounded. It is a common idea here that in attacking a man the bear never uses his paw to strike with like a lion or tiger, which, however, is always the case when it falls upon horses or cattle. Moreover, it is not always the bear's custom when rushing on a man to raise himself on his hind legs, as is generally supposed; but he more often comes in end on end like a fierce dog. There is not much danger incurred from the bear itself in the "skalls," as they are carried on in the midland districts, when a couple of hundred or more men assemble and drive the forests up to the beaters; but much more to be apprehended from the shooters themselves. In the northern forests and fells, however, where men are scarce, the hunters often attack the bear single-handed, or with, at most, one comrade, and the chase of the bear then becomes a hazardous and exciting sport. It is principally in the autumn when the bears lay up in their "ide," or winter quarters, or in the spring, when they wake up from their winter's sleep, that they are killed. Two of these northern peasants, on skiddor (or snow skates), will sally out in pursuit of a bear, whose footsteps have been tracked in the snow, armed, perhaps, with a small pea rifle of the most primitive make, and which carries a ball of about forty to the pound (and yet a bear has often been known to fall dead from one shot, if hit in the right place), but also with a spear, upon which the hunter places his chief reliance, and which to my idea is a far more formidable weapon. This spear consists of a tough pole about ten feet long, armed at the top with a four-cornered steel spike, nearly a foot long, the point and edges as keen as a razor (which is always, when not in use, kept in a sheath), and a strong cross-bar of iron, about eighteen inches long, across the shaft, just under the steel spear. They follow the bear till they bring it to bay, and then attack it. They always try to force the spear into its breast or under the shoulder, right through the heart. As soon as the spear is well in, the hunter plants the end of the shaft firmly into the ground, and holds the spear strongly in an upright slanting position, the bear all the while pressing more and more on to the spear, endeavouring to grapple with the man, but prevented by the cross-bar. As long as the spear stands there is little danger, but the life of the hunter now entirely depends upon his good spear. His comrade, if he has one, now attacks the bear also with his rifle or spear, but if the hunter is alone—and they will always, if possible, be alone, because then there is no other to share the spoil—he finishes the bear as well as he can. I have generally seen the shafts in Lapland made of mountain ash. It must, however, be rather a nervous time for a man, face to face with an enraged monster, and only a slight shaft, and then a steel bar, between himself and eternity; and a man must be possessed of a pretty good share of personal courage who dares to attack a bear single-handed with such a weapon; and yet these northern settlers and little Laplanders often do so.

I used to be much amused at seeing the old parish clerk up at Quickiock, a noted bear-hunter, rehearse the pantomime of a bear hunt, with myself as bear. He was a very little, active old fellow, of about sixty, and he used to hop round me brandishing his spear, the shaft of which was covered with scratches and bites, till he would at times become so excited that I used to beg him to conclude the performance, lest by chance he might forget that he was only rehearsing a play, and had a man instead of a living bear before him.

These rehearsals used to remind me much of some other rehearsals of a rather different sort, when I used to have to stand up in quite another character, the reader will be puzzled to guess—Molyneux, the black prizefighter, and before poor old Tom Cribb. I first knew this veteran when he kept a public-house in Panton-street, but things went wrong with the old boy; and missing him from his parlour in Panton-street, I traced him to obscure lodgings somewhere in Soho, where I used often to pay him a visit. He was confined to his room with rheumatic gout, or something of the sort, but still could hobble about. It seemed as if he was deserted by all his friends, and very hard-up; but his room was filled with trophies of the past, and among them I recollect a silver cup which the old man would fill with ginger-wine, of which he was very fond; and I used to drink this wine out of the champion's cup, and listen to his description of past scenes in which he had been so stirring an actor. Till his great battle with Molyneux came upon the carpet, old Tom would sit quietly enough in his easy chair, only now and then flourishing, and making occasional passes into empty space at some unseen and imaginary opponent. His defeat by one Nicholls he dismissed very summarily, by the trite but energetic observation, that if he had only been in condition, "he could have pumped thunder on fifty Nicholls's;" but when he came to Molyneux, nothing but a *tableau vivant* would suffice. I had to represent the black, and after I had been placed in approved position by old Tom (with my head thrown forward, my left arm straight out, my left fist almost level with my chin), the old man would throw himself into attitude before me, and, despite his bandaged legs and rheumatics, would show me how he dashed the black's left arm aside, and inflicted that tremendous jaw-breaker which won the fight. "Gently, Tom, play light," I used to sing out as the old man became excited; and his fist used to come in dangerous proximity with my head, as he showed me how he finished off his formidable opponent with his favourite one, two. It was a rich play, but one which I was always prudent enough to rehearse upon ginger-wine. "When I go into that question, sir," observed a pompous old stump orator once to me in Australia, who was for closing all the ports, and leaving the colonists to depend solely on their own resources, "I become excited, but I could argue it for hours, sir, upon coffee." And so it was with me. I hardly know which might have been most dangerous, the old Lapland bear-hunter's spear, or old Tom Cribb's fist, if either play had been rehearsed upon anything stronger than ginger-wine or coffee.

SWEDEN.

A SHORT DESCRIPTION OF THE LANDSCAPE, FAUNA, AGRICULTURE, AND FIELD SPORTS OF THAT COUNTRY.

With a few Notes on the Ichthyology of the Great Lake Wenern, and some Remarks on the Northern Salmon Rivers.

It is no easy task to endeavour to give a good general description of the climate, scenery, or fauna of a country like Scandinavia, which extends from $55°$ to $71°$ N. lat., and occupies an area of nearly 300,000 square English miles, diversified with every description of landscape, from the low flat sandy plains and open turf mosses of the south, and the dense pine forests of the midland districts, to the barren fells of the north, whose snow-capped summits afford a scanty sustenance to nothing but the wild reindeer and the ptarmigan. Over so wide a surface we must expect to find soil of every description; and it is the diversity of landscape that adds the great charm to travelling through these northern climes. Still, rich as it is in natural productions, rich as it is in every branch of its fauna, it is a land comparatively little known to the English traveller, while almost every other part of the Continent, whose natural beauties can scarcely surpass this country in the summer, are as well known to the British tourist as the woods and glades of merry England.

Before proceeding into more minute details respecting the agriculture and natural productions of the land, it will be as well to cast a slight glance at the fauna of this interesting country, and the general reader can then be enabled to form an idea of the character of this wide-stretched land of " flood and fell."

Scarcely another country in Europe possesses so many attractions to the naturalist as this; for the varied nature of the landscape, with so few inhabitants scattered over its surface, mark it as a fitting home for such of the rarer species of quadruped and bird as delight in solitude and retirement; whilst its vast extent of coast, its magnificent rivers, and innumerable inland lakes, must render it one of the greatest interest to the ichthyologist. Most of the larger and wilder species of the European mammalia are to be met with in one part or another of this immense continent. The elk finds shelter in the midland forests, the reindeer on the northern fells; the bear, the lynx, the glutton, and the wolf are no strangers in the northern and midland districts; and the marten-cat, the fox, and the squirrel abound in every part of the country. Unfortunately the beaver is now nearly extinct, and the only memento we have of this interesting animal consists in an occasional deserted beaver-dam in some of the wildest of the northern forests. Strange to say, the wild cat is unknown here.

It is on account of the country having so wide and varied a surface that we find so manifest a difference in its fauna; and this is still further supported when we consider the nature of the land— open downs, deep forests, sandy flats, ironbound rocks, and, in the very north, snow-covered fells. These last must exercise a great influence on the fauna of the north, for every species of animal must have its limit from the region of perpetual snow. Nilsson, with his usual acumen, divides Scandinavia into separate regions for different animals and plants. Beginning from the very top of the fells, and following by degrees in a southerly direction the tracts which lie below them, we shall find that certain species of animal as well as plant are only to be met with on the highest fells, among perpetua snow-drifts; and also that other species are met with only in those tracts far removed from the fells themselves; and this will hold good whether we divide these regions in a vertical or horizontal direction—with this difference, that the regions in the latter are much broader than in the former. After these remarks, we will divide the land into the following regions for plants and animals :—

1. The perpetual snow region, which extends from the tops of the highest snow-fells down to the first bushes. In this region the only vegetation are a few ice-plants, lichens, and mosses; and the animals which belong to them are the glutton, the white fox, the northern hare (*Lepus borealis*), the reindeer, and the common weasel.

2. In the willow and birch region, the lemming, two or three field-mice, the fox, the wolf, the bear, the stoat, the common field-mouse, the little shrew (*Sorex pygmæus*), and one bat (*Vespertilio borealis*).

3. Pine and fir region: long-eared bat, parti-coloured bat, the water-shrew, the lynx, the martin, the otter, the long-tailed field-mouse, the common mouse, three or four species of lemming, the squirrel, the elk, and the red deer.

4. The oak region, reckoning from that tract where the oak first grows: the great bat, the hedgehog, the common rat, the grey hare (*Lepus canescens*), the polecat, and the badger.

5. The beech region: Barbastell bat, mole, dormouse, and roe-deer.

6. In such tracts where the black mulberry can ripen (Skania): Here they find fossil remains of the wild boar (*Ursus spelæus*), beaver, the southern species of reindeer, *Bos Urus*, *B. frontosus*, *B. longifrons*, and *B. bison*.

And, as regards the ornithology of the country, we shall see the haunts of the several species of birds just as clearly defined:

1. In the snow region we find the snow bunting, Buffon's skua, the wheatear, the raven, the rough-legged buzzard, the snowy owl, the short-eared owl, the ptarmigan, the white-fronted goose, the golden plover, the redshank, the dunlin, the purple sandpiper, the common gull, and the herring gull (by the fell lakes), and four or five species of diving duck. Nilsson takes his fell tract in West Norway, 60° N. lat.

2. In the willow and birch region, the meadow pipit, the blue-throated warbler, the brambling, the mealy redpole, the black-

headed bunting, yellow wagtail, willow wren, redwing, ring ouzel, redstart, marsh titmouse, Siberian titmouse, water ouzel, willow grouse, common sandpiper, common snipe, hooper, bean goose, wild duck, and teal.

3. In the pine and fir region, the fieldfare, the Siberian jay, the greenfinch, siskin, chaffinch, crested tit, coletit, great black woodpecker, three-toed woodpecker, gold-crest, wren, the crossbills, the redbreast, garden warbler, song thrush, tree pipit, capercailzie, black grouse and hazel hen.

4. In the cultivated districts, the hooded crow, ortolan bunting, yellow bunting, white wagtail, common sparrow, magpie, and swallow.

Thus we shall see that the vegetation as well as the fauna of this country has its defined limits; for, beginning with the cultivated districts in the bottom of the fells, where many of the trees and bushes peculiar to Britain are met with, we come (ascending the fell sides) first to the fir district and then to the pine. Above these we find the birch, and, higher up, the willow and fell birch. Above this we come to the district where nothing but lichen and moss can grow; and, above all, lies the region of perpetual snow.

The botanist can judge for himself what a field is here open to him; and it is no wonder that Sweden is able to boast of many well versed in this science, and the study of the entomologist goes hand-in-hand with it. But, to the geologist and lover of antiquarian lore, Scandinavia possesses still richer attractions. Judging from the fossil remains preserved in the museums of the country, many animals, now extinct, in former days inhabited the south of Sweden; and the bones of antediluvian monsters, which are yearly dug up in the turf mosses of Skania, are evidences of bygone ages. It is easy to carry the reflecting mind back to the period before man appeared on the face of the globe, when probably the waves rolled over the greater part of this land, and we can figure to ourselves monstrous fishes then peopling the waters, and reptiles of misshapen and hideous growth, drawing their slow length along the slimy oozes of the fens. Pass we on to a later date, when the whole face of the country gradually changed; the wild bull tossed his mane in these then secluded forests, the wild sow farrowed in security in regions untrodden by the foot of man, and thousands of gigantic elk and red deer roamed at will over the oak forests and wide prairies of southern Sweden.

"Whatever," observes Dr. Johnson — "whatever withdraws us from the power of our senses, whatever makes the past, the distant, or the future predominate, over the present, advances us in the dignity of thinking beings;" and whoever takes an interest in the history of the early ages of mankind, will here find much to occupy his attention and his thoughts. The rude implements of the chase, and the barbarous weapons of war, carry the mind back to ages when the battle and the chase formed man's constant and only employments. Huge barrows and cairns, and rude but stupendous monuments of stone, mark the site of many an ancient battle-field, or the last resting-place of the old Scandinavian warrior and king; and the rude hieroglyphics cut in the rocks on many parts of the coast, are mementoes at the present day of those savage barbarians who, in the early days of Christianity, spread fire and desolation over so great a portion of Europe; when the "viking's" bark spread her sails before the wind, and bore the dreaded sea-pirate to the opposite shores of Britain.

Our task, however, is with the present, and not with the past; and it only remains for us to add that, let his taste be what it may, whether he be a sportsman, naturalist, or merely a traveller in search of the beauties of nature, the wanderer here will find full employment; and perhaps there is scarcely another country in Europe where a stranger, during the summer months, can travel with so much cheapness, security, and freedom, as in this.

But to return to our more immediate subject. As regards the mammalia of Sweden, two hypotheses will hold good as to their introduction into this land. It is supposed, and with good grounds, that this continent at an early period was landlocked with the rest of Europe, before the Baltic and the Bothnia formed a dividing line of sea. Most of the southern species came over the dry land where the Baltic now flows, and the more northern species, such as the glutton, arctic fox, reindeer, flying squirrel, and some others, came from the tracts lying on the north-east of the Bothnia. Be this as it may, each species seems to be pretty well confined to the limit assigned to it, and only makes occasional migrations to other districts, guided by an instinct which it baffles man's ingenuity to account for.

Not so, however, with the ornithology of the north. The migrations of the feathered race are much more regular and certain; but it may be remarked that many individuals of the different families which, as a general rule, are only summer migrants to the north of the country, remain stationary in the south of Sweden during the winter, especially if the weather is open; and many ducks (although the majority leave the country) are to be seen off the southern coast, and even on the midland open waters during that season. Some other species are only partial migrants in the winter from the northern and midland districts to the south of the country, where they remain during the coldest season, and return to their more northerly breeding haunts in the spring. Among these we may mention the hooded crow, an occasional hawk, the jackdaw, nuthatch, mealy redpole, greenfinch, siskin, goldfinch, mountain linnet, chaffinch, purple sandpiper, spotted crake, dabchick, and one or other of the diving ducks and gulls.

The few that are to be met with in the north and middle of the country throughout the whole winter are the eagles, Iceland falcons, goshawk, all the owls peculiar to the country (with the exception of the short-eared owl), the raven, magpie, all the woodpeckers except the *Picus medius*, which is confined at all seasons to the south of the country; the crossbills, pine grosbeak, jay, Siberian jay, the waxwing, titmice, yellow bunting, sparrow, bullfinch, occasional flocks of redwing and fieldfare, and a diving duck or two, if there is any open water; and we may notice three others, whose slender frames appear but ill-fitted to withstand the rigours of a northern winter, but which I have seen in the Wermland forests during the severest weather—the tree-creeper, the wren, and the gold-crest. Why these little stragglers should remain behind after all their glad companions of summer have flitted to warmer climes has always been a mystery to me.

Some few species, such as the hen harrier, the grey plover, the pigmy curlew, knot, sanderling, and bernicle goose, have not as yet, to my knowledge, been detected breeding in Sweden, but are only seen during their migrations to and from their breeding haunts, as is supposed, in more north-easterly latitudes. With the exception of an occasional rare seafowl, whose peculiar home is in the polar seas, there are no regular winter migrants to Scandinavia.

Some birds are yearly becoming more scarce in the north, for instance, the shieldrake, bittern, ruff, lapwing, blacktern, black-headed gull, and golden plover; and, on the contrary, one or two other species are gradually spreading themselves more widely over the face of the country, such as the shore lark, Siberian titmouse, &c. Many of the summer migrants do not appear in the same numbers on each succeeding year. The nutcracker is a striking instance of this fact; and I could never account for this—it certainly is not altogether owing to a scanty supply of food.

That the British fauna is far richer in accidental varieties than that of Scandinavia may be easily accounted for by the fact of the former country being so densely populated and so closely examined, that it is next to impossible for a strange bird to show itself on the British shores without being at once noticed; whereas, such is the wild nature of the Scandinavian landscape, and so thinly are the habitations of man scattered over its surface, that a rare bird may come and go year after year without being observed by any one. But that Scandinavia is much richer than Britain both in species and individuals during the breeding season may be easily supposed when we consider the vast extent of wild uninhabited country abounding in suitable localities for the wilder, and to the British fauna, rarer species of birds, whose shy and retired habits lead them to seek more secluded and secure breeding haunts than any part of Great Britain can afford. We find, therefore, that out of nearly 360 species known in Britain, scarce 170 breed in the country, whereas, out of 300 Scandinavian species, above 230 breed in the north.

With regard to the Danish fauna, it may be regarded as intermediate between that of Great Britain and the north of Europe; but fewer birds breed there in proportion than in either Sweden or Norway or Great Britain. The climate and general appearance of the country, both in landscape and vegetation, much resemble the British Isles; and I thought I never gazed upon a quieter, richer, or lovelier landscape than when passing through the Belts one summer a few years ago. The country is well adapted to the habits of the southern warblers and many of the waders, and, lying in a direct line, as it were, between Sweden and England, it is more frequently visited by the rarer northern birds than the latter country. The south of Denmark is highly cultivated, and the whole country has a far more pastoral appearance than the opposite shores of Sweden. In the north of Zealand, however, are miles of barren moorland, which, without possessing the rich appearance of the bonnie purple heather of Scotland, are well adapted to the habits of the curlew, golden plover, and many other birds which frequent the British moors. The country, however, is level, and we never, therefore, meet with either species of a ptarmigan peculiar to the northern fells; and the absence of the Swedish pine-forests renders it an unfitting residence for the larger owls and such other species of birds as are peculiar to the forest tracks of Sweden and Norway. That noblest of all game birds, the capercailzie, is unknown in Denmark, and the blackcock is rare; otherwise the Danish fauna much resembles that of the south of Sweden, from which it is only separated by the Sound, a channel some few English miles broad. There are no rivers to speak of in Denmark, but large ponds, well stocked with the common fresh-water fish. However much the agriculturist may long to linger among the neat pastures of the Danish farmers, it is no country for the naturalist or sportman, who will eagerly hasten on to wilder and less-inhabited districts.

I consider the British coasts, generally speaking, to be much richer in the common sea birds than the southern coasts of Sweden; but the wild "skargord," or rocky clusters of isles which skirt the northern coasts, are the peculiar home of the seafowl, and the immense swamps and morasses, and the countless inland lakes with which the interior of Sweden is studded, afford secure shelter and breeding places for every species of inland aquatic fowl. In the very south of Sweden, where the oak, the beech, and the hazel, usurp the place of the pine and fir kings of the northern forest, the different species of warblers find a home as congenial to their habits as the groves and plantations of England; and as regards the general fauna of this part of the country, it differs but little from that of Britain. The severity of the northern winter is here little felt, and the spring migrants make their appearance nearly as early as in England, and generally a fortnight before they are to be seen farther up the country, where the snow frequently covers the ground in the end of April.

In the midland districts, where pine and fir forests of boundless extent rise on high stony ranges (intersected with plains and valleys of meadow and cultivated land, and dells where the birch, the juniper, and the alder vegetate in rank luxuriance), nearly every species of land bird finds a congenial home; whilst vast morasses, many of which can never be traversed by the human foot, rivers, and inland lagoons of every size, fringed with the reed, the bulrush, and the candock, abound in every species of wader and aquatic bird, which resort to the north in thousands at the breeding season. It is now that the British naturalist begins to meet with rare and new specimens, and it is now that the eye of the traveller first gazes on the true scenery of the north—and more beautiful scenery than Sweden displays during the summer months it would be hard to find. I have wandered over many lands, and have scarcely ever seen a European landscape to vie with this.

In the very north the appearance of the whole country becomes gradually wilder and more rugged, and high mountains and barren fells, covered with perennial snow, rising above the limits of vegetation, and towering over the pine forests which skirt their sides, are the home of some few of the very rarer and wilder species, whose habits are but little known to us.

Having now given a short description of the landscape and general features of the country, we will say a few words on the climate, natural products, agriculture, and field-sports of Scandinavia. It is easy to guess that, from the causes above-named, the temperature of this country is subject to great variations—so much so, in fact, that a man may here reside in three climates. It will not be within our present limits to enter upon any description of Lapland; suffice it to say, that in the far north, where the Laplander leads a wandering life, the reindeer are his only riches, and the culture of the soil is not heeded.

We may perhaps take the province of Norbotten, lying in 65° N. latitude, as our northern agricultural limit, and here the farmer has just three months to prepare his ground, sow his corn, let it grow, and gather it into his barn. The summer here is of short duration; but there is no night, and everything springs up by magic, as if to make up for the long winter sleep. The best barley, however, grows up at Calix, in 66° N., and the celebrated *alsike* clover comes from a parish of that name near Upsala. The real Swedish turnip, or, as it is called here, "Rotabaga," from a place in Dalecarlia, is principally grown here in gardens for culinary purposes. Turnip-growing for agriculture is as yet in its infancy here, and the principal sorts which are grown for the cattle are the old-fashioned white globe and yellow bullock; but they are neither by any means extensively cultivated. Of course in a country of such extent and diversity of landscape we may expect as much change in the climate as in the scenery; and the south, the middle, and the north of Sweden have each a climate peculiar to itself. In the very south it differs little from that of the north of Scotland; the cold is rarely very severe in winter; the spring comes on at least a month earlier than in the midland districts, and by the beginning of April all the spring sowing is finished. The country is generally open, and the woods have a true English character. The soil is often rich and good, but there are many sandy plains and deep turf mosses. Along the coasts of the Baltic and Cattegat are some of the best farming tracts in Sweden. The farming here is not amiss; but no attention is ever paid to cleansing the land, and much ground is lost by the wide stone and mud banks and broad ditches that separate the fields. Land is perhaps taken at, throughout the country, ten shillings per acre, and this, I consider, as too dear. The winters in the south are, however, always colder than in England, and the cattle are all kept up in byres throughout that season; but the southern farmer can work his land nearly a month earlier and later than we can in Wermland, and as a proof of the variability of the clime I may mention that in the Christmas week, 1860, our thermometer, up at Carlstad, was as low as 25° cold Celsius, while at Gothenburg, perhaps 200 miles south, it hardly exceeded 9°.

As to the farming in the very north, the reader may be able to form his own idea if he reads what I have written above as to the length of the season; and, merely remarking that Wermland is certainly *not* one of the best districts for farming in the middle of the country, and very much inferior to the south, I shall nevertheless give a description of the farming in that province, because I know more of it than any other; and, moreover, my short notices being as it were general ones, will pretty well apply to the Swedish farming throughout the country, allowing for heavier crops in the most favoured districts.

In the middle of Sweden the winter is long and severe, the spring delightful, and the summer generally hot and dry. When the thermometer falls as low as 20° Celsius it is considered cold, but is not unfrequently as low as 25° to 30°; farther north 40° is not rare; and the heat in summer is occasionally, but not often, as high as 25° Celsius. The snow generally covers the ground deeply from the beginning of November till April, and this is a long, dull, monotonous season; about six hours' daylight to eighteen of dark. Beautiful as is a winter's landscape, it loses half its charms when we have to gaze upon it for five months; and at this season a man can reckon upon getting little outdoor exercise on foot, and often for two months you can hardly even get into the forests, for the snow is generally too deep; but the sledging is then first-rate. Bleak as the prospect, however, is without, there is nothing cold within; every country house is thrown open—glad *réunions* of families and social meetings of friends celebrate this festive season. The tinkling of the sledge-bells ring cheerily through the frosty air; and nowhere are the hospitable rights of old Father Christmas more strictly observed than in these northern climes.

Now is the time for getting the timber out of the forests and the iron down from the mines. Driving out dung and peat-earth on to the fallows, thrashing and delivering corn, keep the farmer in full occupation during this season. The cattle are all snug in the byres, gates thrown off the hinges, the tops of the fences scarcely apparent above the snow; high roads are now little heeded, and short cuts across the country are made for sledging over the snow and frozen lakes as straight as the crow can fly.

Nearly all the birds have left for more genial climes, and all nature seems wrapped in a still deep sleep. But sudden as was the change when the cold north wind, drifting over the dreary deserts of the North Cape, buried the landscape beneath its icy mantle, it is no less sudden when the mild west wind of April comes with "healing on its wings," and the first summer migrant appears as the glad harbinger of spring. A few dull misty days, with rain and warm wind, and the whole face of the country changes as if by magic. The trees suddenly burst into leaf, the green rye appears from under the snow, and no one who had looked upon the country a few days back could believe that so much beauty lay hidden beneath the waste of snow. Now all is bustle out of doors—animal as well as vegetable life seems suddenly to wake up, and the farmer has not a day to spare in making preparation against another winter, which he knows will surely come again in due season.

Although the principal riches of the north are the forests and the iron mines, the country is much dependent upon agriculture; and to prove that great improvements are yearly taking place, we may judge from the fact that twelve or fifteen years since 36,000 tunna of corn were yearly imported into the province of Wermland, whereas now the export exceeds the import by 6000 tunna.

Every Swedish country gentleman is something of a farmer, living upon and cultivating his own estate. The principal part of his produce goes to the support of his household, and the sale of his surplus corn and timber from his forests covers incidental expenses. Thus he passes his time quietly and happily in the bosom of his family—a country gentleman or squire in every sense of the word, with just enough employment to keep his time occupied; and if he is not rich compared to the British landowner, his expenses are much less; and his estate supplies him and his family with all the real necessaries of life. But do not let the reader suppose that the gentleman farmer works here as in England. An inspector or bailiff is kept on every estate; and, as to the farmer himself, his knowledge is principally theoretical, as no one above the class of a peasant understands much about the practical part of the affair. It is not to be wondered at that we see true pictures of domestic happiness in the Swedish homes, where the members are so much more closely thrown together than in England. Hospitable and kind-hearted, a stranger is treated as "a friend and a brother" wherever he comes.

It is much to be regretted that the youth of this country take little or no interest in athletic games, such as cricket, rowing, &c., and the many other outdoor manly exercises in which young England delights (and which, whatever your soft-hearted carpet-knights may say, have tended more than anything else to bring England to the high position she now holds), for a finer, handsomer race of men than the upper classes in Sweden, take them altogether, it would be hard to find—generally large grown, and the average standard certainly above that of the English. And, as to the females, it is without the slightest flattery when I say that I have certainly seen more fine women, in proportion to their numbers, in this country than in any other; and the proud beauties of England would find it hard to "hold their own" when brought side by side with the fresh, healthy beauty of the north. And, rough and uncouth as the Swedish peasants may be, they are as "hard as nails;" and the thought struck me, as I saw about 100 of these hardy foresters marshalled together at an elk "skall," that it must be a bold enemy who would attack such men in their native woods.

The Swedish peasant is an original. It has been observed that "a Yorkshireman was the hardest study of man, not even barring a Scotchman; but a Yorkshire *farmer* out-Heroded even Herod." For the Yorkshire farmer substitute a "*Swedish peasant.*" You need never try to drive him out of his way. If you want anything done for you, you must let him do it after his own fashion; but on one thing you may depend, *it will be done.* There is something, to my fancy, very sterling and good in the character of the true "bondes" of the north; always civil and friendly, hard-working, cheerful, and honest, he generally farms his own little estate, and nearly always contrives to lay by a little money. He is proverbially inquisitive, and covetous after money; and it is wonderful, for a trifle, how far he will go to serve you. But the real key to his heart is a glass of corn-brandy.

And I may here remark that the principal drink of the country is a fiery kind of spirit distilled from potatoes or rye, about half the strength of our gin. This is called finkel or branvin, and can be bought for about 1s. 6d. the Swedish kanna or gallon, which contains four English bottles. This is the nectar of the Swedish peasant; and it has one great advantage in his eye, that he can manage to get comfortably drunk on it for 3d. The Swedish peasant is often a heavy drinker and a heavy swearer.

It is singular that, although a drunken peasant is no uncommon sight, it is a very unusual circumstance to see any one of the better class in Sweden intoxicated: they like their social glass, but they do not drink in the business-like manner of the English; and, moreover, somehow or other, they all seem to have found out the secret which an old friend of mine used to say he had been sixty years trying to discover, which was, "when he had had *just* enough."

For hard work commend me to a Swedish female servant. Her wages will probably not exceed 30s. per year and a few clothes, and yet on this she contrives to dress well, often to look very smart and pretty; and it is a pleasure to see the cheerful way she goes about her work.

Besides the peasant who farms his own land, and who represents the British yeoman, we have still another class, the "torpare," who is, as it were, attached to the estate, and does the principal work of the farm. Every large estate has so many of these "torpare" on it. They have a house and a bit of land on the estate; and, in consideration, are bound to work so many days in the year for their landlord. This I consider a most objectionable system, for these "torpare" never have a shilling to enter upon their little holding, which is too often in wretched condition. It is generally let far too high, and their day's wages are proportionably low; they have little time to work their own farm, and as they must buy everything from their landlord, because they scarcely ever are able to go elsewhere, they live completely on the tally system. They are almost always in debt. A poor "torpare" once in debt is never able to work himself out again. The system is certainly good for the landlord, for he gets a hard-working man in return for a wretched house and a poor little patch of land; but I am certain the day labourer would be far more independent and better off here if he received his wages weekly, and hired a small cottage to live in. But labour every year in Sweden is becoming of a higher value. That the Swedish labourer is just now in a better condition than the English labourer, is proved by the fact that in the winter of 1864 and 1865, the labourers round us, who were free and not tied down by this "torpare" system, were earning from 8s. to 9s. per week. Rye was not above 1l. 10s. per quarter, and pork not 5s. for 20lb.

The religion of Sweden is strictly Lutheran; and the Swedish priests exemplary, hard-working, and too often ill-paid men. There are no religious schisms or dissensions in this country, and the priests are far more respected among the peasants than at home. The education of the poor is much better looked after, and no one can take the sacrament without having first read with the priest. The consequence is, that nearly every peasant can read and write—all can read ; and this, I think, is rather a clincher against the argument that it is not prudent to teach the working classes too much. Nowhere do we see a more honest, hard-working, quiet race of men, taking them in general, than the peasants here. Even " in his cups" he is pleasant and good-natured; and there certainly is not in this country one-third of the crime in proportion to the number of inhabitants, which we hear of in England.

It is very difficult to give any idea of the value of property here. Very little is rented; almost every Swedish proprietor farms his own land. Estates are, however, always in the market; and a man with capital has no trouble to suit himself, and often at his own price. I have seen a 2000 acre farm, in Wermland, sold for 2000*l.*, and many others, not half the size, for double the sum. I should say, however, that 5*l.* per acre would buy most of the estates in Wermland; and 5*s.* to 10*s.* per acre (when lands are let) is, perhaps, the standard rent; and, in my opinion, this is their full value, considering the present state of the land.

There is a perfect mania in Sweden for buying estates, and I do not believe there is a landed proprietor here who would not part with his estate, if the price tempted him. Not one estate in 1000 is entailed; and, as most of the estates are fully mortgaged, and half of them bought on speculation, to be parted with again directly land rises in the market, the landed proprietor in the north does not feel an interest in his land equal to that of the British landowner, whose estate has been in his family for centuries. This is the true secret why the farms are made so little of in the north. Scarcely any gentleman thinks of renting a farm—his great object is to become a landed proprietor; therefore, if he possesses 1000*l.* or 2000*l.*, instead of renting just as much land as he can well manage, and throwing his capital into his farm, where he would be sure to get a safe return, he at once buys an estate for from 2000*l.* to 4000*l.*, puts what money he has into the purchase, and borrows the remainder at 6 per cent. He has therefore nothing left to come in with and improve his farm when he has once entered; and hampered with a debt which keeps him poor, he is unable to make any improvements on his farm which would increase his yearly returns. Of course this is not always the case; many clear-sighted men will make a good thing of it; but it is the general rule. If every man (unless, indeed, he saw it was a safe speculation) would limit his purchase to half his capital, or rent his land upon a long lease, we should then see agriculture flourish in this land, and not till then. When a man can help his farm, and stick to it, it is sure to give a good return; and this is proved by the peasants, who, notwithstanding their generally slovenly state of cultivation, by careful living and industry always contrive to lay by something. Do not, however, misunderstand me. I do not in the least blame a man for buying a farm, if he sees he can make more out of it as interest for his capital than he can get elsewhere. But this speculation is carried on almost to gambling; and many a man who buys an estate knows very little how to cultivate it to the best advantage. There is a loan society here which will always advance one-half of the purchase-money, but they have the first claim on the estate, and the mortgagees who lend the other half (for very often land is mortgaged up to the whole of the sum that it costs) have, I should fancy, a very poor security for the remainder. There are more ways of entering a farm here than one. Very often the cattle and implements go with the estate, and, in the case of renting, the whole stock is taken at an inventory, to be replaced at the expiration of the term, by which means it is possible for a man to come into his farm with scarcely a shilling. But I think that a tenant who really means to start right, and stock his farm properly, should enter it with about 2*l*. or 2*l*. 10s. capital per acre, and in this case, if he understood his business, he would be sure of a good and certain return. One great advantage a good working farmer would have in taking a farm here is this—he would pay only for the cultivated land; and as there is generally nearly as much waste land on each estate as that which is under the plough, but equally good (wanting only working), he could if he got a long lease (which every British farmer would of course insist upon) in a few years double the area of his cultivated land.

Of course, throughout this wide land, there is as much variety in the soil as in the climate, and there are few estates of any size upon which you will not find nearly every variety of soil which the farmer requires; but of course, like England, Sweden has its rich and its poor districts. Taking the land in general, I should say it was a stiff, useful, but poor and hungry, soil, with much deep good land by the sides of the river and lakes everywhere capable of great improvement by ground drainage and care. The standard crops of the country—rye, oats, clover, and artificial grasses—appear to grow well on every farm.

Rye is the principal corn grown in Sweden. In Wermland it should, if possible, be in the ground by the beginning of August, and the harvest will generally fall in that month. The measure in use here is the tunna, and on a rough calculation we may reckon this as equal to four English bushels, or half a quarter. The land is measured by the tunneland, which is rather more than an English acre. It is next to impossible to give a general average of the crops in the midland districts, for so much depends upon the weather and the seasons; and most of the land is in such bad heart, that, unlike the farmer in England, who can generally calculate upon his return with some certainty, the Swedish farmer can hardly ever reckon, when he sows his corn, how much he may get back. I know no country which wants it more, or which could be more improved by ground-draining than this, and the expense of ground-draining here is not dear—about 2*l.* to 2*l.* 10*s.* per acre. Artificial manures are coming much into fashion, although the peasants stick to "muck," and muck only. Guano answers well for an autumn dressing, but the summers are generally too dry to use it in the spring. I wonder, considering how much they are wanted at home, at the quantity of bones that are annually exported from Sweden.

A tunna of good rye will weigh from 260lb. to 300lb.; and its market price is always 15*s.*, and sometimes as high as 1*l.*

When properly done by, I have seen some rattling crops of wheat in many places, which proves that, with care, the land might soon be adapted to its culture; and I wonder it is not more attended to. An average crop will probably be about eight tunna, or four quarters, to the acre; it should weigh 300lb. per tunna, and average 25*s.* in the market. Red wheat is generally sown three-quarters of a tunna seed to the tunneland; and spring wheat, if they can get it in early enough, generally does well.

Wermland is not a barley province, but by good draining it might be made to carry good crops. It is impossible to give an average of this crop, which varies from six to twelve tunna per tunneland, and will average about 12*s.* per tunna, weight 260lb.

Oats, however, appear to be peculiarly adapted to this soil and climate. They are generally sown three years in succession on the same land, in many places six, and sometimes ten—just cast into the land, without any manure; and, notwithstanding this lazy-bed culture, the return will sometimes be six tunna to the acre; but we see often wretched crops, and it is not to be wondered at, considering what state the land must be in after such close cropping. The principal oats grown here are both white and black, and potato oats. They will weigh from 160lb. to 200lb. the tunna, and the price varies from 8*s.* to 12*s.*

Potatoes will average 3*s.* to 6*s.*, and turnips (Swedish) 4*s.* per tunna. The land seems well adapted to potatoes. On Gardsjö they generally plant fifteen tunna on three tunneland, and get back seldom less than 150 tunna. On good ground, carrots grow well up here, and occasionally the crop will yield 200 tunna to the tunneland.

Beans are but little grown, nor do I think the country adapted to them—certainly not at present. Peas, however, grow well in many places.

The clover crops are excellent; and as there is in this country no rich old natural meadow-grass, like the English meadows, it is the standard hay crop here, and very heavy crops they get. The seed is white clover, alsike clover, and timothy grass, mixed, 30lb. to the tunneland, sown always on rye or wheat early in the spring, often on the top of the snow, seldom on oats. A good crop will often yield as much as fifteen loads to the tunneland, and the price of a load of such hay weighing 400lb., will be 8s. to 10s., sometimes more. The general price of oat-straw is 5s., of rye-straw 3s. per 400lb.

The natural meadow-grass is coarse and rough, growing by the sides of the lakes and swamps, and there is no old swarth for pasture such as we see in England.

As I said before, the growth of turnips is but yet in its infancy; and, till the land is in a better state by drainage and manure, I do not expect they will make much head.

The general rotation of crops here is: 1st, A dead summer-fallow, followed by rye or wheat sown in August; 2nd, Grass and clover seeds in the spring, and this will stand two to four years; 3rd, Oats; 4th, Oats or barley; 5th, Oats or tares; and then a fallow and rye again.

I will now proceed to make a few remarks on the live stock of the farm, and wind up with some observations on the subject generally.

The beef is but poor, and little wonder, seeing that the principal cattle which are slaughtered are either worn-out oxen or cows past milking. Such beef costs about $2\frac{1}{2}d.$ per pound. The calves are killed when a few hours old, and such veal is worth 2d. per pound. It is a nasty sight to any one who has been accustomed to the neat, clean appearance of the meat in the London butchers' shops, to see the carcases brought into the market here in the peasants' carts. The pork and mutton are, however, excellent. They seem to have a curious idea, however, here, that " pigs will not pay for fatting." A good pig will generally weigh, when slaughtered, 400lb.; and the sheep often 70lb., when of English race. Mutton is worth 3d. per pound, and pork about 6s. for the 20lb. In the country every family kill their own meat, and October and November are the slaughtering months.

It is strange, considering butter and milk are the two staple commodities here, that the cows are not better looked after. The cow-byres are in general low, dark, and dirty, and the cows scarcely ever well done by. In the middle of Sweden they come in about the beginning of October, and hardly ever leave the byre again till May. During the summer they pasture in the forest and grass lands; and during winter their food is often little more than rye-straw, with a small proportion of hay. The race of cows peculiar to the country are small, hardy little animals, and the general yield of milk is 300 kanna (one kanna is equal to two-thirds of an English gallon) per year; but when taken care of they will often double that. About 3*l.* to 4*l.* is the price of an in-calver here. Milk with the cream in the country may be averaged at 3*d.* per kanna; butter 6*d.* to 9*d.* per pound, and cheese at all prices from 2*d.* to 9*d.* They say the annual yield of every cow is 5*l.* I confess I can hardly see it. And in general they seem to think much more of the produce of their cows than of their crops. Many shorthorns are imported from England to improve the breed, and I have no doubt, with care, the desired end will be effected. But these fine-bred English cattle will require a little different treatment from the rough Swedish cows, or, to use a horsedealer's phrase, they will soon "fly all to pieces;" and were I going to stock a farm here to-morrow, I should stick to the native breed, feed and tend them better, and I am very doubtful in the long run whether they would not be found to answer best. As long as milk is the principal desideratum, I am convinced, with the keep they now get, the little Swedish cows are the best; but when they get the land to carry better crops, and commence stall-feeding, the large English breed will, of course, improve the meat.

The sheep, however, have been much improved by crosses with our Cheviots and Leicesters; and considering the price of wool, and the immense quantity that is annually required for warm winter clothing, I wonder that sheep-farming is not more attended to. I don't suppose that in the very north they could live; and in the midland districts they will sometimes be under cover for six months out of the twelve. Their principal food at this time is hay and birch branches gathered and stacked in the autumn; and in the summer they find excellent picking in the woods and plantations, and on the heather.

The Swedish horses are compact, docile, hardy little fellows, showing no great breeding, but well adapted for this climate and these roads, and, like the cows, can rough it upon any pasture and in any quarters. They average about 14 to 15 hands. The carts they draw are small, and doubtless, if the larger English cart-horses and our common carts could be introduced into the country, the farmers would get through their work quicker and easier. But I don't believe they would stand either the climate or roads, except, perhaps, in the very south; and instead of trusting too much to foreign aid to improve their breed of cattle, or system of farming, I should recommend the Swedish farmer to do more justice to his own breed, and modify his own style of farming, which is best suited to the country, without introducing fashions and cattle from other countries, which probably would be very unsuited to this. Much as we must applaud the spirit of enterprise and improvement, we should always bear in mind that there are certain laws of nature which man cannot overstep without paying the penalty.

Horses are dear here; about 15*l.* is the price of a useful country nag, such as we should see in a butcher's or grocer's light cart in England, but without the style. Riding on horseback is not fashionable here, and, except the military, you rarely see a Swedish gentleman "outside a horse." The military seat is in vogue here, and, as there is no racing or cross-country work, when you do see a man riding he seems as if he was trying to take as much out of his horse as he can. Our English cross-country seat, and our style of riding, where the rider tries to ease his horse as much as he can, not being understood, is laughed at here. There is not much work for the veterinary surgeon in the country-stables, for the horses being more naturally treated are much healthier than in England. I believe the Norwegian horses are considered the best, and though they boast of some rattling trotters in that country, I don't believe they could find many to do the English mile within the three minutes.

Domestic poultry is but little attended to, although eggs will occasionally fetch 1s. 6d. per score. In my opinion, both poultry and tame rabbits would pay well in the south and midland districts.

They have very much improved lately in the fashion of their agricultural implements, as they get all their models from England. Wood and work are cheaper here; and a Scotch plough, in every respect equal to one made at home, can be bought for 40s., and other implements in proportion. Timber is cheap, and houses and outhouses cost but little putting up in comparison to England.

The taxes are moderate; all the relief of the poor in our district was out-door, and the poor-rates are levied in grain, after this fashion. Early in spring an auction was held, to which all aged and helpless paupers are brought in order to be let for the year. Each pauper is put up to bidding, to see who will take and keep him or her for one year at the lowest price, and a good deal of speculation goes on among the assembled farmers. A helpless old pauper out of whom they can get no work will perhaps be rented out for the year at ten tunna of oats; while one who appears to have a little work left in him will be taken perhaps for three. This annual quota of grain is levied among the farmers of the district. I have heard this practice much condemned, and it certainly does appear to be a kind of traffic in human flesh. But I cannot see what other plan could be adopted in this thinly-populated country, where the houses lie so wide apart; and I really believe that the Swedish peasant is always kindly disposed towards the unfortunate, and these poor old bodies are perhaps as well treated as the paupers in any of our parish unions, and are certainly much freer. But there is something melancholy in the reflection that one can live long enough to be of no use to any one, and to be hawked about at the end of one's "journey," and let out to the man who will undertake to keep you for the lowest price. I recollect two or three old gentlemen who were rented out in our neighbourhood, and they appeared cheerful enough; all they seemed to want was tobacco, and the poor old boys used regularly to waylay me in the woods when I was out, to beg for a little bit. They at length became regular pensioners, and many a time in after years, when I have been out of tobacco in the Australian bush, have I thought of these old men, and become a beggar in my turn of any stock-rider who might casually canter by.

It is a pity, in most places, to see how badly the forests are looked after, and how much waste yearly takes place. In many of the more populous districts even firewood is becoming scarce, and most of the forests in the midland districts are becoming sadly thinned by the woodman's axe, especially where water-carriage is near. Timber is consequently rising yearly in value. The fences in the midland districts are a kind of light snake-fence, composed of split palings stuck obliquely in the ground one above another. It is one of the ugliest fences imaginable, and has nothing to recommend it; and, to form a mile of such fencing, many hundreds of valuable young trees are sacrificed. However, in many places they are substituting neat single posts and rails.

That agriculture is every year making head in Sweden, is certain. Farming associations are held in every town, and a farming school is established by Government in every district, where a dozen or so young men are sent every year to work on the farm, and go through a course of agricultural study. But at present theory is more in fashion than practice. As the Swedes, however, are peculiarly gifted with that most inestimable quality, common sense, things will be sure to come right in the end. Few countries in Europe have greater natural capabilities than Sweden as an agricultural land, and although the two great drawbacks are want of capital, and the severity and uncertainty of the climate, that farming must pay is proved by the fact that more than two-thirds of the gentlemen's families are brought up by it. But a stranger settling on a farm in this country would at first have much to contend with. A total ignorance of the language and habits of the people, the severity of the climate, and the very different manner in which the farms are managed here to what he has been accustomed, would sorely try a

British farmer. A young working farmer, however, coming over here with a small capital, and really setting his mind to acquire a knowledge of the language and the habits of the people, which he could do in a twelvemonth by living for that time on a farm where the owner spoke English (and there are many such places where he could live very cheaply), would soon find an opening.

Happily, however, no men are more averse to leaving England than the farmers, and no wonder at it. I spent my early days much among them, and since then I have mixed much with farmers of other nations; but in no other country under the sun have I found a class of men who lead such truly happy lives as the farmers of England. No matter whatever new country he may seek, the British farmer is sure to leave behind him home comforts which he can never replace abroad. Whatever faults he may find with Old England, and however much he may grumble at her taxes, her institutions, and the imaginary ruin which too often stares him in the face, he loves her at heart perhaps better than any other of her sons. He is as it were peculiarly a part and parcel of her soil, and transplanting him to a foreign land is like lopping a branch off the old British oak. His native village church, in which so many quiet Sabbath mornings have been spent—the innocent occupations of his early rural life—the neat homestead, the well-tilled fields, the cattle which it was his just pride to gaze upon, the social meetings at the market or the covert side—will haunt his memory to the last, and every one of these must be relinquished the moment he turns his back upon Old England. The adventurer or man of business leaves his native home with scarce a sigh of regret, and, in the thrill of adventure or the all-engrossing pursuit of money-making, will soon forget the land of his birth, and, like a true citizen of the world, accommodate himself at once to the manners and customs of the strangers among whom he is thrown; but not so the farmer.

Still, there must be many young farmers in our overstocked country who, through necessity (not, we will trust, through choice), yearly leave the British shores to seek their fortune in foreign climes, and to such men I will fairly say, that of all countries in Europe,

I know of none that presents a fairer opening to a farmer possessed of a small capital, but with a good knowledge of his business and a hearty will, than Sweden. There exists, over all, a good feeling between the Swedes and English. There is scarcely a farm in the country which could not be improved doubly with a little capital and a few years' proper management; and when he once acquired a knowledge of the language and manners of the people, the emigrant would have no trouble to get on.

I have endeavoured above, as far as I am able (for I must fairly confess to the reader, that, like old Jorrocks's boy Benjamin, " I don't profess to be a farmer,") to give a general insight into the agriculture of the country, and I have been careful rather to be under the mark than over it in my farming statistics. All I can say is, if this should meet the eye of anyone who is about to emigrate to more distant climes, I think it might be worth his while to turn his attention nearer home; and I can only add, that Sweden just now offers a good opening for a practical, hard-working farmer, with small capital; but I should never recommend a man to invest one shilling in land here in any way until he had spent a year in one of the numerous farming schools which exist in the country, for it would not be the slightest use a man commencing farming operations in Sweden till he understood something of the language and habits of the people among whom he intended to settle—that is, if he means to conduct his farm like an English farmer, and manage it himself.

We will now turn to another subject, and say a few words on the ichthyology of this land, which is as rich in "flood" as it is in "fell;" and as I resided for some time in its neighbourhood, I will commence with a short description of the Lake Wenern.

The Wenern is, next to Ladoga, the second largest inland lake in Europe, lying between 58° and 60° north latitude, and about sixty English miles from the North Sea, into which it empties itself through the Gotha river, running into the Cattegat at Gothenburg. The length of this magnificent lake is about seventy English miles, its breadth in places about forty, and it is computed to cover a surface of 360 English square miles. It lies about 150 feet higher than the sea, is fed by twenty-four tributary streams, although its only outlet is through the Gotha, a river not so wide as the Thames at Kingston. Its greatest depth is 360 feet, and ships of a fair tonnage ply on its surface in the summer, bringing down from the northern districts of Wermland and the Dalecarlian forests iron, timber, and corn to Gothenburg for export. The Wenern lies also on the summer high road from Gothenburg to Stockholm, and at this season a line of communication is open through the middle of Sweden by means of lakes and canals, and travellers may run from one town to the other in about four days, passing through a picturesque and beautiful country in small steamers, which, for appointments, cleanliness, and cheapness are second to none in the world; their captains, being all " old salts," speak and understand English well, so that on such an excursion the tourist may dispense with the nuisance and charge of a courier.

The small but remarkably neat town of Wenersborg lies at the southern extremity of the Wenern, and the clean, well-built little town of Carlstad at the north; and here the Clar, one of the largest rivers in the middle of Sweden, empties itself into the Wenern. The Clar rises far up in the Norwegian fells, and runs through the wild forest districts of Dalecarlia and North Wermland. A little distance to the north-east of Carlstad is another smaller town—Christineham; Mariestad and Lidkoping stand on its eastern shores, and Amal on its western. At any one of these towns cheap and good accommodation may be had; but, as a fishing station, I should recommend Christineham or Amal. In addition to these towns, the margin of the lake is studded with small villages and farms, while gentlemen's seats, peeping out of avenues of lime and birch extending down to the very margin of the lake, form pretty objects for the traveller's eye as he glides over the glassy waters of the Wenern on a fine summer's morning. As is always the case in the north, the land just round the lake is of a far better quality than elsewhere; and if it was only made the most of, the farmers round the Wenern might soon be rich men;

but the land of course lies low, and as the farmers are as slovenly with their dyking and banking as they are with their other farm operations, thousands of acres of land are wasted, and thousands of bushels of corn lost by sudden rises of the Wenern, though they might be all saved by a little management and judicious application of capital. The edges of the lake are bounded with large flats of coarse meadow land, beyond which rocky forests, rising all around, form a grand natural panorama. Just out of Wenersborg, to the right, are two singular mountains, Halle and Hunneberg, rich in old Scandinavian lore, while half way up the Wenern the beautiful mountain of Kinnekulle, rising about 800 feet above the surface of the lake, forms an imposing object in the distant landscape. In many places the Wenern is studded with little rocky isles, some of them well timbered, which, as well as the extensive reed-beds on the sides of the lake, afford safe and undisturbed haunts for the numerous waterfowl that visit these regions in the spring for the purpose of breeding. We have said that the Wenern is considerably higher than the sea, and at Trolhattan, about six English miles below Wenersborg, the Gotha dashes over a precipice about 120 feet high, divided into five falls, through a narrow channel between the massy rocks which beetle over the foaming waters of the falls themselves, and the dark pools that lie at the bottom of each. Of course these falls proved a stopper to the navigation of the Wenern; but the difficulty was at length surmounted, and a canal was hewed out of the solid rock parallel with the river, and fitted with sluices, up which the ships gradually "walk" from the bottom to the top, and *vice versâ*. The scenery around the falls is picturesque in the extreme, but I have no doubt we have much grander falls in the north than these. The canal is, however, a stupendous undertaking, and a great triumph of art over nature. Of course not even the gamest salmon can come up the Trolhattan falls, consequently we never take a real sea-salmon (*Salmo salar*) in the Wenern, although the sea-salmon, as well as the bull-trout (*S. Eriox*) and the salmon trout (*S. Trutta*), all come up from the sea to the very bottom of the falls. A few miles farther down the river are some smaller falls, and the same "dodge" of the sluices on a smaller scale is again called into requisition.

Parallel to the Wenern lies another lake, the Vettern, at a distance of about thirty miles, through which a canal runs between the two lakes. The Vettern is nearly as long as the Venern, but not half so broad, and its area is little more than 120 square English miles. The water of the Wettern (for it is immaterial whether we spell these lakes with a V or a W) is clearer and deeper than that of the Wenern—in many places above 400 feet—and I should fancy the bottom must be different, for no charr are taken in the Wenern, whereas the largest charr in Sweden are met with in the Wettern; otherwise I should fancy the fish fauna of the two lakes differs but little.

Having now slightly sketched the locality, let us proceed to its fauna; and, first, I will notice such species of birds as to my own knowledge breed on and around the Wenern.

Of the gulls, they have the common gull (*Larus canus*, Lin.) in all parts; the lesser black-backed gull (*L. fuscus*, Lin.) common; and the greater black-backed (*L. marinus*, Lin.) by no means rare in some places.

Of the terns, I never could identify more than two species breeding here—the common tern (*Sterna hirundo*, L.), and the large Caspian tern (*S. Caspia*, Pall.), although in the fall of the year I have met with the black tern (*S. nigra*, Briss.) evidently bred in the neighbourhood, and Richardson's skua (*Lestris Richardsonii*, Sw.) shot on the Wenern.

Of the divers, we had both the black-throated (*Colymbus arcticus*, L.) and the red-throated (*C. septentrionalis*, L.); and, as far as my observation goes, the black-throated diver is the most common in the north of the Wenern.

I never heard of a wild swan or any of the wild geese breeding here, although we had plenty of both during the seasons of migration.

Indented as the shores of the Wenern are with small shallow

Sweden.

bays or inlets, choked with bulrushes and reeds, edged with low, swampy, undrained, sedgy meadow flats, the wildfowl shooter in the autumn, if he only understood his business, could reap a good harvest here, even at the price that wild ducks fetch (under one shilling per couple); and as for snipe-shooting, I do not believe the far-famed bogs of Ireland can beat (in a good season) some of these marshy meadows in September. No one here cares a pin for killing a snipe; but, unfortunately, every duck-shooter goes for the "pot" not for the sport; and as the duck season commences in July, the young birds are cleared off by "family shots" before they are more than half-grown—in fact, as soon as they can rise above the rushes, most of the sportsmen here shut up duck-shooting. But then for a few weeks a man who can shoot may get some rattling sport, if he has only a good fellow to sprit his punt quietly through the reeds. I have more than once known twelve couple of full-grown ducks killed in one morning's shooting as they rose snugly from a patch of reeds of no great extent; and although about fifteen couple of snipe is the most I have ever myself bagged in a day, I am certain I have been out some days here when two good men might have picked up their fifty couple and been home to an early dinner. And the reader will bear in mind that this is on unpreserved ground, where a stranger who has not the character of a pot-hunter, has only to ask leave, and obtain permission to shoot. But by November all the sport with a shoulder-gun is over. The snipes have left, the ducks are packed and as wild as hawks; they leave the rushes, and congregate in the open waters by hundreds—wild-duck, widgeon, teal, golden-eye, all mixed; sailing about in perfect security, well out of gun-shot. Now would be the time for a punt-gun—a thing that never was seen on these waters.

The only ducks that commonly bred round the Wenern, to my knowledge, were the common wild duck (*Anas boschas*, L., as they are called here, the grass-duck), the widgeon (*A. Penelope*, L.), and the teal (*A. crecca*, L.) The golden eye (*A. clangula*, L.) breeds in holes of trees in the forests on the north-east of the Wenern, and the goosander (*Mergus merganser*, L.), and the merganser (*M.*

serrator, L.) sparingly over all. Of course in the spring and autumn we had the scoters, pintail, and some others, on their way to their northern breeding haunts.

Of the grebes I could never identify more than one species on the Wenern, namely, the great-crested grebe (*Podiceps cristatus*, Lath.), and this was by no means rare. It is a curious fact that, in such a locality, so admirably suited to the habits of these birds, the coot *Fulica atra*, L.) is only very rarely killed on the Wenern; and as to the water-hen (*Gallinula chloropus*, Lath.), it is unknown here. I never myself (nor can I hear of anyone else who has) killed the water-rail (*Rallus aquaticus*, L.) here; but the spotted crake (*Gallinula porzani*, Lath.) was common in all the rushy meadows throughout the summer. I once shot a red-necked phalarope (*Phalaropus hyperboreus*, Lath.) on the banks of the Wenern in full summer plumage, but they don't breed here. I have shot Temminck's stint (*Tringa Temminckii*, Leisl.), and the greenshank (*Totanus glottis*, Bechst.) more than once in the summer time, although I never obtained the eggs of either from these parts. The peewit (*Vanellus cristatus*, Mey.), the golden plover (*Charadrius pluvialis*, L.), the curlew (*Numenius arquata*, L.), and the common snipe (*Scolopax gallinago*, L.) are all common breeders here; but I never yet took the nest of the dunlin (*Tringa alpina*, L.) As to the great snipe (*S. major*, Gm.) and the jack snipe (*S. gallinula*, L.), although I never took the eggs of either here, I feel pretty confident that they both bred somewhere in the neighbourhood, for I have shot the young of both far too small to have travelled down any distance.

The little ring dotterel (*Charadrius minor*, Mey.) was, in my opinion, more common on the northern banks of the Wenern than its congener the ring dotterel (*C. hiaticula*, L.), although both bred here; but I never detected the Kentish plover (*C. Cantianus*, Lath.) breeding anywhere in Sweden on the margin of the freshwater lakes, although common on the southern coasts. The common sandpiper (*Totanus hypoleucus*, Tem.), the redshank (*T. calidris*, Bechst.), the green sandpiper (*T. ochropus*, Tem.), the wood sandpiper (*T. glareola,* Tem.), all bred commonly with us; and I think this completes my list of the waders—at least, if I have omitted any, they must be looked upon as accidental and not regular visitors.

The crane (*Grus cinerea,* Bechst.) occasionally bred in the neighbourhood, but this is not a favourite district, for the mosses are hardly large enough here. I never heard of a bittern being killed in the middle of Sweden; and although a few specimens of both the stork (*Ciconia alba,* Briss.), the black stork (*C. nigra,* Briss.), and the heron (*Ardea cinerea,* Lath.) have been shot here, none of them can be considered as indigenous to these districts.

I once saw the common guillemot on the south of the lake close to my boat while lake trout-fishing, and one specimen of the black guillemot was once picked up on the banks of the Wenern in a state of decomposition. It fell into the hands of a friend of mine, a keen collector, who immediately added it to his list as new to the fauna of the Wenern. I had my doubts about such a bird having been ever brought up here by wings; and with that characteristic jealousy which prompts every collector to sift out all particulars respecting a rare species which falls into any other hands but his own, I felt it my duty to make inquiries as to how such a bird ever could get up here. The consequence was, I discovered that the specimen in question had been brought up from the southern coast of the Baltic in a schooner along with a lot of gulls and such like rubbish, as sea-stores, but having been kept too long, the cook cast it overboard, and it was picked up on the beach by the peasant who carried it in triumph to my friend. Oh, the jealousy of collectors! I do not consider myself particularly maliciously or evil-disposed towards any man, but I cannot help owning that I felt much gratification in undeceiving my friend respecting this black guillemot; however, this circumstance, trifling as it is, might bear with it good results, for there was certainly very good ground for his supposing that the bird in question had by some means or other found its way up to the Wenern while living; and it is not improbable that other rare birds which are added to local faunas from specimens being picked up on beaches, &c., may have been transported there by other means than through the air.

However, two specimens of the little auk (*Mergulus alle,* Nob.) a bird which I should have as little dreamt of seeing up here as the black guillemot, were killed during one winter (and both I believe on the ice) on the Clar, a little north of Carlstad. How these birds came here, and which way they were steering, is a mystery to me; one thing is certain, however, they came without the aid of man.

Of land birds we had every species inhabiting the middle of Sweden, and one bird peculiar to the south, whose northern limits end here, the melodious willow warbler (*Sylvia hippolais,* Lath.). It is superfluous, therefore, to go through the list. I will only add that the rarest nests which I have obtained in this neighbourhood have been those of the osprey (*Pandion haliaëtus,* Sw.); honey buzzard (*Pernis apivorus,* Cu.); goshawk (*Astur palumbarius,* Bechst.); peregrine falcon (*Falco peregrinus,* L.); kite (*Falco milvus,* L.); eagle owl (*Strix bubo,* L.); Tengmalm's owl (*Strix Tengmalmi,* Gm.); great black woodpecker (*Picus martius,* L.); nutcracker (*Caryocatactes graculus,* Nills.); crested tit (*Parus cristatus,* L.); parrot crossbill (*Loxia pytiopsittacus,* Bechst.); common crossbill (*Loxia curvirostra,* L.) I never took an eagle's nest by the side of the Wenern, although I know that the white-tailed eagle (*A. albicilla,* Cuv.) breeds there.

Till the last three severe winters and heavy snowstorms swept off all the partridges in Wermland, excellent partridge as well as blackgame shooting might have been obtained in many places on the shores of the Wenern. The capercailie and hazel grouse are also pretty common in many parts, and lots of foxes and hares, both on the fast land and the little islands in the lake.

Now let us proceed to the Ichthyology of this magnificent lake; but, as a preface, let me say that the same pot-hunting spirit prevails among the fishermen as among the shooters out here, and the fish are so persecuted, swept off when they come up from the deeps of the lake on to the spawning-grounds—taken wholesale in nets, the meshes of which are so fine that fry of three inches long cannot escape—in fact, exterminated by every possible device that the ingenuity of man can invent, that, as a natural sequence, the fish are every year becoming scarcer in the Wenern, and more difficult to catch; and miles of valuable water are, as it were, lying fallow, only for want of a little common prudence in keeping up a breeding stock of fish. How sad it is that man is ever too eager to kill the goose that lays the golden egg! Pisciculture is in every man's mouth up here; but no one will give himself the slightest trouble to keep up the breeding stock which we already have, and which, if only well looked after at the proper seasons, would afford a sufficient supply without calling in any artificial aid.

Without restricting ourselves to strict scientific classification, I will slightly notice the different species of fish peculiar to the waters of the Wenern, beginning with the trout.

Much confusion still exists about the classification of the Wenern trout, or, as they are erroneously called here, the "salmon;" and, without entering further into the subject, I will only observe that, in my opinion, we have two distinct species, and only two, of the great lake-trout in these waters—the common lake or grey trout (*Salmo ferox*, Jard.) identical with the British lake-trout; and another species, which we call here "the silfver-lax," or silver salmon (from its bright silvery appearance), at present not identified in the British waters. The real *Salmo ferox* is taken in these waters up to thirty-two pounds; the silfver-lax (I can give no Latin synonym, seeing that none of our ichthyologists can decide what species this really is) from seven pounds to twenty pounds, and even larger, but generally, especially in the south of the Wenern, under twelve pounds. The real lake-trout are caught, I may say (whenever they are taken on a hook), invariably by spinning-bait, a bleak, or small roach; whereas the other species rise freely to the fly. In many parts of the Wenern very good salmon or trout fishing is to be had at the close of the summer, and many heavy fish are caught just when the ice breaks up in the spring. The wholesale salmon-fishery, however, is in the end of June or July, when the fish ascend the streams to the north of the Wenern for the purpose of spawning. The common trout (*S. Fario*, L.) also runs to a fair size in the Wenern and many of its tributary streams. The average price of the Wenern trout is three-pence per pound, when the season is well on.

I never saw or heard of a charr (*S. alpinus*, L.) being taken in the Wenern; but the Wettern's charr (*S. Salvelinus*, Bloch)—at least both Mr. Lloyd and Nilsson consider this fish to be identical with the *Salmo Salvelinus* figured and described by Bloch—run to a large size. I have myself seen them five pounds weight; but, according to Nilsson, they are taken in the Wettern up to ten or twelve pounds weight. I used to fancy that this was nothing more than a large variety of the common charr which we took up in some of the forest lakes in Wermerland, to my knowledge as heavy as five pounds; but now I think that is a true species. It is considered so by the Swedish ichthyologists, and also by Dr. Günther in his notes on the "charr," who, in alluding to a large specimen from this very Lake Wettern, says, "This species is not represented by any of the British charrs that I have examined." One thing I can, however, say, that if Bloch's diagnosis—"the first ray of the anal and ventral fins white"—is to be considered as a characteristic and specific mark of distinction of the *S. Salvelinus*, we have both species in the same lake, for on March 3rd, 1862, I made a charr-fishing trip to this very lake. We fished in holes cut in the ice. Baits, a white grub taken out of the dead fir bark. We had some capital sport, although on this occasion two pounds was our heaviest fish. But we caught several specimens with the front ray, or sometimes rays of both anal and ventral fins, white, and these I took for diseased fish.

The smelt (*S. Eperlanus*, L.) remain in the Wenern throughout the year, but are never seen except just when the ice breaks up in the spring; and then immense shoals come up from the deeps of the lake to spawn on the shallows. Directly, however, the spawning is over, they return again to deep water, and we see them no more till the next spring. We have two varieties: the smaller one, called here the "nors," which rarely exceeds four inches in length; and a larger one, the "slom," about eight inches. The slom is precisely the British smelt, and although many consider the nors a distinct species, in my opinion it is clearly nothing more than the young of the slom. I certainly once did hear of a smelt being caught out in deep Wenern in summer, but this was quoted as a very rare occurrence.

I have known the grayling (*S. Thymallus*, L.) to be caught in the Clar close to Carlstad, but I do not believe they ever come into the lake itself.

Respecting the different species of gwynniad (*Coregoni*), or, as they are called here the sik, nearly as much confusion exists as in the genus *Salmo*. This is not, however, the place to enter into a piscatorial controversy. Suffice it to say, that the gwynniad, be there three or only one species, is one of the commonest fishes, and they are taken by thousands in many of the bays round the Wenern during their spawning season in the autumn. It is the opinion of our best ichthyologists that there are three distinct species of gwynniad in this lake, and strange to say it does not appear to be at all clear that any of them is identical with any one of the British species. The gwynniad is in my opinion a capital eating fish, especially a fat smoked gwynniad; but they afford (here at least) little sport to the angler, being altogether taken in nets. I never but once heard of a gwynniad taking a bait, and this was a small fish on a night line in the Wenern. They run to a large size in the Wenern, six to ten pounds being not uncommon.

The vendace (*C. Albula*, L.) or, as they are called here, the sik loya, is also very common in the Wenern. They, however, run to no large size, the largest I have seen rarely exceeding seven inches in length. Like the rest of the family, they spawn in autumn, and are justly considered with us to be capital eating. I have seen them exposed for sale in Carlstad market from the beginning of October to the end of January. Like the smelt, the Wenern fishermen consider that there are two distinct species of vendace. The smaller fish, which rarely exceeds three inches, they call the "dattor." These come in fresh, and I never by any chance saw either spawn or milt in any of these small fish. I have carefully examined many specimens of both, and I can come to no other conclusion than that these smaller fish are only the young of the vendace.

The burbot (*Lota vulgaris*, Cuv.) is common in all parts of the Wenern, and runs often to a very large size, although fourteen pounds is the largest I ever saw, and this was taken on a night line in the middle of summer. They are usually taken in stake-nets under the ice in winter, when they come up on to the shallows to spawn. In a good season, the burbot can be bought in Carlstad market for 1s. 6d. the Swedish pound (about twenty pounds English). The burbot is only in season when it is spawning, and then the liver and caviare are indeed delicacies.

The pike (*Esox Lucius*, Cuv.), notwithstanding the persecution he receives at all hands, still battles his way bravely, and holds his own in every water where food is to be obtained. The Wenern pike run to a large size, and in the months of June and July a score might be caught in a day by a man seated in the stern of a punt, a bait and swivel dragging after him. No rod is required for this sport, and a spoon bait, I fancy, answers as well as any other. This may certainly be termed "fishing made easy." The rower pulls slowly and gently round all the reed beds where the pike lie in summer. When the fisherman is single-handed he rows, and holds the line in his mouth.

The perch (*Perca fluviatilis*, L.) also run to a large size in the Wenern, and there are certain grounds where almost any quantity may be caught in a summer afternoon's fishing. A perch of three pounds is not at all uncommon, but I once caught one nearly five pounds.

The ruffe (*P. Cernua*, Cuv.) is common in the Wenern, but, as in Britain, runs to no great size.

The pike-perch (*Perca Lucioperca*, Cuv.) is another famous fish in these waters, affording excellent sport to the angler, and capital eating when caught. In fact, in my opinion, a pike-perch caught in the summer, when they are best in season for firmness and whiteness of flesh, beats all the Wenern fish. They are principally taken on the long chain lines. These chain lines are in great use here. They are rigged up with 300 to 1000 hooks, about six feet apart, baited with worms or pieces of fish, floated here and there with bits of wood to mark the whereabouts, and sunk with stones at every 200 to 300 yards. I may mention here that all the fishing on the Wenern is wholesale, and hardly any man goes out for the sake of the sport. Even when a few do go out together in a boat, the principal attractions are the company and the "prog," and, as may be supposed, these fishing parties are anything but "the contemplative man's recreation."

That the tench (*Tinca vulgaris*, Cuv.) is taken in the bays on the north-east of the Wenern in considerable numbers, and of a good size, I know for a fact. I am told that the common carp (*C. Carpio*, L.) is also common there, but of this I have no positive proof.

It is said that before the construction of the canals and sluices at Trolhattan, the eel was unknown in the Wenern; whether or not such was the case, of course I cannot positively say, but it is certain that in many parts of the lake they are now common enough, and of a large size, and appear to be gradually spreading over the whole of North Wermland.

We have a species of bream here unknown in the British waters, common enough in many parts of the Wenern, the *Cyprinus Wimba*, Linn. Its shape, however, is much more elongated than the common bream; and, as Mr. Lloyd properly observes, "it much resembles in appearance the young of the *Coregoni*, but is readily distinguished from them by the absence of the adipose fin." Whether or not there are two fish of this name I cannot say, but, on referring to a small treatise of the fish found in the Lake Malare, near Stockholm, the author describes the *Cyprinus Wimba* or *wimban*, and (I quote his own words) says, " But it must not be confounded with the wimma (*S. Wimba*) which is taken in the Wenern." Now, many naturalists here suppose that we have a second species of vendace peculiar to the Lake Anim, which lake is connected with the Wenern. This fish is the *S. Wimba,* Linn., or Anim's wimma. By some the existence of this fish is looked upon as a myth, but I consider it a good species. It is, however, a matter of conjecture with me whether these Anim's wimma, of whose existence Nilsson seems to entertain no doubt, may not be identical with the Irish pollan, for Yarrell's description and figure of that fish seem to tally well with Nilsson's description of the Anim's wimma.

The common bream (*Abramis Brama,* Cuv.) in the Wenern run to a very large size, and are taken in many places in astonishing quantities; six pounds is a common weight, and I once saw a monster as large as a large pair of bellows, which pulled down eleven pounds. Cold bream, steeped in vinegar, with fennel, like pickled salmon, is a capital summer dish here, and bream tongues are another Swedish delicacy.

It is a disputed point whether or not the Pomeranian bream (*Cyprinus Buggenhagii,* Bl.) inhabits the Wenern; but I am inclined to think that it does.

The bream-flat (*C. Blicca,* Bl.) is also very common in the Wenern, but always small. This bream-flat is often, doubtless, confounded with the young of the common bream, but the red colour of the ventral and pectoral fins at once distinguishes it. On this account it is called here the "red fin."

Another species, unknown to Britain, is very common in some parts of the Wenern, but very local. This is the *C. Ballerus,* Lin., which appears to be confined to our northern waters. It runs to no large size here, being rarely taken above one pound in weight. This species may at once be distinguished from the common bream by the deeply-cloven tail, and by the long anal fin with forty-one rays.

The roach, rudd, and bleak are common over the whole Wenern, and I think the rudd here are the largest and handsomest I ever saw.

The dobule roach (*C. Dobula,* Lin.) appears (on the authority of Mr. Lloyd and Yarrell, who identified specimens taken in the Wenern) to be by no means uncommon in this lake, as well as the chub (*C. Cephalus,* Lih.); but, strange to say, much confusion has existed hitherto in the identification of all these fish, some naturalists here appearing to confound the dobule roach with the chub, and others the real dace with the dobule roach. According to Mr. Couch, the Swedish *Cyprinus Grislagine* (Stamm). is nothing more or less than the true dobule roach, and this is very common both in the Wenern and the Clar. The British dace has not yet been identified in Sweden. I think it would avoid confusion if it were to retain the old synonym of *C. Cephalus*, for the common chub. Nilsson's Swedish name for the chub ("Bred-pannad Id," broad-forehead ide) is not bad. The fishermen in the north-east of the Wenern describe to me a fish which they call the stam, and for the life of me I can't make out what it is, unless it be the asp (*C. Aspius*, Lin.). They say that this stam comes up from the Wenern every May to spawn in a small stream near Christineham. They remain only a few days on the spawning-ground, and are never again seen or taken by them out in the Wenern. They describe them as large fish, from ten pounds to eleven pounds, so it is clear they can't be the dace which we call the "stam;" and unless it is the asp, which they assure me it is not, I cannot make out what it is.

There is, however, no mistake about the ide (*C. Idus*, Lin.), which certainly is commoner in these waters than the chub, call this latter fish by what synonym we may. The ide runs to a large size here: five to six pounds is a fine, bold fish, gives excellent sport both with the bait and fly, and, in my opinion, is no bad fish for the table. The chub may be easily distinguished from the ide, which it much resembles in shape, by the round anal fin and the large scales. According to Kröyer, Yarrell's ide is not the same as the ide which he figures in his Danish fish, which species, although he says it is identical with our Swedish fish, he also says does not belong to Britain.

The asp (*C. Aspius*, Lin.), another fish unknown in Britain, is common in some parts of the Wenern, but local. It is a fine fish in shape, rather resembling the chub, but more elongated, of a more silvery colour, and its distinguishing peculiarity is the long under-jaw, which protrudes far beyond the upper one. They run to a large size, from ten to eighteen pounds, are tolerably good for the table, and appear, unlike the rest of this genus, to prefer animal to vegetable food.

The miller's thumb (*Cottus Gobio*, L.) is common in the Wenern, and I have seen specimens of the horned bull-head (*C. quadricornis*, L.), taken in the Lake Wettern.

I believe the lampern (*Petromyzon fluviatilis*, L.) is to be met with in the Wenern, although I never saw a specimen; but at Fryksdalen, a few Swedish miles north, I found Planer's lampern (*P. Planeri*, Bl.) as well as the pride (*P. branchialis*, L.), common in every small stream.

Of the sticklebacks (*Gasterostei*) we had the common three-spined in all its varieties, as well as the ten-spined (*G. pungitius*, L.). I have still my doubt whether our common stickleback is exactly identical with the common British stickleback; but, for fear of seeking a mare's nest, I shall give no opinion.

I never, to my knowledge, met with the common loach (*Cobitis barbatula*, L.) anywhere in the Swedish waters; but the spined loach (*C. tænia*, L.) is very common in many parts of the Wenern.

The little minnow (*Cyprinus Phoxinus*, L.) completes my list. Strange to say, I never myself took this fish in the Wenern itself, although I am told that it is met with there; but a few miles north, in every water where the common trout is taken, I have met with them in shoals, and certainly the largest I ever saw in my life.

The above list, which, from my own experience, I believe to be strictly correct as far as regards the Lake Wenern, will also give a very fair idea of the ichthyology of the middle of Sweden. It will, I trust, prove as interesting to the angler as to the naturalist; giving him some idea as to what sport he is likely to obtain in these waters. For salmon-fishing, doubtless the Norwegian streams beat any waters we have in Sweden by long chalks; but salmon-fishing in Norway has lately become such a fashion, that if, as we are told, all the good waters are rented by rich Englishmen, a poor wanderer like myself would have no more chance of wetting a line in the Namsen than of fishing the best salmon streams of Scotland. But of this, more hereafter. If a man has only a full purse, he can always obtain sport go where he will, and requires but little information or advice from anyone as to where he had best pitch his tent; but there are many other men quite as enthusiastic, and probably equally good with the rod, whose means are limited; and to such men I would say, try our Swedish waters before going up to Norway.

The expense of a Norwegian trip is no trifle, what with guides, &c.; and of course living in that country rises in proportion to the number of rich Englishmen that visit it. I suppose on some of these Norwegian streams, if a man goes for nothing but salmon-fishing, he may kill any quantity of fish, but the expense of the trip will be commensurate with the sport obtained. On referring to Mr. Lloyd's "Scandinavian Adventures," we shall read that a friend of his, in 1842, from the 15th of June to the 8th of August, killed on the Namsen 323 salmon, weighing in the aggregate 3840 lb., and was obliged to leave off for want of tackle. And in the same book we find an account of one season's fishing at Ronnum—Mr. Lloyd's fishing-station on the south of the Wenern—where that gentleman killed with his own rod, in one particular season (although, as he himself remarks, he had others nearly equally good)—

120 trout, heavy	1796 lb.
75 do., smaller	201 lb.
15 perch	15 lb.
364 pike	827 lb.
1 pike-perch	4 lb.
5 ide	21 lb.
580 fish.	2864 lb.

It must, however, be borne in mind that few better fishermen have ever come into Sweden than Mr. Lloyd, and also that the Ronnum water is not now what it was in his day. But, to my fancy, there are still many places on the north-east of the Wenern quite as good as Ronnum ever was. And as I do not in the least doubt that every pound of the Namsen salmon cost at least six times the money to kill that Mr. Lloyd's fish did, I will leave the reader to judge for himself, looking at both sides of the question, which water he would prefer to visit.

I will conclude this chapter with a few remarks on the northern salmon-rivers, which may not be uninteresting to the British angler. One of the most curious facts connected with the ichthyology of the north (if it is proved to be a fact) is this: that whereas all the Norwegian rivers flowing into the North and Polar Seas, on the north and west coasts of Scandinavia, from Christiana Fjord to the North Cape, are full of salmon, which will rise readily at the fly, I can never hear of any salmon-fisher who has had sport with the rod in any of the hundred magnificent streams on the east coast of Sweden, which empty themselves into the Bothnia, between Stockholm and Tornea. Now, no one denies that there are plenty of salmon in the Bothnia, and precisely of the same habits as the North Sea salmon, yet we seem to have an extent of nearly a thousand miles of coast, through which, perhaps, a hundred salmon rivers flow into the sea, lying, as it were, waste and dormant to the salmon-fisher. And as we are told that nearly every mile of water on the Norwegian coast is taken up by some rich Englishman or another, it will be seen that it is apparently of very little use for any stranger to visit either Sweden or Norway now for the purpose of salmon-fishing.

I believe it is quite true that, although many good salmon-fishers have tried these Bothnian streams, all declare that they could get no sport in them, either with the fly or the bait; and yet all say that the Bothnian salmon run quite as large, although inferior in taste, to those taken in either the Cattegat or North Sea. This may probably be owing to the water of the Bothnia having so much less salt in it than that of the North Sea. But the difference of the water would, we should imagine, make no other difference in the feeding habits of the fish than that there might be different crustacea and insects on these coasts, and the fish might require a different bait.

Mr. Lloyd observes that the only solution of the mystery which he has heard is—that the fish in the rivers in question may not be

Sweden.

the genuine salmo salar, " but a huge trout, exactly resembling it in appearance." Even if this were the case, why should not these large trout take a bait as freely here as in other parts of Sweden? But it is not the case; because, although I believe that far up in most of these Bothnian rivers they have both species of large lake trout peculiar to the Wenern, I also know, from my own observation, that both in the Tornea and Lulea rivers, the true sea-salmon, as well as the salmon-trout, are taken every year in very great quantities when they come up to spawn, so we must seek for some other cause for the solution of a mystery which, I must confess, has puzzled me more than anything else in the ichthyology of Scandinavia. When in Lulea Lapland, I made many inquiries into the habits of the salmon in the great Lulea river, and doubtless they are the same in the other rivers along the coast, as well on the Swedish as on the Finnish sides. Both the salmon and the salmon-trout begin to ascend the large Lulea river soon after the middle of June, and the spawning season in this river is about the middle of October. They ascend the river as far as Lockmock, perhaps 120 English miles from Lulea, and between Lockmock and the sea there are eight falls, but none prettier or more fitting for the habits of the salmon than the Leclel fall close to Lockmock, which, however, apparently they cannot ascend, for the true sea-salmon never comes up as far as Quickiock, above eighty miles farther up, although I believe there is water communication so far, but broken probably with lakes and tracks. I never myself wetted my line here, but I was told at Lockmock that salmon are taken by a rod and line under this fall during the summer. As far as I could learn, the salmon fishing in this magnificent river is much spoilt by the large salmon traps set across the stream at Ederforss, a little distance from Lulea, and the salmon taken here belong to the town of Lulea. At six of the other salmon traps on this river, the yearly catch of salmon, I was told, would average as follows:—At Sands, 40 tunna, or about 160 bushels; Luarts, 50 tunna; Gaddock, 70; Balinge, 50; Lunnerley, 30; Annan, 40. The value of the salmon fishing in the Lower Tornea river is averaged at about 3500*l*., reckoning the average value of the salmon at 4*l.* for the four bushels. I do not exactly know how far the sea salmon run up the great Tornea river, but I think as far at least as Munro. According to Widigren, the bed of the Lulea river consists of sandstone and clay, without any vegetation—only in two places are to be found one species of pond weed (*Potomogeton gramineus*), and the banks are lined with different species of willow and hedge, which are of very little advantage for the spawning of any of the members of the carp genus, because it is only at very high tides that they are under water, and on this account but few of our commoner species of white fish are met with in the Lap rivers, especially far up. The medium temperature of Lake Saggat, near Quickiock, mostly may be taken at about 50° Fahr. in an ordinary season. The stream is filled with falls and still water; the depth is considerable, and but very few different species of crustacea, except *Entomostraca, Porcellanidæ* and *Lerneæ* are met with; but these, however, abound in such quantities, that these streams are peculiarly rich in all the species of salmon and gwynniad. In the great Tornea river the inferior water animals are met with in prodigious quantities, affording even a readier supply of food for the fish. The temperature of the water in the Tornea river is considerably higher than in the Lulea river, and this may probably be accounted for by the fact of the springs in the Tornea river being lower than in the Lulea river, and that the Lulea is much the deepest. The consequence of this is that the supply of fish in the Tornea river is double that in the Lulea river.

Although the individuals of each may be numerous, not a very great many species of fish are met with in the Lap rivers running into the Bothnia, and at their outlets. Widigren's list includes the perch, the ruffe, the pike-perch, four species of bullhead, two species of stickleback (*G. aculeatus*, Lin., and *G. Pungitius*, L.), the viviparous blenny, the dobule roach (*C. Erislagine*, L.), stamher, which goes up the Tornea river as far as Munco, but not far up the Lulea river; the ide, the roach, the minnow, the winnow (*C. vinelia*, L.), the bream, the bleak, the pike, the salmon, the bull-trout, the salmon-trout, the great lake trout, the common trout, the charr (*S. alpinus*, L.), only in the fell lakes, the smelt, the grayling, the gwyniad (*C. oxyrrhinchus*, L.), the vendace, the herring (*strömming*), the burbot, the flounder, the sturgeon, the eel, and the lamprey.

Thus we see that thirty-two normal species of fish are met with in the waters of Norhotten and Lapmark, of which three (the pike-perch, the ruffe, and the smelt) belong exclusively to fresh water. Twenty-four are fresh-water species, but are met with also in the brackish waters on the coasts. Two species (the salmon and the eel) are met with both in fresh and salt water. Of the true salt-water fish only two species are met with in the very north of the Baltic—namely, the herring and the viviparous blenny; while on the Stockholm coasts fourteen species of salt-water fish are normal, by which we may judge that the Bothnia has more the character of a large Arctic lake than a true sea. It may be very probable that the food of the salmon in these Bothnian rivers is different to that in the Norwegian streams. Yet it seems singular that they will not in both rivers rise to the salmon fly, which certainly in general is a resemblance of no insect that ever crawled or flew; and even if the fly failed, it does seem strange that these Bothnian salmon, which certainly are precisely the same species as those taken in the rivers running into the Cattegat and the North Sea, should not be tempted to take a small herring-bleak or vendace (the most killing of all baits for large lake trout), if neatly spun.

Now, from a perusal of the above, it will be seen that as far as regards the true sea-salmon, the Swedish waters, except just three or four rivers running into the Cattegat in the south of Sweden (and which I believe are all taken up by some of the rich " timber lords" in Gothenburg) offer not the slightest attraction to the salmon fisher; and as we are told that all the Norwegian waters are rented (but of this more by-and-by), the whole of the Scandinavian continent, whose waters the salmon fisher at home is foolishly led to believe offer the finest and freest sport in Europe, and, as it were, a complete dead letter, save to a very few; for there seems to be an opinion that all along the Eastern coast there are no means of taking the fish, which are to be met with in abundance, while the whole of the fishing for hundreds and hundreds of miles along the Western coast are monopolized by a few rich Englishmen, who perhaps never see the country except during a month or two in the summer, who never spend a shilling among the poor inhabitants, except just at the fishing season; who have not the slightest interest in the land further than as a means of gratifying their love for sport, and yet have assumed a power to warn other older residents in the country off water (a good deal of which, if the matter was looked into, has really no private owner), which surely in their wild tracts, at least, we should have imagined, would have been as free at least to one *stranger* as another. Is it possible that such can really be the case?

And now for a word or two on the practice of monopolizing fishing in this wild land. I observed in 1864 some letters in the *Field*, in which we were told that the River Alten up near the North Cape from the Lea to the Fors, is leased by the Duke of Roxburgh, the Hausen by Sir Charles Taylor and his friends, and that there is not a *river of note* in *Norway* that is not now protected by English lessees. This is a wide statement; and without for one moment denying the full right of any man in any country to let his fishings or his shootings to whoever he chooses, or for any other man to rent them; but when we are told that *not a river of note* in Norway but what is protected, it naturally leads us to ask, " What is meant by this protection ?"

I do not exactly know how the law stands in Norway as regards fishing; I fancy, however, much the same as in Sweden. Now in Sweden no man has the least right to interfere with the middle of the stream. Every proprietor has the sole right of fishing in one-third of the water—that which abuts upon his own land. Thus two-thirds of the river can be preserved—one-third on each side; but the middle-third, which is here called the king's highway, is open to all. It must, moreover, always be kept open not solely for the purposes of navigation, but for the sake of the fish passing up and down. Not a stake, net, or any obstacle, may be placed across it, under a heavy penalty; moreover, many of these Lapland and Norrland rivers (and I should not wonder if this is the case with the greater part of the Alten) are altogether crown property, and no one, save a crown bailiff, has a right to interfere with any man fishing there, and this no crown bailiff would do, if he met a foreigner fishing with a rod and line. In fact, I am pretty certain that half of their northern rentings are a mere myth, and other fishermen are only kept off because they are told by the London fishing-tackle makers, or others that know nothing about it, that Lord So-and-So has hired the water, and has the exclusive right to fish. Fancy the whole of the water in such a land as Norway being all taken up by about half a score of men. Why, the statement is too absurd on the very face of it to be believed for a moment.

I am not a salmon-fisher myself. I have neither the time or the money to throw away upon it; but I well know if I was, that I would soon see how many of their rentings would stand good; and even if I wished to fish on so-called preserved water (unless it was strictly preserved by a native for his own fishing, and then I could always obtain leave by paying) I would do so without asking any one's leave. It is perfectly absurd to talk about preserving either shooting or fishing through the agency of a northern peasant. All I should require to fish the best water in Norway would be a good interpreter to parley with the peasants—and there are plenty such to be found in Christiania who would like the job—a good guide or two who knew the river and the peasants well, a nine-gallon cask of Bianvie (on which I should place by far the greatest reliance), and just an "inkling," as the Scotch say, of the sun. The lessee, whoever he was, paid in rent for his water. Moreover, if a trespasser is caught, the peasant or owner of the land will always accept the fine at the time (the owner or guardian of field or water has a right to seize a man's gun or fishing-tackle, and hold it till the fine is paid); but I should trust entirely to my nine-gallon cask and the "soft sawder" of my guide, and I never yet knew a Northern peasant able to withstand these. Moreover, the middle of the stream is always open to me, and it would be very odd if, with a couple of good rowers,

I could not dodge in and out when I liked on to any preserved water on the sides of the stream.

I never, however, set foot on any gentleman's or peasant's ground in Sweden without first asking leave, and the proprietor was always welcome to a liberal share of the game or fish which I might kill; and I recommend every foreigner in a strange country to do the same as regards the *real owner* of the soil. But somehow or other I regard a proprietor who preserves his own land on which he is residing, in a very different light from a rich Englishman, who probably owns hundreds of acres of good sporting at home, but not content with this, comes over to a land of which he knows nothing and cares less, when I, a poorer man, but quite as good a sportsman as himself, have settled among the people, have become, as it were, one of them, and am hoping to enjoy a little sport in freedom which, on account of my means, is denied me at home. If such is to be the case, a dozen or two rich lords will have it in their power to monopolize the whole sporting in Northern Europe.

This nuisance is now becoming rather too much of a good thing, and I would seriously advise any sportsman before he leaves England, never mind for what out-of-the-way country he may be bound, first to advertise in the columns of the *Field*, and beg to know, not whether the *inhabitants* of the country he is about to visit have any objection to his doing so, but whether any countryman of his own objects.

Now, I therefore advise every man who has the dream or inclination to try a little salmon-fishing in Norway, not to be the least deterred or frightened by the interested reports he may hear in England of all these northern waters being taken up. I am certain that there are lots of places where he will find open water, if he only has a good guide; and even on the preserved waters he will, I fancy, always get fishing, if he is willing to pay for it. These peasants have not the least conscience or sense of honour in a bargain like this. Moreover, most of this fishing and shooting is paid for by a very nominal rent, and so badly looked after that—although it may sound all very grand when a man tells you in England that he rents so many thousand acres, or so many miles of water in Norway—yet it would not appear such a great renting if he told you the rent he paid, and how many keepers were employed to look after it. Moreover, I cannot yet believe that the Bothnia salmon altogether refuse to look at a fly or a bait; and I feel certain that if a good salmon-fisher were to come to Stockholm properly equipped, hire a good guide in that town, and fish his way up to Tornea, he would not be altogether disappointed. Anyhow, he would probably gather some interesting facts and information relative to the habit of the salmon on that coast, and throw some light upon an enigma which has hitherto puzzled our best ichthyologists and fishermen.

There seems, however, to be a very erroneous opinion in England respecting the cheapness of travelling in these Northern countries. I think I can safely say that there is no country in Europe where a man can enjoy a *little* sport so cheaply and freely as in Sweden, *when he once gets used to the country*. To the casual traveller, I believe, Norway will be found quite, and Sweden pretty nearly, as dear now as any other European country; and wherever the English have found their way, prices have risen 100 per cent., and are every year rising, and good fishing and shooting are both hard to obtain by the stranger, for the simple reason that he does not know the right locality to pitch upon. No man can be more covetous after money than the Northern peasant, and, as he has now begun to find out that the English are always willing to pay for their sport, in Norway he is every year becoming more and more extortionate. It seems a great question to me now whether the English salmon-fisher would not be able to obtain nearly as good sport in many parts of Great Britain as in Norway; for although, doubtless, some men who know and are used to the waters do occasionally kill a great many fish here, I hardly believe a *stranger* would find the sport compensate him for his trouble and expense—certainly not without a good guide and interpreter, and such a man will be found a very expensive companion.

DUCK-SHOOTING IN WERMLAND, SWEDEN.

I HAVE, I think, already observed, that in the part of Sweden where I reside we have none of what the English game-shooter would call open shooting. Our partridges were all destroyed by two severe winters a few years since, and the breed has never been got up again. The capercailly and hazel grouse, as in all other parts of Sweden, are confined exclusively to the forests, and here, at least, I only occasionally find the blackgame lying out in the open, although we have some tolerable ground, and the hares are always in woods or plantations. The forests are so much thicker than in England, that one rarely gets a fair flying shot. It is, therefore, impossible to make a heavy bag in any of the woods round us, and the English sportsman would find but little amusement in a day's covert-shooting in Sweden, except, perhaps, just in the very south, at woodcocks.

But although, as I have said, we have no open shooting at game, we have round us some of the finest duck and snipe grounds that any man would wish to shoot over, and I will describe two localities in my own neighbourhood over which I have full right to shoot, and these will give the English sportsman a pretty good idea of hundreds—I may say thousands—of places in Sweden of the same description.

As a word of preface, I may as well say at starting that, except just for duck and snipe, my game-book would show a very poor return when compared with that of most English sportsmen; but then we must remember that I do not pay one shilling rent for either my fishing or shooting, and *exactly that* sum per day is the cost of my man, who rows and attends me in all my little trips.

Duck-shooting in Wermland, Sweden.

The two places to which I have alluded lie at equal distances from where I live, about five English miles; and as this is almost too far to shoot the grounds properly in one day, I have a boat at each place. We drive over in the morning (the horse and cart cost me ninepence), take our things with us, shoot all day, camp out at night, shoot next day, and home in the evening. I enjoy these little outings greatly—not so much for the sake of the shooting we get, but because they are the nearest approach to the dear old bush life that we can make in these civilized countries. The ground to the right (excuse the bull) is a bight of the Lake Wenern, studded with islands, and there are several small inlets fringed with reed-beds, in every one of which we are sure to pick up a pair or two of ducks; but the best bit of all is a large plain of bulrush flags, and the great water horse-tail grass (in which the ducks are sure to be in the early season), of about a couple of hundred acres in extent. It is impossible to wade this, although the water is not deep, for the bottom is spongy—in fact, a kind of shaking bog; and in many places the reeds are so thick and high that it is next to impossible to get the boat through them. Of course, this place being almost tabooed ground, is the resort of all the ducks in the neighbourhood. There is much luck in shooting this reed-bed; but it does so happen that if we find the ducks out in the horse-tail grass (and this often happens if we are on the ground a little after daylight) we do get some rattling shooting. There is a capital snipe country round here, and six couple of snipe and four to five couple of ducks is my average day's work on this ground. I have done more, and I have done less. I have got a capital camping-place here on a little island; plenty of wood and good water at hand; no rent or taxes to pay, and no questions asked; and I have often wondered—as I have lain out on a warm night on a bed of dry grass under the lee of an old stack of dry bulrushes (wherefore it was put here I never can tell, because I have known it here as long as I have known the place), with my face turned up to the heavens, watching one little star after another twinkling in the clear blue sky—why the whole tenor of our lives should not flow on as smoothly as the hours we spend in these lonely, out-of-the-way spots.

When we shoot this ground we have a goodish deal of water to row over; so, as we always hang a swivel out behind the boat, we are certain of a dish of fried pike or perch, or, it may happen, even a pike-perch (the sander)—respecting which there was a discussion some short time back—to our suppers. However, as this is uncertain ground, and very heavy work both to get to it, as well as shoot it, I do not go here half so often as to my other more favourite place, which I will now try and describe.

Imagine a river about 200 yards across, backed by magnificent forest scenery on either hand, on one side of which the ground is partly cultivated, but on the other one unbroken swampy meadow, an English mile broad, stretches for about four English miles, bounded towards the river by a bed of flags and bulrushes, along its whole extent, in many places three-quarters of an English mile across, and some idea will be formed of a Swedish duck and snipe ground. I can fancy an old fen-man standing on the deck of one of the little steamers which ply up and down this river, catching sight of this swamp, and if his first exclamation was not, "What a magnificent place for a decoy!" I'll never again place faith in early association. And he would not be far wrong either, for if you can only get a windy day and highish water, so that you can sprit your punt quietly through the reeds without the birds hearing you too soon, I'll back a good man to have such a day's sport here on duck in the middle of August as he wont forget in a hurry. He can wade in many parts of this ground; and the man who wades will always beat the man in a boat.

Water-boots are of little use far out in the rushes, for the bottom is uneven, and I don't think I ever remember a single day on this ground, when I really waded, even in good boots, that I came out of the rushes dry. Still, if a man only keeps on the edges where he can see and feel the bottom well, a pair of water-boots towards the end of September, when the water gets cold and the evenings chilly, are very comfortable, especially in flight-shooting; and if you could get a pair of boots to come right up to the fork, and fit the thigh tight, they might be useful. I never, however, had a pair of water-boots even that came high over the knee, which did not, after a few hours' wading, wrinkle down, so that every step you took, the water flew up behind into the bend of the knee, and ran down the leg till the feet were soon as wet inside the boots as they would have been had you waded barefooted and much more uncomfortable. However, as our best duck and snipe and shooting is in August and September, when the water is warm, a pair of flannel trousers, low shoes, and a change in the boat, if one means camping out, is the very best dress; for one never feels chilly after wading in flannel.

I don't care to boast of my own performances, for I never do make a very heavy bag. I once killed in these rushes twenty-three strong flyers in one day, and eleven snipe, but I saw a friend of mine knock down twenty-eight full-grown ducks one after the other. I did not shoot that day, for I wanted him to have the sport. I fancy, however, if a man were to beat these rushes *every day* (and a good duck-shooter should, because it makes no matter to the birds in such a tract of rushes as this how much they are shot at in the beginning of the season—they never leave them; and, strangest of all is, that they do not become wild till about the end of September, when, all at once they pack, and as soon as ever a gun is fired, they rise in clouds and go right away), he might average, with flight-shooting, twenty couples of ducks a week throughout August and September; and that's no bad work for one gun. He would, however, kill most of his birds at flight, especially in the end of the season. At this time the ducks all appear to leave the swamp in the day—where they go to I never could make out; but, I fancy, to the large open waters. But they come back in hundreds at night to feed, and this is the time I nail 'em. I poach the holes in the reeds with floating trimmers in the day, and, as soon as I have got my night-lines all out, and just before I can see the evening star, I go to a favourite place, right in the line of flight, and set myself high and dry, and "wait the coming storm." And I have not to wait long. Firs a flight of teal dash by as pioneers, and I know I have not long to wait now. The first intimation of the approach of the general flight is the "whish, whish, whish, whish" of wings high in the air overhead. Scouts, I suppose, on the look-out, for I invariably remark that, as soon as I have heard this, the birds begin to drop down. Backwards and forwards they dash by sometimes singly, sometimes in twos and threes; and for about an hour the shooting is first-rate —especially if you are well in the line of flight; and it takes some little knowledge of the swamp to get this. No doubt the birds drop down into the rushes in many places, but there is one high road, and the man who can find this out may lie on his bunk and smoke his pipe all day while his mates are beating the swamp; but as soon as he sees the sun go down he will take his stand, and in two hours' time will probably come back with as many birds as it would take another a whole day to kill. This flight-shooting lasts, perhaps, not more than an hour, and you can follow it any evening. And, mind, I do not mean, when I use the term "flight-shooting," shooting the birds on the water as they pitch to feed. For this work you must have a moon, and the light is so uncertain when a man is sitting low on a large swamp, which is bounded on both sides by high ground, that perhaps scarcely ten nights in the month will do for it. However, if you can find a good place where the birds feed really well, you will kill double the quantity you can in flight, for you may get two or three at a shot; and shoot as you may, it seems next to impossible, here at least, to drive the birds from a favourite feeding-ground. However, this sport is over by about ten or eleven, and you may then go home. And I will now tell the reader how I got home one night from this very swamp.

It was in the third week of this last month of September, just at the new moon, and although of course the moon gave no light, still the twilight is always clearer just at this time, and after the flight was over I went down to a good bit of feeding-ground, and, sitting with my face to the west, I managed to see the birds tolerably clear, if they came in pretty close, and, although I had but little sport, I was loth to leave the ground till the birds had done feeding. There is to me a kind of fascination in this quiet, solitary sport, which I never find in any other. The dead silence which reigns over all, unbroken save by the calls of the different night-birds as they pass over (and these are real music to the naturalist's ear), the consciousness that no prying observer is "touting you through the hedge," and the excitement of the sport, all give it peculiar charms in my eye; and if a man gave me the choice of the best day's covert-shooting, or a good night on duck-shooting on a favourite feeding-ground, I should without hesitation choose the latter. There is a singular little island butting into the river in the middle of this swamp. It is not a natural island, but evidently a large heap of gravel rising like a pinnacle, perhaps 100 feet high, several hundred acres in extent. It has evidently partly been thrown up by the hand, and many suppose that in the early days an old cloister stood here, which supposition is doubtless correct, for the village church stands on another height not far distant, and this valley was probably peopled when all the neighbouring district was one wild unbroken forest. Be this as it may, this immense mound is now all grown over with fir and juniper, and this is my camping-place when I shoot the swamp—and a more picturesque camping-place it would be hard to find. I had drawn my punt up on to the strand of this island when I rowed over, but unfortunately had not pulled it high enough up, and while I was in the swamp it had drifted away, and when I came down to row myself back over the river I found no boat. This was pleasant; I did not much care to camp out, for a jolly friend on the other side of the river was waiting up for me, and I much preferred a glass of his hot brandy-and-water and a cigar to a "night out" on "the dismal swamp." Moreover, it was dark, and some heavy drops of rain were just beginning to fall. I could see the light twinkling in his window about half a mile down the river, on the other side, as if to tantalize me. However, I was not going to be beaten just like this. There was a stand of boats about 500 yards down the river on the other side, which the peasants used for rowing over the river to church and for fishing; so I stripped (for the stream was strong, and I durst not try to swim over in my long boots and shooting-coat), and slipped in to swim over to these boats, and row back for my clothes. It was a stiffish swim, for the current was powerful. However, I got well over. We have a plan here of locking up the oars on an iron bar, which comes out at the back of the punt; and, as every boat was locked, I had to break a pair of oars off with a stone. This was a longish job, as Swedish iron is proverbially tough, and these peasants do their work pretty strong. The night was not too warm, and it was rather chilly work, as I stood *in puris natura-libus* for about a quarter of an hour tinkering away at this old iron bar. But I got the oars free at last, soon rowed over for my clothes, dressed, and was at my friend's house by midnight. He belonged to the "Peep-o'-day Club," so we had a couple of my ducks roasted, and made a very jolly night of it. I walked home next morning, and thought no more of my little adventure; but I had not seen the end of it yet. Three nights after I came home from shooting, and all at once my head began to throb as if it would split, and every joint in my body ached. I knew what was up, for I had felt this before. I turned in directly, took a hot cup of coffee and brandy, and in half an hour was shivering like an aspen leaf, my teeth chattering like castanets. I had a touch of our Swedish "frossa," or ague—one of the nastiest sicknesses I think it is possible for a man to have, and one against the attacks of which not the strongest is proof. The fit lasted two hours. I was all right next morning, and had only to wait to see whether the fit was to come on every day, or every second, third, or fourth. My next fit did not come on till the third night, so now I knew that it was the tertian ague, and as the fit always comes on precisely at the same hour, I knew when to look out for it; and as, luckily, my first fit came on at night, it does not cause me much inconvenience, for I just turn in an hour before I know it will come on, take a good dose of coffee and brandy, and wait for the shivering fit. It is a horrid complaint, for it pulls a man down so; and although, except just when the fit is on you, you can work as usual, a kind of low, listless feeling hangs over a man the whole while the ague is on him. It often hangs about people here for years. The spring ague is always the worst. Luckily, mine is not a very severe attack; and as each fit appears to become weaker, I hope in a short time to be all right again.

The sport upon the swamp I have described, depends in a great measure on the state of the water. If the water is high we have not only more ducks, but we can shove the boat along better; and if the water is low, the contrary is the case. In a dry season we have scarcely any snipe, and I have remarked one thing as curious regarding the snipe here. As I said before, it is one line of snipe-ground along the whole extent of this meadow, perhaps four English miles long, every yard of which appears to be good lying for snipe; and yet I only know five places on the whole swamp that are worth beating. In these places the snipe lie in wisps, and often far out in the water, and if they would only lie well, a man would have little trouble in killing five or six couples in each place; but as soon as ever you flush your first bird, his "scape, scape" puts all his comrades on the *qui vive*, and all at once they keep rising round you, till I am certain that I have seen considerably above a hundred in the air at one time, flying round and round, rising higher and higher, a sure sign—as every old snipe-shooter knows—that he is pretty certain never to see those birds again that day. Still, when the wind has been blowing fresh, I have had some capital shooting on this swamp, and one day this very September I ought to have bagged twenty couple, for I had forty-five shots, but only picked up thirty-one birds. In fact, I begin to fear very much that I am fast going off my shooting. There is always something wrong now, either with the gun or the ammunition. The powder is bad, or the shot is either one size too large, or one size too small. It never used to be so; and depend upon it when a man begins to make all sorts of excuses when he misses, he is either a pottering shot, or his nerves are not in tune. I would rather by half see a man miss ten shots clean running and never say a word about it, than see another man kill five out of ten, and bother you with a hundred reasons and excuses why he missed the other five. However, on this day I had some little excuse, for half a gale was blowing from the south, and as of course I shot against the wind, I often really had trouble to get my gun up and hold it steady. I never saw so many snipe in one day in my life, nor did I ever see them lie so well. I had a rare steady retriever with me, and never lost a bird. And now a word or two about this aforesaid retriever.

Some few years since I recollect reading in the *Field* the following remarks from, I think, the Hon. G. Berkeley, " That if he had a dog to break, he would trust it to no one's hands but those of Anthony Savage." I always had the greatest ambition to become possessed of a first-rate retriever. Luckily, chance brought me in correspondence with this very Mr. A. Savage (who, by the way, is a very good ornithologist). I was therefore very much pleased when I came in correspondence with Mr. Savage on ornithological matters, and more pleased still when the result of that correspondence led to his sending me over last May a fawn-coloured retriever bitch, which, as far as I can see, is a perfect retriever both by land and water. I have not lost a *single duck or snipe* this year, and that is saying something in this country, where the reeds are so thick. Our season begins early, long before the birds are strong flyers, and although such a thing would not do in England, when we are at Rome we do as they do at Rome ; and as I argued upon the principle, if I don't get the birds now, some one else will, and, moreover, as all our duck-shooting parties among the gentlemen take place just at the commencement of the season, I joined many parties before the 1st of August, and it was a caution to see Sutt (as we call her) catch the young birds about three-quarters grown, and bring 'em alive to me one after the other. This just suited the Swedes, who, so long as they get the game, hardly care much how they do get it. This, however, was not likely much to improve my lady's steadiness, and she got worse when the old birds were losing their pinion feathers, and, though they could not fly, could scuttle along the water at a good pace. I once heard the late Bill Scott remark, in his usual energetic manner, in reference to a horse who some one said would "walk over" for the Derby,—" Will he ? well, he must walk quick to walk out of my way, that's all." So it was with the poor ducks—they could not even walk away from Sutt, who, I am certain, I have seen chase a mallard for an English mile, and bring it back alive to me. I fancy, if Savage sees this, he will say, "Well, if I had known how she would be used, I should have thought twice before I sent such a dog over there;" and I must confess I began to wonder myself how it would be when the snipe season came on, and I wanted her to hunt within shot. But as soon as ever the birds became strong flyers, and the snipe came down, she forgot all these tricks, and settled down to one of the steadiest dogs I ever shot over, and never ranged out of shot. It was a real treat to see her huggle up a rail or a little bothering jack out of a bit of thick grass; and she retrieved so tenderly, that I never saw her rumple a feather, except the first lark I shot to her when I tried her. I suppose this was new to her, for she mauled it terribly, and I began to fear she was hard-mouthed, but she soon proved the contrary. She became quite a noted character round here, and I am certain I could have shot over half Wermland only for the sake of my dog. I once recollect coming down Fleet Street, when I was accosted by a corkscrew-curled gipsy-looking fellow, carrying a pretty little Skye terrier, who asked me if I wanted to buy "a nice little toy tarrier dawg," adding, as a recommendation, "sweet as a nut—clean in the 'ouse, *and wonderful tricky.*" And I soon found out that this was the case with my new retriever. I soon taught her to do almost anything—fetch a cap off a person's head in a moment, if I only pointed to it, drop my powder-flask in the reeds and send her back for it; hide my handkerchief in a room full of people (often in another person's pocket), and set her to find it; all which, and a dozen other such tricks, made her a general favourite, but on two occasions nearly brought me into serious disgrace. On one occasion, in a little party was an old gentleman who wore a skull-cap, as old gentlemen often do here. Sutt was in the room. The old gentleman was leaning back in a chair, talking to a friend. I had occasion to cross the room by the back of his chair, and in so doing laid my hand on his shoulder. Whether Sutt took this as a signal or not I cannot say, but in less than half a minute after she sprang up behind the chair, dragged off the old gentleman's thatch, and triumphantly brought it to me, amid roars of laughter from all the company, save the old gentleman, who clapped his hands to his head, wondering what the deuce was up. On another occasion, in the same house we had a little music, and a celebrated violin player, whose fiddle was a real old Cremona of a fabulous date, electrified us with his fiddle. He laid his old fiddle on the piano, and walked to the other end of the room to talk to a friend. Two little boys were larking with Sutt, and one or other of them managed to pull the cover off the piano, and the old Cremona fell. Judge my dismay, as well as that of the whole room, when Sutt sprang forward, seized the old fiddle by the handle, and brought it up to me, as proud as a peacock. I jumped up, and took it out of her mouth as tenderly as I could, and put it into the old professor's hands, who stood the very picture of misery and dismay. There was no laughing on this occasion. No one spoke a word, for if the old fiddle had been destroyed, I really think the good old owner would have scarcely deemed life worth living for. He never said a word, but walked out of the room with the fiddle under his arm. As soon as he got into the passage we could hear him run through the gamut in all directions, backwards and forwards. I never did hear such extraordinary music in my life. But in five minutes he returned with a smile on his good-humoured old face to tell us it was all right, and patting Sutt on the head, told her in Swedish that she had frightened him more than he had ever been frightened in his life. I would not have had that old fiddle injured by my dog for a hundred pounds.

I said that we were in the habit of dropping a floating trimmer here and there in the open places among these bulrushes, and now I want Mr. Francis to read this.

At the back of the island I have mentioned above is an open place in the bulrushes considerably deeper than the water in any other part of the swamp; it is probably between four and five hundred yards long, and less than one hundred broad, and has all the appearance of having originally been a fish stew; and this favours the supposition that a cloister originally stood on this mound, for we know that the old monks in all ages were desperately fond of fish. This hole is now fringed with reeds all round higher than a man's head, and choked up in all parts, save the bottom, with thick cow-docks and waterlilies. It is, in fact, the very place of all others where a large pike would lie; and my poaching experience in the still waters of our midland British streams told me so the very first time I saw it. No one had ever thought of wetting a line here; I was at once determined to try it, and the first night I had thirteen lines out with nice lively bait, and the result next morning was three pike, the one eight pounds, the other two about five pounds. This looked very promising. The next night I got another of eight pounds, and a smaller one about two pounds. The latter was dead on the hook, and when I took it off I saw its sides were mutilated, and scored here and there as if cut through to the bone with a razor. I knew "my gentleman" was now at home, and the very next night I baited with the largest and liveliest roach I could get, and went next morning to take my lines up with every anticipation of great success. However, it was a blank—one fish of about 5lb. was all we got. I did not visit the swamp again for a week, and on that day, strange to say, although we fished for some time, we could not catch a bait longer than three inches. These I fancied were no use, and thought it hardly worth trying, but luckily a fellow rowed up in a boat who had been taking up a long chain line which had been out all night, and in the bottom of the boat lay five or six half-rotten roach of three-quarters of a pound to one pound each. I got a few of these, and laid out seven lines. In the morning as soon as we spritted into the hole I saw one of the trimmer-sticks drawn fast into the candocks; and whilst I was thinking whether I had laid out a line in that spot, I was startled by a splash close to the stick, just as if you had thrown a dog in. We got to the place as soon as we could, and then I saw such a pike standing in the water, with his head to the boat (the trimmer hook just in the side bone of the jaw, and the line wrapt round the candocks), as I never fancied I should live to see. I was fairly startled, and hardly knew what to do, for I could plainly see (he was not two feet below the surface) how slightly he was hooked. I pulled up the candocks and loosed him, and he ran out into the middle of the hole, and again got fast. I will not tire the reader with all the chases we had backwards and forwards after that pike. I suppose it was at least half an hour before I got the landing-net under him, and lugged him into the boat. I never saw such a monster of a pike; he was not so very long, but so broad in the back, and darker-coloured than any pike I ever saw before. He was as fat as butter, and just weighed thirty-nine pounds Swedish, which would be somewhere about thirty-eight pounds English. I dried his head as a trophy, and I hope to have the pleasure in autumn of showing it myself to Mr. Francis, along with the hook that took the fish. I don't mean to say that he was put into the stew by the monks that owned the old cloister, but there was something very wicked and monkish in his appearance, and, judging from the length and size of his tusks (I can hardly call them teeth), might have been of any age you pleased.

We often have a night leistering in the shallow water on the open places where the reeds have been cut. We get nothing but pike; plenty of them, however, for the last night I was out I stuck twenty-seven pike. They were, however, not very large, the lot weighing together about seventy pounds. I have, however, often killed one cwt. here in the night. This is a sport (groans from the opposition) which I greatly delight in; and let me say that it takes some little skill to guide the boat single-handed, attend to the fire, and strike the fish well.

No other ducks breeds with us, as far as I can see, save the wild duck, the widgeon, and the teal; and of these the former is by far the most common. No wild geese breed with us, and, strange to say, I never even saw a flock pitch during their migrations. Towards the middle of September, the ducks get very strong and wild, the old mallards are then assuming the full plumage again, and when a shot is fired the birds rise from all parts of the reeds. About the end of September they leave the reeds, and large flocks assemble by day in the wide open water, but returning every night to the swamps to feed. It is now almost impossible to approach them without a punt-gun, and even this would hardly be safe in our wide waters. Towards the middle of the month the golden-eye come down, and the common wild duck begin to travel coastwise. A few golden-eyes remain in the open water during the winter, but no wild duck. The weather now begins to get chilly and inclement, the duck-shooting season in Sweden may be considered at an end, and with it the shooting season in all the midland districts, except an odd shot at a hare or other forest game. I never could make out which way the scoters, scaup, or geese come down from Lapland. It must be along the coast, for they certainly do not pass through the midland districts, and the same remarks will apply to the principal part of the waders.

I have only seen one double snipe this year, and that I could not kill. I do not know what is the cause, but the double snipe seem to be gradually disappearing in this country. When I first came into Wermland I killed seventeen double snipe in one afternoon in a rough, dry tussock meadow at the top of this very swamp. This was, however, a very exceptional case. The double snipe comes down to us the earliest of all the snipes, and leaves the soonest. I generally expect to find the first about the middle of August, and never kill one after the third week in September. The common snipe begin to draw down early in September, the jack towards the end of the month, although you may flush a few jacks up to the middle, even up to the end of October. The cream of the snipe-shooting here ends by the middle of October.

Take it altogether, I consider with us the past has been an excellent season for all forest game, especially capercailie; and although I never do much this way, I have killed more this year than ever I did before. My new retriever is an excellent bitch for the forest, where a pointer would be little use, and where a close-hunting, well-broken dog is the very thing, for it is wonderful how close both the capercailie and black grouse lie in the cranberry and bleaberry bushes, which form the undergrowth of the Swedish forests.

Everything now warns us that the Northern winter is approaching. The winter migrants are fast coming down from Lapland. Many of our summer birds have left. The night frosts have set in, and, as I sit and look out of my window on a forest tableau, painted in every shade of red, yellow, and green, I think of the beautiful lines of the American poet—

> "It is brilliant autumn time, the most brilliant time of all,
> When the gorgeous woods are gleaming as the leaves begin to fall—
> When the maple boughs are crimson, and the hickory shines like gold,
> When the noons are sultry hot, and the nights are frosty cold;
> When the country has no green save the sword-grass by the rill,
> And the willows in the valleys, and the pine upon the hill;
> And the pippin leaves the bough, and the sumach fruit is red,
> And the quail is piping loud from the buckwheat where he fed;
> When the sky is blue as steel, and the river clear as glass,
> When the mist is on the mountain, and the network on the grass;
> When the harvest is all housed, and the farmer's work is done,
> And the woodlands are resounding with the spaniel and the gun."

MY FIRST STEEPLE-CHASER.

"The merry men of Lincolnshire were foremost in the fray,
 When 'Walker' rode the 'Gaylad,' and 'Skipworth' steered the grey;
 Over any line of country 'Old Discount' was a trump,
 And only felt at discount in 'the mare's' rear round the clump."

I ONCE heard an old gentleman, when complaining bitterly of his son's extravagances at Oxford, wind up a long tirade against picture-dealers, dog-dealers, horse-dealers, and all other dealers, by declaring energetically that he thanked God *he* had never possessed a taste of any kind in his life. Now I have no doubt, on an abstract view of the case, he was right, for doubtless to indulge in any taste (unless it is that of money-making) dips sadly into a man's pockets, and perhaps, after all, those men will rub through life the easier who have not a single taste to gratify. It is true, nevertheless, that such men must be looked upon as mere automatons in the great drama of life, and as such are certainly more to be pitied than envied.

Now I will suppose that scarcely one of my readers agrees with this old gentleman, but I will, nevertheless, ask him one question, which is—Has he ever indulged in a taste for screw dealing? If he does so, I will candidly ask such a one whether he has not taken more interest in watching the progress of that one screw (for, screw as he may be, the owner always fondly believes that there is a hidden value in him) than in all the rest of his stud, whose capabilities he knows to a pound? There is a sort of mystery attached to the screw which is truly delightful. His greatest charm lies in his very unsoundness, and, "Oh! if I could but only get *this one* right, what a plater or hurdle-racer he would make!" is the owner's constant theme.

My First Steeple-chaser.

It is certainly now many years since I had anything to do with this class of horse, but I must confess that once on a time I never grumbled to give 15*l.* or 20*l.* for a good-looking "screw," when I should have thought twice about 35*l.* or 40*l.* for a horse which I knew was all right. This dealing in screws is, however, after all, a dangerous and expensive taste to indulge in, for I really do think that it brings a man into fellowship with more of the pariahs and outcasts of the sporting world than any other. No one can deny that it is the very lowest step in the horse-dealer's ladder. Sporting butchers, broken-down dealers, rough-riders, even the very cads of the stable, can all meet on an equality in this game, and all distinctions are levelled by the talismanic go-between of the screw.

Now mind, by screws, I do not mean old, worn-out rips, which have gradually passed through every phase in a horse's existence, worked hard in all, and at length become worn out in the service— nor the horrid screw you see in the hands of a blackguard coper at a country fair, but I mean the real "casualty horse" (and I do think no name can be more appropriate than this for the class of horse which I am describing), still in his prime, who shows good points and good breeding, but who has been disabled or blemished in his youth; perhaps has broken down in training, or been thrown up on account of his temper, or some unlucky accident or latent disease, which has baffled the keenest of the faculty, yet being too good or too handsome to be knocked on the head, he has been sold out of the stud probably for a 10*l.* note, with all his faults, and found his way into the hands of a man of whom there are dozens in every hunt, who having but little money, yet rare eyes to the good points of a horse, and who, with an intuitive love for a screw, always prefers seeing the beginning of a run in a good place, on a raking, showy, unsound bit of blood, than the finish of it, on a steady, sound old hunter. The great ambition of such a man is to endeavour to find out where the fault really lies which has baffled so much veterinary lore, and his waking and sleeping thoughts are concentrated upon his screw; no matter if the horse has only three legs to go upon, the hidden nugget lies in the fourth; and visions of county cups, hurdle-races, and it may be even a heavy steeple-chase, loom in the future—if his screw can only be once got right. I really do not know, as such a man hustles his screw up to the three or four first fences (which he is sure to clear gallantly), whether he envies a single man in the field, let him be mounted how he may. The screw can probably beat the most of them, even in his present state, ridden in the reckless manner of a man who only cares to see the first mile; and there is no saying what he may do after he is once got right, for the owner of a screw invariably feels confident that this day must come, sooner or later.

I have but to cast my mind's eye back through the dark vista of years that have fled—choose any good hunting morning in the season, by the side of a well-known covert, and the very man and horse I am describing stand revealed. A little apart from the crowd, on the grass by the roadside, a small knot of grooms and sporting, hard-riding young farmers, are gathered round a man and horse, whose prototype was to be met with in my day at every covert side in the kingdom. A rare-topped, blood-looking nag, a little queer on his pins, whose neat head is set off to advantage by a heavy snaffle-bridle, is standing in the middle of the ring, undergoing the strict scrutiny of the "horsey" crowd by whom he is surrounded. It is certainly hard to detect a flaw in the horse, except upon a very close examination, as he stands there quietly champing his bit, and swishing his long thin tail backwards and forwards, as a warning to the crowd that they had better keep clear of his heels; and, save that he looks rather more ragged and staring in his coat, we can see but little (as far as good points and breeding go) to choose between this screw (for, good as his looks are, we can tell at the first glance that he is a screw) and that magnificent satin-coated 200-guinea chestnut which has just been walked by in charge of the groom with a cockade in his hat. The rider is apparently well-known to all; has a joke for one man, a quiet bit of chaff with another, and the knowing wink and careless, but meaning, nod of the head with which he answers the inquiry of a jovial-looking farmer as to "What have you got there *now*, Tom?" tell the horse's history plainer than words can speak. A few strokes of our pen can describe the rider after a fashion as we have already attempted with the horse, but it would require the pencil of poor Leech to do the whole picture justice. There he sits, as I have seen him scores of times before, the very personification of "the right man in the right place." He is certainly not one of the upper ten thousand, but there is a confident, determined look about him which strikes the eye at once, and a quiet sporting cut about the whole man which must be bred in the possessor if he will wear it properly. Every member of the hunt, from the noble owner downwards, has a cheery word to say to him, and the quiet respectful manner which he assumes to his betters proves that he knows his place as well as his business. Originally a small farmer, but a far keener judge of the points of a horse than a bullock, a constant attendant at every race meeting and steeple-chase for miles round, his farm became neglected, and Tom was perforce obliged to look to horses as a means of gaining a living, instead of affording him a noble amusement. A reckless, devil-may-care, open-handed, open-hearted sort of a fellow, of whom the worst that could be said was that he was nobody's enemy but his own, he was a general favourite; and as he always rode as if he had a spare neck in his pocket, and possessed a cool head, a firm seat, and a fine though strong hand on a horse—the three best qualifications of a cross-country rider—he won the affections of a rich old uncle, who had already made a fortune at the very trade which Tom was only just commencing, who took him into his employ to show off his "casualty nags," and occasionally to ride steeple-chases and hurdle-races for him. And no one better fitted for the task; for if he only did mean going—which was not, however, always the case —no one harder to shake off than Tom, however he might be mounted. He was truly one of that sort immortalized in the old hunting song, who,

> " Spite of falls and bad horses, undauntedly still,
> Rode up to this motto, 'Be with them I will.'"

The whole appointments of both man and horse may perhaps

appear a little shabby when scrutinised through the eye-glass of a swell, but they are all good. The neat 10lb. hunting saddle may have seen some service, but the model and the fit are perfect; and the side loop on each flap for the surcingle to pass through prove that it is not only in the hunting field where that saddle is required to do battle. We all know that nothing sets off a screw so well as a neat-fitting saddle. A plain dark hunting martingall, and a heavy snaffle with broad reins, which look as if they would hold an elephant, complete about as workmanlike a turn-out as is to be met with at that covert side.

The dress of the man is in perfect keeping with the rest of the picture. The broad, baggy, brown cords, meet a pair of long, plain, faultless jack-boots; a tight pepper-and-salt surtout, buttoned close up to the throat, reveals in front a few inches of a long, striped groom's waistcoat; a head, which seems as if made expressly for charging through a bullfinch, is "tied on" by a neat check scarf; while a strong napless hat shades a handsome, close-shaved, weather-beaten face, in which sturdy resolution and good-nature strive for the mastery. His riding weight may be about eleven stone; and his broad shoulders, sinewy arms, and hard brown gloveless hands, added to the firm short seat, all form the very beau-ideal of a cross-country jock; and although there are perhaps scores of better-mounted men in that field, many a scrutinising eye is turned towards him as he quietly wends his way to that corner of the covert where he expects the fox to break; and more than one hard rider inwardly wonders where the deuce Tom picked up that "goodish-like horse, what he gave for him, and where his fault lies"—for the very fact of being in such hands condemns him at once. And well may they scrutinise this nag, for he is destined ere long to be a sharp thorn in many of their sides; as on this occasion Tom is mounted on "my First Steeple-chaser." For the first few fields after they have gone away the screw leads them, and the way in which he came over that ox fence in the corner of the field leading from the woods is in the mouth of every one. However, it does not suit his rider, on this first appearance with a new performer, to let all the field see where the screw is loose; so at the first check he quietly turns his horse's head homewards; and, as he gently walks him home towards his uncle's stables, picking all the soft places by the roadside, he keeps continually asking himself the oft-repeated question, but for which he has never yet been able to find an answer—What this horse really would be worth if he was not such a confounded screw?

Having introduced the nephew to the reader, we will now say a few words about the uncle. He was a small but independent gentleman-farmer, living in the same village as ourselves, well-to-do, but a very saving card; and it used to be a standing joke in our hunt when he appeared at the covert side—always showingly if not perhaps well mounted—that it was even betting which was the greatest screw, the horse or the rider. He was a pleasant, merry little fellow, and considered to be the best judge of a horse in our county: and this was saying no little, for every farmer round us was a breeder, and the names of Lottery, Gaylad, and Peter Simple were a few samples of the many nuggets that were turned up at our "diggings," where everything was dated from the year when so-and-so won the Leger or the Brockelsby. He was a beautiful light weight, with the finest seat and hands on a horse in the world; but he had unfortunately been lamed for life by a tremendous fall. His left leg had been not only broken, but perfectly shattered; and although the doctors saved it by a miracle, they could never get it straight again; and from that day he was a cripple for life, and ever after walked with a stick. I do not know, however, whether this misfortune had not its advantages; for "Pray take care of my poor leg, sir," was a rare password when the old fellow was working through a crowd up to a horse of which he particularly wanted to take stock. I sometimes used to drive him to Lincoln fair, for he bought many a sound horse on commission, though never for himself, and one of his dodges amused me much. We used to seat ourselves upon the bridge, and whenever a horse was led by which he fancied, I was started off to stop him and keep him in price, and thus give the old boy time to hop up and look the horse well over, while I was apparently attempting a deal. And it was worth something to see the polite way in which he addressed me, as I turned away, just as if he had never seen me before: "If you're quite done, sir, perhaps I can try and deal." His lameness certainly did not interfere with his equestrian powers, when once he was firm in his saddle, and although he was obliged to ride two holes shorter on his left stirrup-leather than his right, and used only a single spur, with which he was continually higgling at his horse's side, he had such a marvellous knack, to use poor old Dick Christian's words, "of catching 'em up and putting 'em at it," that he was generally in his place. I may mention that Dick Christian was a perfect oracle with the old man; and "if Christian only had that horse for twenty minutes from Ashby pastures, he'd sell him to a swell for a little fortune," was constantly in his mouth. Not that he used to risk his neck upon every "casualty hoss" that passed through his hands: the nephew did the rough work, and when he had taken the sharp edge off the screw, the uncle drove it home. He could probably have afforded to ride as good a nag as any man in the hunt; but the love for a screw was born in him, and he owned candidly that he never cared to buy a horse whose value every dealer could tell to $5l$. Always chopping and changing, swopping and higgling, he was never seen half a dozen times on the same horse; and I once heard him lament, when he was completing a little chop, after his old principle of drawing as much to boot as both the screws were worth, "It's very hard: I never get a horse that suits me but some one comes and takes a fancy to him, and I'm fool enough always to part with him." Of course the word "warranty" was not to be found in his vocabulary, for, as he told me, he never but once in his life warranted a horse sound, and that was returned on his hands; so what was the use of a man's word in horse-dealing? Still there was nothing of the low dealer or coper about him. Scrupulously neat and clean in his dress and appearance, his manners, whenever he could sink the shop, fitted him for any company. I never heard an oath or a coarse word pass his lips; his pew in the little village church was never vacant on the Sunday morning; and, strange as it may appear in one of his trade,

I do not believe he'd have told a lie to save his life. Mind, I don't always mean to say that he "told the whole truth" on all occasions; but whatever he did tell you was a fact; his style of dealing did not require to be pushed by the aid of lies and crooked prevarications. No one ever dreamt that a horse was sound when he had one to sell, and he never wished anyone to think so; but he never was known to deceive a man when he bought a horse for him on commission. He was strict enough then about the warranty, which he handed over to the purchaser with the receipt, charged his commission, and, as far as he was concerned, the matter was at an end, and I never once heard a man find fault with a horse which had been bought through him. When he had, however, a horse of his own to sell, his style of doing business was this:—"I had him of so-and-so, but he's wonderfully improved since I got him" (which was generally the case). "I know nothing about him, mind; but it's my opinion, if he only gets into the right hands, and shakes off that lameness, he'll make such a horse as we have not had in our county for many a day. Now you know as much about him as I do. They do tell me he's got by so-and-so, and that looks likely enough. Thirty pounds is his price, with all his faults; if he was sound, I should ask you 100*l.* Why, his very looks would sell him, if he were lame all round." And he was considered such a rare judge of what a horse really was and might be made, that I don't know whether many a man did not rather prefer buying one that was a little screwy out of his hands in preference to a sound one from a regular dealer. Blood and bone were what he most looked at. 15.1 was his lowest height, and 20*l.* the highest price that he gave, except on extraordinary occasions. He had a perfect horror of a fast trotter; his pace was always a sling canter along the green turf by the roadside, and although no one was fonder of setting a parcel of young farmers larking across his own farm, he detested it in the field, unless a horse was sure to be sold by it; and his standing motto to the young ones used to be, that he never knew a horse have one jump too many left in him at the end of a long run. A country racecourse was his delight, especially when, as was generally the case, he had some rip or other to run. And although he had never missed a Leger since he was twenty, he rarely laid a shilling on a race. He was a perfect walking racing calendar, knew the pedigree of every stallion out, and the fund of turf information he possessed was extraordinary. Like all good judges, however, he was shy of giving an opinion; and "I'm told, mind you, although I know nothing myself, that such a horse will see a better day," was his quiet way of " putting a friend on ;" and it generally turned out well for those that took the hint.

Now, after all this long rambling preface, I fancy it is about time that I told the reader something about my first steeple-chase horse. Well, it was, as near as I can recollect, in the end of July, 184— that I had to go down from our place to York upon some business. I met the night coach on the North-road, and as there was plenty of room, I got the box-seat alongside of the coachman. At our first stage, the coachman—who, like the rest of the craft, dabbled in horses a little himself, and, of course, knew my old friend— begged me to look at his near leader, when we got down to change, for he fancied he was just the sort of nag to suit him, "for, although," added the man, "he certainly is a little groggy, I'll eat my hat, if he only got into the right hands, a pot of money might not be made out of him." At the next change we stopped to supper, and I then had lots of time to examine the horse in whom lay such hidden treasures. His looks certainly did not belie the coachman's words. Apparently as thorough-bred as Eclipse, sixteen hands high, with lots of bone, and a nose which, as his owner observed, might be got into a quart pot, while rather drooping quarters and a long thin swish tail gave him quite a varmint appearance. Indeed, I think I never set my eyes on a much more taking horse than this —his very poverty only brought out his good points into bolder relief; and were it not for an unfortunate twitch apparently in the near hind leg as he limped towards the stable, he would have been perfect. But the secret of his being in this team was accounted for by this very lameness, which had baffled all the best veterinary surgeons in the North, and was destined to remain incurable till the patient underwent a course of charges and "inflammable iles" under the hands of a queer, eccentric, but very clever country horse-doctor, who was attached to the stables. I could well believe the coachman when he told me his horse's pedigree: how he had gone lame in training, and no one could find out the seat of the disease; and after the usual vicissitudes in such a horse's career, he had come down to leader in a night coach, where he seemed likely to end his days, unless by some lucky accident his enthusiastic driver should succeed to some property, when he was at once to be released from slavery, and again put into training; "and if only that hind leg would stand, he was to win the Liverpool in a canter." I may add, that amongst his other accomplishments he had carried a whip, was a perfect fencer, and could be ridden by a lady in a packthread.

There is one good thing when one buys a horse with all his faults—it saves a deal of trouble in examination and no end of lies. This examination is often great humbug, for two-thirds of the buyers who look into a horse's mouth, punch his ribs, pass their hands down the legs, do so only because they have seen others do the same—but as for any idea of how old the horse is, or whether he is sound or not, after such a scrutiny, they are just as wise as they were before. It however gives them an importance in their own eyes at least, for to be considered "horsey" is the height of many a young man's ambition. But don't let any of these unfortunates fancy that the real dealer is deceived by all this: he knows at once the sort of man he has to deal with by the very way in which he walks up to a horse, just as surely as a gunmaker knows at a glance only, by the manner in which a man handles a gun in his shop, whether or not he is a customer with whom he can take liberties. There is only one point to be settled when buying a screw, and that is the price; and as the coachman did not open his mouth too wide (he had given, he told me, 15$l.$ to his brother, who was stud-groom to Lord ——, for the horse, and as he wanted to get a box-coat and a new hat out of him, he thought 23$l.$ would not be too much) after about five minutes' chaff—for of all bargains none is so prolific in the latter commodity as one like the present—the bargain was struck, and the horse that was to win the Liverpool in a canter became mine, at the nominal price (according to the seller's idea) of 23*l*.

In this instance there was a little more chaff than usual, for every strapper and horse-keeper in the stable (which, perhaps, turned out some sixty coach-horses in the day) seemed to be particularly interested in this bargain, and everyone had some remarks to make on my new purchase. I am sorry to say that these remarks in general, directly the bargain was closed (for, of course, no one opened before) were anything but complimentary to old "Dot-and-Go-One," as the horse had been facetiously christened in this stable; and one ugly old fellow, who answered to the characteristic name of "Ginger," and who was evidently the wit of the stable, was particularly annoying. "So you've bought our steeple-chase hoss, have you, sir? well, he's a rare bred 'un— got by Golumpus, dam by Highflyer, I should say, for he's quite old enough. You'll want a stud-groom, sir, when he goes down to Liverpool: better take me along with him." This was a specimen of the badinage in which he indulged, as soon as the coachman had bustled away to see after his way-bill. And, as I left the stable, I just caught his last remark—"Ah, he looks like a steeple-chaser, *he* do! Should not wonder if that swell means to ride him hisself;" which was the signal for a hearty guffaw from the assembled strappers.

However, old Dot-and-Go-One had now become my property; and as I went towards the bar to look after the coachman and settle for my new purchase, I walked with a dignity befitting the owner of the winner of the Liverpool in prospective. After I had paid for him, I was determined that he should never again look through a collar in my possession, so I bargained with the landlord to keep him till I returned; and I deemed it prudent to make friends with old "Ginger" before I left, as most probably he would have charge of the horse during my absence. This was very soon effected by the gift of a gallon of ale, and the promise of half-a-crown more when I returned, if I found the horse well cared for. The man now became very civil, but he could not altogether drop his chaff. Such an opportunity for the display of his wit had not occurred for a long time, and he was determined to make the most of it. As he drank success to my new bargain, he confidentially asked me to let him "stand a fiver in the first race I ran him for," and he kept continually following me about for orders as to how he was to treat the horse during my absence—what bandages he should put on; whether I would have his mane plaited, or his tail banged; in fact, it was quite evident he regarded me as "a muff," and nothing else. This, however, I cared little for at that time—the days had long passed by when the slightest imputations on my pretensions to be a sportsman would have been regarded as a personal insult; and although I never went so far as the old betting-man we read of, who declared that he would willingly give 100*l*. to be taken once again for a flat at Newmarket, I had much rather, when having anything to do with horses, be regarded as a fool than not.

On a lovely August morning, about a week after making the bargain as already narrated, I again pulled up at the door of the little roadside inn, to take possession of my new purchase. A week's rest had done wonders for the old cripple—he did not appear to go a bit lame as he walked out of the stable; and even the landlord, of whom I borrowed a bridle and saddle (for I intended to ride the horse home myself), seemed struck with his good looks, as he was led to the door. I must say, screw as he was, I was much pleased with my new bargain. He cantered so corkily along the grass by the roadside, that I was tempted to have a shy at some rails by the side of a gate, which we so often see across a country lane, and he popped over them like a bird. There was not much in this leap, it is true, but there was a good deal in the style he jumped it, which showed that he could do twice as much, if it was asked of him.

It was early when I reached my friend's house; but laziness was never one of his faults, and he stood on his lawn to welcome me, in company with the very two men of all others to whom I wished to show the new nag—his nephew, the rough-rider and the vet. I pulled up close to the trio, and the two questions, "What have you got there?" and "Well, what do you think of this one?" passed each other, as it were, on the road. I was soon out of my saddle, and Tom in my place. The old gentleman hopped two or three times round the horse to look him well over, but never spoke a word; he hardly cared to look into his mouth. His quick eye soon detected where the screw was loose, directly Tom walked him round him, down the gravel walk, and "There, take him round to the stable, and come in and have some breakfast," was the only sentence he uttered till we got into the snug little parlour, which I so well remember, with the sporting pictures arranged round the walls, the bookshelves filled with odd volumes of the sporting magazines, and the perfect museum of hunting-whips, jockey-whips, and other sporting paraphernalia in the different corners. And then the cheering, substantial breakfast! I soon told the history of the horse; and although I had rather exceeded the regulation price, the old man did not seem to think that I had done wrong. We all visited the stable after breakfast, and had a careful examination of the horse, who, I was sorry to observe, was now pulled out as lame as ever. Notwithstanding all their knowledge, not one of the three could decide exactly where the horse was lame. The vet. fancied the lameness laid in the pastern, and was for firing at once; the nephew fancied it was in the hock; while the old man declared he was lame all round. Still they all agreed that he was a very likely horse, and the vet. quite deemed that it lay within the powers of his science to bring him round.

Now, it so happened that in our hunt we had an annual steeple-chase every March, of 5*l*. entrance, with 50*l*. added, and it was the ambition of every hard-riding member of the hunt to win this steeple-chase. The old man had attempted it twice and failed, notwithstanding all the powerful assistance of his nephew, who was certainly by far the best cross-country race-rider in the hunt. He fancied that he saw in this horse the very thing he had long been looking for; and without aspiring quite so high as the coachman, his late owner, he still thought him good enough to win this race, if he only once came right; and the old man was not deceived. One of the conditions of this 12st. steeple-chase was, that every horse must have been hunted one season with the hounds, and be ridden by a member of the hunt. Now, here was just the thing to hand.' We had certainly the services of the best jockey. It wanted full three months to the beginning of the hunting season to try and bring the horse round. The risk was not great; so a bargain was struck at once. The old gentleman was to take half the horse, and we were to be part-owners; share the expenses and the winnings. He was to have the sole management of the affair; I was only to be a sort of sleeping partner, and not to interfere in the least with the training. Tom was to ride, and have a share in the stakes, if he won, and we agreed to put the Vet. on at 25l. to nothing in his first race, if only he could get the horse right to the post.

Certainly if our hunt steeple-chase was destined ever to be won by a screw, it did seem as if old Dot-and-Go-One was to be the lucky horse, considering the hands he had now got into. Of course we were all bound to secrecy: the horse was to have a run in one of the old man's meadows, and then to be brought up and got into hunting condition. Although part owner, I knew no more what mysterious operations that horse went through than the very coachman of whom I had bought him, but I believe both the old man and the vet. had an anxious time of it. Sometimes the horse would come limping out of the stable at a pace which the old man, with the aid of his stick, could have beaten, down the gravel-walk; sometimes he seemed to go lame on one leg, sometimes on the other, and sometimes all round; at others he would come bounding out of the stable as if he had never been lame in his life. Scores of times did the old man declare he would give treble the value of the horse if he could only discover where the lameness really did lie, and many an anxious hour did he spend in watching him and thinking what a triumph it would be if he only could carry off this much-coveted prize with a screw, of whose existence no one in the hunt had the least idea. But, wherever the disease lay, or whatever remedies were applied, the horse certainly did get better, and by the middle of November he was seen at the covert-side.

The winter passed over, and the old horse kept much about the same. On his sound days nothing could beat him, when Tom chose to send him along—for he was riding to orders, and never took the horse through a whole run; and sometimes he would appear at the covert-side so lame that chaps began to wonder what reason Tom had for persevering with such a screw. Still he was now in rare condition, and as the stable had found out the secret that, however lame he might start, he always managed to shake off his lameness in about the first mile, and as he was a splendid fencer and had a great turn of speed (for Tom had managed to get the length with him of some of the best horses in the hunt), it began to look quite on the cards that the much wished-for prize would come home to these stables at last. Although part owner, I had never got on the horse since the day I rode him home, but I now and then saw him out with the hounds; and one morning when I rode home by his side, Tom informed me confidentially that he had the cracks safe enough, and if the race was to be won by an outsider, old Dot-and-Go-One would have it.

In these hunt steeple-chases there is usually very little mystery, and it is pretty well known months beforehand what horses will be entered. In fact, the owners are generally proud of their horses, and boast of what they are able to do, and, as they know they have to meet nothing but what they have seen out many times before, they have more confidence than in a great open race; in fact, these steeple-chases used to differ not in the least from a usual run, save that the men wore jackets instead of coats, and instead of choosing their own line had to ride over a certain number of ordinary hunting-fences between two flags. There was, however, on this occasion, one horse which puzzled all the hunt, and this was the screw. Of course Tom was as close as wax about him, and all that his nearest friends could get out of him, when they tried to work the pump, was, "I can't think whatever the old fool (his uncle) means, by sticking to this screw for so long. I never can see the end of a run on him, and if he goes ever so sound for the first mile, he's sure to shut up before the end of the second." But there were a few old hands who had watched

Master Tom very closely, and had seen him pull up and leave the field, when old Dot-and-Go-One was full of running. They, moreover, knew very well that the old man (his uncle) had always some good reason for what he was doing, and it did not surprise them in the least when the entries for the Findon Steeple Chase "came out" in the county paper a fortnight before the race to see in the list of fifteen entries Mr. ———'s br. g. Dot-and-Go-One, aged, blue body, white sleeves and black cap. The mystery of the brown screw was partly cleared up, but no one was a bit the wiser as to his capabilities. He was never seen out in the field again after the entries were published, for his owner declared in the words of the old Yorkshire trainer that, save a little gentle exercise on his own farm, "the old horse should never sweat again till he sweated for the brass." However, it was nothing new for the old man to run a screw and get beaten; and the two cracks of the hunt—the one a magnificent chestnut gelding by Priam, belonging to a farmer who had won this steeple-chase in the two previous years, and the other a wiry little bay mare, nearly thorough-bred, the property of a half-pay captain—were made hot favourites, and backed at very short odds against the field. 12 to 1 could be had about any other, and two or three who placed unlimited confidence in the old man's judgment went about quietly picking up these odds wherever they could get them about the screw; and although it was never a very heavy betting race, one young fellow, "just out," who had taken great liberties with the horse, in consequence of a trifling dispute he had with Tom about a favourite hunter which he rode, and which Tom had declared to be nothing better than a pig, found himself upon the eve of the race to stand to win 500*l.* on either of the favourites, but to lose about 1500*l.* if Dot-and-Go-One pulled through, of which 300*l.* would find its way into Tom's pocket.

The little village of Findon lay in the best and stiffest-enclosed part of our hunt, about twelve miles from us. The village itself stood on a gentle rise, and the old ivy-covered church-tower was a landmark for miles. The snug parsonage, embedded in a clump of large elms, where the rooks had held undisputed sway for centuries, stood close into the church, while neat farmhouses and well-filled stack-yards scattered around, bespoke the agricultural wealth of the district. The village, of course, boasted its blacksmith's shop, its pound, and its one public-house, the " Rutland Arms," where good accommodation was to be obtained for man and horse, and whose excellent loose boxes never stood empty on the night before a Findon Toll-bar meet. As a man gazed from the hillside by the church upon the valley below, his eye wandered over a panorama such as few countries could display—a panorama such as is never seen out of merry England, and which stretched for miles over perhaps the best agricultural as well as the best hunting country in the world. The little river Swift—which here dwindled to a brook, but a brook of formidable dimensions—wound its tortuous course through rich meadows, which bounded it on either side ; while ploughed fields of stiff, useful clay-land, and large enclosures of old swarth, which had never been turned up by the plough within the memory of man, separated by bull-finches, ox-fences, strong post-and-rails, and splashed stake-and-bound growing blackthorn hedges, with a ditch on each side, all formed the *beau-ideal* of a stiff hunting-country.

The start for the steeple-chase was in a meadow close to the village, and the brook, or river as it was called, which was the third fence from the first flag, was here, perhaps, eighteen feet wide, and eight to ten feet deep. After this the line went on over large enclosures of grass and plough, with some excellent galloping ground up to the flag, placed in a grass field about two miles distant, round which the horses had to come ; and then back again over much the same line of country, down to the brook again—which, however, was not nearly so wide on returning; and then on to the finish between two flags placed in the starting meadow, giving a straight run-in of about four hundred yards from the last fence. The whole line, including twenty-seven good hunting fences, and the brook twice, was beautifully chosen ; and as almost every man and horse who went for the race knew the country well, and had crossed the line some time or another with the hounds, it was a far more open race than many of the crack steeple-chases, where horse and rider, perhaps, never see the country before the morning of the race. Our friend Tom, who had ridden in this steeple-chase twice before, and knew the line to an inch, was very confident this time, for the country was deep, and he considered old Dot-and-Go-One just the sort of horse to pull off the race. The old horse had certainly wonderfully improved, and, although he still went at times a little lame, such was his strength and bottom that it seemed scarcely to interfere with his going, especially in deep ground; added to that, he rarely made a mistake at his fences, and had a good turn of speed over the flat. Of course, as in most steeple-chases, the brook was the centre of attraction, for it was pretty certain that on this day more than one nag and rider would have a cold bath; but the fence which all the old hands considered the most dangerous in the race was the fourth fence from home coming back, leading out of a ploughed field into the meadow where the brook had to be crossed for the second time. This was a new, strong, splashed blackthorn hedge, above four feet high, with growers and binders thicker than a man's arm, on a bank, with a wide ditch on both sides. If a horse made the least mistake here he must be thrown out of the race, for it would neither bend nor break. It was well known to all the hard riders in the hunt, and more than one had come down a tremendous cropper at this very fence. Not one place in it was weaker than another, so it must be taken in the line; and as the horses before they came back to it would be naturally distressed, it was clear that more than one would come to grief at this stake-and-bound rise—as the country people here called it. A lane ran parallel with the side fence of the meadow where the right hand flag was placed; and here all who had the most interest in the horses stationed themselves, for it was pretty certain that at this point it would be decided who had the race in hand.

It is needless to dwell upon the bustle and excitement that prevailed throughout the little village on the evening before the steeple-chase. It would be tedious as a thrice-told tale. Ten horses had arrived; and as two horses from the village were sure to go, and one or two more were expected in the morning, the probable starters were calculated at thirteen or fourteen. Every farmhouse was filled on this evening, and even the parsonage had its mild coterie of hard-riding black coats, each of whom had some interest, although he did not care to show it, in watching how young So-and-so (a farmer's son, probably from his own parish) would perform on this memorable occasion. The Rutland Arms was full of grooms, horse-dealers, and hard-riding outsiders, who had not exactly the entry of the better houses, and here the fun was fast and furious; while each jovial farmer and comely farmer's wife and daughter did the honours of the table to a company as jovial and as truly British as themselves. Not much talk about agricultural distress on this evening! The prices of wheat or oats were never once quoted; and if £ s. d. were ever touched upon, it was merely to inquire the price of such and such a horse for the next day's race. The little village was in a perfect blaze—lights streamed from every window and open door, the stable lanterns flitted across the different yards like meteors, as anxious grooms or owners visited their favourites, to see if all was comfortable for the night; while every now and then the stentorian chorus of some good old hunting song would break upon the ear, disturbing the stillness of the usually quiet street. Oh, these happy *réunions* of jovial manly spirits! the remembrance of which no distance of time can ever obliterate! By midnight, however, every light was extinguished, every voice hushed. Young jockeys were restlessly tossing in their beds, wondering what luck the morrow had in store for them; while the older ones were riding the race over mentally, and weighing their own chances against those of other good rivals whom they were so soon to meet. A loose box had been engaged for our horse at the Rutland Arms; but night closed in, and, to the surprise of many, he had not made his appearance. Not that I was a bit surprised, for there was something mysterious about all that my old friend did, and I, moreover, well knew that the horse was standing comfortably bedded up at a farmhouse about four miles distant. "They'll see us quite early enough in the morning, depend upon it," was the old man's remark to Tom as he locked the stable-door for the last time that night—a remark which even elicited a grim smile from old Sam, who was stud groom on this occasion.

About eleven next morning the little cavalcade walked up the village street, "the observed of all observers." The old horse in neat blue and white body-clothing, with all the accompaniments, in true sporting marching order, led by Sam; Tom (in full jockey costume, his colours, however, hidden by a blue pilot cloth pea-jacket, his silk cap stuffed into his hat), and the old uncle, following on their ponies. I never remember seeing old Sam look so respectable or so pleasant as he did on this eventful morning. He never once contradicted his old master, never interfered with orders, and the only remark I heard him make to Tom as he gave him a lift-up in the stable-yard of the inn was, "There, God bless you! the old man's told you what to do. I don't want to see you again till you come back to weigh in;" and Sam kept his word, for he never moved from the public-house parlour, where he sat stoically ruminating over his pipe, till an ostler breathlessly rushed in with, "Your horse has won!" And then, "I knew he would," was the only comment he made, as he bustled out to lead the winner back to scale.

There was no denying it, that as Tom rode down to the starting-meadow, he and old Dot-and-Go-One looked a very dangerous couple, and the jockey of the favourite hurriedly whispered to his owner, as they passed him, "I should not see a bit of fear if we only had that fellow and his screw safe in the brook." However, the last jockey's hand had been shaken, the last instructions had been given, and thirteen horses, ridden by thirteen of the best riders in our hunt, were all drawn up in a line, anxiously waiting for the signal to start :

> "All good 'uns to look at, and good 'uns to go,
> And if put at the pound-wall of Ballinasloe,
> There was not one among them would ever turn—no."

MY FIRST STEEPLECHASE.
"'I'll give you a lead over,' shouted Tom."—P. 91.

The day was fine, and country people mustered strong, every hard rider for miles around was there, and a cheer burst from the crowd as the clear manly voice of one of the stewards (over whose farm the principal part of the line ran) shouted " Are you all ready, gentlemen? Then off you go." And away the lot went, like a flock of pigeons floating over a dovecote top. The three fences leading down to the brook were cleared by all in their stride without a mistake; but directly they got into the meadow, three or four of the older jockeys were seen to take a pull at their horses as if to steady them for what was coming. " I'll give you a lead over," shouted Tom, as he came through his horses, and old Dot-and-Go-One skimmed over the brook like a swallow on a summer evening. As he turned in his saddle after he had landed, to see who had followed him, five horses and riders were struggling in the brook. while seven were in the meadow with himself. As soon as he had seen our horse well over, my old friend and myself, with a crowd of well-mounted farmers, galloped across to the lane to watch them come back over what the old man called the " casualty fence " in the race; and we, therefore, did not see much of the horses again till they had turned the middle flag. Only two of those that got in the brook came again into the race, and they did not catch the other horses till they were half way round. One of the Findon horses—a great, strong, fine-looking hunter—had rushed to the front, after crossing the brook, and made the pace tremendous, closely followed by the favourite and two others. Tom lay about fifth, the whole time inwardly wondering how long it would be after they had rounded the flag before the leaders came back to him. Strange to say, there was hardly one of the front division that he was the least afraid of; but there was a great raking chestnut mare who had lain close to him throughout the race, taking every fence just behind him as surely and safely as himself, but who never tried to pass him, which he began now to consider dangerous. Tom had taken no notice of this chestnut at starting, nor could he for the life of him call to mind either the mare or her rider. The young farmer who steered her was evidently riding to orders, and those orders clearly were to let Tom lead, and keep close behind him. No matter whatever fence he went at, the chestnut took it exactly in the same place; and if he tried a bit of a spurt, it was all the same, she stuck as close to him as his shadow. As soon as he rounded the flag, the horses began to change places. Two of the leaders fell back, while Tom gradually crept to the front, followed closely by the mysterious chestnut; and when we saw them again, within three fields of the great fence, Tom was leading, the chestnut and four others well up, but nothing else in the race. In the field leading down to this fence the favourite and one of the Findon horses drew up to the two leaders, and the four came down to the hedge together. The rider of the chestnut now changed his tactics, and, instead of following Tom over, charged the fence in a line with him. Probably he was afraid of Tom coming down right before him; in fact, it was a very awkward place either to lead or to follow over, and one which had much better be taken alone. The Findon horse got down to it first, but swerved at the crowd in the lane, and had to be turned and put at it again before he cleared it. Tom and the chestnut went over beautifully side by side; the favourite fell a burster. The Findon horse could not be got over till the leaders were nearly down to the brook, and only two of the other horses came on to the fence, one of whom fell, the other scrambled over. The race was now left to Tom and the chestnut: they cleared the brook so near together that their knees almost touched on landing. Tom took a pull at his horse, and the chestnut passed him and went on with the running. This was bad policy, and just what Tom wanted. Whether the young farmer thought he had the screw safe, or whether he now fancied that he could win as he liked, and wished his friends at the winning flags to see by how far he could win, there is no telling; but he pressed his mare on over the fence into the straight run-in, and then set to work with her; Tom all the while lying close to him, but so straight behind him that the jockey on the chestnut could not see him till they were within a hundred yards of the winning flags. It was now Tom's turn, and rousing up old Dot-and-Go-One with three overhand cuts that might have been heard all over the meadow, he closed in with the mare and won on the post by a short length. "A magnificent finish!" shouted the bystanders, but there were a few in the crowd who saw but little in the finish except a splendid waiting race on Tom's part, who, they felt confident, could have won by twenty lengths if he had pleased; and directly I heard the old uncle's remark, as he shook his hand upon winning, "You did that monstrous well, my lad," and saw the nephew's quiet smile, I was of the same opinion myself.

Every one cheers a winning jockey, and of course Tom came in for his share; in fact, he was a pretty general favourite with all, and many who had no pecuniary interest in the race were really glad that he had won. The old uncle was in a state of great excitement, and it was a treat to see him as he rode by Tom's side back to scale in a barn, belonging to one of the stewards, gracefully bowing right and left, in acknowledgment of the cheers, which he understood quite as much for himself as for the old horse and its plucky rider. As for Tom, he bore his honours very meekly; the expression of his countenance rarely displayed the workings of his mind; but I observed him suddenly change colour as he approached a little pony-carriage, standing close to the gate leading out of the winning-field. My eye involuntarily followed his, and, on looking in that direction, I saw a respectable but very surly old gentleman sitting in that little carriage, who stared at our party, but without taking the least notice of any one of us, and by his side a dark-eyed, dark-haired girl, apparently his daughter. The girl was pale as death, but her black eye flashed fire as it caught Tom's, and a deep red flush mantled over her cheek and forehead as she slightly waved a white handkerchief which she held carelessly in her hand. No one observed this dumb show save Tom, myself, and, of course, the lynx-eyed old uncle, whose eagle glance nothing escaped; and as we rode together up to the scales he confided to me that this girl, the daughter of one of the richest farmers in the county, might have been Tom's wife long ago, if he had only been tolerably steady; but the old man her father not exactly approving of Master Tom's goings-on, had peremptorily forbidden him his house, and threatened his daughter with penalties far worse than those of a convent, if she ever spoke to him again. The girl obeyed her father at the price of a broken heart, but she silently registered a vow in heaven, that if she could not become Tom's wife she would never become the wife of another man; and this vow she solemnly kept, perhaps living on in hope, but gradually dying of despair. The old uncle wound up his little history with "Mind you, her father's an old fool, for if the girl had married Tom she might have kept him straight; anyhow, she could never have been more miserable than she is now. There's many worse-looking fellows than Tom; and if he is a little wild, all I can say is, there is not a more straightforward chap or a better rider in our hunt." The old gentleman evidently thought it impossible to say more in his favour.

After the steeple-chase came a hurdle-race, but although two of the steeple-chase horses went for it, one of them winning, the old gentleman would not enter our horse, as he had a better plan in his head, which he brought about in the evening. All left the course well pleased with their day's fun. Many went home that night, but we all stayed; and Sam had strict injunctions to see after the old horse, as he might be wanted again in the morning. The owner of the chestnut was not half satisfied with his defeat, and his son, the jockey, was very sore at having been out-ridden by Tom. In the course of the evening party-feeling waxed high, for both horses had their supporters, and after a great deal of personal chaff a match was made for 50*l.* a-side, to come off next morning at eleven, over the steeple-chase course. As Tom quietly closed a 10*l.* bet with his rival rider, his sarcastic remark of "Just see what an example I'll make of you in the morning, young man. You shall ride a waiting race to-morrow, whether you like it or not," raised the hopes of our party; and he kept his word.

The match came off as agreed. Tom jumped away with the lead, and kept it the whole way round, gradually improving it up to the big fence, where the chestnut fell, and the screw cantered in by himself.

At three o'clock we left the village for the farmhouse, where we meant to stay the night; and as old Sam led our horse in triumph out of the inn yard, he pithily observed to a group of stable-men and grooms who had gathered round to see him start, "There, I don't fancy you'll want us again at Findon for a twelvemonth." Just as the old horse was leaving the yard, Tom walked up to his head and pinned on each side of the head-stall a blue and white rosette, which the old uncle mysteriously whispered to me had been sent him in the morning by " that party." There was certainly some value attached to these little cockades, for on going into Tom's bachelor apartments a short time after the race, I observed them pinned up over the bracket where his whips hung; and whenever afterwards he left home to ride the old horse in a race, they accompanied him as surely as his whip and spurs, and generally decorated the horse's head as he returned home a winner.

After lunch the stakes for both the steeple-chase and the match were handed over to my old friend, who generously left 10*l.* behind him for the poor of the parish (" Reads well in the country paper, don't you see ?"); and after deducting 25*l.* for the Vet., according to promise, and 5*l.* for old Sam, he divided the rest into three parts, for himself, Tom, and me. He had now gained the long coveted prize—he had won "the Findon," and that with a screw, which he flattered himself no one could have doctored but himself. Tom had made a very good day's work; his share in the stakes, and about 300*l.* in bets, came to enough, as the old man observed, to stock a little farm with. But " if you'll be a little more steady, you may marry that girl yet, and do well," only met with a sad shake of the head from Tom, as he tossed off a bumper of sherry and left the room. As for myself, not a word of praise fell to my share for having been the original purchaser of the horse—in fact, I was a real sleeping partner, in every sense of the word, and had no more to say in regard to the management of the old screw than the coachman of whom I bought him.

As soon as we got home, an important ceremony took place—that of re-christening our horse. He had now distinguished himself; 150*l.* had been bid for him, in two places, as the auctioneers say, before we left Findon, and we considered he was fully entitled to a less plebeian name than Dot-and-Go-One. Now the christening of a horse who has three or four masters is not an easy matter; each one of us had a fancy name of his own. I thought "Splinter Bar" appropriate, on account of his having been bought out of a coach. Tom leant to "Rory O'More," or "Donald Caird," probably from having some kindred feeling with these worthies. The Vet. had hardly a mind on the subject, so long as he was consulting physician, and Tom was jockey. He fancied the old horse good enough to win under any name, so we just left the choice to the old man, who, to our great surprise, went at once into the classics, and thought Hercules would "look very well on paper." I fancy it would have puzzled him to tell us who Hercules was, for, as old Baron Alderson observed to one of the witnesses in the noted Running Rein case, when the counsel asked him where they got the name of Maccabeus from, "Oh! that name comes out of a book which your party very seldom look into." However, Hercules it was, and three weeks after Mr. ———'s br. g. Hercules (late Dot-and-Go-One) figured in the entries for a steeple-chase in Warwickshire. This time, however, Hercules came home without the cockades, for he was beaten cleverly by Powell on the Grey (I believe, candidly, through jockeyship, though none of us told Tom so, as we did not much mind, for we had little or nothing on the race, and saved our stake). His work, however, now began in earnest. It did not suit my old friend when he had a good bit of stuff to work upon to let him stand idle, and throughout the whole summer Hercules and Tom had a merry time of it, flitting about the country like two Will-o'-the-Wisps, from one little race meeting to another; and wherever there was a small plate or hurdle-race to be run for, they were sure to make their appearance on the morning of the race, sweeping off everything before them till they became almost as notorious in our district as old Isaac and Sam Darling used to be on the Warwickshire side. As he never went for any very great stake, the old horse rarely met with company to make him gallop; and although the stakes he won were generally small, they paid expenses and a little over, and gained my old friend a kind of notoriety which he had so long aimed at.

Yellow-leaved autumn, however, came round again at last, and the old horse, who now scarcely ever went lame, but who, strange to say, notwithstanding all his knocking about, seemed to keep as fresh on his legs as ever, and who was always, to use a favourite expression of old Sam's, " A rare doer," made his appearance for the last time at Findon gorse, early in November, just to show himself to his old friends once again, previous to his going down into a remote western county—which my old friend, whose knowledge of geography was limited to " the sheers," as he called them, fancied was altogether out of England—to run for the great event of his life, the Grand Annual Aristocratic Bideford Steeple-chase (this was not exactly the name, but it is near enough for our purpose), of 20 sovs. entrance, with 100 added, and in which Vanguard, Peter Simple, Gaylad, and a host of other cracks, were to meet as competitors. Hercules was now in a racing stable, for, as my old friend observed, the horse was public property, and the responsibility of bringing him out for this great race was more than he dare undertake himself, so he was placed for about six weeks with one Mr. Snaffle, to put the final polish on him. The weekly bulletins were favourable; and when it became generally known that he was meant for the race, every member of our hunt felt interested in the old horse's success, and many a quiet commission was sent up to London to back him by men who rarely hazarded a shilling on a race. Now, although old Hercules was well known as a good horse among a limited circle, his fame had hardly spread beyond that circle, and however good he might be among platers, with country jockeys on their backs, it was quite a different thing when he had to meet the best steeple-chasers in England, with regular professional jockeys up, and twelve or fifteen to one could be easily obtained about him. But the stable-money was on him, Tom declared himself equal to the task of steering him, and, as the journey was long, the old horse started about ten days before the race, in charge of Mr. Snaffle's head lad on a mule, for we had no railroad conveyance direct at that time, and we could hardly stand the expense of a van with posters. He reached the little town about three days before the race, and when he took gentle exercise on the racecourse the morning after his arrival, was observed by more than one lynx-eye, who was watching him, to *go a little lame.*

The race was fixed for the Wednesday, and it was agreed that our party should take the night coach up to London on the Saturday night, and reach Bideford comfortably by the Tuesday morning. The old horse travelled across the country, and in less than half the distance. On the Saturday our hounds met at Waverley Wood, and Tom rode over to meet them on another " casualty nag," which my old friend had lately picked up cheap. He was not a bad topped horse, and perhaps less of a screw than the generality of horses that came into these stables, but he was a vicious, hard-mouthed brute, a regular "mistechst" devil, as old Sam used to observe (I never could define this mysterious word), who could do almost anything he liked when in the humour, but, if he were not, was just as likely to take the bit between his teeth and walk through a gate, or flight of rails, without rising at them. We were to start at eight to meet the up night-coach on the north road, and Tom promised not to do more than just to show the horse the hounds and be home to dinner (which always on hunting days consisted of a beef-steak pudding) by two. I never saw him in such high spirits before. He was in rare condition, and just the steeple-chase weight to a pound. He quite longed to meet some of the cracks, and inwardly hoped that he might be able to turn the tables on the Grey this time. During my connexion with this steeple-chase horse, I had been brought much into contact with Tom. I had come to know him better, and the more I knew him the more I liked him. Under a rough exterior and the veil of wild reckless manner, there was a vein of simple, warm-hearted kindness running through his character which atoned for many a fault; and when, in his calm moments, I could draw him away from the only subjects he cared much to talk about, I was struck with the justice and soundness of the remarks which fell from his lips. He was, in fact, but one specimen of a class unfortunately too common—a class of men who have been well brought up in their youth, but having abandoned all to the fascinations of a sporting life, find themselves in a few years drawn into a vortex from which they can never extricate themselves, and linked in irrevocably with associates whom they can never shake off. Study the private history of a hundred such men, and we shall find that in ninety cases a woman has accelerated the fall. So it was with Tom.

The morning was dull and mild; a heavy dew hung on the hedges, and little globes of water, pure and clear as crystal, stood on every turnip-top. The old uncle prophesied that it would be very nasty riding in the deep woodlands this day, and thought Tom was as well at home; but he wanted to see a friend or two before he started for the race, and he left the house at nine as gay as a lark. I was to spend the day and dine with the old man, and to while away the time I took up my gun and strolled over his farm. But the turnips were like a river, the birds were as wild as hawks, and in an hour or two I came back with an empty bag. The old man was a little nervous and fidgety the whole day; and old Sam did not mend matters, for he went croaking about, abusing his old master for buying horses which were fit for nobody to ride, and prophesying that the new nag, which he hated the sight of, would be the death of some one or other, before they had done with him. There's more truth than we are aware of in the old saying, that "coming events cast their shadows before;" and the dulness of this morning was a fitting prelude to the melancholy finish of the day. Two o'clock came, without Tom making his appearance, and after half an hour's grace we sat down to dinner without him. Just before we sat down, however, a red-coat pulled up to tell us that the hounds had found in Waverley Wood a ringing fox, who hung about it the whole morning, and as he did not see much chance of their getting him away, he had left them in the wood. Soon after two more red-coats pulled up to tell us that the hounds had whipped off and gone to another small gorse about twelve miles distant. They casually observed that they had seen Tom; that the new horse seemed to give him a good deal of trouble, and then they rode off. Our dinner this day was a dullish affair, and it was not till we had got fairly settled to our pipes that the old man began to cheer up. He was just proposing to me that after this race, win or lose, he would buy my share in the steeple-chaser, and settle, give him to Tom, when a man, whom we both knew well, cantered up, and, throwing himself out of the saddle, begged to see some of us directly. We could tell by the expression of his face when he entered the room that something was wrong. He was luckily a man of few words, and did not keep us long in suspense by useless preface; he said a bad accident had happened to Tom; his horse had fallen at a flight of rails and broken his back; Tom had been picked up insensible, and was now lying at a farm-lodge, which was luckily close to where he fell, and that we had better run over to him as soon as possible. It did not take us much time to get ready, and, although the lodge was about eight miles distant, we reached it well within the hour. I hardly think we exchanged twenty sentences during the whole of that ride; and the only observation the old man kept making aloud to himself was, " Strange that they should have taken him in *there*." And strange, indeed, it was, for the accident had happened close to the lodge where the old gentleman lived whom I had noticed at the steeple-chase with his daughter, and Tom's lifeless body had been carried into the very house in which he had so strictly been forbidden ever to enter while alive. His horse had rushed at a small flight of rails leading out of this very farm into a lane which ran in front of the house; they both rolled into the ditch beyond; the horse broke his neck, and poor Tom, who fell under him, was dragged out on to the bank a corpse! (Strange, I have seen three fatal accidents in the hunting field, and every one of them has been at a small fence which the rider has taken carelessly and heedlessly, when the hounds were not running, but going from one covert to another.) They placed the body on a gate, and carried it up to the house.

The girl, who might have been Tom's wife, stood at the window and saw him fall, and the stern old father met them at the door with their lifeless burden.

No time now for any display of passionate feelings. The faults of the dead man were all forgotten in his sudden and violent death, and the old man, with a faltering voice, bade them carry the body upstairs, and hurried back into the parlour to endeavour to console his only daughter, but with a heart nearly as heavy as her own. What his feelings were at this moment it would be hard to say. Did his thoughts recur to that fearful passionate scene, when with a dreadful oath he bade the young man leave his house, and prayed that God would strike his daughter dead before his very face, sooner than see her become the wife of a man whom he designated as a reprobate and an outcast? Did he think of all the bitter anguish, of the many sorrowful days and nights which the poor girl had suffered since that fearful oath was recorded? Or did he feel that now the fatal curse had come home to him? His only daughter lying on the sofa insensible before him; the man upon whom her sole affections were placed, a corpse in the room above his head; himself a powerless, sorrow-stricken, grey-haired old man, who had tried to measure his strength, as it were, against the Almighty One, and had failed. But we will draw the veil over this sad scene.

As the old uncle and myself galloped up to the door, the groom who took our horses whispered to us that Tom was dead, and, as the old father met us in the passage, he grasped our hands, and led us upstairs without saying a word. On a bed, in the best room, lay poor Tom, just as he had fallen. His death had been instantaneous, and, apparently, painless; at least the expression of his features was unaltered, and his face wore the same determined look of resolution which so well became it when living. A little blood had oozed from his nose and mouth, but this had been carefully wiped away; and no one who gazed upon that calm and quiet face, could have guessed that he had died by a violent death some two hours before. It was painful to watch the countenances of the two old men as they stood in silence by that bedside, and more painful still to think what feelings were working in their breasts at that solemn moment. It was a relief to leave the chamber of death, and go down into the parlour. The daughter had been carried to her bed-room in a swoon, and the little parlour was filled with men who had seen the accident, and who had stopped at the lodge till our arrival. From them we learnt the full particulars. The old uncle was now anxious to get home and make arrangements about the removal of the body. So, after leaving particular instructions for them to cut off a hoof of the horse before they buried him, we rode home. There was but little outward exhibition of grief during the whole of this sad scene—the principal actors in it were made of sterner stuff than to show the sorrow which struck inwardly, but deeply, into their breasts; and as for the poor girl, she lay, during the whole time, happily unconscious of all that was taking place around her.

What was to be done about the steeple-chase now that poor Tom was killed? Of course the old uncle could not go down to the meeting; but the horse was there, heavily backed by many of his friends. And when the old man asked the company in the parlour how he should act, the unanimous reply "Just as if Tom was alive," decided him, and at ten o'clock the Vet. and myself took our places in the night-coach to go down to Bideford, engage another jockey, run the horse, and do our best to win.

We reached London by twelve o'clock next day, and Bideford by the Tuesday morning. The journey was a dreary one, far different from what we had expected it would be. Just before starting I went up into Tom's room for the jacket and cap; but I had not the heart to take down the two little rosettes which hung up over them, now that he who had so fondly cherished these valued remembrances would never see them again.

The coach was filled, outside and in, with steeple-chase riders and betting-men, and the conversation the whole way down was slangy and turfy. When we entered the little town of Bideford the place was in a bustle, and as we pulled up at the Woolpack in the market-square (the principal sporting inn), the coach-office and the steps outside were thronged with a group of knowing sporting-looking characters of every grade and description. Our horse was standing at this inn stables, attended by the lad who had brought him down, who was anxiously waiting our arrival. Great was the lad's distress when he saw only two of our party alight from the coach, and greater still when he heard of poor Tom's sad accident, for he had backed the old horse up to nearly the whole of his year's wages, more on the strength of Tom's jockeyship than anything else. His spirits sank within him when he heard that we had come down to seek a strange jockey in a strange town, where, as the lad said, they did not speak even in the same language as ourselves. However, the first thing was to see after lodgings, and then try and engage a jockey for the morrow. As I picked my way to the bar through a crowd of sporting-men to engage beds for the night, "our Jem," as neatly got-up and looking as handsome as ever, was chaffing the pretty barmaid on the very same subject. She was trying to persuade him that for one night he must put up with the inconvenience of a double bed with a friend. To which Jem strongly objected, adding something in an undertone to the girl, which caused her to laugh heartily and turn away quickly (evidently, however, not displeased), under pretence of serving some other customer. I was quite prepared for her reply of "all engaged," when I asked if I could procure beds for myself and the Vet.; but I thought she need not have regarded us quite so contemptuously as she did, although we might both look a little travel-soiled and seedy after our twenty-four hours' journey outside a night coach. She treated us, however, very differently next day, when the race was over—but not to anticipate. We considered ourselves lucky in procuring the loan of a bed-room for half-an-hour to put ourselves a little straight, and to this we at once retired—my friend, the Vet., anxious to arange a toilette with which he was bent upon astonishing the good people of Bideford, and the sporting part of the community in particular. And it certainly was a magnificent "get-up," built expressly for the occasion, of which none of us had the least idea. A bright-green, long-waisted cutaway, with gilt buttons as big as half-crown pieces, a very staring red plaid waistcoat in the long-approved grooms' style, a pair of bran new white cords and mahogany tops, a yellow belcher neckerchief, and new white hat, which he had decorated in London with a black crape band out of respect to poor Tom, completed a costume which would have shone brilliantly at a country fair. But when I noticed how his clothes hung about him, as if they had been thrown on with a pitchfork, and looked at his broad freckled face, sandy hair and whiskers, and brown, gloveless hands, I fairly groaned in spirit when I reflected that I should have to be leader to such a bear among men who of all others, perhaps, aim at a neat and quiet costume. There was, however, no help for it now, so I just made the best of it, and affected not to hear the remarks which greeted us as we made our appearance again in the passage before the bar. " Halloa, Jennings !" asked one man; " whose colours are bright green and tartan ?" " Why, the gentleman has made a mistake, the race does not come off till to-morrow," added another. " Devilish neat style of thing, and by no *manes* gaudy," drawled out the prince of the Irish steeple-chase jockeys to a friend, as he eyed the burly figure of the Vet. from top to toe. Such were among some of the compliments which fell on my ear. But when I heard one fellow whisper to another " It's the other one's the jockey; him in the green coat's a rich Yorkshire farmer, owner of that lame brown horse standing in No. 10," I took my cue directly, and determined to play second fiddle myself, leaving to the Vet. all the arrangements of what promised to be rather an intricate affair. He was immensely gratified when I told him this, and it was quite pleasing to hear him order an ostler to send to him directly the lad who looked after the brown horse in No. 10, and to watch the deferential manner in which the man obeyed him. The old horse seemed to know him again as soon as he entered the box, and testified by a faint neigh his pleasure at seeing him; but there was evidently one other he missed out of the little group, and that was his favourite jockey who had so often steered him to victory, for, after we had carefully locked the door and began to strip him, the old fellow kept turning his head every now and then in that direction, as though he expected to see it open every minute and poor Tom walk in. However much he might be out of place in the crowd that thronged the bar-passage, the Vet. was "all there" in that loose box, as he threw off the "bright-green cutaway," and proceeded carefully to examine the horse. More than a dozen times was his hand slowly passed down that treacherous hind leg, and severe was the cross-examination which the lad underwent as to how the horse fed, how he galloped, &c. The examination was apparently satisfactory, for, after he had given some directions about fresh bandages, and to have the horse ready for gentle exercise at three in the afternoon on the race-course, he remarked, on leaving the stable, "If we had but poor Tom here to ride him, we should be very near pulling through."

When we returned to the inn to lunch we were regarded as objects of curiosity by the assembled crowd. Our horse had been standing there for three days, and beyond his being the property of a midland farmer, and that a country jock was coming down expressly to ride him, nothing was known about him. Nothing could be got out of the lad who looked after him—he was too well tutored. The idea of sending a lame horse (for he was most decidedly a little lame, although it was hardly perceptible) to run for such a stake and in such company, added to the mystery, which was in no degree lessened by the countryfied appearance of his owner and jockey, as we were taken to be.

When we sat down to lunch, however, a little of the mystery was cleared up, for one or two jockeys had now arrived who had seen the horse run in Warwickshire; and it was whispered about that, notwithstanding all his lameness, he would prove to be a very dangerous outsider. But the strangest thing was nobody had yet seen his old jockey. It was well known that the man who rode him in Warwickshire was always in the habit of riding him, and Tom was personally known to many of the jockeys, which we were not. It is true I knew every professional jockey in that room by sight, and many to speak or nod to, but I was not on what might be called friendly terms with any one of them; and as not one of them was likely yet to have heard of Tom's accident, I did not care to tell how it was that we had come down alone and had not even yet engaged a jockey to ride the horse. I knew very well that all the crack jockeys were sure to be taken up, and moreover I did not fancy that any one of them would care for such a mount as this, unless to suit some purpose of his own. But where were we to find a jockey at the eleventh hour, in a distant town, where we scarcely knew a soul to speak to? This was the question which spoilt my lunch. The Vet., of course, was out of the question, for I suppose he walked fourteen stone. There was but myself and the stable lad. Now I certainly could hold my own across country, and had even once ridden in the Findon race, where, as an old Yorkshire trainer observed, "I made a very poor *tew* of it;" and I did not therefore much fancy measuring lances with such men as Oliver, Mason, and some others whom I saw taking lunch with us, and chaffing each other across the table with that quiet, self-satisfied air which proved that they were perfectly at home here, and that the coming event to which I was so nervously looking forward was an every-day matter to them. I did not see one of the "Lincolnshire division" present, or I might have found a friend. It is true that both "Old Peter" and Gaylad were expected to run, but they had long since passed into other hands than those who bred them, and Lincolnshire knew them no more. As to the stable-lad, he had never ridden a steeple-chase in his life. Besides, he was probably three stone too light. Moreover, as he told me afterwards, he had come down to look after, not to ride, the horse, and he did not know how Mr. Snaffle might take it if he got the mount. That worthy had sent word down that he would be there on the morning of the race, if possible; but as he placed implicit reliance on the lad to see after the horse, and of course concluded that Tom would be there to ride him, he gave the matter very little further thought, and it was hardly likely that he would leave his business and come down so far to see a horse run in which he had only a temporary interest.

How different were my feelings on the afternoon when I rode into Findon before that steeple-chase, to what they were on the present occasion! Then, every second man I met was a friend. I knew our horse would be properly and fairly ridden, and we were all of us very confident in his success. But now, we were in a strange country without a friend. It wanted but twenty-four hours to the race, and we had not even engaged a jockey for the horse. Poor Tom's recent death sat heavily on my mind, and if it had not been that others at home were anxiously waiting for the result of the old horse's performance, I declare I would have sent him back that afternoon by the lad, and left the town by the night coach, without even staying to see the race in which, strange to say, I had now lost all interest. The Vet., bold as he might be at home, was a very different man here; and I could plainly see, notwithstanding the brightness of the new green coat, he sat very ill at ease at that table, among men whose deeds of daring he had so often seen recorded in the *Life*, and whose chaff and inuendoes he could plainly see were covertly directed against himself. He was by no means destitute of pluck, and had proved himself an awkward customer on more than one occasion; and as I saw that he was burning to get into a row with some one, I was right glad when lunch was over, and he proposed a stroll through the old town to buy a new ash stick. I thought this would be a good opportunity of getting the correct weight of the lad and myself, and as we passed a butcher's shop, at the door of which a very jovial, good-humoured looking man was standing, I asked him if we might just step into his scales. The request was at once granted, and after we had got our weights, the butcher, who was evidently a sporting man, civilly asked us into his little back parlour, to have a glass of ale, and on following him in we saw two other men sitting there smoking their cigars, evidently talking over the coming race. One was a fat, jolly-looking fellow, apparently a country farmer; the other was the very counterpart of poor Tom, save that his hair and whiskers were sandy, and his face pock-marked and freckled. His clothes fitted him as tight as if he had grown in them. Coat, waistcoat, and trousers were cut in the approved sporting style, back-stitched, double-stitched, and strapped. It seemed as if nothing could tear them; and upon the Vet., who was by no means shy, requesting if he might feel the thickness of those fine trousers, and remarking upon the apparent excellence of the quality, the man good-humouredly remarked, "You're in the west of England now!" His low-crowned hat and a formidable cutting whip lay on the table, and I felt certain, at first sight, that the man was a jockey. The whole performance of weighing had been watched from the back parlour by these two men through the little window which commanded the shop, and they were now eager to get at the bottom of what they began to consider a mystery. They soon told us all they knew about the coming race, how many horses were likely to start, who would ride them; and in the course of conversation, the brown screw came upon the carpet, but about him they were quite in the dark; they had all seen him, and watched him at exercise; knew that he had come from a distance, and as they could well see that his slight lameness was of old standing, they naturally thought that he would not have been sent so far, if it was likely to interfere much with his going. Great was the jolly butcher's surprise when I told him this was our horse, that we had no jockey for him, and that I had come into his shop casually to weigh, in case the forlorn hope of steering him should fall to my lot. Words can hardly express my delight when I heard him remark, "This mount would just suit you, Jem;" and when the young man replied, "I should very much like it," I felt as if luck had turned right in our favour. It is true, I knew nothing of either men, but I felt relieved of an immense responsibility. Anyhow, Jem could hardly be a worse jockey than myself. There was something honest and straightforward about both men; and the very fact of their being ensconced in that little back parlour, instead of joining the noisy crowd which were assembled at the Woolpack, proved that, like ourselves, they were outsiders. We soon learnt Jem's history. He was indeed a second Tom—a farmer, living about ten miles from the town, a capital rider, had figured in one or two previous steeple-chases on this course, but never in a crack one, and had come down to Bideford on this occasion expressly on the off chance of getting a mount.

He gave the old horse a rattling spin for half a mile on the racecourse in the afternoon, and his remark of "he'll do," as he got off him, satisfied me that there was no mistake about our new jockey. The jolly butcher himself was bursting with importance. Such a strange thing to happen in his little back parlour; it seemed just as if it was to be! And although we all agreed to keep the thing as dark as possible till next morning, he could not help confiding the secret to a few friends, and when I went into the long room at the Woolpack in the evening, I heard "What'll any one lay a*gin* Har*cules*?" and observed two or three men quietly booking the long odds against the old horse, who could hardly be said to have come into the betting. The Vet. and myself walked over part of the steeple-chase course that afternoon; there was not a fence in it to compare with Findon, but as the country was pretty heavy, we fancied it would suit our old horse, whose forte was in deep ground; but then the same remark would apply to some other of the cracks, especially "old Peter," who was a familiar acquaintance, and we were far from confident about the result of the race. We got beds at the civil butcher's, and, as all anxiety was now off my mind, I slept well that night.

About eight next morning we sat down to certainly the most substantial breakfast I ever saw. Of course the chops and kidneys were perfection—we were in the right shop for them; but I certainly never expected to taste such ale—for we all fancied the Findon tap was not to be equalled in England. All were in high spirits. Jem had tried on the blue-and-white jacket and cap, and liked the colours. The Vet. had been about the horse ever since five, and his broad, good-humoured Yorkshire face beamed with delight as he entered the little room and saw a breakfast laid out, to which he was quite prepared to do ample justice. The jolly butcher and myself had become very friendly. He was a little bit of a screw dealer himself, but his line lay among the trotters, and he had taken me into his stable to show me three nags, either of which, he declared, could trot the two miles under the six minutes; and when I told him I fancied I had one at home who could beat either of them, he swore that he would travel all the way to Findon to see her, which he did.

    It was a lovely morning, as mild as May, and the sun shone brightly out of an unclouded sky; the jackdaws were cawing high in air round the old church tower, whose bells were ringing out a cheery peel, and over whose battlements floated "the red-white-and blue," in honour of this day. The steeple-chase was evidently a gala-day in the old town of Bideford. A brass band paraded the streets as on an election day. The county families were flocking into the town (for there was to be a grand ball in the evening), well-mounted men on strong useful hunters rode up the high street towards the course, and the town was crowded with country people, who had come miles to see the race. All was in a bustle. Every one you met seemed full of importance; but it was easy to distinguish who were the *real actors* in the play about to be performed. The race was fixed for two; the horses were to saddle in the inn-yard, parade through the market-place, and then proceed to the racecourse, where the start was, about a mile out of the town. It was a pretty and a national sight to see eleven of the best steeple-horses in England, ridden by the crack jockeys of the day, meet in that market-place; and old Hercules, with his new jockey on his back, walked every bit as proudly through the crowd as the best of them. They were marshalled to the racecourse by the clerk of the course, in a bran new pink and leathers, and the whole affair was very well arranged. The racecourse was very prettily situate, and from the top of the grand stand the eye wandered over a wide tract of champaign country, with very little plough, through which the silvery Wye wound its placid course, while the dim blue outline of the Welsh mountains could be distinctly traced in the distant horizon. Nearly the whole of the steeple-chase course, dotted out with white flags, could be seen from the stand, and though there were as many fences as at Findon, and a fair brook twice, the fences were of a very different description; there was much more grass than I had expected, and I was fearful that some light-weighted thorough-bred (for the days of handicapping had just commenced in steeple-chasing) would gallop away from the rest, for this course was just suited to such a horse.

I paid my half sov. and took a place on the stand; but not so the Vet.—with his usual Yorkshire caution he stationed himself at the brook, and invested his ten shillings, at twelve to one, as the old horse came down to it pulling double. The start was very pretty. The only orders Jem received were, to follow one or other of the favourites—and these he obeyed to the letter, never leading himself, but sticking to the leaders as close as wax. It was a very fast run race; and at a mile from home only seven horses were left in it. These soon dwindled down to five, and only three of them came up, with anything like a chance, to the large brushed hurdle across the racecourse, the last fence in the race. But the blue-and-white colours were there. They all three rose together at the hurdles, and when they landed safely the struggle began. "Vanguard wins!" "Peter wins!" "Hercules wins!" were shouted by a thousand voices. Half way up the run in, however, the gameness of the old horse told; he struggled manfully to the front, and as they shot by the grand stand, close to which the winning flags were placed, he was two lengths ahead, Jem hard at work with whip and spurs, and the judge's fiat was—Hercules by three lengths.

What a curious thing is popular favour! Here was a strange horse, which but few on this course had backed for a shilling, and which scarcely a dozen men knew, and yet a hundred cheers greeted him and his jockey as they came back to scale; and a score of burly-looking squires and country farmers slapped me on the back, and shook me by the hand, as they congratulated me on the old horse's success. There were very few there who knew how little chance old Hercules stood of winning twenty-four hours before; and I met the good old butcher with a thoroughly cordial handshake below the stand, for without him the race would probably never have been ours. The Vet. was in a high state of excitement, and his bright-green coat and white hat could be seen struggling through the thickest of the crowd to get up to the horse's head; and he eyed the curious gazers with a fierce glance as they crowded round the winner, and pertinently asked them, "What they thought of the lame horse now?"

It was singular that on this very afternoon they buried poor Tom, and as the shouts at the success of his old favourite were rending the air on that racecourse, the solemn, measured knell of the passing bell from a quiet little village church, nearly 300 miles distant, tolled the last requiem of one who, a short week before, had fondly hoped that those cheers would have been lavished on himself instead of a stranger.

Of course we attended the race ordinary at the Woolpack. The chair was taken by one of the head men in the county, the dinner was excellent, and all passed off capitally. We had lots of health-drinking and speechifying. The Vet. broke down in returning thanks to the winner, but came again further on in the evening and astonished the company with a tremendous Yorkshire hunting song, which was loudly applauded, and which I was very fearful would be encored. The owner of the second horse, who had already been beaten in Warwickshire by Tom, declared that the old horse had won that day upon his merits, and that he always feared him, although he did not say so. Not much money was lost. Our horse was a good one for the bookmakers. The old butcher and his friends stood well on him. I had not backed him for a shilling; but the Vet. had managed to win fifty pounds, and as a good deal of it was in pounds and fivers, it took him some trouble to collect. But he carried away with him a trophy from Bideford, which he valued even more than all the money, and this was a large roll of the celebrated west of England drab, the identical stuff from which Jem's trousers were built. He had ingratiated himself much in the good butcher's favour, who gave him the cloth in return for the receipt of the noted " inflammable iles."

The stakes were paid over to us next morning. We gave Jem a

very good present for his excellent riding, and 10*l.* to the lad for having so manfully stuck to the old horse throughout. Just before we left, the pretty barmaid presented me with two grand blue-and-white rosettes to decorate old " Hercules's " head, declaring that these were her favourite colours—a pretty good hint, as my friend the butcher observed, that she would like a silk dress of the same. And as I thought that in all probability we should never see the old town again—certainly never take away so much out of it—I went out and bought her the richest blue silk piece that I could find; and I'll do her the justice to say, that I felt certain she would well become it.

About an hour before we left, old Hercules was led out of the town in triumph. We had a parting bottle of champagne with the civil butcher and Jem, without whose aid we should have left Bideford "unhonoured and unknown," and after promising Jem that he should have the mount if our horse went for any other good race while I had anything to do with him, we mounted the outside of the up-coach, and left Bideford in very different spirits to those in which we had entered the old town.

There were no telegraphs down to our remote county in those days; and as we lost no time on our journey, we had the pleasure of bringing the news of the old horse's victory home ourselves. Hercules came back from his training-quarters as soon as he got home, and I took him to meet the hounds a few days after (my first mount, by the way, on a horse which I had now owned about eighteen months), to receive the congratulations of his friends. We ran him for one more steeple-chase in our county, with the odds of ten to one on him; but the hawbuck of a country jockey who rode him managed to go on the wrong side of a flag, and lost us the race. We were all of opinion that he sold us.

My old friend became quite an altered man after poor Tom's death; he had lost his right hand, as it were, and he cared little now to bring a horse to the post under the pilotage of a jockey whom he could not trust. Grief shows itself in various forms, but the old man's sorrow took a very disagreeable one; he became ill-natured

I

and snappish, and could scarcely bear a word to be spoken to him, and old Sam and the lads had a weary time of it. I have no doubt Tom's death affected him deeply, for he had the hoof of the horse that killed him mounted in silver, which, with the whip and spurs he used in his last race, together with the little Findon cockades, hung up ever after over his mantelpiece till he died. The Vet., moreover, took to bad ways; to use a favourite phrase of his own, he could not "carry corn;" the little money he had won during his connexion with the old horse, and the excitement of the racecourse, upset him, and he took to company and drinking. He still, however, stuck to his favourite "inflammable iles," and one night a tremendous explosion was heard in his little back shop, and when the neighbours rushed in he was found lying insensible on the floor, with a candlestick grasped tightly in his hand, and a two-gallon jar, which had doubtless contained some dangerous ingredient or other used by him in his mysterious mixtures, shattered into a thousand pieces at his feet. The window of the little room was blown out, and every jar and bottle on his shelves broken. He never recovered that smash. My share in the horse I sold to my old friend, who kept him through the summer without once running him, and sold him again for a hunter the next season. The old gentleman died shortly after—it was quite clear that his silent but deep-rooted grief wore him out; and his little farm and stables passed into other hands. The poor girl, who should have been Tom's wife, never looked up after the sad accident; she lingered on through the winter, but the next spring saw another little headstone in the village churchyard, not far from where Tom lay, and the simple initials, "J. H., ætat. 25," was all that told the sad history of many years' patient suffering.

THE TROTTER.

"Oh! he's such a one to bend his knee and tuck his haunches in,
And to throw the dirt in flats' eyes, he never thinks a sin."—OLD SONG.

"IF there is *one* thing I *ken du*," a Yankee captain once drawled out to me, "it is, sing our almighty national song, 'Yankee Doodle;'" and if there was one thing I flattered myself, when a young'un, I could *du* better than anything else, it was, sing the then popular (at least among my *set*) song of "The Trotting Horse," two lines of which head this chapter; and the way I learnt it is worth telling. I took my singing lessons on the coach-box, by the side of one of the patriarchs of the road, when a journey to London from our remote parts occupied the whole day, thus affording me ample time to practise my singing lessons—my preceptor being a Jehu of the true old school, and after his fashion the neatest dandy on our road. The old boy had once possessed a beautiful voice, now, however, grown rather husky through age and constant exposure to the weather. Still there were few to beat him at this song; and when the chairman at the little "free and easies" which the members of his craft were wont to hold on the Wednesday evening at the old Magpie and Stump, gave the order—"Attention, gentlemen; Mr. Jarvis will oblige us with the 'Trotting Horse,'" the applause was, to use a popular phrase, "unbounded." Unlike many selfish men, who, if they possess a better knowledge of anything than their fellows, or a secret of any kind, are only desirous of carrying it with them to the grave, nothing seemed to give this old man greater pleasure than to find that I improved under his tuition. He even tried to get me up in "A southerly wind and a cloudy sky;" but, according to his quaint phraseology, I could never "come the dog language right," and he gave up the task in despair.

Poor old boy! I dare say he has dropped off his perch this many a year since. The box which he last mounted when alive was a melancholy one to him, for the old Regulator was driven off the road by the rail, and the last time I spied my quondam tutor he was perched on the box of a 'bus near the Mansion House. "Bank, Paddington—jump in, sir," shouted the cad. There was room on the box, so I clambered up, and was by the old man's side before he recognised me. I made four journeys over the stones that day alongside the veteran, who was still as great a swell as ever, although a shade seedier than when last I saw him; and we agreed at night to look in at the old Magpie and Stump for the last time.

My old tutor's name was Jarvis—Frank Jarvis—but he was known at that day all down the road as old Joliffe, on account of the peculiar boat-shape build of his hat; and a neater, cleaner, little old man never mounted the box. Although I always style him the old man, he was not so very old, but he had one of those faces which always look old and thoughtful, and never guide one as to the age of the man; and men considerably older than himself, when alluding to him, always used the term "old," although, perhaps, they would have repudiated it themselves. He was invariably scrupulously clean and neat in his dress, and his manners might have gained him admission into the B. D. C. His clothes were always of the same cut and pattern, only the style varied a trifle with the seasons. The neat, hard, close-napped Joliffe was white in the summer, black in the winter (the former he generally managed to win on the Derby, the latter on the Leger). The neckcloth at all seasons was spotless white, as pure as snow. A long brown Newmarket coat, very wide in the skirt, and with pockets very low down, reached to his "hocks," as he would have termed them; and a long striped black-and-white stuff waistcoat came down below his hip bones. His breeches were always the same, light drab kerseys; and the neatest, best-fitting pair of brown top-boots—the creases of which natty little Arthur Pavis himself might have envied, but which in winter he encased in fustian overhauls—completed the attire of one of the neatest-dressed, most obliging, and gentlemanly old coachmen of his day in England. When his well-shaped buckskin glove was off, a plain black and gold mourning ring gave an aristocratic finish to a hand as clean, as white, and as well-shaped as a lady's.

I never heard his early history, nor did anyone in our part know it, but I gathered from occasional slips in his conversation that he was born to fill a higher station than the box of a coach; and his manners, with all the true genuine polish of the old school—and two or three exquisite little studies of hounds, and one favourite hunter, done in oils, which graced the walls of his little parlour—all bespoke the fact.

He had come down to our little town from London some ten years previously, and started the old "Regulator" on his own account. He drove the whole journey up and down himself, on each alternate day; and as "three wheels and the hind boot of the coach" belonged to him, and as he was an accommodating old fellow, willing to oblige anyone, and a great favourite with all the gentry and farmers round us, his coach was always full; and it was wonderful to witness what a miscellaneous freight the old Regulator used to carry.

She was truly and literally speaking a family coach. Anxious mothers would trust their children up and down to school with old Joliffe, and feel quite satisfied that the old man would treat them as a father; and jolly country farmers would hand over their wives and daughters to his charge with every confidence that they would be well looked after on their journey. The jovial squire would stop the coach himself at the park gates with, "Well, Frank, you have not forgotten that little bit of fish;" and the pretty barmaid of the Cross Keys would exclaim with her sweetest smile, as he handed over to her across the bar counter a mysterious-looking brown paper parcel (not, however, a crinoline then), "Well, now, that is kind of you," and bustle away to fill him a glass of the best pale sherry, the only liquor the old boy ever tasted. Everybody on the road seemed to know him, and everybody respected him. This sort of thing has all gone by now; but I dare say many of my readers can remember the day when one solitary coach drove up three times a week to London from the neighbourhood, and there was no way of getting any commission done in town save through the coachman. What an important personage that coachman used to be, and what a general favourite he was with all!

Accommodating, however, as she might be, and useful as a luggage van, the old Regulator still had her faults; and perhaps the one which would have been looked upon as the greatest in this go-ahead age was that she was always behind her time. In the winter, no one could tell at what hour she might come in; and if I happened to go down to the booking-office at seven (she was due at six), I hardly cared to ask if the Regulator was in, but my commonplace question as to what time do you expect her to-night was always met by the same stereotyped answer, " Impossible to say, sir."

And this may be accounted for in many ways. In the first place, she was a heavy coach in every sense of the word, and over her best ground was never timed at more than eight miles in the hour. Moreover, her old driver had many little private ventures of his own, and had often to pull up by the roadside three or four times in one stage, to transact a little business on his own account. He was a kind of country general dealer, and nothing which he could by any possibility stow away in the old drag came amiss to him. I have known him buy a plough which was standing at a blacksmith's shop by the roadside. It was hoisted on to the roof of the coach and carried twenty miles down the road to an old friend of his, who had long been looking out for such a pattern. I believe we should have had a pair of harrows also, but to find room for them beat even the old boy. He did fancy he could lash them on under the coach, if he only had time. As for live stock, this coach often resembled a menagerie on wheels—geese, poultry, pigeons, nothing came amiss. In fact, there was not an article in general use which, to use a phrase of his own, he did not know "where to plant if he could only buy it right." He was fond of asking your opinion as to what you thought of his purchases; and now and then, if I happened "to beggar my looks, and hint something not very complimentary," he always had his answer ready, " Well, I dare say I was a fool to buy it; but I think I know a bigger fool to whom I think I can sell it again." He did not, however, confine his little speculations alone to such things as he could carry on his coach. If he by a chance saw a promising colt or a likely-looking heifer grazing by the road side, he never forgot it, and if it was for sale he generally, sooner or later, managed to find a customer for it. Many a time have I known him pull up at the gate of a field by the roadside, hand me over the ribbons, and leisurely walk down the field to inspect some animal or other he fancied would suit him. We never passed through a toll-bar but some rough rider was waiting to show him a raw colt, some farmer to talk to him about a bullock, or some old woman with a basket of geese, poultry, or eggs. He was a great horse dealer in a small way; and as he worked best part of the ground himself, was always shoving some new purchase or other into the team, which certainly had no business there. He was always chopping out and in; and not a team on the whole journey, except the first two and the two last, could be said to be properly matched. In vain did strange passengers grumble at all this (as for his regular passengers, we all knew the old man's little foibles too well ever to say a word); he was incorrigible, and this I think the reader will admit, when I mention two circumstances which fell under my own observation. We were coming up one day after a large Midland fair, and for half the journey, when we had a team which he dare trust in my hands, the old boy gave me the reins while he got inside to have a little bit of loo with three horse-dealing friends. And on another occasion, when some leather plating stakes were being run for in a park which we had to pass by, he coolly drew his coach into the park, saw one race run, then drove out again, and resumed his journey.

There was a standing joke against him, that he once bought three live pigs somewhere down the road, shoved them into the hind boot (which, wonderful to say, was empty on this journey), and sold them to a pork butcher near Islington. He dare hardly bring them into London. Unfortunately, a little of the straw left in the bottom of the boot told its own tale. I should never have known this had I not been standing at the Peacock one evening about Christmas to see the old man come up. He was, as usual, two hours behind his time. A group of cads and rough fellows, whom we always see hanging about such places, were gathered close to my elbow. When the lamps of the old Regulator bore in sight, one of the roughest of the lot was the first to notice it, and he communicated the fact to his fellows in the following complimentary sentence, growled out in a voice husky with gin and London fog, " Here comes the old Slow and Dirty. I wonder whether old *Boat Tile's* got any more pigs up to-night!"

However, with all her faults, the old Regulator was a safe coach, and, notwithstanding all the " bokickers " which helped to swell her team, very little went wrong on the road. Moreover, she paid well; and as most of her customers and passengers were regular ones, who all knew and liked her old driver, if a complaint from an outsider did reach head-quarters, it was taken very little notice of by the coach-masters, who worked the old coach the two first stages out of London.

Well, as I said before, it was on the box of this old coach that I took my first lessons in singing, and, I may add, in driving also; for as soon as we were well clear of the place where we changed, it generally used to be this: " Here, catch hold of 'em; we'll change places now and have a little harmony."

Our first song, as soon as I got the horses well together, was the " Trotting Horse," and the driving and singing-lesson commenced after this wise : " Now, keep that off-side leader well in hand." Old Boy sings : " I ride as good a trotting-horse." "There, don't you see that near wheeler's doing all the work ?"—" as any man in town." " Have you got that right?" " He'll trot you sixteen miles an hour." " Keep that off-wheeler up to his collar." " I'll bet a hundred pound," and so on; and the " Trotting Horse" usually lasted us over the best part of the stage. The next on the programme generally was, "A southerly wind and a cloudy sky," and here the old man had the whole performance to himself, and many a gaping rustic would leave off his work and stare at us in stupid astonishment as we drove by him, the old man waving his whip in all the ecstacies of " Have at him," " hi, wind him," " my steady good hounds." I recollect one evening at this very part of the performance we happened to meet the hounds coming home from hunting. They turned down a by-lane into the turnpike. Just as we drove by, a scream from the huntsman, which seemed to rend the skies, caused the old bokicker to start and nearly pull the reins out of my hands, and a poor old lady, who was sitting just behind me, almost jumped off her seat as she screamed out, " La', let me get down, I think you're all mad." We pulled up, not, however, to let the old lady down, but to allow the old man to give us one whole verse of the song; and as he had now the huntsman and two whips to help him find his fox he soon got away with him, and the rattling view-halloa which the second whip hurled after us as we drove off, rings in my ears to this very day. "There's dog music for you," exclaimed the old boy, in his seventh heaven, as he waved his black Joliffe triumphantly. This was a standing joke down our road for years after.

"Tom Moody" used to come next on our list, and here I was allowed to join in chorus; and there was something rather novel in the way we used to get through " Harry Bluff" as a *duet*. The old man's fund of songs appeared to be inexhaustible, and he never seemed happy except when singing them. They were chiefly, however, of the sporting order; and, except a few old national English ballads, such as " The Death of Nelson," " Harry Bluff," and a few others of that sort, he did not care much to sing any one which had not a little dog language in it.

Thus the milestones were merrily passed, and thus our journeys used merrily to roll on. Oh, those were happy days and happy journeys, deny it who can; and although we certainly did not get over our ground quite so quickly as in these days of steam, we had a deal more fun on our road; and a drive on the old Regulator did not wear the uniform monotony of railway travelling, for in those days a journey up and down to London furnished us simple rustics with incidents and matter to talk over for weeks after.

I was very young and very green when I took my first singing-lessons, and at that time did not even possess a horse of my own; it is true I had often been at the covert side on one of the old carriage horses, and had been once or twice well up on an old pony, who had a perfectly marvellous knack of scrambling and thrusting through places which no horse in the world could get over. But I had never seen the hounds on anything like a real hunter. However, the lucky day came at length, and, through the kindness of the old coachman, I became the fortunate possessor of a little flea-bitten grey, wall-eyed Irish mare, which the old man swore could leap over anything on which she could lay her chin, and for whom, as he emphatically concluded his little chaunt, no hounds were too fast, no day too long, and no country too heavy!

She was standing at a public-house by the roadside, and one afternoon we pulled up the coach to look at her. She was brought out into the yard by a bare-headed, coatless, rough-riding lad, who looked after her. A gate was set up in the yard, over which the boy rode her bare-backed three or four times, much to the satisfaction of the old man and a group of assembled horsekeepers. This *only* caused us a delay of some ten minutes, but that was nothing on our road. However, it made about our tenth stoppage that day, with which the business of the coach had not the slightest concern; and some of the passengers were "exceeding wroth," for they could see our whole performance from the coach. There was only one objection to my buying the mare, or I would have done so at once, and this was, I had no money. I knew where I could borrow a 10*l.* note, but the price of the mare was 45*l.* On stating this difficulty to the old man, he generously agreed to let me have the mare on receipt of this 10*l.*, when I got it, and to trust me for the rest.

I was a nice weight then; and although I had, I fear, but little judgment, I rode with plenty of pluck; and I suppose this just suited the hot Irish blood of my new purchase. I hunted her for two months, and never was carried better in my life. I rode to a leader, and this leader was one of the best men with the hounds, though I did not at first know it, for I was a perfect stranger as yet in that field. I well recollect that first run; we had as sharp a forty-five minutes as I ever rode to; and though I got three falls, I was one of the nine who saw the fox pulled down. This was on the Monday, and on the Saturday I was out again. I soon recognised my leader, a hard-riding farmer, in a green coat, this day mounted on a powerful black horse, with strength enough to carry a church. As soon as we found I "at him again," and in a very merry burst of twenty minutes, in which I only got one fall, he left me but a field behind. On my third appearance he good-naturedly noticed me, told me to stick to him as close as I could—he was not afraid of my riding over him; and seeing I was but a young performer in the saddle, he gave me a few hints as to riding at my fences. A third good run, and the wall-eyed Irish mare again in a good place. I rode home with the farmer to his house that night, where I slept, and, through the instrumentality of the Irish mare, formed a friendship which remained unbroken for years. I hunted her for two months, when I had to leave the country. The last day we were out the farmer bid me 60*l*. for the mare, which I took. The old coachman and I shared the "boots," as he called it, and I may reckon I got my first two months' hunting for nothing. But this was not all: I did not require to buy a horse the next season; with the old coachman on one side of the country, and the hard-riding farmer on the other, I had a mount whenever I wanted it. I don't say I got the pick of the stud; but, as I was riding to sell for them, they never put me on a very bad one. That was a merry winter for me; and I enjoyed that season much, and not the less because I rode cheaper and better than ever I did in my life, other men's horses with my own spurs.

I know not whether it was that the constant repetition of the old song of the "Trotting Horse" gave a bias to my tastes, but this I do know, that from the time I first heard it, I have always dearly loved a fast trotter; and for some few years in my early life I generally owned one which could hold its own among our country nags. I don't mean to say that I ever possessed a Peerless or a Flying Cloud, but I once had a Welsh mare (whom I shall presently introduce to the reader) who did her two two-mile heats in five min. fifty-three secs. and five min. fifty-seven secs., and pulled up "neither sick nor sorry;" and it must be acknowledged that this was not bad travelling. I can truly say with Sam Slick, "I must confess I am fond of a horse. I have made no great progress in the world myself; I feel, therefore, doubly the pleasure of not being surpassed on the road. I never feel so well or so cheerful as on horseback, for there is something exhilarating in quick motion; and, old as I am, I feel a pleasure in making any person whom I meet on the way put his horse to the full gallop to keep pace with my trotter."

This taste for trotters might have been an inherent one, and, probably, like most other tastes, would have developed itself in due time; but I question much if it would ever have taken so strong a hold upon me, had I never heard that rollicking free-and-easy old song, the "Trotting Horse." If such is the case, all I can say is that old Jarvis has much to answer for, because of all kinds of racing, trotting matches are certainly the lowest; and the possession of a fast trotter is sure to keep its owner in a continual state of excitement, squabbles, and disputes; and it used to appear to me that "to win, tie, or wrangle" was the sole motto that must continually be borne in mind in bringing a trotting match to a satisfactory result.

On the afternoon of the last day of the fair, the owner of the drove, who spoke and understood English well, and who had probably heard of my taste for trotting horses, asked me whether I would buy the mare he rode, which he thought, if in condition, could trot fast enough to beat most that she met. She was not for public sale, so was not with the drove, but standing at a little public-house in the town. When we went to look at her I could see nothing very striking in her appearance, and certainly very little that betokened the fast trotter. She stood about fifteen hands, was eight years old, of a rusty-black colour with a blaze down her face, a beautiful blood-like head, and sweet fore-hand, but ugly drooping hind quarters, and a swish tail very low set on; she had rare good flat legs, as hard as iron, big knees, and large open feet, and, save her poverty, was without a blemish or a fault. The man said he was sure she could trot a mile in three minutes, and he wanted 30*l.* for her. I liked the looks of the mare much, and bid 25*l.* at once. After a little wrangling he proposed to take her out of the town next morning, ride her himself, and, if she trotted the mile to my satisfaction, I was to give him all he asked. To this I agreed. No one knew anything about the matter, and next morning, at five, the Welshman, who certainly walked over eleven stone, and rode in a saddle the like of which I never saw before or since, was mounted, and all ready for the start. We rode gently about two miles out of the town, and I sent a friend on with him to the third milestone to start him, and stand myself at the second to see him come in. Very few were astir at that early hour, and we had the course to ourselves. I waited some little time rather anxiously, for the appearance of the mare at my end, when at length an unearthly screech broke upon my ear, to which the shrill "coo'ee" of an Australian stock-rider would have been as nothing. This was followed at intervals by another and another, gradually drawing nearer; then the clatter of hoofs became more distinct, till at length the mare came flying by me (followed by my friend at top speed, both enveloped in a cloud of dust), pulling double, at a pace which I thought I never saw bettered in a trotter. It was not, however, a clattering hammer-and-pincers trot, nor a high-actioned trot with the knee doubled up to the chin, but just a lengthy, low, stealing pace—much after old Alice Hawthorn's style of galloping. As the man pulled up I could not help thinking of "Old Jolifle," and how much he must have admired the way this Welsh mare "tucked her haunches in" as she shot by the milestone. We made the mile two seconds under the three minutes, but I will not say we were right

to a second. This, however, I did not care a pin for. If she could
travel at that pace with twelve stone on her back (for I am certain
the old saddle weighed a stone), and in her present state, I fancied
that, with about ten stone on her, and in top condition, she would
be "hard to hold." I gave the man the price he asked, and a pound
for his trouble, and led the mare back to town, the proudest man in it.
I was forty miles from home. Not a soul but myself and friend knew
anything of the trial; and "Now, my boys," I thought, "I'll drop on
some of you when I get home. You little think what's coming." Before
parting the man told me that they fancied she was by a thorough-bred
horse, out of a Welsh pony; that she had never been caught up
till six years old; that he never found out she could trot till the
previous autumn; and that he had christened her "Patty Morgan."
He, moreover, gave me the following instructions which I was implicitly to follow: always to ride her in a snaffle; never use a whip
or spur, but get all out of her I could by shouting. I could, of
course, not catch her scream exactly, but after a few lessons, I managed to make a pretty good imitation of it, and we parted.

I have had a good many horses through my hands, but never one
about which I felt so anxious as this mare. I saw in her something
better than common, and I was rather at low water just then, not
having a trotter which was worth backing for a shilling. It is true
I had a tidy little punchy cob, a fair second-rater, but he had been
lately beaten so often that they had facetiously christened him "The
Drum," which is never heard except when it is beaten—so they explained the pun. I dare say it was a very stale one; that it was a very
poor one, I think the reader will allow; anyhow, of course I never
could see the wit of it. However, "The Drum" might be put out
of commission now, and my new mare come forward to the sound
of kettledrums and trumpets. I think I visited her in her stable a
dozen times before I left the town, and I hired a man expressly to
lead her gently home, where she arrived on the evening of the next
day. The fellow had particular injunctions not to come up with
her till after dark; and depend on it I was waiting for him on
the road when he did lead her up. By ten, Patty Morgan was

comfortably suppered up in a loose box, and the relish with which she turned to her corn, after indulging herself in one hearty roll, proved that English air had by no means destroyed her Welsh appetite. I did not sleep much that night; I was tormented with all sorts of fears concerning my new purchase. However, she was all right when I went up to the stable next morning, and greeted me with a kind of whinny which asked for breakfast as plainly as her language could speak. We gave her a double measure of corn to make up past shortcomings. I think I never did see so greedy a feeder; she "went into her corn," as the groom observed, "just like a terrier into a rat." The Welshman had told me that nothing in this world would hurt her but scarcity. After breakfast we had her and the Drum out; I rode the mare and put the groom up on the cob. We took them to our favourite "trysting-place," a mile on the turnpike-road which ran by the top of our village, as straight as a two-foot rule and as level as a bowling-green. The mare did just as she liked with the cob, and I sold him that afternoon to a sporting butcher who had long been nibbling at him, under the plea that I *rather* fancied I should have nothing more to do with trotters.

We soon changed Patty Morgan's looks. Her long rough coat was just coming off in patches; and when I bought her, her colour rather resembled that of a very old rusty black bombazine gown, such as you will occasionally see on decayed old ladies, or, more often still, on London lodging-house keepers *en déshabille*. In a short time, however, she "moulted out" into a beautiful black, glossy and soft as velvet; and good keep and gentle exercise wrought such a change in her, that at the end of two months her old owner would never have known her again. She soon became a general favourite with all. I think I never saw so quiet a horse; you could do anything you pleased with her, except ill-treat her; but if you did that, then "look out for squalls." One of the lads cleaning out the loose box once struck her rather sharply with the handle of his fork, to make her turn round. My lady's Welsh blood was then up. She rushed at him like a bull-dog, seized him by the shoulder, and worried him as a terrier would a cat. The groom, who was luckily in the stable, hearing the boy scream, rushed to his help, and it was just in time, for she had got the lad down, and was kneeling on him. The groom afterwards said he never in his whole life saw such a picture of savage rage as she then presented. However, strange to say, directly he halloed to her, her passion seemed to subside in an instant. She rose from the boy, and the groom dragged the lad out with a shoulder not only broken, but literally crushed. This was a warning to us all. She had far more the manners of a dog than a horse, and soon got to know me so well that I believe she would have followed me anywhere, especially if I carried an apple in my hand or pocket.

The reader must not think that during my first two months' possession of that mare my bed was a bed of roses. I felt like one who is in possession of a momentous secret, which a slip of his tongue may reveal at any moment. One great object was to keep this mare as dark as possible till the proper moment, and this was no easy task. By some means or other it got whispered about that a new trotter had come home to our stable, and my parting with the cob just at the time looked very suspicious. Miss Morgan's early habits of life had not been those of idleness, and she required a deal more exercise to keep her from breaking out than our other horses. She had, I believe, never looked through a collar in her life, but this did not seem to make a pin's head difference to her. The first time we put her into a dung-cart to try, she walked away with it like the steadiest old team-horse on the farm, and after her first lesson in harness gave us no further trouble. I took a contract to lead gravel from a pit, about two miles off, on to the turnpike-road; and often and often, when she has been standing quietly by the side of the gravel-pit—all her best points hidden by blinkers, collar, and breeching—looking as rough and dirty as the men who were shovelling in the gravel, have passers-by—members of " the prying, inquisitive clan"—pulled up, attracted by the name on the cart, and tried, by pumping the labourers, to see if they could not glean a little information about the new trotter, which so many had heard of, so few seen. Little did they think that "Patty Morgan," whose name they were often to see afterwards at the top of the poll, was then and there standing quietly in the shafts under their very noses. But we did not neglect her education for all this. Twice a week we had her out on our "convincing ground;" and often in the grey twilight of morning, or in the deep, full, quiet moonlight, the labourer going out to his day's work, or the jolly farmer on his way home from the neighbouring market, would be startled by the thundering clatter of hoofs as Miss Morgan and her schoolmaster came rattling by him at a pace which hardly gave him time to pull up and turn round before we were out of sight.

I was not quite certain on what stage the new actress should make her *début*, and this, like many other more important events in our lives, was decided by accident. I very rarely rode the mare out by daylight, and if perchance I did, I took good care that no one should ever fancy she could trot; and notwithstanding all their suspicions that I had something or other a little better than common, not one, even of my oldest associates, knew anything about the capabilities of my new mare. But my whole life, during the first three months I owned that mare, was one of prevarication; and glad enough was I when the day arrived that all further secrecy was unnecessary, and Miss Patty Morgan was brought out at the tenth milestone on the Nottingham road, and her colours—Lincoln green and white sleeves—hoisted in defiance of all comers.

I had ridden her over one day to see a friend who resided at a few miles' distance, and I did not leave his house till latish in the evening. There was no moon, still it was not dark; but it was towards the end of September, and the twilight bore that haziness which is so peculiar to an English autumn evening. I was riding very gently along the crown of the road, for I had it all to myself, when I presently heard the rattle of wheels, and the clatter of hoofs behind me. The mare pricked up her ears, and with a sharp "Hi!" there shot by me a gig (in which sat two men), drawn by a horse which, as far as I could then observe, appeared to be one of the most magnificent steppers I had ever seen. They came upon me so suddenly, that if I had been a believer in the supernatural I might almost have thought they had sprung out of the very earth; but there was something perfectly natural in the jovial laugh of one of the men just as they passed me, and something completely human in the whiff of cigar smoke which the night air wafted to me after they had driven on. I think I should have taken no notice of them, but the mare began to get very fidgety, so I gave her her head and rattled after them. I dare say they had full a hundred yards' start, but I was soon close behind them; and as the mare was now on her mettle, I shot alongside of the gig almost before they had heard me come up. I was on the off-side; the man who was driving saw me at once, and the defiant manner in which he threw away his cigar, rose a little higher in his seat, and pulled his horse together, with a "Hi! Morgan, go along, old boy!" proved that he was fully prepared to accept the challenge I had so presumptuously thrown out. The horse made a magnificent spurt, and the gig drew clear of me in an instant, but it only needed a very slight pressure of my knee, and one "Hold up, Patty!" to bring her alongside of him again. This time I reached the horse's head, and here I kept for about a mile; once, indeed, I shot ahead, and I daresay I had got a clear length, but he soon overhauled me, and for a mile and a half we were head-and-head. I don't know whether the horse was doing his best—I fancied he was; and I fancied, moreover, that I could have gone by him when I liked. But I did not think much of this; for in the first place I was not sure that he was doing his best, and moreover, he was drawing a gig, which, as far as I could see, contained two heavy men. Now there was a toll-bar about a mile ahead, and, above all things, I did not want to keep their company so far, for at this gate I knew we must stop, and anxious as I was to find out all about my unknown opponent, I did not yet want the secret of my mare to be "blown." Luckily, however, a lane led up to a farm lodge out of the high road on my side, and when we came to this I pulled up, and politely bidding them good-night, I turned up it.

I waited quietly under the hedge till the sound of their wheels had died away in the distance, and then walked the mare gently up the grass by the roadside to the turnpike-gate. The gig had, I should fancy, driven by about ten minutes, and the old pikeman had turned in for another snooze; but I soon pulled him out again, and when I asked him who it was that had just gone through, his answer was, " Sam West and Morgan Rattler, sir."

" Did he ask you any questions ?"

"Well, sir, he did ask me who lived up at Maple Lodge; and when I told him Mr. Johnson, he asked if he had not got a fast trotter, and I told him, ' Not as I knew on.'"

" And what did he say then ?"

" Why, he just d——d my eyes for a stupid, know-nothing old fool, and drove on."

Sam West and Morgan Rattler have now to be introduced to the reader; but to do the subject justice will require a chapter to themselves.

Mr. Samuel West, or, as he was always called, " Sam West," was a character, and, if report spoke true, a very bad character too; and when it is added that his old dun horse, Morgan Rattler, had been the partner in one-half of his scrapes and escapades, we may conclude that the old saying, " Like master like man," would have held as good in their case as in any other. Before, however, we touch upon their histories, they may as well both of them give us one brief sitting for their portraits.

Sam West at this time was a fine, handsome, gentlemanly-looking man of about fifty, stood six feet high, had a commanding figure, with a very broad chest, and arms that indicated immense muscular strength. His face bore a manly, open expression, and his bronze cheek was tinted with the florid glow of rude health. His features were regular, and, had it not been for a slight indentation of the bridge of the nose and the loss of two front teeth, would have been faultless; and no one who looked at that mild blue eye, and quiet, generally thoughtful countenance, could ever have guessed that so much devilry lurked under so handsome a mask. His whole dress and appearance, clean and strict to the letter, without a shade of dandyism, all bespoke the English country squire. The low-crowned hat covered a head as white as snow, and the tight-fitting drab trousers sat close to a thigh and leg which a sculptor would have longed to model.

His old horse, Morgan Rattler, was a wonder—a great raking, upstanding brute, fully sixteen hands high, of a light dun-colour, and though eighteen years old (for Sam had bred him) as quick on his legs as ever he had been. A more savage, vicious horse was, perhaps, never foaled; yet in his old master's hands (but in no one else's) he was as quiet as a lamb. "There was nothing that old horse could not do," as Sam used to observe, "except pay the turn-pike-gates." He could live with the best horses in the hunt across the stiffest country, could jump a gate standing, was a splendid gig horse, and, stranger than all, was the fastest trotter in our county. I have said that the old dun had been partner in many of his old master's scrapes, and so he had; and I dare say the Sandford Lock, the Wooton toll-bar and the six-barred gate with the *chevaux de frise* out of Norbury Wood, are still standing to bear witness to this very day of some of the desperate leaps which the old dun had carried his daring master over. He was a fine, handsome-shaped horse, but had a drooping off ear; and the way he got this was curious.

He was bringing his old master home in the gig one night from a neighbouring fair. As usual, Sam was "market merry," and, as was his accustomed wont, was sitting on the low cushion on the near side of the gig, as being the easiest seat, and half asleep. When in this state he always placed implicit reliance on the old horse, who never made a mistake with him. Within about five miles from Sam's house was a steepish hill, and here the old dun pulled up into a walk. Luckily the stoppage woke up Sam, and they were going gently up the rise, when, by the hazy indistinct light of the young moon, he saw a man on the near side of the road, apparently getting over a gap in the hedge. Sam took no notice of this, for poachers abounded in those parts; but on reaching the crown of the hill, he saw another man a little ahead of him standing in the middle of the road. His suspicions were now excited. He had a goodish sum of money about him; and he never travelled without a pistol stuck in between the cushion and the rail of the gig on the off-side, to be ready to hand at a moment's notice. It did not take him many seconds now to shift into the driving seat, and he was just waking up old Morgan, when the second man sprang at the old horse's head, to which he clung like a bull-dog, shouting all the while to his comrade, who was running up the hill after the gig, to come on. Sam was an excellent pistol-shot: his pistol was levelled straight at the man's head in an instant, and he fired. The man fell like a log of wood; old Morgan sprang up into the air with a bound as though he was going to fly away with the gig, and then set off at a full gallop, which he kept till he pulled up short at a turnpike-gate, about two miles distant. Just as Sam had fired the pistol, the man behind, who was now within a few yards of the gig, hurled a hedge stake after him, which struck him across the back of the head, and knocked his hat off, fortunately without stunning him. When he got to the gate, Sam, as usual, began to abuse the turnpike man for keeping him waiting, when the old fellow, happening to look down, saw that the horse was standing with his off fore-hoof in a little pool of blood. The old man called Sam's attention to this, and, on jumping out, he found that the pistol-bullet had passed clean through the root of the old horse's ear. Sam fancied he must have missed the man altogether, who fell through the horse giving so violent a plunge; but this they never could make out, for no body was ever found. It was a lesson to Sam, however, never to trust again to a *single* pistol; for, as he truly observed, had he chanced to have shot the old horse dead he would have been left unarmed at the mercy of two ruffians, who would, doubtless, have knocked his brains out before he could have cleared himself from the gig. Sam could never make out how he missed that man, for he always boasted, and with good reason, of his skill as a pistol shot.

Sam West lived about fifteen miles from us, on his own estate, called Ashby Grange. The estate was a good one, and the old house, in other hands, might have been one of the finest in the country. No saying what traditions were connected with that old building, or what historical lore was attached to Ashby Grange. At the time of our tale, however, it was little better than a domestic ruin, and the iron finger of decay was fast completing a wreck which neglect had commenced. Built some centuries back, the old house presented a glorious specimen of the architecture of that day, but now fast crumbling to decay. How preferable (as some antiquarian has observed) is the aspect of the fragments of some once great edifice to that which such a house as we are now describing presents to our view. *There* the tall gable reaches its chimney-stack bleakly to the sky, and the green banks scarcely mark out the obliterated gardens. Time has done his worst *there*, and the death struggle is over. One can trace the terraces of the gardens restored to grazing land again with the calmness with which one walks over the grass-grown grave of a friend long dead; but *here* we see the very action of decomposition going on—the crumbling stucco of the ceiling in all (save the few rooms which are still kept inhabited), feeding the vampire ivy, the tattered tapestry yet hanging on the walls, the picture flapping in its broken frame, the machinery of the clock fallen through the roof into the chapel, and the fresh ferns sprouting out in the choked gutters, and yet the masonry in all its firmness, without a stone displaced, the sculpture as sharp as the first day it was carved, the solid oak staircase yet entire—this is a melancholy without a redeeming touch of hope or comfort; and yet, desolate as it appears now, within fifty years Ashby Grange was a habitable and comfortable house, and a moderate outlay a few years ago would have saved all the time-honoured associations connected with the old building, and preserved a house that thousands could not now restore.

Such was Ashby Grange when I first saw it; but there were old labourers living in the parish who could remember the days when it wore a very different aspect. The estate had been in the family for generations, and the house of West was as old, and at one time as honourable, as any in the county. Sam's grandfather was a true specimen of the old Sir Roger de Coverley school, and in his day the Grange was the resort of the best county families. A justice of the peace, a kind landlord, a good neighbour, and in every sense of the word a pattern of the true old English country gentleman, the old squire was beloved and respected by all; and when the hatchment frowned over the massive gothic doorway of the Grange, many an eye was wet and many a heart was heavy, for it told the rich, in mute but eloquent language, that they had lost a true friend and kind companion, and the poor, a charitable and generous protector.

Sam's father was a soldier, a greater portion of whose early life had been spent abroad, and his tastes possessed little in common with the old country families among whom he now came to reside. He was profligate and dissipated, deeply addicted to play, and his habits were just such as those which quiet country gentlemen would detest and despise. Very changed was the aspect of affairs at the old hall during the time he reigned over it to what they were in the days of the good old squire. The country gentlemen of the oldest and best families gradually withdrew themselves from his companionship, and the prestige of the old Grange was fast waning. But there was a certain set who still associated with the colonel. Men whose standing in society was tarnished but not utterly blemished, and for whom the loose, free-and-easy habits which had now full licence at the Grange possessed abundant attractions. They were, however, *gentlemen*, and the nightly orgies in the colonel's day had not yet sunk to the gross debauchery of those that characterized the reign of his son. The colonel was a widower, with one son—our hero. He was killed by a fall from his horse, after having lived at the Grange for nearly a quarter of a century, and Sam, at the age of twenty-five, succeeded to an encumbered estate worth about 2000*l.* per year.

Sam might have commenced life with the fairest prospects in view; but the school in which he had been brought up was a bad one, and quiet country gentlemen shook their heads when they heard of his accession to the property. Ever since the day he was expelled from Oxford, he had been running wild down at Ashby amidst scenes of riot and dissipation, and it could hardly be expected that the son of such a father could turn out any other than a profligate and a spendthrift. And so he did. But had he *strictly* followed that father's example things might not have been so bad; for, with all his wild, licentious habits, that father was a man of sense, and though extravagant and fond of play, was still an excellent manager. It is true he might have been looked coldly upon by the country gentlemen, and many declined his invitations, alleging that the boisterous merriment of the Grange was too much for them. Still no one actually cut him, and he met his neighbours upon neutral ground as an equal, and with a show of friendship on either side. He was a perfect gentleman when he chose it; and although strange tales of the nightly doings up at the old hall got whispered about, he never shocked propriety by any outward breach of decorum. Surely, he argued, if he gave away a dinner, he had a right to ask whom he pleased to eat it; and if old Squire Langley or the Hon. Mr. Compton did not choose to accept his invitations, they could stop away.

But Sam's bane was a decided and innate taste for low company, and he followed his father's footsteps to the shadow, but among associates ten times lower and more degraded. Even the few country gentlemen who had, as it were, tacitly acknowledged the father, and occasionally visited the Grange, could not but view with repugnance the low tastes of the son. They gradually fell away from Sam, and in a few years none but the outcasts of society would associate with him. Broken-down horse-dealers, gamblers, the lowest hangers-on of the racing-stables, prize-fighters, touts and black-legs, were now the only company that were met at Ashby Grange; and if those old steel-clad, corsletted knights and warriors, or ruffed dames of high degree, former proprietors of the estate, who looked down grimly out of the canvas from the walls of the ancient banqueting-room, could but have started into life and joined one of Sam's nocturnal revels, they would have been rather struck with the altered aspect of affairs. But for all this Sam had a kind heart and generous disposition, was a first-rate sportsman, and possessed a spirit of daring and energy which would have been invaluable if directed in a good cause. He was positively afraid of nothing; had immense strength, and a power of endurance such as few could boast. Scarcely a month passed without some fresh lawless or daring exploit, in which he had figured, being recorded in the county paper; and he was being continually bound over to keep the peace for some assault or another. Up to the age of thirty-five he was unmarried, but suddenly a new actress came upon the stage to reign as queen over Ashby Grange. Where he picked her up, who she was, or what she had been, no one at the time knew; but she was one of the most beautiful women that had entered those old portals for many a year, and her grace and manners might have adorned a Court.

There was a good deal of "the tragedy queen" about her; her manners were quiet, composed, and lady-like, her carriage dignified and graceful, and she was altogether the very last sort of woman that any man who knew Sam West would have dreamt of his taking as a wife. Her age might be about twenty-five; she was above the middle height, superbly formed, and her long glossy ringlets, black as jet, clustered round a brow and over a neck and shoulders as white and pure as alabaster.

It turned out that she had been a second-rate actress in a low London theatre, which Sam had happened to visit in one of his nights about town. Whatever he did was generally off-hand. He rarely gave up much time to reflection. If he liked a horse he bought him at once without further parley; and fancying he saw something about this woman a little better than the generality of his female associates, he procured an introduction to her, and after trying her with proposals which she indignantly scouted, he married her at once, and brought her down to be the mistress of Ashby Grange.

And he did right; for if any mortal hand could save him from the ruin which was just then hanging over him, it was hers. What-ever her antecedents, she was well fitted to fill the post to which she was now elevated. She soon found that she had given her hand to a man who, as his friends pleasantly used to observe among themselves, " could not live another mile at the pace he was then going," and had come down to an estate heavily encumbered, to preside over a house which was now the resort of all the spendthrifts and broken-down sporting men in the county. But she never quailed —the greater the perils which menaced her husband, the greater pride did she feel in helping to extricate him from them ; and, like a true woman, her courage rose as fresh difficulty after difficulty stared her in the face. It was nothing to her that not a lady in the neighbourhood ever noticed or called upon her ; it was nothing to her that when in her visits to the little neighbouring market-town the county ladies whom she met crossed over the road, or gave her the path with a chilling politeness and a cold haughty stare such as only high-bred ladies can assume—God help them ! Judged fairly by their intrinsic merits, there was hardly one among them who could hold a candle to her. Kind and generous in her disposition, warm-hearted almost to a fault, with a character as stainless as her brow, grateful to her husband for having rescued her from the pollution of low London life, and dragged her from an existence which she detested and abhorred, she loved him with all the fervour of a woman's passion, and she had now but one sole aim in life, to endeavour to render herself worthy of the position to which he had raised her. She soon saw his faults, but she never blamed him. She had been brought up in a hard school, but a school in which she had good opportunities of reading the human heart; and if but few gleams of sunshine had hitherto illuminated her rugged path, she had studied the dark side of life in all its phases. She saw at once that it was in vain to endeavour to clean the " Augean stable " at a single sweep. She knew that complaints and remonstrances would avail her nothing. She saw that her only chance of accomplishing the task was by kindness, affection, and patience, and she set about that task with a tact peculiarly her own. She never reproached her husband for excesses which she had not the power to stem. She never looked coldly upon his dissolute and abandoned friends ; she received them with a courteous grace that was bred in her, and although in her inmost heart she might have despised them, she never gave the slightest outward indication of the fact. But, courteous as her manners were towards them, they all saw at once that she knew and read them thoroughly, and not one of them ever felt at his ease when that black eye flashed upon him. One by one they became less frequent visitors at the Grange, and the old house began to wear a quieter and a more respectable aspect than it had done for years.

"Can't stand the missus, Sam," was the answer of Tom Woodcroft, the steeple-chase rider—who always rode for Sam, and who, although a wild, harum-scarum fellow, was by far the best and least dangerous of all his acquaintances—in reply to Sam's question as to why he saw so little of him up at the Grange now. "She's always too —— civil for me; and yet I know that she reads us all like a book."

"Sorry for you, Sam; sorry for you," observed Captain Morris, who was Sam's most intimate friend, and had lived on him, riding his horses, winning or borrowing his money, for the last six years; "but, excuse me, old fellow, you've quite lost your position in society by bringing that woman home."

This friendly and disinterested little speech was made on the evening of the day in which Sam had introduced the captain to his wife. The captain was a keen hand, and in one hour had read her character, just as truly as she had read his own, and he saw plainly if that woman was allowed to have the upper hand he would soon be obliged to look out for lodgings elsewhere.

"Tell you what it is, master," growled out Jemmy the tout one day to Sam, on leaving the stable-yard, "if you don't soon get rid of that filly" (jerking his thumb knowingly in the direction of the house) "you'll be losing all your old friends."

And even Tom G——, the prize-fighter, who used occasionally to run down to Ashby to blow the London fog off him, as he called it, candidly remarked: "She is a stunner. I've no fault to find with her, in the least; but my name's Walker. I never yet met the man that I was afraid of looking in the face; but as for that woman, I could not stand her eye full upon me for half a minute if you'd make me champion of England."

Sam was a little worried by these remarks at first, but her uniform kind and affectionate manner towards him soon put him right; and when blunt, honest farmer Jones met him for the first time after his marriage, driving his new wife round to show her the parish, and shook his hand, with "Well, Sam, my boy, you've done the best thing now you ever did in your life," his face beamed with inward satisfaction, and he looked down upon the beautiful creature that sat by his side as a kind of protector, and felt that, if only she was true to him, he could well afford to make any sacrifice for her sake. He never cared when, by chance, he heard of any of the spiteful reports which were spread round the neighbourhood respecting her. However they might sneer at her, however they might scandalize her out of hearing, no one in the neighbourhood could help allowing that she seemed born for the station which she filled; and as Sam proudly walked by her side for the first time through the little market-town near him, all agreed that it would be hard to find so handsome a couple, pick the whole county through; and bold indeed must have been the man who would have dared to breathe a word of scandal against her fair fame in the hearing of the stalwart protector who now walked by her side.

Things soon began to wear an altered aspect at the Grange, and the simple villagers one and all agreed that, if there was an angel on earth, it was the Squire's lady. It is true that, except the good clergyman's wife (who had read and appreciated her character from the first) and some of the neighbouring farmers' wives, she had but few female friends; still she was never dull or lonely. Her whole time when her husband was at home was occupied in amusing him, and when he was absent the cares of the poor villagers were her sole concern. So matters went on for a few years, and Sam's wife was a happy woman. She gloried as she marked the change for the better, for she well knew it was owing to herself. But darker days were in store for her. Whether Sam began to tire of the monotony of the respectable life he was then leading, or whether he became weary of a submission which was yielded to him without an effort to gain it, it is hard to say, but he gradually grew restless and uneasy; and although it was very rarely now that any of his old associates came home to him, he by degrees got into the habit of meeting them at neighbouring public-houses and taverns, till at length he scarcely passed at home, in his wife's company, one evening out of the seven. The poor woman saw the change, but she never repined. She had now other cares and anxieties to contend against. They had no children until five years after their marriage, when a little son was born. The poor child was sickly from its cradle, and by degrees sank into a helpless idiot. One would have thought that such an affliction would have bound any father closer to a wife, whose fondest earthly hopes were thus rudely dashed away; but it had a contrary effect on Sam. He loathed the very sight of that child, and as for the poor mother who bore it, he appeared to regard her as the sole cause of the calamity. He now seemed to shun a home into which she had brought the only ray of pure sunshine which had entered it for years, and he took again to drinking deeply—a vice which for some time he had abandoned. "Cuss them bad shillin's," says Sam Slick, "they are always coming back to you;" and now, as his poor wife, whose spirits were gradually becoming broken, was nearly always confined to her room in charge of her idiot boy, and was rarely seen by any one, his old acquaintances one by one returned; and on the night when I had my first spin with Morgan Rattler on the turnpike-road, Sam West, though past the age of fifty, was a wilder and more reckless man than ever, without the excuse of youth to palliate his excesses.

Such was the history of Sam West and Morgan Rattler; and I only hope I have not tired out the reader, for I have got a little more to say about both of them yet.

On reaching home, after the chance contest between my new mare and Sam West's well-known favourite, I told my groom Jem of my little adventure. Now this groom had lived at Ashby Grange for a year before he came to me, and knew "Old Morgan" well, for he had both ridden and driven him, and he also knew by this what the mare could do. The name of Morgan Rattler was a name of dread around us, and although there were doubtless many trotters in England to beat him, there was not one in our country-side could live with him; and as surely as ever a little cup or trotting sweepstakes was advertised in our district, so surely did old Morgan put in an appearance and carry it off.

"And so you think you could have gone by him, sir?" asked the man, after I had finished.

"Yes, Jem; but then I don't think much of that, because I'm not so sure that he was doing all he knew."

"Ah, but you may depend on it he was," answered the shrewd fellow. "You may take your oath Sam was half drunk, or he'd never have let a stranger on the high road get the length of old Morgan for a mile for nothing. I know what Sam is when he's on the spree; and the old horse is as bad as he is just then. He'd never have let you get to his head if he could have helped it. I wonder he did not try and savage you when you came by his side. I've ridden both horses, now, and I know there's not a deal of difference between them. At catch weights I'd even back the mare; for there's not a boy in the country can ride or drive old Morgan, and a child could hold Patty. If we can only keep this dark, we shall make something of it yet."

But we could not keep it dark from such a wily old fox as Sam West. By noon the next day he was back again to the turnpike-gate, found out from the old man who kept it who it was that had passed through just after him on the preceding night, and obtained a pretty accurate description of my mare.

Now, Sam was a man of decision, and drove at once down to our village; he did not come straight up to me, but put up at the little public-house. I was in the stables, when a message was brought to me that two gentlemen wished to speak to me up at the Rising Sun directly.

I went down at once. A light cane-bodied gig with remarkably high wheels and straight shafts, the corduroy-covered driving cushion nearly level with the rail, was standing at the door without a horse; and I walked straight into the little parlour, where Sam West and his friend Captain Morris sat discussing a large dish of eggs and bacon.

Nothing could be more polite than the manner in which Mr. West greeted me. He apologized for thus troubling me, but said, as he had just learnt that it was I who had ridden by his side the night before, he had a great curiosity to see my mare, and hoped it would not be asking too much if he begged me to show her to him.

I now saw that the plot was thickening, and that the time would soon come when all secrecy must be laid aside. I therefore cheerfully complied with his request, and took him to my stables to show him the mare.

Keen was the scrutiny to which Patty Morgan was subjected on that morning; and, although he said but little, I could see that Mr. West regarded her with more interest than he cared to show. He merely asked if she was for sale, and, when I answered "No," left the stable. He recognised his old helper, and, as he tossed him a half-crown, observed to me, "You've got one of the best men in the county there, if you can only keep him sober."

We went in and had a glass of sherry, and he gave me a most cordial invitation to come over to the Grange, and take pot luck with him any day I had nothing better to do.

About a fortnight after this, the following conversation took place between Jem and myself:

"I think I shall ride over and see Mr. West to-day, Jem."

"Do you, sir? Well, mind what you're about, that's all. You know I've lived there, and am up to all their tricks."

"I'll take care; so just put the saddle on the new mare, and bring her round in twenty minutes."

"Not if I know it, sir," answered the fellow.

I looked at him in blank astonishment. "What do you mean by that?" I asked.

"Why, you don't mean to say you're ever going to take the mare over there, sir! As sure as ever she gets to the Grange, they'll either do you out of her, or else get a fair trial out of old Morgan. I know what Sam meant when he asked if our mare was for sale. No, sir, no; take my advice, and ride the pony over, but leave the mare at home. I should like to see her meet old Morgan dearly, but not till the money's down."

There was good sense in the man's advice, though not given very respectfully, and I took it.

Now, I had a great curiosity to see Mr. Sam West "at home," for although, in common with every one in the neighbourhood, I could not but know him, I was not intimately acquainted with him, and had never once set my foot in Ashby Grange. I wanted to see the old house of which I had heard so much; I wanted to see his wife; and, above all, I wanted to try if I could not get a match on between old Morgan Rattler and my new mare. I was confident now that she would take some beating. I must begin with her somewhere, and why not as well with old Morgan as any other horse? If she was beaten by a horse whose name was in every one's mouth, she would not be disgraced, for I was sure she would run well up.

I mentioned my project to the groom, and he approved of it. He was certain old Morgan must be getting stale, and he felt quite convinced that nobody would drive him but his master. So he advised me, if we did make a match, to be sure and have it at catch weights, and to make it two-mile heats. As I rode off, he added, "I shan't feel easy till you come back, for I know where you are going. Keep your eye on the captain—he's a bad 'un; and be sure and remember me very kindly to the missus."

I reached the Grange about eleven; and when I first caught sight of the old house through a long avenue of elms more than two centuries old, I was not a bit surprised at all I had heard in praise of it. There was something truly imposing about that venerable building, seen from a little distance (for I was not near enough to detect the ravages which the hand of neglect and time had committed), as it burst suddenly upon my view, a glorious memento of past ages, in all the grandeur of ancient British architecture, its outline clearly defined in a cloudless blue October sky, which formed the background of the picture. It needed now very little stretch of the imagination to fill the *tableau* with living forms—the bold crusader, the stalwart knight armed for the tournament, and the lady of high degree with falcon on her fist—all seemed to meet me as I rode over the old bridge that spanned the moat which encircled the house and gardens. But as I approached nearer to the building, the signs of dilapidation became more apparent; the place seemed deserted, the clatter of my pony's hoofs, as I rode across the large, empty, grass-grown court-yard, struck a chill to the very heart; and the only living actor in the scene, save some poultry and pigeons, appeared to be my pony, myself, and a purblind old mastiff, who was chained under a horse block by the stable-door, and who greeted me with a deep-mouthed bay, the echoes of which fairly startled me. This brought out a helper from the stable-yard, who took my pony, and I followed him to the stables, anxious to see what they were like, and how they were filled.

However much the house and the rest of the premises might be neglected, this was not the case with the stables. They were new, capitally arranged, and kept in the greatest order. Four hunters, which had just been straightened up after their morning's exercise, in first-rate condition, every one of them up to sixteen stone, were standing in clothes and bandages; and a perfect model of a gig-horse occupied a fifth stall, while, on the door of a loose box at the end of the stable, I read the redoubtable name "Morgan Rattler," written in gold letters under one of his plates. One of the prettiest little fox-terriers I ever saw came bustling down the ladder from the loft above (where he was very busy hunting after rats) to welcome a stranger; and under the manger of the gig-horse lay a favourite otter-hound bitch, suckling three puppies. I never was in a better six-stall stable in my life, nor one that seemed to be kept in better order. The stalls were roomy, the partitions high, and each stall could be immediately converted into a loose box by hanging a gate on between the pillars.

Old Morgan was at home, and I asked if I could see him.

"Certainly, sir; but you'd better not go in to him," was the reply.

His box was closed by two half doors, the top one of which we opened. The old horse was standing lazily in the middle of a very roomy box up to his knees in straw, apparently half asleep.

"The old boy does not get much sleep o' nights. I often don't get him suppered up till three o'clock," observed the man apologetically.

When the door opened, he came sidling up to us, with his ear laid back and a cunning look in his wicked old eye, as if he was half debating whether he should rush at us and seize us with his teeth, or whether he should lash out his powerful hind legs at the door over which we were leaning. But, "Now, old man, none of your nonsense!" and he came quietly up to receive the accustomed carrot, without which the groom never, he said, entered his box.

He certainly was a wonderful-looking old horse. His dun colour and his hanging ear gave him a peculiar appearance; his shape was unexceptionable; and, although they had been deeply fired all round, his legs now seemed as hard as four oak posts. He had a very clean, blood-like head, well set on, and he carried his flag (to use the dealers' term), in the shape of a long swish tail, gallantly. He stood above sixteen hands, and was altogether a real varmint-looking horse. He had neither clothing nor bandages on him; nothing but a plain, heavy headstall. He carried no flesh, but appeared to be one compact mass of bone, muscle and sinew.

"Wonderful horse that, sir," observed the man, as we closed the door of the box; "there's nobody can do anything with him but the guvnor and me. You'd never believe what that horse has done, and yet he's as good now as he was at six years old."

"He can trot a bit, too, can't he?" I carelessly asked.

"Trot! I believe you—there's nothing in this county can touch him. There was a chap, however, tackled him the other night as the guvnor was coming home from Retford fair, and the guvnor did say when he come home that old Morgan's stockings were tied tighter to shake him off than ever they were in his life before. The guvnor was not half pleased about it, and could not rest easy till he found out who it was."

"Well, and who was it?"

"Oh, why, a dealing chap on the other side of the county. It was a mare he was riding. The guvnor's seen her."

"And what did he think of her?"

"Why, he rather liked her; but he did not seem to think a deal on her, for I heard him say to the captain as they were looking at old Morgan, after they came home, 'That little Welsh mare's a neat little thing, and not half a bad 'un for a mile, but I should like to get a match on between her and old Morgan for two. It was a deep trick of that chap's turning up the lane when he found he was beaten. He's no fool, that fellow, anyhow.'"

I never listened so eagerly in my life to any conversation as I did to this; and if the man had given me ten pounds, I should not have felt half so gratified as I did when I learnt so unexpectedly and by chance the "guvnor's" opinion of my mare. But he was a little out in his reckoning this time, for we had tried the mare to be quite as good at six miles as at one; beyond that we had never gone. I was now in high spirits, for, to tell the truth, I had begun to "funk" a little when I saw those stables and their appointments, for I then knew I had to deal with a man who, whatever irregularities could be laid to his charge, was not very likely to make a mistake in anything about horses, and a man, moreover, on whom the experience of every phase in sporting life for thirty years was not likely to have been thrown away. At first I felt as if I had come on a foolhardy errand; and, as Mr. West was out in the village and was not expected back for an hour or two, I had half resolved to sneak home again, and leave old Morgan to the quiet enjoyment of the honours he had so bravely won and so manfully maintained. Directly, however, I heard what the groom said, I began, like Nick Bradshaw in "The Clockmaker," to feel "quite encouraged like," and now determined to wait till Mr. West came home, and let matters take their course.

Like all good stablemen, this man was remarkably civil. He took me into the saddle-room, which, of course, was as well appointed and in as good order as the stables, took me to see the greyhound-kennel, and after that showed me the most magnificent brace of heavy pointers I had ever looked at. In fact, whatever might be the internal arrangements of the old Grange, the sporting appointments were complete, and everything I saw bespoke the sporting tastes of the owner. Every fowl (except a few of the sweetest little spangled bantams) were thorough game, and the man pointed out to me a magnificent "ginger pile" which had been champion in a main at Nottingham the year before. Every pigeon we saw was a fancy bird of some strain or other. Two tame foxes were kennelled in the yard. The coach-house door was covered with pads and muzzles, while three or four gilt plates on the stable-door proved that it was not alone hunters and trotters that had come out of these stables.

I did not care to go into the house till the owner came home, so I thought I would amuse myself while waiting for him by a stroll round the premises. I went down a long flight of stone steps which led from the back of the house into what had once been a splendid garden, now a perfect wilderness. Originally it had been laid out with the greatest taste and care; now you could not distinguish the flower-beds from the walks. I never saw so sad a picture of gross neglect, and the further I strolled the more I grieved to think what this place might be in any other hands than those of the present owner. It was the same over all—

> "Nightshade, on each border glowing,
> Said a rose might here be blowing,
> If I left her room to grow in.
>   Fruit-trees tottered to their fall,
> And their virtue sapped with ivy.
> Here and there an empty hive I
> Saw, but not a bee alive; I
>   Found the wasps had killed them all."

The pedestal which had once supported the sun-dial had been snapped in half, and the old sun-dial itself lay buried in a bed of nettles. Several statues which had once been handsome, but every one of which was in some way or other now mutilated or disfigured, were scattered here and there. One chubby little leaden Cupid had apparently been used as a target for Sam's pistol practice; while a pond perhaps a quarter of an acre in extent, originally a famous fish-stew, but now choked up with weeds and filth, the surface covered with a thick green coating of slimy duckweed, formed a rare breeding-place for myriads of frogs and water-newts.

By the side of this pond was a little kind of summer-house, in a tolerably good state of repair, and a well-trodden path down to it proved that it was more resorted to than the upper part of the garden. I walked up to it to have a peep in, and found that I had stumbled on one of the greatest curiosities of the place, adorned in a manner which the old squire, Sam's grandfather, would have little dreamt of. It was apparently fitted up as a smoking-room. A little, jolly-looking, three-cornered table stood in the middle of the floor, and a couple of lockers, fitted into the walls, doubtless contained the materials for a jovial evening's carouse, and many a jovial carouse had those old walls witnessed. It was to these old walls that my attention was particularly directed. They were not decorated with pictures of any kind—Sam had a soul above the flashy daubs which generally adorn the walls of smoking-rooms or bachelors' apartments—they were not even papered, as we commonly use the term; yet I question much if the most splendidly-furnished drawing-room in Portland-place cost more (reckoning by the square inch) to paper than the walls of that little summer-house; for nearly two whole sides of the room were covered with copies of writs and summonses, collected with the greatest care and during upwards of a quarter of a century, by a man who had been in continual hot water during the whole of that time—civil, but still most pressing invitations for Samuel West, of Ashby Grange, in the parish of Ashby, gentleman, to appear before every judge who had ruled supreme in any one or other of her Majesty's Courts of Queen's Bench,

Exchequer, or Common Pleas during that period, at the suits of so-and-so, "greeting." A large square patch on the middle of the third side was devoted to summonses to appear before one or the other of her Majesty's justices of the peace for the county, for assaults, poaching, trespasses, or (crime of crimes) for having, when in a state of intoxication, obstructed a policeman in the execution of his duty. There were some few declarations pasted here and there among the civil processes, but most appeared to have been settled as soon as the first shot had been fired; while on the margin of every summons was written how the case terminated—for instance, " Fined 5l.," "Discharged with a caution," "Bound over to keep the peace." I have examined collections of various kinds in my life, but I never saw half so curious a one as this.

By a careful study of these walls, one read Sam's whole life as plainly as any biography could tell it. The summonses which contained the gravest charges bore dates during the ten years that elapsed between Sam's succession to the property and his marriage (a few were even antecedent to that period); many of the writs were issued at the same time, and I was sorry to see that many were dated within the last five years, and that each succeeding year seemed to beat the last in number. For the first few years of his married life, not a summons appeared, and very few writs. The earlier summonses were principally to answer charges of "assault and battery," some of them of a rather grievous nature; but of later years Sam's principal offences seemed to have been of a more venial kind—trespass in pursuit of game; and the keepers of the Right Hon. the Earl of —— appeared to have had many a merry dance after him, according to the statements contained in these summonses. I observed the copy of the last writ bore date just three days prior to my visiting the summer-house. I could not but help thinking that Sam must be a tolerably profitable client to whatever attorney he might honour with his patronage. It was not so much through inability to pay as through a careless inattention to all matters of business that Sam always required to be summoned before he paid a debt; and I have met with more such men than one during my journey through life.

However, from all accounts, affairs at the Grange were now wearing a threatening aspect, and they did say that Sam was only nominal possessor, living in the hall of his ancestors on sufferance, for that the mortgagees held all the title-deeds, and that Capt. Morris had a bill of sale over all his personal property.

On leaving the summer-house I branched off into the labyrinth of trees and rubbish with which I was surrounded, anxious to see the extent of this wilderness, when I suddenly came upon a little spot, a perfect oasis in the desert. It was a small patch of garden-ground, laid out and tended with the greatest care. The flower-beds were kept in the neatest order, and stocked with the choicest varieties of hollyhocks, dahlias, and other autumnal flowers, which now blazed showily out, in strange contrast with the weeds surrounding them on all sides. Working in one of the beds was an old man, and by his side stood a lady, and a boy about ten years of age. I had little difficulty, from what I had heard of her, in recognising in this proud-looking, handsome woman (for she was still handsome, notwithstanding the years of suffering and neglect which she had passed through), the lady of the mansion; and the vacant unmeaning stare with which the boy regarded me, as I approached, told me plainer than words could speak that this was her idiot son.

The lady looked me over with one long, keen, searching glance, as I introduced myself and apologized for my intrusion. I said I was waiting for Mr. West, and had strolled quite by chance into the garden to pass away the time.

"Not much to see at Ashby, I fancy, except the stables," was her reply; adding in a tone of bitter irony, "unless it is a proof of what waste and neglect can accomplish. A friend of Mr. West's, I suppose; you want to see him something about a horse?" glancing at the jockey-whip in my hand.

"Well," I said, for her keen black eye was on me, and I felt that prevarication was useless (I had heard of Tom the prize-fighter's remark, and I could not help thinking that he was about right, and that, if she had only been born a man, what a splendid

Queen's counsel she would have made), " I certainly had a curiosity to see old Morgan Rattler, of whom I had heard so much; and Mr. West having kindly asked me, I had taken the opportunity of the fine weather to ride over this morning."

Her manner was courteous enough, but rather chilling; and no wonder at it. I thought how that woman must detest the very name of horses, and hate the sight of anybody connected with them. She, however, asked me politely to walk in and wait for Mr. West, and, taking her boy by the hand, led the way up to the house. The poor child clung to his mother's side, apparently frightened at the sight of a stranger. He, however, kept furtively eyeing me, and seemed to regard my silver-mounted whip with great curiosity. After a little coaxing, I put it into his hand for him to look at. The bright gleam of satisfaction which shot from his lustreless eye as he showed the coveted treasure to his mother proved that the lamp of light even yet glimmered in that darkened mind; and I ventured to remark to her that there was still hope, and that, in my opinion, the child would outgrow the malady.

God knows, I spoke at random; but even that random speech shot a ray of comfort into the poor mother's blighted heart, and that one simple action, and those hap-hazard words, placed me upon a far better footing with that woman than the most sycophantic compliments I could have paid her, or the most studied politeness I could have shown towards herself would ever have done. How true it is that the way to a mother's heart is through her child's!

The poor boy seemed to have taken a great fancy to my whip. I happened to have an old repeating watch in my pocket—not one of the diminutive, waistcoat-pocket affairs now in fashion, but a regular old-fashioned gold hunting watch, nearly as large as a small turnip. I pulled it out to show the boy; and when I rung the chimes in his ear, his delight knew no bounds. From that minute we were sworn friends, and I walked up the old stone steps with the child's hand in mine, and his mother by his side, as though we had all been on terms of intimacy for years. When we got in, the lady apologized for leaving me, and, showing me into a long old banqueting-room, which now served for the sitting-room and parlour, left me. The boy would not part with the whip, so I let him carry it away with him.

It was a splendid room, and the wainscot and polished floor were altogether of old British oak, now nearly as black as ebony. This room was in tolerable repair, for it lay in the best wing of the house; and as the chamber above had been converted by Sam into a granary, the ceilings were sound. The walls were garnished with old-fashioned portraits of Sam's ancestors and other celebrities of bygone ages. Mighty bold did those old knights look, as they frowned down upon me, many of them clad in mail, with his gloved hand upon his sword hilt. And mighty fine were those high-born dames in ruff and bodice, who with meaningless eyes seemed to follow me wherever I went. But there was not a knight or lady in any one of those old frames who for proud, manly, real English good looks and bearing, could compare with the two that seemed fairly to stand out of the canvas at the far end of the room, representing the present squire and his lady, taken as large as life, at the period of their marriage. Old Morgan hung over the mantelpiece; and one or two old-fahioned hunters, in the short dock and crop-eared style of the last century, kept him company.

Presently a bold, fine-looking, over-dressed female servant brought in the materials for a substantial lunch, and about ten minutes later the squire and his friend the captain came in. He welcomed me most cordially, hoped I had made myself at home, and we sat down. Mr. West was looking as fresh and handsome as ever, and the way in which he went in at the cold pigeon pie and pheasant proved that his appetite was still unimpaired. It really seemed as if no amount of dissipation could ever undermine that iron frame. Of course we had some ale, such as you cannot get out of "the shires;" and we topped off the heartiest lunch I had made for a long time with a glass of brown sherry, of which Sam remarked, "You wont find a headache in a hogshead of it."

After lunch we went the round of the premises. It was a treat to go round the stables and kennels with such a conductor as Sam

West. It was a treat to see the way in which he walked up to a horse; and if the roller or the body clothing was the least out of place or deranged, how soon his keen eye detected it, and his hand set it right. It was, moreover, a treat to see how every dumb animal about these premises loved him, and how they recognised him directly they saw him. The old mastiff bayed out his honest welcome, the little terrier came bounding up to greet him, the foxes tugged at the end of their chains to reach him, even the old "ginger pile" flapped his wings and sent forth a shrill crow of defiance, as if he recollected who had handled him in his last main. The pigeons seemed as if they would almost settle on his shoulder; and, as for old Morgan, as soon as he ever heard the well-known voice, he sent forth a wild neigh of delight, as much as to say, "I am quite ready if you are." Ah, well, I thought, this man is not half so bad as he has been represented. There must be some good in that heart—dumb animals and children never make mistakes. As we were walking to the stables, the captain asked me whether I had brought the little mare over; and on my answering "No,"

"Pity," he remarked; "we might have had a mile spin with old Morgan; it would have amused Sam. He does not seem in good spirits."

And many others had made the same remark during the last ten days; for since the day on which he had handed over that bill of sale to the captain, giving him the power to seize every horse he had at a day's notice, the squire had been an altered man, though no one, not even his wife, knew the exact cause, although many guessed it. His farms were well let; and although the estate, over which he had unlimited control, was mortgaged, there was always sufficient left to maintain him, and respectably, too, with care, after the interest was paid. Moreover, the railroad was about to run right through the heart of his estate. His compensation would have been something handsome, and he could have struggled on against his just debts till this compensation money would have set him free. His principal creditor was the captain, and the greater part of the money owed to him was for money lost at cards at Sam's own table, not one shilling of which could ever have been recovered in a court of law. In an unguarded moment, the captain persuaded him to sign a bill of sale to him of all his personal property as a security—" merely as a matter of form;" and from that moment he had placed himself in the power of as unscrupulous a sharper as ever existed.

At five we sat down to an excellent dinner. Sam did the honours of the table with the manners of a true gentleman, which all the contamination of low habits and low associates had not effaced. His wife seemed far more cheerful, and her manner was much more cordial towards me than when I had first met her in the garden. Sporting subjects seemed avoided by tacit consent, and dinner passed off amid a desultory conversation on general topics such as all could join in. But when we quietly settled down in Sam's little sanctum (for there was a fireplace in the old summer-house which rendered it very comfortable now the nights were beginning to get chilly), we fairly opened. We were now joined by Tom Woodcroft and a sporting friend. We talked of " horses and hounds, and the system of Meynell." Sam gave us a graphic description of two or three famous runs in which he had distinguished himself; and his account of the manner in which old Morgan carried him over the lock pound and the spiked-gate out of Norbury Wood, formed not the least interesting topics in that evening's conversation ; but not the slightest allusion did he ever make to any of those little patches which adorned the walls, the history of which I was longing to hear. In fact, as they observed, Sam was a cup too low on this occasion.

We passed a remarkably pleasant evening—nothing like excess. I was on my guard, but there was no occasion for it. Tom Woodcroft could not drink, having just risen from a sick bed, to which he had been confined for the last three weeks, by a broken collar-bone and two broken ribs. The captain, like his craft, was careful, and I followed suit, and there was no pressing. Sam merely observed, when he saw me fill my glass, that I was drowning the miller, adding, that if he did drink a glass of grog himself, he liked it strong. To my surprise, old Morgan's name was never mentioned, till at length, during a pause in the conversation, the captain turned suddenly round to me, with—

"And so you think your little mare's good enough to beat old Morgan, do you?"

Now, if I had ever thought anything of the kind I had never given him the slightest intimation of the fact; so I observed quietly that I hardly knew enough of the old horse to give an opinion, but that if Mr. West had no objection I should not mind trotting him for two miles if he gave me one hundred yards' start in each mile.

Sam directly answered, "I've nothing whatever to do with the old horse now; he belongs to the captain, who, I dare say, will accommodate you." And he never made another remark on the subject.

The captain and I soon came to terms. It does not take long to make a bargain when both parties have made up their minds about it; and after far less wrangling than is usual on such occasions, I matched my black mare, Patty Morgan, to trot against Captain Morris's dun horse, Morgan Rattler, at catch weights, the best of three two-mile heats, the mare to have one hundred yards' start, for 50*l.* a side, the match to come off over two miles on the Nottingham road, half-way between my place and Ashby on that day six weeks, between the hours of two and four. We each of us placed 10*l.* in Tom Woodcroft's hands, to bind the bargain, and we agreed to meet three nights after at the Woolpack, a coaching inn, which stood on the very ground, to draw up articles and stake the money.

I never made a match so quietly or so pleasantly in my life, and the only bet we booked upon it was one even 10*l.*, which the captain laid me, that although old Morgan was to give me one hundred yards' start, he would beat my mare in the first heat by that distance. Sam certainly did not seem in his usual spirits that night. He appeared to be in that frame of mind when drink takes no effect upon a man; for although he drank glass after glass without any stint, he rose from the table as sober as any man in that company. About eleven we all retired to our bedrooms, after spending a very different evening from what I fancied I should have done from all that I had heard of the doings at Ashby Grange.

I slept on a sofa in Sam's study, and I think it would have taken an auctioneer some time to appraise the miscellaneous contents of that room. The shelves were filled with just such books as we might have expected to find in such a man's library; and every other article in the room bore some testimony to the sporting tastes of the owner. His three favourite double-barrels hung in a bracket on the walls; a case of " saw-handles," by Nock, stood on the mantelpiece; while tandem whips, jockey whips, boots, spurs, boxing-gloves, single-sticks, and even a battered policeman's hat, with other articles " too numerous to mention," were stowed away in every corner.

I left the old Grange at about eleven the next morning, after receiving an invitation to repeat my visit, which I promised to do, and which I certainly should have done; but I little knew, as I shook hands with both Sam and his wife on parting, what a sad calamity was threatening them; and I should have regarded that poor woman with far deeper interest if I could only have known what would be her fate within one short week from that day.

As to my whip, the little boy, with the cunning peculiar to his class, had hidden it away, and no one could find it; but Sam gave me another to keep as a remembrance of him, telling me that it had been in good hands, for that " Sim" had won the Queen's guineas with it at —— for him, on his old mare, Maid Marian.

Jem was very pleased when he saw me come home so early, and heard that I had so easily made the match on better terms than it had expected. He would hardly believe me when I told him what sort of an evening we had spent, and opened his eyes with astonishment when I said that the captain was now owner of old Morgan. He could scarcely think it was all on the square, and was not satisfied till we drove down to the Woolpack on the appointed night, drew up articles, and staked the money in the landlord's hands. However, when I read over the articles to him next morning, he observed, "Ah! that looks like business : and now, sir, I think if I was you I should send over for Mr. Jones and hear what he says about it."

Mr. Jones was a small country trainer who lived a short distance from us, on the edge of what was even then called "the forest," although all traces of forest land had been long swept away, and corn grew in glades where a couple of centuries ago herds of red deer browsed at will under oaks coeval with the Druids. He was a great man at all our little country meetings, as trainer and jockey, and perhaps there were few men in England at that day who could bring a trotter to the post more fit, or ride him better when there, than this Mr. Jones.

He was a very respectable steady man, a man on whose word you could always rely, and in whom implicit confidence could be placed. His dress and whole appearance was peculiar—a dash of the nag with the pulpit. The low, broad-brimmed hat, white neckcloth, and black surtout, always buttoned up to the throat, summer and winter, gave him rather a clerical look; while the neat drab kerseys, and light jockey boots or long drab gaiters, smelt of the stable. He was a little, wiry, attenuated, cadaverous-looking old man, of whom Mr. West once facetiously observed on Nottingham race course that he looked "for all the world just as if he had come out of his grave for a glass of cold water, and could not find his way back again"—a remark which Mr. Jones never forgot or forgave. He knew a horse well, could easily get up at a little over 8st., was an excellent judge of pace, a very fair rough-race rider, and in figure and style very much resembled "Auld Tommy Lye," especially when mounted. He had both ridden and trained for me before, and I had every confidence in him.

I sent a special messenger over for him directly (I had no fear of his being "retained" on the other side, because I knew his animosity against Sam), and about noon he rode up. He was a man of few, indeed I may say, very few words, and never wasted his breath in useless remarks. I knew his peculiarity. I told him what I had done and what I wanted him to do. He never made a comment, but merely asked if he could see the mare. I dare say he stood looking at her for full five minutes without saying a word, during which time he chewed up about a foot of straw, bit by bit; and we then left the stable. He followed me indoors, but never spoke till I poured him out a glass of sherry to drink the mare's health in.

"Well, sir" (he always began an important sentence with "well, sir"), "that I'll do with pleasure; and now will you show me the articles?" After he had carefully gone through these word by word, he returned them with this remark—

"Any how the captain was not drunk when he drew up these articles."

"Do you mean to say that I was, then," I asked him rather hastily?"

"Well, sir, I did not say so."

"You have done well in making the match at catch weight, for I know nobody can drive Morgan Rattler properly but the squire, and he walks 15st.; but you ought by rights to have had 250 yards' start in the two miles to bring the horses level, instead of 100."

"Oh, then," I remarked, "you fancy there's so much difference between the two, do you?"

"Well, sir," answered the old man, "I never said exactly that; I know what old Morgan can do, but I don't know yet anything about the mare. But still, you know, in trotting, four inches make a great difference, and in making a match you should always try and get all you can. However, send the mare over to-morrow. I'll do my best with her, depend on it, and in a week's time I'll let you know what I think of her."

I knew it was no use trying to get any more out of him, and we parted. The next morning Jem took the mare over, and in a few days the old man discovered, to his great satisfaction, that Patty Morgan, with his weight on her back, could travel the two miles quicker than even old Morgan Rattler had done in any match in his life; but then all his matches had been in harness, and he had been driven by his old master, who walked, as we have before said, nearly fifteen stone.

It was on a Tuesday morning that I left the Grange, and on the following Monday Sam agreed to drive his wife over to dine and spend the afternoon with one Mr. John Robson—or as he was always familiarly called, Jack Robson—a sporting farmer, a very old friend of his, who lived about six miles from him. It was clear to all that Sam had become quite an altered man since he gave the captain that unfortunate bill of sale. He was silent and reserved, appeared to seek the company of his wife much more than he had done for years past, and seemed to hang about her as if he had some secret to disclose, but could hardly muster courage for the task. Her woman's tact soon discovered this. All her old affection, which had, as it were, gradually become blunted during so many years of cold neglect and suffering, appeared to revive, and the last week of that unhappy woman's life was a happier one than she had known for years. What seemed strangest of all was that from the day Sam made over his property, he never again either drove or rode old Morgan Rattler. He would lean over the half-door of his box for half an hour at a time talking to his old favourite, and feeding him with bread or carrots; beyond this the partnership between the two seemed dissolved. But of course, as yet he was apparently master over all, and took a horse whenever he wanted one, and it was the gig-horse which he drove on this eventful day. The day was clear and fine, the fresh air brought back some of the colour to his wife's faded cheeks, and her eye once again beamed with its old lustre, for ancient memories of happier days long since buried in oblivion and forgotten, rushed upon her mind with their full force, as she once again and for the last time sat by her husband's side in that gig. As Jack Robson came out gallantly to hand her out of the gig, he honestly declared that the squire ought to be proud of her, for that she was looking as handsome as ever she had done in her life. They spent a pleasant afternoon, and it was late before they started for home. The weather had by this time completely changed. The wind had risen and was blowing in violent gusts; heavy masses of scud and cloud drifted across the stormy sky, while

> " The moon, as if in malicious mirth,
> Kept peeping down on the ruffled earth,
> As if she enjoyed the tempest's birth,
> In revenge for her old eclipses."

The horse was very fidgety at starting. It is probable that he did not like to face the storm, which was then raging at its full height; and it was some little time before Sam could get him settled down to a steady trot. Even then he would not go pleasantly, but kept breaking, fidgeting all over the road, shying at every stone heap, till at length Sam lost his temper.

"Confound the horse, I never knew him like this before." And he drew the whip sharply across him, with " Now steady, will you?"

This was all that was wanted to fire the train. As soon as the horse felt the lash, he gave one sudden plunge as if he would have snapped the traces and went off at the rate of twenty miles an hour. All Sam's strength of arm was of no avail now, and all he could do was to try and keep the horse in the middle of the road; but his coolness and presence of mind never left him.

"Sit still, and for God's sake don't scream: leave the horse to me," was all he said to his wife, as she laid her hand, as it were imploringly, on his arm.

Luckily the road was straight and good, and there was little fear of meeting anything on it at this time of night; but there were rocks ahead which Sam never saw till he was close into the breakers. For the first mile and a half the road was straight, and ran apparently right down to a backwater, which carried the stream from a neighbouring mill into the main river; but when it reached the water, the road suddenly branched off at right angles, followed the side of the stream for about one hundred yards up to the mill, and then turned sharp again to the left, over a bridge, and so straight on. As far as the road ran parallel with this mill-stream, the sides were built up with flat coping stones, which faced the water, and, as it were, edged the road; but no wall protected the road from the water, only a single rail extending along the whole length. It was a nasty bit of road, to say the best of it, even with a steady horse by daylight, for there were two sharp turns to be made within a hundred yards; and for a runaway horse I don't think a more dangerous place could be found in England. The backwater, when the stream was full, reached nearly on a level with the top of the coping stone (in the spring floods the water often came up into the road); and if a horse should by any accident dash over that single rail, in an instant he was in ten feet of water— the stream, when the mill was going, running down like a " mill-race." Sam's horse never slackened his speed, but came on in mad career right down to the water. He never tried to turn, but dashed straight at the rail, which he breasted; the rail gave way, and horse and gig plunged headlong into the stream. Whenever Sam was driving he invariably kept the apron unbuttoned on his side, to be ready to spring out at a moment's notice. The consequence was, that when the horse dashed up against the rail, he was thrown out of the gig by the concussion, and although he pitched in the water, he fell clear of the gig. His poor wife, however, was fast in her seat, and no human power could save her. The mill was going, the water came rushing down with an irresistible force, and gig and horse were rapidly carried down the stream. The horse fought bravely for a short time, but the heavy gig soon pulled him down; and the struggle, although violent, was a short one. The moon was now completely obscured by heavy clouds, and the night as dark as pitch. Sam, who was a strong swimmer, struck out instinctively for life, and reached the opposite shore (for the stream was narrow), but with some difficulty; he dragged himself up the bank, and then sank down exhausted in a kind of swoon. Whilst he was battling against that angry current, nothing could be seen through the murky pall that surrounded him.

The waters hissed and bubbled in his ears, and he was deafened with the roar of the stream as it came rushing and tumbling down the narrow channel under the mill wheel. But above all the din and tumult of the storm, one long wild piercing shriek of agony rose upon the chill night air—a shriek the like of which is scarcely ever heard once in a life, but if once heard, is never forgotten. It was the last imploring call for human aid, where human aid was none; and with that wild shriek, a pure and gentle spirit winged its flight from a world of grief and pain to that happy land where sorrows are unknown—where the "wicked cease from troubling, and the weary are at rest."

A light was dimly burning in the mill, and to this West directed his steps as soon as he could rise from the ground. The miller and his men gazed with terror upon his spectral figure, as, dripping wet and without a hat, he staggered into the mill and sank down upon a heap of sacks. "My wife, my poor wife!" were the only words he uttered; and it was some time before they could gather from his incoherent speech any particulars of the sad accident. They had heard nothing, for all outward sounds were drowned in the rattle and roar of the mill.

The miller immediately stopped the wheel; lanterns were lighted; one man went down the stream in a boat, the rest followed on the bank. They had not far to go. About a hundred yards down from the place where the horse breasted the rails was an osier-bed in the middle of the stream; and here the gig and horse had been borne by the current and brought up on the muddy bank. The body was still in the gig; they dragged it out and carried it up to the mill. But the vital spark had fled for ever, and the dishevelled tresses, wide, staring eyes, and pale, bloodless lips gave a ghastly, death-like appearance to a countenance which had so lately beamed with animation and life. A messenger was despatched in hot haste for the nearest doctor, and another to Jack Robson, with the melancholy intelligence. Both arrived before midnight; but the time had gone by when human assistance would have availed, and the words of consolation which they kindly uttered to the bereaved husband fell coldly upon ears which scarcely heard them. The body had been carried up to the miller's house, and such restoratives as were at hand had been applied. West never left that bedside where lay the only human being he had ever really loved—the only true friend he had ever possessed on earth; but sat with his dead wife's hand convulsively clasped in his own, without speaking a word. Not a tear did he shed—not a lamentation escaped him; but the tightly compressed lips, the heavy breathing, the fixed, stern, determined look, and the spasmodic shiver which would every now and then convulse his whole frame, all sufficiently indicated the fierce struggle that was raging in his breast.

Early in the morning the body was removed to Robson's, where it lay till the coroner's inquest was over. They then carried it to the Grange to place it in the family vault; and the poor, low-born actress was laid in the same grave, side by side, with the mouldering remains of haughty beauties who, during their lives, would scarcely have deemed her worthy to wipe the dust from their feet. Sam was the only one of that proud family who had formed, what the world is pleased to call, a *mésalliance*; and of all the arrogant mistresses that had ever yet ruled over Ashby Grange, not one but could boast of a pedigree as faultless as her face; but there was not one among them all who had ever played the true woman's part like her on whom the vault was just closing. Not one but might have felt honoured by the acquaintanceship of as true a lady, and a woman as beautiful as the most beautiful among them all, and whose only earthly fault lay in her obscure origin.

The Grange was now no longer a home for Sam, and, leaving his poor idiot son in the charge of the good clergyman, he went up to London on the day after the funeral—an altered, but a broken-hearted man. The only mementoes which he carried away with him were his wife's picture and that of old Morgan; and from that day he never saw the old Grange again. He gave notice to the mortgagees to foreclose the mortgage at once, and sell the estates; and the captain took possession of all the personal property under his bill of sale. All was, however, brought to the hammer, except old Morgan, whom the captain claimed as an independent gift from the squire; and no one gainsayed him. The estate realized a far larger price than was expected, on account of the anticipated railroad. The personal property also sold well; for so many were anxious to secure some remembrance of Sam West, whose name for the last five-and-twenty years had been a household word in our parts. An eccentric sporting baronet bought the old summer-house as it stood; it was carefully removed and set up again in his park. It fetched a high price; in fact, as the auctioneer observed, it was the most "sportin' lot" in the whole catalogue. After the mortgages and all the debts were paid, there still remained about ten thousand pounds; five of this was invested in the funds for the maintenance of the poor idiot boy, of whom the good clergyman kindly undertook the charge, and with the other five thousand Sam emigrated to Australia. No one in our parts ever heard from him again; and the name of Sam West, by degrees, became forgotten.

The Grange passed into the hands of a rich railway director, originally a shoeblack, now a millionaire. He renovated it after his own vulgar taste; and it was a question in the neighbourhood whether the old house had not better have remained as it was during Sam's reign, and been left to crumble into ashes.

As soon as I heard of the sad accident, I wrote over to the captain to know whether he might not wish to declare the match off, or at least postpone it a little out of respect to his old friend, stating my willingness to meet him either way. I received a laconic reply to my note, in which he said that he certainly expected that the match would come off according to articles. He added, " that he was not aware that Mrs. West had nominated Morgan Rattler, or, probably, I might have been in a position to have claimed forfeit; that Mr. West had nothing whatever to do with the horse, or the match; and, moreover, he felt certain that nothing would cheer him so much in his present affliction, as to hear that old Morgan had added another to his list of victories." I may add that the captain had taken up his residence at the Grange till Sam's affairs were settled; and, if all accounts were true, the old house was just then anything but "a house of mourning."

When I read the letter over to old Jones, he quietly remarked, "Well, sir, if the captain thinks it is such a good thing, try and get a pony more on the mare with him, and let me stand your halves"—which I accordingly did. The mare went on capitally; old Jones declared that she was the sweetest goer he had ever crossed. Nobody ever mounted her but the old man, and his beautiful light hand just suited her tender mouth.

Not so old Morgan. He was always a savage, hot-tempered, impetuous brute, and would never do his best except in the hands of his old master. The only man who could ride him at exercise or in his trials, was the groom who always looked after him; but he had no idea of match-riding. The old horse, moreover, had now got into a habit of breaking—a thing he had never done in Sam's hands—and, in fact, went so rustily and unpleasantly, in any hands he was not used to, that when the jockey who was engaged to drive him (the best jockey in England of that day to put up on a savage horse or a trotter) came down to the Grange a week before the match, to get a little used to the horse, he candidly declared he dare not back him for a shilling, because however good he might be, there was no dependence to be placed in him now; for as sure as ever he got to his top speed, so sure he was to break. This was true to the letter. There was but one man in England who knew exactly when that old horse was at his top speed, and who, moreover, knew, from long experience, that the slightest mistake of his driver then would be fatal—and that was his old master. He knew just when to press him—when to let him alone—and as long as old Morgan felt Sam's firm, but steady, pull on his bit, he knew that he was doing all that was asked of him; and, as for breaking in his hands, to use Mr. West's expression, "the old horse did not know how to do it."

The evening before the day appointed for the match, both horses were on the ground, and stood in the Woolpack stables. Although only quite a local affair, this match excited considerable interest, for old Morgan was known to so many, and his name was connected with so many daring exploits, that he had become quite a public character; and although it was known that the squire had no longer any interest in the old horse, and was not even going to drive him, still the names of Sam West and Morgan Rattler had been so long connected, that hundreds who had not the slightest interest in either horse came, and many from a long distance, as much to see the famous Morgan Rattler as anything else.

The night before the race he was favourite at about two to one, but there was not much betting. His backers would have felt far more confidence if his old master had been going to steer him; and although very little was known about the mare, no one liked to take liberties with old Jones, who did not often make a mistake.

Early in the morning, Patty Morgan went over the ground, ridden by old Jones "in mufti," and, although of course she did not do her best, she pleased most who saw her.

At ten, old Morgan was brought out in a bran-new light-match-cart, driven by one of the best trotting jockeys in England, and attended by a crowd of admirers. The old horse looked well, as hard as beans, and his magnificent action and proud, lofty carriage obtained him a host of friends. He was sent over the first mile pretty sharply, brought gently back, and taken again to his stable. He became a hot favourite now, and many laid three to one on him; but there were a good many there who had seen the old horse pull off many a previous match, and who had now ridden by his side and watched him carefully. They had not forgotten how freely he used to step out when "the squire" held the reins, and they soon saw that his style of going in a stranger's hands was very different to what it used to be with his old master up. This was not lost upon them, and, although it seemed like deserting their old colours, they could not believe it was safe laying three to one on him. They preferred to take the odds rather than give them; and even Jack Robson—one of the old horse's staunchest admirers, and Sam West's best friend—booked 100 to 300 on the mare with the captain, remarking as he closed the bet, "If the old squire was up, mind, capten, I should lay the other way." Mr. Jones went quietly wandering about among the crowd, saying nothing, but hearing everything. He felt quite easy after he had seen the fashion in which the horse went with his new jockey, and remarked quietly to me, "I'll lay he breaks three times in the first mile."

The start was fixed for two, from a milestone which stood about five hundred yards below the Woolpack; and the conditions of the match were that the horses should trot two miles straight away for the first heat, rest half an hour, and then come back over the same ground for the second heat; and, if it came to a "who shall," the odd trick was to be played out over the same ground as the first heat.

As the time drew near, I dare say a couple of thousand people had assembled—country gentlemen, hard-riding farmers, fast tradesmen, sporting butchers, on what they deemed fast-trotting cobs—jostling each other and talking loud, with all that freedom of speech and manner so peculiarly characteristic of the horsey mob which one usually sees brought together when a trotting match takes place, and last, not least, all the roughs in the neighbourhood, with whom Sam had always been an immense favourite, and who came prepared to give old Morgan an ovation on winning, for they could never believe that anything living could beat the old horse. These latter gentry formed no inconsiderable a body in the ranks of the spectators, and I almost feared that, should our mare get the best of it, they would bring it to a wrangle. However, nothing of the sort happened, and the match was run fairly out from end to end.

At about ten minutes to two, old Morgan was driven slowly down to the starting-place; and directly his well-known colours—crimson and black—were seen, a cheer rose, which proved that, among a certain set, his old master was still a popular man.

"Pity t' auld squire don't drive him hisself. Ay! but he's a grand hoss," was passed from mouth to mouth.

He was soon followed by the mare, old Jones looking quite smart in his new Lincoln green and white cap. Although not greeted with any enthusiasm, she still had her admirers, for she stepped along as a rough observed, "as spry as an eel;" and "Ay! but she's a bonny little thing, though she has not got the stretch of old Morgan," was the verdict that was passed on her. The old man rode without whip and spur, in a plain ring snaffle.

They took their places, Patty Morgan a hundred yards ahead. The umpires were all ready, the watches set, and at the word "Go!" both went off at a slashing pace, accompanied by, perhaps, a hundred horsemen who wanted to see the race run throughout. Some of the longest winded of the roughs also ran by them for a hundred yards or so, cheering old Morgan with all sorts of yells and strange noises. From the very start the old horse overpowered his jockey, and came thundering after the mare at such a pace, that at the end of the first mile there was scarcely a length between them. But the mare had been going quietly within herself, old Jones's hands down the whole time; while old Morgan was fretting and fuming, shaking his head, yawing, and boring at the bit as if he would pull his jockey's arms off. After passing the first milestone, old Jones pressed the mare with his knees, and shouting to her, "Come up, old woman!" she shot out at her best speed. Old Morgan now broke; it was plain his temper was gone, and the heat was no longer in doubt, for the mare went stealing away from him and shot past the milestone more than one hundred and fifty yards in advance, having done the two miles in 5 min. 53 secs.

The backers of the old horse looked blue; it was clear that the name of Morgan Rattler was no longer a name of dread unless coupled with that of Sam West. The betting for the second heat was even, the mare for choice. This was a very hollow affair; old Morgan broke three times, and the mare won at least by three hundred yards, and was never pressed.

This was Morgan Rattler's last performance in our county. The captain left the Grange as soon as Sam's affairs were wound up, and took old Morgan up to London with him. Whether he ever trotted him again, I don't know; but I fancy he set up a brougham on the strength of the money he had won of Sam, and drove the old horse in it—at least I judge so from the following fact.

About a year afterwards, I happened to be in London, and passing along the top of Farringdon-street one afternoon, I saw a crowd assembled. When I got up I observed two or three policemen taking charge of a horse in harness, with a pair of broken shafts hanging at his sides. Little groups of bystanders, as usual in such cases, were standing round, discussing what had taken place. It was quite plain that there had been an awful smash, for I observed two or three more men lifting up a cab, which had apparently been upset also. I ventured to ask a beery stableman, who stood smoking his pipe at a little distance from the crowd, backing and filling like a ship in stays, if he could tell me what had been the matter, and I received from him the following graphic account of the transaction, much in the words of the "Confused individual," in *Punch*, but uttered with such volubility, and in so thick a voice, that I could hardly follow the narrator—

"Matter, sir! gentleman's 'oss run away with a broom, sir. Never see anythink like it in all my born days. Down he comes the 'ill with the sharves a danglin' all about his legs—knocks a butcher's cart into a linendraper's shop—bangs up agin a carridge-and-pair—smashes the pannels all to bits, hupsets a phe-aton, and, if he 'adn't a run up agin this here cab and dashed it right over, and stopt hisself, blowed if I don't think there'd ha' been some haccident!"

I thanked my informant, and pushed through the crowd to get a nearer view of the horse who had so much distinguished himself, and great was my surprise when, in the hands of two policemen—talking to the captain, with (apparently) his groom—I recognised my old friend Morgan Rattler. Yes, I could not be mistaken, even if I had not known that well-bewhiskered, foxy face at a glance; for there were the drooping ear, the deeply-fired legs, the fine shape, and peculiar dun colour to swear by. And there the old horse stood, apparently as fresh as on the day when he met Patty Morgan at the Woolpack; and, as he defiantly looked round him, seemed to intimate that he was quite ready for such another burst if they would only put him into harness again.

"Game to the last, old boy," I thought; "I only wish your old master was here to see you now;" and I walked away. This is the last I saw of old Morgan Rattler.

As to the little mare, she did me good service. I kept her for two years, during which time I got a good deal of gig work out of her, besides running fifteen matches, winning eleven. It was true they were most of them country matches, and for no great stakes. Occasionally, however, she flew at higher game. I ran her one year for the Manchester Trotting Sweepstakes, and although she did not win, she finished well up with Lady Sale. I was getting her ready for this race on the following year when she broke down incurably, and I chopped her away to old Jones for a slab-sided, spindle-shanked, three-cornered blood filly, which the old man always fancied would do great things. For once in his life, however, he was mistaken. I kept her for two years, and, with old Jones up, ran her for many little country stakes; but she never got higher than No. 2, generally 4 or 5, and she managed to lose me more money than Patty Morgan had ever won for me. Old Jones kept the little Welsh mare for breeding, and she threw a colt to Mulatto, which he sold for a long price.

And what became of Sam West? Well, if the reader is not already tired out, I will tell him. I said he went to Australia, and about fifteen years afterwards, when the diggings had broken out, I followed him. I was not long on the gold-fields, but went into the bush kangarooing. I was camped with two mates, about thirty miles south of Melbourne.

Now, we rarely had more than one change of clothes in a bush tent; we used to buy a suit of ready-made ones in Melbourne, which we wore till they were no longer decent, and then went up to Melbourne again for a new rig. There was something very comical in the manner in which a digger or a bushman at that day used to "cast his skin." He would come down to Melbourne in his old suit, walk into a ready-made clothes shop, and select a whole new suit, even to shirt, boots, and stockings. He then walked off into the clothier's back-yard, with his bundle of new clothes, a bucket of water, and some soap. Here he performed his toilet, cast away his old "slough" on to a huge heap of old clothes which lay in the corner of the yard, and walked out of the shop, in all the pride of a new cabbage-tree hat, jumper, and moleskins, so altered that his most intimate bush friend would hardly know him.

We used in our tent to "change our coats" about once a quarter. On one occasion we all three walked up to Melbourne together for that purpose. Not one of us had a shilling in his pocket, but we had money to receive when we got to town. We left the tent in the afternoon, and walked up through the night. It was in March (the Australian autumn), and the morning sun rose in a clear cloudless sky, so peculiar to this beautiful country. It was a lovely morning, and by about seven we had reached Brighton, a little suburb, then six miles from Melbourne, now, I suppose, annexed to it.

As we were tired, we threw ourselves down and lit our pipes under a large gum tree on a piece of common land, for there still remained signs of the bush, even so near town, although the country round was studded with pretty little villas built with the greatest taste, surrounded by small parks or gardens. We rested just in front of one of the prettiest of these. A neat flower garden faced the road, on the grass plot of which lay some of the very largest pumpkins I ever did see in my life. We lay smoking our pipes, speculating as to the weight of the pumpkins, when a tall, handsome, portly, florid-looking old gentleman, in a dressing-gown and straw hat, walked out of the house, apparently to get a sniff of the fresh morning air. He had all the look of a man who was perfectly at home, and appeared to survey his little house and garden with great satisfaction. We were just wondering what the "old bloke" was going to have for breakfast, and wishing he would ask us in, for, as we had no money, we knew we must wait till we came to Melbourne before we got a "feed." All at once his eye fell upon us, and he stepped out of the wicket to have a nearer view of us. Our looks certainly were not prepossessing, for our clothes were ragged and dusty, and no man looks the fresher in the early morning for having been up all night, no matter how he may have spent his time. In fact, our appearance was in strange contrast with that of the neat, fresh-looking old man who was now approaching us.

"Here comes old Cockatoo to ask us in to breakfast," growled one of my mates, the roughest of our lot.

"No such luck!" I said. When the old man, after he had taken good stock of us, accosted us with—

"Are you looking out for a job, my lads?"

"No," one of us answered, "we are looking out for some breakfast."

He did not, however, take the hint. It is one of the privileges of declining years to be garrulous and inquisitive; and this old gentleman certainly took every advantage of his privilege. I can hardly say how many questions he asked us. "Were we sheep-shearers?—were we splitters?—where were we bound for?—where did we come from?"—&c., &c. But when I told him we were neither one nor the other, but kangaroo-hunters living down in the Western Port district, the old man became quite interested. "And what part of the old country do you come out of?" was one of his numerous questions. My rough mate's patience was now fairly exhausted, and with, "What the h—— is that to you?" he rose up, saying, "Come, my lads, it's time we were in Melbourne."

I was rather sorry he had answered the old man so roughly, for his questions were harmless enough, and his grey hairs and venerable aspect warranted a certain degree of respect. He seemed hurt at it, too, as I could see when he answered, "Well, mate, you need not cut up so rough, I meant no harm;" but, with a pertinacity which an Old Bailey barrister could scarcely have equalled, he turned round to me with, "Well, what was your county at home?" I directly told him.

"Did you know Ashby Grange, then?" he hurriedly and excitedly asked me.

"Yes," I answered, "I should think so; and Sam West and Morgan Rattler, too."

"Come in! come in! all of you," said the old man; and turning to me, said, "I'll introduce you to an old friend."

He took us into his little parlour, where over the mantelpiece hung the very portrait of old Morgan which I had seen at the Grange the last and only time I was there.

I recognised the horse at once, and when I turned round and looked the old man well over, I had no difficulty in recognising in him the once renowned and notorious Sam West. He was, of course, considerably aged, for he was getting on then for seventy. But the beautiful climate of Australia suited him, and his years sat lightly on him. He had bought a bit of land, built himself a little house, and was passing the few remaining years of a wild and stormy life happily and quietly in growing pumpkins and breeding Cochin-Chinas.

I soon told him who I was, and it was a jovial meeting. No fear of our breakfast now—such a silvery round of cold beef! The old gentleman carved at a side table, and his knife and fork knew no rest for the first twenty minutes.

"It does me good to see you chaps eat," said he, as he filled our plates for the third time; adding, "don't be offended when I tell you that when first I saw you I took you for three bushrangers, and little did I think that a man lay there who had once beaten old Morgan."

He could not do enough for us. Did we want money?—would we have a dozen pumpkins?—anything he had we were welcome to, except old Morgan's picture. Before leaving, he beckoned me out of the room, and when I got into the passage, he eyed me intently from top to toe, and at last broke out—

"You don't mean to say you are going into Melbourne in that state! Oh, dear! if any of the old friends at home could see you now. Don't you think"—and here he paused as if not liking to go on—" a suit of my clothes would fit you?"

The Trotter.

I laughingly thanked him, but declined his kind offer. I told him I would call upon him quite a different figure when I came back from Melbourne; which I did. As long as I remained in that part of the country we were sworn friends. Our kangaroo-cart never went up to town without leaving him a hind quarter of a kangaroo, or a bunch of game; and it never came down again without a little present of some kind or other, if it was only a large pumpkin.

So strangely do old acquaintances meet in this world when they least expect it; and so strangely is something or other always turning up in after years to revive within us the memories of our past lives?

THE FISHING DAY.

"I shall stay the reader no longer than to wish him a rainy day to read the following discourse; and that, if he be an honest angler, the east wind may never blow when he goes a-fishing."—IZAAK WALTON.

It was a beautiful sentiment, whoever uttered it, that "to transmit the first bright and early impressions of our youth free and uninjured, to a remote period of life, constitutes one of the loftiest prerogatives of genius." And although the task of transmitting such impressions, in all their original freshness, is an impossibility, yet which of us is there who will not gladly, at times, snatch a minute from the hours which are engrossed in the hurry and bustle of the world, to turn back to the early chapters of his "book of life?" How fondly then does memory love to dwell upon the pages which are written in the free, bold characters of boyhood!— perhaps the only pages in that mysterious book which are written without a blot!

Such, at least, is the case with me; and although I well know it is useless now to sigh for

> "The returning bloom
> Of those days, alas! gone by,
> When I loved, each hour, I scarce knew whom,
> And was blest, I scarce knew why——"

still the remembrance of those happy days will haunt me to the last page of life's chapter; and many a trivial and careless incident of my boyhood stands out in bold relief upon the tablets of the mind, while graver and more momentous passages of after years have passed away and left no impression.

Which of us can ever forget his first pony or his first gun?

Although many years have passed since that day, I could even now find the very spot in the rough sedgy meadow where I killed my first hare; and whatever may be the standing crop now in that field, if I were only once again in it I fancy I could find my way to within a hundred yards of where I shot my first partridge. As for my first run with foxhounds, why, that red-letter day in my calendar will keep its freshness to the last. But whatever may be our favourite sport in after years, there is one which I think I may safely say was the dearest and most treasured of all the pastimes of our boyhood, to every one of us who had the opportunities of enjoying it : I mean that of angling—at once the most fascinating, innocent, and least selfish of all field sports, and one whose quiet recreations are so peculiarly adapted to our earliest youth or declining years.

Moreover, there is less jealousy existing between the members of the gentle art than among sportsmen of any other class Let the north country angler boast of the Tweed, the Coquet, or the Till; let the richer and more aristocratic brother tell of the salmon he has taken in the magnificent rivers of Northern Europe : the true bottom-fisher of the Thames envies neither of them; while the trudging tinker, as he sits by the side of some favourite bream or chub hole in one of our sluggish Midland streams, quietly watching his float, and even the little shoeless urchin whose only treasures consist in a "willow rod, some thread for line, a crooked pin for hook," are both happy and contented in the full belief that theirs is the only sport worth enjoying.

And why is this ? Because, in whatever locality, in whatever manner the sport is pursued, there is a quiet calm infused into the angler's mind, when following his favourite pastime, which no other sport can offer; and whatever the prey, whatever the scenery amid which the angler roams, he sees the hand of God written in every flower, in every blade of grass, and, unlike those who follow the more boisterous pursuits of the chase, he has full time and leisure to observe and reflect on all the beauties of nature which are so profusely spread before his eyes.

Early associations lend a greater charm to the angler's sport than perhaps to any other; and the scenes among which his early days have been passed leave a far deeper impression on the angler's mind than the sport itself. My early days were spent in the quiet of a secluded village by the side of a sluggish inland stream; and the only fish met with in it were the pike, perch, chub, bream, gudgeon, roach, eel, and a few other kinds, which the scientific fly-fisher would despise. But the village was, perhaps, one of the prettiest in England, and the stream gently wound its crooked, Scheldt-like course through a lovely pastoral landscape. I have since that day wandered over many lands, and fished in mountain streams which came dashing and tumbling over beds and masses of rock in all the magnificence of wild, untamed nature, through scenery of the grandest description. I have seen the lordly salmon quivering in his last death-throe by the side of the dark pool, whose waters hissed and bubbled at the bottom of the fall which carried the upland flood with a resistless force down to the sea. Yet the old mill, the staunch, and the lock on my own native stream, are far dearer to me than all these: and if I only had my choice, I would rather by far spend one afternoon in again watching the perch as they sail to and fro around the piles of the old rustic bridge across the backwater, or the chub, as he lazily rises in the still, deep hole under the old pollard which overhangs the little stream where my first angling lessons were learnt, than see the largest salmon killed in the finest river, which is bound to me by no early associations, and in a land where all men are strangers to me.

It would be a difficult task to choose any individual day from the many spent so happily by the side of our own favourite little stream. Let us take any one towards the end of July (which used to be our favourite season for perch), and all we shall require to aid our sketch will be a dark, cloudy morning, wind S.W., with just such a breeze on the water as slightly rustles through the flags and willows which fringe the margin of the river, and curls the ripple on the dark waters of our favourite pit or hole.

The evening before an excursion like the present was generally a busy one. The minnows and gudgeons had to be looked over and sorted; the tackle to be overhauled; lines tried, hooks spliced, gut bottoms proved; and many an anxious eye was turned towards the setting sun, and two or three journeys made to the river-side to ascertain the colour and the height of the water. Before these arrangements are concluded, the sun has sunk behind the old wood which bounds the western horizon on the other side of the river; and as "early to bed and early to rise" should ever be the angler's motto, we are soon in full enjoyment of that undisturbed repose which few of us can ever hope for after the days of boyhood have passed. At seven in the morning we leave the house with our factotum—an amphibious sort of fellow, half gamekeeper, half fisherman—laden with the minnow kettles and the landing net—and, not the least important thing on a day like the present, the basket of provisions.

We have to call on an old friend who lives just outside the village, to breakfast; and, although we are pretty punctual to our time, he is already awaiting our arrival. His cordial greeting as he meets us at the gate is as cordially exchanged, and, as we set down our rods and tackle in the little trellised porch before his door, we all agree that, had old Izaak himself bespoken the day, we could not have been more fortunate in the weather. Our friend, who is this day to be the captain of the party, is a veteran both in "flood and field;" and, although a slight bend in the shoulders and the scant silvery locks proclaim that he is travelling in the downhill of life, the firm step, the bronzed, ruddy, healthy, weather-beaten cheek, and the keen eye, prove that the ravages of time have had but little effect on a frame so well seasoned by the healthful pursuits of a country life.

We are too anxious to be off to waste much time at breakfast; and while we are at the boat-house getting the punt in order, the deep, full-toned chimes ringing forth the hour of eight from the tall spire in the distance, strike upon our ear "with voice prolonged and measured fall," mellowed by the water over which the sound passes.

The ripple on the stream is beautiful, and the sun can scarcely make his way through the heavy clouds, the screaming swifts chase each other high in the air above our heads, while the swallows skim over the margin of the river in pursuit of the gnats and flies, whose brief ephemeral existence is cut off almost ere they have begun their short-lived enjoyment. The little sedge-warbler keeps incessantly hopping about the flags and willows in which the boathouse is sheltered, uttering its merry and ceaseless note; while the kingfisher, startled from the willow on which he was perched, dashes down the stream with the speed of an arrow. The dense mass of candocks and water-lilies to our right are the secure resort of many a jack, who lies there in grim repose awaiting his daily prey; and by the muddy bank of the osier-bed which faces us is the best tench-hole in the whole river. Oh! these are all every-day sights and scenes familiar to the angler and lover of rural life, and, trifling as they may appear to be to the careless observer, the true lover of nature treasures them in his heart; but it is not until, perhaps, far absent from the spot where he has so often observed them, that their beauty is fully appreciated. It is then that "distance lends enchantment to the view," and when, in after years, the thoughts for a moment recur to these pleasant visions of youth and home, do they rush across the mind with their full force. But, like the bubble on the stream, they are seen only for an instant before they burst and disappear in the headlong currents of the waves of life.

We sprit down in the punt to the old locks, about a mile down the stream, dropping a trimmer or two behind us on the road. We leave the punt at the top gate; and, as the locks are closed, the deep still hole at the bottom gate is the spot where we commence operations. The stream runs slow, the water is dark and low, and all promises well. Rods are soon put together, each one chooses a bait to his own fancy, and takes his place. For a while not a word is spoken, each being too much occupied in watching his float. At length, after a slight move, one float disappears under water, and in a few seconds a perch of about one pound is struggling on the bank —first fish, upon which a little jealousy has depended. Another, and another, soon succeeds. As we proceed down the stream, the lock-pound, the head of the staunch, the mill-tail, are all successively tried, and each yields something to help to fill the creels; but *the* fish of the day, a perch of two and a half pounds, is taken by our veteran friend, with a paternoster, in a deep hole against one of the piles of the old wooden footbridge that crosses the backwater.

The sun has all the morning been obscured by clouds, and, as the fish have all been well on the feed, by twelve each creel holds its share. But the evening's sport has yet to come. We now cross the river in the punt, to the osier holt on the opposite side, where we propose to lunch in the shade, screened from the oppressive rays of the mid-day sun, which has now found its way through the clouds. The creels are emptied, fresh flags put into each, the fish carefully repacked, and laid in the shade till lunch is over. The minnow-cans are sunk, the provisions are spread out upon the grass; and, as ceremony is unlooked for on an occasion like the present, each man for himself. Thanks to the provider of the feast, no one can grumble at either quality or quantity—the bottled ale, which has been sunk in the river all the morning, is excellent, and no one finds fault with either the cold pigeon-pie or the lamb salad. Not a breath of air is now stirring; the cattle stand lazily up to their knees in the shallow ford a little way down the stream; the haymakers have left their work in the meadows, and are now seated under the tall hedge-row, resting from their toil, during the heat of the day; and as the fish are now altogether off their feed, the margin of the stream is as smooth as glass.

But hark! a hail from the opposite bank, and the jolly miller calls to us to bring the punt across. As he says, we can have no fishing for an hour or so, but if we will come up to the mill and smoke a pipe, he promises us that he will stop the wheel in the evening, when we shall be sure to have some rare sport, both in the head and tail water. This is too good an invitation to be refused, more especially as the miller is "one of us," although his line lies more among the bow-nets and eel-traps. A rare evening's sport winds up a happy day, and it is not until the sun, fast nearing the western horizon, "proclaims it high time to get home," that we leave off.

We unscrew our rods, pack up our tackle, and turn out the fish on the grass for inspection. We have had a very fair day's sport: a dozen of the perch will average one pound each, and several from a half to three-quarters of a pound; three or four heavy chub, and a good-sized pike or two make up the catch; and each one, as he packs up his creel, feels satisfied with its contents.

After a parting glass of ale, just to keep the night air out, and a hearty good-night from the jovial miller, we start for home. The deep crimson streaks across the western sky mark a glorious sunset, and the pale moon has already begun to cast a silvery light over the tranquil stream which, but an hour ago, seemed almost alive with fish rising at the evening flies, dancing up and down over its surface. The bat flies so close by us, that we can distinctly hear his sharp snap as he catches at a gnat. The last waggon has left the meadow with its load; and the silence of the evening is broken by the voices of the haymakers, dying away in the distance as they slowly follow it home.

Our homeward walk lies through the meadows, now almost obscured by the heavy mist, which, rising up from the river, shuts the landscape from the view. Our steps may not be so pliant as they were in the morning, but our hearts are as light; and although our creels are well filled, no one feels their burthen. The lonely heron, startled by our laugh, rises from the river side, and as he wings his measured flight to the old heronry in a distant park, the air resounds to his hoarse, discordant scream; and the pewit, as it wheels in airy rings over the fallow to our left, "wakes the echoes with unwearying cries."

We soon reach the village, guided by the twinkling lights in the cottage windows, which shine like beacons to guide the weary traveller on his homeward track. We enter our old friend's gate, and, having doffed our creels in the hall, are soon in his snug little parlour, where supper is awaiting us. When this is finished, the old man lights his pipe, our tumblers are filled, each man's catch is talked over, and many a discussion takes place on the merits of a superior bait or a favourite hole; and many are the tales told of the weight of fish taken upon such a gravel or at such a staunch.

Happy as are the recollections of scenes like the present, how much of that happiness is tinged with regret as we look back upon them, through the dark haze of time! Many years have now fled, still it seems like yesterday as I recall to my mind the last evening I sat at my old friend's table after a fishing-day like that above described— one of the happiest of that happy party of four brothers, all tried companions in every rustic sport and amusement. Within a year of that evening, our old friend was taken from us, and his place was filled no more. Out of the four brothers, the youngest now sleeps his last long sleep in the old churchyard, against the wall of which the quiet waters of his favourite stream continually ripple—meet resting-place for one whose earliest and happiest days were spent upon its margin, and

> " The others are dwelling far apart,
> With coldness in each selfish heart.
> Happiest far that stripling boy
> Who died in the hours of peace and joy,
> Who passed in the flush of his beauty's bloom
> From his ' happy village ' to the tomb !"

The window is open, and the night-breeze as it sighs through the leaves of the sycamore at the gate, wafts the perfume of the jasmine and acacia into the room. All is still save the never-varying hum of the distant mill, and the monotonous " crex, crex," of the corn-crake from the opposite meadow. The moon rides high in the pale blue atmosphere; not a cloud overshadows her brightness, and her light silvery beam dances upon the rippling waters of the river which flows on silently at the bottom of the garden.

The quiet tranquillity of this evening is felt by all, and each, as he silently gazes on the river, seems lost in his own thoughts. The evening is fast waning, and a happy one have we spent, listening to the tales and maxims of our good old friend. His manly features wear a thoughtful cast, and he utters a sigh as he shakes the ashes out of his last pipe. We rise to depart, and each, as he warmly grasps our hands on taking leave, truly feels that

> "The evening breezes chill
>   Now close our joyous scene,
>   And yet we linger still
>   Where we've so joyous been;
>   How blest were it to live,
>   With hearts, like ours, so light,
>   And only part to give
>   A last, a long good night.
>   Good-night!"

THE BEST FOURTEEN-HANDER IN ENGLAND.

It used to be a saying in my day "that there was but one best horse, one best dog, and one best gun in England, and that everybody had them." And as there is a good deal of covert truth in this observation, it may appear a little presumptuous on my part when I make the bold assertion that once in my life (but only for twenty-four hours) I was really the lucky possessor of the best fourteen-hander in England, in the shape of a little one-eyed rat-tailed galloway, who won three races for me in one day, beating what we considered the best ponies in England, after which, for two years, she went through the length and breadth of the land, sweeping away every prize that was run for by horses of her standard; and the reader will probably inquire wherefore, when I had become possessed of such a treasure, I did not keep it? This question he will find very satisfactorily answered if he reads on to the end of my story.

The tale is this. One evening in the end of June, a pretty good many years since, seated on one of the coaches which then ran between Birmingham and Leicester, I entered the little half-town, half-village of Hollerton, on the eve of the annual feast and pony-races. At this time, races for horses under fourteen hands were, I fancy, much more the fashion in England than at the present day; and, although called "pony-races," they brought out a very different class of animal from what are generally understood by the word pony; for I have seen perfect racehorses in miniature saddled for a galloway stakes, in as good training and very nearly as well-bred, but deficient only in size, to any of our thorough-bred racers. No place was more renowned in my day for its pony-races than Hollerton; and the Hollerton Cup of 15 sovs. with a Sweepstakes of 5 sovs. added, often brought to the post twelve to fifteen of the very best and handsomest little racers in England; and the distance (nearly the same as that of the Derby) would perhaps be covered by these little flyers considerably under the four minutes. I fancy, moreover, that "leather-flapping," as these little half-bred racers were contemptuously called, was more followed in the midland counties than elsewhere; and, although the practice was considered by many as being greatly open to fraud (which it probably was), I do not fancy that the turf is in a bit more healthy state now than it was then; nor do I believe there was half so much "roping" or "milking" carried on then as there is now. Be this as it may, I know that these little meetings used to afford many a happy day's amusement to the country people, who, but for them, would probably have never seen a day's racing in their lives. They brought together neighbours and friends; they infused a little spirit of racing emulation amongst the farmers and breeders of each particular district; and, if they did not lead such men to breed a better class of horse, they certainly gave them opportunities of finding out when they had a good one, and, moreover, of making the most of such a horse when they did possess it.

At all events, this kind of racing just suited my pocket and tastes, and for a few years it was very rarely that I had not a "little one" in for the "Hollerton Cup." Once I had won it, and once I had run second, and on the present occasion I had a share with my friend "the screwdealer" (mentioned in my sketch of the "Steeple-chaser") in a little pony called The Rejected, with which the old man was very confident of winning the cup this year.

I got down at the "Dolphin" (the principal sporting inn in the place) about eight in the evening, and as this was just the hour when the entries were closing for the morrow's races, not only the pavement in front of the inn, but the inn yard itself was crowded with burly farmers, horse-dealers, country jockeys, and second-class racing men, who either had something to run or felt an interest in a pony belonging to a friend. There was nothing very aristocratic about the looks of the throng, but there was something truly British ; and many a cordial shake of the hand did I receive as I elbowed my way through the crowd to look for my old friend, who I knew had arrived that afternoon, and was somewhere about the premises.

Whilst pushing my way through the crowded inn passage I ran against a man who was forcing his way out, and whom I instantly recognised as one "Joe Cox," by some considered the biggest blackguard in our parts. As soon as he saw me he seized me by the arm, dragged me out again into the inn yard, and when we were clear of the listeners, accosted me thus: "You're the very man I was looking for, sir. If you want to buy the best fourteen-hander in England, now's your time."

I must, before proceeding with my tale, introduce Mr. Joe Cox to the reader. He was, to use the words of my old friend, a very "equivocal" sort of character, and the very last man in the world to part with the sort of horse he had just named, if he luckily owned such a treasure, which was very unlikely.

He was a low, horse-coping kind of a fellow ; a stout, muscular, goodish-looking man, of about thirty-five, who kept a little beer-shop, the "Crooked Billet," on the edge of "Merry Sherwood," the resort of all the broken-down horse-dealers, poachers, sheep-stealers, and vagabonds in the neighbourhood. He was a man possessed of considerable acquirements, such as they were—a capital judge of a horse, and a rare bruising rider for his weight. He was an excellent pigeon-shot, and an incorrigible poacher ; could fight, wrestle, throw a quoit, play the tambourine, and kick a football with any man in Nottinghamshire ; was renowned throughout the county for his breed of terriers, game-cocks, and ferrets, and, as he was just the sort of fellow who could be very useful to country gentlemen of certain tastes, and was, moreover, hardly the man one would care willingly to offend, he was in a certain degree patronized by many. Although not exactly what we should call a "steady character," Joe was not a bad sort in his way, and would go any lengths to serve a "pal," or even a gentleman who trusted him. He was a jovial, hearty fellow, with a peculiarly English yeoman cut about him, could sing an excellent song, and tapped as good a glass of ale as any man in the county. He was always remarkably civil and respectful to his betters, and, as nothing beyond a predilection for any kind of fun or mischief, and an innate propensity to get the best of any one in a deal (a very venial offence, by the way, in our horsey neighbourhood), could be brought home to him, he reigned unmolested at the " Crooked Billet " over subjects who particularly delighted in "a shiny night at a season of the year," and whose ideas respecting the rights of *meum* and *tuum* were probably hardly so strict as they should have been. In fact, although the old forest might be very much changed since the days when bold Robin Hood roamed at will through its merry glades and pastures, there was still a very lawless, roving, Robin Hoodish spirit remaining in the characters of the inhabitants of that district; and if the bold outlaw could have arisen from his grave to revisit the scenes of his former exploits, the " Crooked Billet" would assuredly have been his house of call. But all Joe's multifarious accomplishments were as nothing compared to his consummate knowledge of every phase in the chicanery of low horse-dealing and "leather-flapping ;" and although it naturally happened that out of the many horses which yearly passed through his hands, a good one must now and then turn up, I hardly ever heard of a man who cared to venture on a second deal with him.

Such was Joe Cox, such were his accomplishments; and a "very respectable sort of acquaintance!" I fancy I hear the reader exclaim. Probably this was correct, but, nevertheless, I must candidly confess that I did not altogether dislike the man; and although, as I shall presently explain, he had left his mark pretty deeply upon me in the first and only horse transaction I ever had with him, still there was something so talismanic in the words, "The best fourteen-hander in England," especially just at a time when to be the possessor of such a treasure would ensure my winning the Hollerton Cup; and, moreover, as there was evidently some mystery to be solved, I did not, as most prudent men would have done, tear myself away from him, but, merely answering his question as to whether "I wanted to buy the best fourteen-hand pony in England?" with, "Not if it be anything like the last I had of you, Joe," I quietly waited to hear his explanation of the mysterious sentence.

Before, however, I proceed with my story, I must beseech the reader's patience, and travel back over a period of more than a twelvemonth, in order to explain why I answered Mr. Cox in the manner I did, and I trust this digression will be pardoned, because it touches upon rather an eventful episode in my life, and one which, if it had turned out right, would probably have given quite a different influence to my future career. It will at least describe a race such as very few of my readers have probably ever ridden in, and, moreover, a race for a heavy stake—a wife and a fortune.

Early one fine morning in the beginning of May, in the year preceding the meeting just alluded to, I espied Mr. Joe ride up to my gate, leading one of the very prettiest little chestnut mares it has ever been my lot to cast eyes upon. That she was as handsome as a picture, I could see with my own eyes, although I might be a little sceptical as to whether she strictly answered Joe's description; for according to his account she was such a treasure as no man could hope to possess more than once in his life, and very few, even that. According to his account, she was nearly thorough-bred, perfectly sound and free from vice ; and had for the last two years been carrying a young lady, who, however, had become too consumptive to be allowed horse exercise, and who was therefore reluctantly obliged to part with her favourite pony. It was beautiful to listen to Joe's pathetic account of the parting between this "dear young lady" and her little pet. He declared it was solely on account of his solemn promise that he would put her into the hands of a man who would use her kindly, that he ever became possessed of her ; and it was with the laudable wish to keep his promise that he had troubled himself to bring her over a matter of twenty-five miles for me to look at. And the cunning rascal wound up with, "I had you in my eye, sir, when I bought her; and when I mentioned your name to the 'dear young lady,' as one who I knew, of all other men, would take charge of her pony and use her kindly for life, she clasped her hands together and said, 'Bless him!' And if you could only have seen her at that minute, sir, you'd have said she looked as much like an angel as anything you ever see in your life, sir!" Joe had a habit of speaking quick, and running his sentences into each other, which rather detracts from the pathos of a tale; but he spoke all this with an air of such feeling, and, moreover, threw in his little bit of flattery so well, that I had almost made up my mind at once to try and buy the mare. His last shot, however, decided me: "And besides, don't you see, sir, if you can't find any nice young lady friend where you can place her, you've nothing to do but to put her into training, and if she don't win you the Hollerton Cup, why I'll return you every shilling of the money, and take her back again, sir." There was another little circumstance which also helped my decision: the night before I had been kicked out of my gig by a vicious brute which I neither dare put into harness again or sell in my own neighbourhood, but which I felt certain Joe would tackle. He did not seem to think a bit worse of the horse for having played me this trick, so long as it was considered in the price, and after a little higgling I agreed to take the mare as she was, giving him my kicker and 15*l.*; and as I well knew the value of a warranty from such a character, I merely took a receipt for the money, and Joe rode off apparently thoroughly satisfied, although he was taking away with him about the most dangerous brute that ever looked through a collar. Perhaps he was consoled by the reflection that he was leaving nearly as dangerous a one behind. Just as he rode out of the gate, he turned to remark, "You'd best ride the little mare in the bridle she's got on now, till you get a bit used to her mouth, sir, for if she has a fault it is that she hangs a *little heavy on the bit*. Not that that makes twopence difference to a man like you, as knows a hoss; fact, I dare say, like myself, sir, you would not care to ride one if you could not feel his mouth. Keep 'em well on the bit, that's my motto, sir;" and with a polite wave of his hat, Mr. Cox rode off. I never heard so neat a description of a regular bolter in my life.

When I turned the little mare into the loose box which the kicker had just vacated, and looked at her meek, dove-like eye, sleek satin coat, and faultless symmetry, I felt quite pleased with my new bargain. If there was such a thing as love at first sight, I certainly experienced that feeling in this instance; and when the beautiful little creature came sidling up to me to take some oats out of my hand, and nestled her velvet nose against my breast, I inwardly thought of the "dear consumptive young lady" whose pet she had so lately been, and vowed that Joe's solemn promise should never be jeopardized by any treatment her little favourite would receive at my hands. The mare had not been in the stable an hour before I put her under the standard, and found, to my delight, that she was the very height for Hollerton; and I now began seriously to think of abandoning a project which I had half formed, and of sending her instead to my old friend's stable, to get her fit for the Hollerton Cup. But my first project was one well worth entertaining; and when I cantered the mare two or three times round a small paddock close to the stables, sitting lady-fashion on the saddle, with a counterpane tied round my middle and dangling down her side, and found she took not the slightest notice of it, I began to put some confidence in the story of the consumptive young lady, and to fancy that really, for once in his life, Joe might have told the truth on this occasion. I deemed it prudent, however, to stick to the bridle which she had been used to (about as coarse and sharp a looking curb as ever I had seen) and a strong martingale, and though, as Joe said, she certainly did hang rather heavier in hand than I should have fancied a consumptive young lady would have liked, I had not the slightest fault to find with either her going or her paces. My old friend was away at a fair, and would not be home till the Saturday following, so I could not get his opinion on my new purchase; but I sent directly over for the vet., and, after a careful examination, he passed her as sound in every respect. Although he shook his head when he heard of whom I had bought her, he declared that, as far as soundness went, she was all right, and as to vice of any kind, if such a lamb-like little thing was not to be trusted, all he could say was, he never again would place faith in any horse's countenance.

I must now explain to the reader the project to which I have above alluded. To use Joe's words, I certainly did "know a kind young lady friend where I could place this little pet," and, perhaps, advantageously for all parties. Moreover, upon serious consideration, I did not feel quite sure whether I was not bound in honour to the "consumptive young lady" to place her late favourite in hands which I felt certain would use her well instead of sending her into a racing stable. There lived in a village about four miles from us a young lady, into whose custody I could deliver my charge with a safe conscience, and who, whenever we met, was continually pressing me to buy her a pretty little pony for her own especial use. She was the only daughter of an old, sun-dried Indian officer, who had come to reside and end his days in the quiet of this little village, and whom we young ones had irreverently christened " old Mullagatawny." He was evidently "warm," judging from the style in which he lived, and, as he was an hospitable old fellow after his fashion (though desperately passionate and tyrannical in his own house), he was always glad to see a friend to help him eat his curry, smoke his cigars, listen to his tiger stories, and join him in the evening at a quiet rubber at whist. His daughter was a fine, dashing girl, with a goodish spirit of her own, rather fast, and very fond of riding about the country with an old groom behind her; but what I most liked in her was that she had a plain way of saying just what she thought, without caring a pin whether it offended you or not. I was a good deal at the old nabob's house, and, of course, thrown a good deal into the society of the daughter, so that at last I had the vanity to flatter myself that, as the novelists would say, I was "not altogether indifferent to her." Moreover, I began to think that Chunee Villa (as the nabob's residence was called), a fine, dark-eyed girl, and a lac of rupees (which was the very least we fancied in our rural innocence that her old father could possibly have amassed during his Indian campaign), would be very well worth dropping in for. Having talked the matter over with my old friend, who, although unmarried himself, was a great advocate for seeing us young ones settled in life, he strenuously advised me not to throw such a chance away; and, as he had heard that she was an excellent horsewoman, he thought it would be a masterstroke of policy if we could pick up a quiet lady's horse, on which I was to ride over, and, if she admired it, as would most probably be the case, I was to open the campaign at once by begging her acceptance of it. That she must admire the little chestnut mare, I felt certain; and although there may not be much in a name, I thought there was something delicate and lady-like in that which the "vet." and I bestowed upon her, namely, "The Evening Star."

I had formed my plan of proceeding, which was, that on the following Sunday morning, I would ride over to the old nabob's house on the little mare, go to church with the old man and his daughter, or (if he was confined to his easy-chair with the gout, which was often the case), better still, with the daughter alone; and in the afternoon press her to accept the little mare as a present, which, although not altogether a disinterested one on my part, I flattered myself would be accepted, and, if matters only went on smoothly, then, " hey for a wife and a lac of rupees !" As I sat and ruminated over my future prospects, I felt quite amiably inclined towards Mr. Cox for having put me in possession of the stepping-stone to such luck, and I inwardly resolved, if things turned out as I trusted, that I would, out of gratitude, do something very handsome for him.

Youth is naturally impatient, and I really began to fancy that Sunday would never come (it was on a Wednesday that I bought the mare). The reader will probably ask why I did not ride over with the little mare directly, and perhaps that would have been the most cavalier way of doing business; but, must I confess it, I was rather selfish, and I wanted to see my old friend first, and, in case he should fancy that the Evening Star would prove of any use as the second string to the fiddle which we were intending to play at the next Hollerton races, why, then I would enter into a sort of compromise with the young lady, and give her the mare with the reservation that I should run her first for the cup, and, if she won it, her value would be greatly enhanced. How beautifully and how easily in life can we form projects for the future, and how rosy do they appear till some unforeseen accident scatters them like chaff before the wind.

The Sunday came at last, a lovely morning, ushered in with that calm, refreshing quiet which so peculiarly characterizes an English Sabbath in the country. All nature seemed at peace. As I opened my bedroom window, the loud carol of the thrush was heard from a neighbouring spinny; the swallow flew backwards and forwards from her nest, which was built over my very window; and the blackbirds were hopping upon the little grass-plot before the house as if at least they feared no disturbers so early on so quiet a morning. It was only a little after five, but I was soon dressed and in the stable to see that every care was taken with the little mare who was, perhaps, destined on that day to be the maker of my future fortune. I meant to leave about eight, breakfast with my old friend, whose house I must pass on the road, and then canter on to Chunee Villa, about two miles distant, and arrive there just in time for church. I never was a very "heavy swell" at any time, but this morning I got myself up with a little more care than usual—neat but not gaudy; and as I knew my lady's horsey propensities, I did not fancy that a new black "cutaway" and a pair of tight-fitting drab trousers would offend her. I felt in a very pleasant humour, and as I cantered away from my own gate I was at ease with myself and the whole world—and that is what very few of us can say after the days of youth have once passed. I rode up to my old friend's door; he had spied the new nag from the window, and he soon hopped out to welcome me. He was delighted with the little mare, and very gratified to learn that I had borne his instructions in mind, and was about to open the campaign as he had recommended. He could not find a fault or flaw with the new nag; and the only thing that spoilt her in his eye was that I had bought her of "that Joe Cox," whom he hated like poison. However, strict as was his examination, he was bound to declare that he fancied she was all that Joe had said, and he only trusted this latter worthy had come honestly by her, for he never could believe, unless there was some fault which we were unable to detect, that such a little beauty could have come into his hands fairly. He saw no reason why I should not part with her at once, as, however good she might be, he fancied the one we then had in training was good enough to "lick her head off." However, on one thing he insisted—that I should take the breaker's bit out of her mouth, unless I wanted to "crab" her off hand; and when one of the lads led her round to the door after breakfast, she was decorated in a neat new racing snaffle with a blue-and-white plaited band on the forehead. The martingale was taken away, and then she looked, as he triumphantly observed, a nag fit to be shown to any lady, even if that lady was the Queen of England.

Among his other tastes the old man was a bit of a florist, and his tulips, carnations, anemones, and dahlias, when they were in season, were the envy of all the gardeners round us. In front of his house was a large round bed, divided into little squares, in which his favourite flowers grew, and in the middle of which stood one of the largest and handsomest rhododendrons I ever saw. This bed was fenced off from the gravel walk which led round it by a light iron fencing just high enough to keep a dog out, and trellised with iron netting to prevent his game fowls from intruding; for, like many of the old school, he had a strong *penchant* for "the sod." Beyond this bed was a lawn as soft as velvet and smooth as a Turkey carpet, in the middle of which stood the old chestnut tree to which I have alluded in a former sketch; and at the back of this was a thick plantation of fir, hollies, laurel, and Spanish chestnuts, which screened the house from the road, from which the plantation was divided by a deep, bricked "haw-haw," flanked with spiked slanting palings about three or four feet long. This flower-bed, lawn, and shrubbery were the old man's chief delight, and, it is needless to say, were scrupulously kept; and, if I had wanted to offend him, I do not think I could have chosen a more effectual mode than by riding over this lawn, where every horse-print would have left an indelible mark. Even to pluck a flower without first asking leave was a grave offence. I mention all this that the reader may be acquainted with the premises, and in some measure prepared for what is to come. One of the stable lads, as I said, led the mare round, and the old man hopped down to the gate to open it for me, that he might see her canter along the road and watch her action. I do not know whether it was that a change in the bridle wrought an entire change in the mare, but I had no sooner got settled in my saddle than she broke away from the lad at her head, reared up, and then, suddenly flying round as if on a pivot, lashed out her hind legs within a few inches of his head. She then sprang over the little iron fence, right into the old man's very finest hyacinth-bed; dashed through the rhododendron bush, crushing his favourite flowers right and left, with as little remorse as if they were only so much gravel; jumped out on to the lawn, and then rushed into the plantation, through which she dragged me, dashing me first against one tree, then against another, till we came down to the haw-haw at the bottom, which she cleared at a bound, and, as soon as she felt the turnpike-road under her feet, went off, with her ears laid back and her head stretched out, at a speed which the old man declared (as we shot by him, standing with the open gate in his hand), if it would only last, was good enough to win all the Hollerton Cups in England. I have been through some thickish bullfinches in my time, but never through such a "stitcher" as this. It is a miracle that I kept my seat, and, as the sequel will prove, it would have been quite as well for me if I had not. But I did not come off scathless—my new hat was flattened just as if I had been "bonneted;" and, had not my nose prevented it, my head would certainly have come through the crown; one arm of my best black coat was torn completely off, at least hung on only by a thread; the coat itself was ripped up the back, and my trousers split open at both knees. A pretty figure I must have cut as I came shooting out of that shrubbery, to the amazement of a quiet country family, who were just passing on their way to the church in the little neighbouring town! However, when I got on to the turnpike, and saw there was no help for it, I pulled myself together as well as I could, pushed my battered hat up over my eyes, and this gave me a still more rakish appearance, and, as I saw the road was pretty clear, I thought it best to let my lady have her fling out, feeling confident that the pace would soon kill her with my weight on her back. But I little knew her pluck and bottom; and as little did I know what I afterwards learnt, that this was not the first time by many that she had bolted in this way. In fact, the whole tale of the dear consumptive young lady was a "pleasant conceit" of Joe's, for it turned out that this meek, dove-eyed lady's hack had passed into his hands from a farmer on the Belper side—one of the best judges of a pony in England, who would never have parted with her if he could have found a lad to hold her, for she had shown herself good enough, when in the humour, to beat anything of her size; but after having bolted with himself and all his boys, he reluctantly threw her up, and sold her to Mr. Cox for about a fifth of her value, if she had been quiet. But, strange to say, at times she was as quiet as a lamb, and then a sweeter little horse was never crossed; but there was no saying when she might take it into her head to bolt, and when the fit was on her, no arm or bit in England could hold her.

This was the history of the little mare, and I never was more regularly sold in my life. However, I had no time now to think about whether I had been done or not, for I was within a couple of hundred yards of the turnpike-gate, which, as usual on a road where, except on market-days, there was but little traffic, was shut. Now this gate was a strong ash one, more than five feet high, with bars so thick that an elephant could hardly have broken them. There was a stiff stile by the side on a high, broad causeway, and although not quite so high as the gate itself, this stile was pretty nearly as nasty a leap, for it had two foot-boards, which crossed each other, projecting more than a yard on each side. There was a legend that one "Jack Russell," a hard-riding, drunken farmer, had cleared this very stile when coming home from market at night, and when its white bars could hardly be seen, for it was one of the conditions of the wager that the lamp which blazed over the turnpike-door should be extinguished when he took this dangerous leap. He, however, cleared it well, and the stile for ever afterwards went by the name of Jack Russell's stile. This feat was naturally much talked of in our hard-riding neighbourhood, and Jack Russell became a sort of hero in my eyes. Scores of times when riding along the turnpike-road have I been tempted to have a shy at this very stile myself, and try if I could not do as much as Jack Russell, but it looked such a desperate stiff bit of timber, and, moreover, the causeway was always as hard as iron, so that if the horse should make a mistake, certain death seemed to stare me in the face. I have, no doubt, often cleared as large a jump when out with the hounds, and thought nothing of it; but then I had soft ground under me to fall on. The little mare appeared to see the closed gate as soon as I did, and made up her mind in an instant, for she flew up on to the causeway, which was, I dare say, a foot higher than the road, set her head straight at the stile, and cleared it apparently as easy as she would have done a sheep hurdle.

I turned back in my saddle with a look of triumph as the old pikeman was hobbling out to see whatever it was that had just shot by his house. "Gentlemen," as the public speakers say, "this was the proudest moment of my life." I had now done as much as Jack Russell, and that on a pony which I had never ridden over a hurdle. There are many grades of ambition in this world, and I had now reached the summit of mine. "Oh! you little jewel," I thought, as the pony went sailing along the smooth causeway, as fresh as ever, "I'll forgive you all now, and never for a moment regret the 30*l.* you cost me. As soon as I can get you pulled up, I'll turn you gently home, for it's out of the question thinking of the nabob's daughter to-day." But I very soon had something else to think of. Being a fine Sunday morning, many country people were on their way to the church in the little town, which was now within half a mile or so, and whose glorious peal of bells distinctly floated upon my ear. They naturally chose the causeway to walk on, under the shade of a row of magnificent chestnuts, which extended along the road right up to the town. Now it is clear that I had no business there; and I began to get rather nervous as I saw little groups slowly wending their way ahead of me, and who, not having yet heard the clatter of my horse's hoofs on the hard causeway, had little idea of the danger which so closely menaced them. As for pulling up, or even turning the mare into the road, that was out of the question; she had a mouth of iron, and the little bit which was in it was but a plaything to her. Moreover, my hands were almost paralysed, and I had no more power over her than a child. I had lost my whip in the shrubbery, otherwise, as I now saw what a frightful risk I was about to run, I should certainly have knocked her down by a blow with the handle between the ears. As to throwing myself off at the pace she was going, on a hard road, I dare not risk it; for even if I cleared her, I might be killed by the fall, and if my foot should happen to hang in the stirrup the consequences were too dreadful to think of. All I could do was to shout.

The first group I came down on was a country lad and his sweetheart. They luckily heard me, and, being young and active, sprang on one side as I passed them like a shot. The next was a corpulent, elderly, " Sairey Gamp" looking old lady in a stuff gown, carrying in her hand a formidable cotton umbrella and pattens. (There was not a cloud in the sky; but no saying, it might come on to rain before night, and she doubtless thought it as well to be prepared.) Luckily she was not deaf, but heard me shout, and scrambled into the ditch before I was down on her. The old lady was game, for she viciously struck at the mare's head with the cotton umbrella as I went past, and screamed out, " Cuss you! for a bad 'un, whoever you are"—words which rang in my ears for days after. The next was a more formidable lot—nothing less than a ladies' school of girls, walking demurely to church in Indian file; as poor Tom Hood has it—

> " Two and two,
> Looking as such young ladies do,
> Trussed with decorum and stuffed with morals."

I scattered them right and left, like a hawk swooping among a lot of pigeons, without doing any harm; but hardly was I clear of them when the worst of all stared me in the face. It was two nursemaids indolently dragging along two children in a little sort of four-wheeled carriage (it was before the days of perambulators). Now they had lots of time to get out of the road, for they both saw and heard me coming; but, with a stupidity for which it would be hard to account, they left the little carriage standing slanting across the causeway, and jumped down screaming into the road. If I had felt a little nervous at the turnpike-gate, that was nothing to what I felt now. But if I had only known what a rare bit of stuff I had under me, I need not have been in the least apprehensive, for she seemed hardly to think such a leap as this worth rising at, but cleared it in her stride, never looking to the right or left. I certainly shouted to the mare to "come up" as she rose at the leap, for I thought this might urge her; and I mention this because it was afterwards brought against me to prove what a reckless character I was, for one of the girls swore that I purposely jumped at the little carriage, and exultingly shouted "tally-ho!" as I cleared it. I just caught sight of one of the little children's faces looking up at me as I was in the air, and I think I never saw such a curious expression of countenance in my life.

I was now close to the town; and just here a lane branched off which led straight up to the village where the nabob resided. I had now this pleasant alternative staring me in the face—either to gallop through the town just as the people were flocking into church, or else to go through the village right past Chunee Villa. I could hardly say that I had much choice, but perhaps the latter was the best, as I fancied the mare must pull up before I reached the village; and so she probably would have done, had not everything conspired against me on this eventful morning. She turned up the village lane as sharp as an eel; and when I got a hundred yards up it, who should I see cantering slowly along before me but my friend the vet. He was perfectly astonished when he saw who it was, as I galloped past him, and could hardly believe that I was on the same mare that he had but a few days before pronounced as quiet as a lamb. Anxious to see the end of this wild-goose chase, he clapped spurs to his old Rozinante, and followed me. The clattering of hoofs behind her sent my mare along, and in a few minutes I was in the village, in the middle of which the church stood. Chunee Villa was right opposite; and just as the old nabob was coming out of his gate, with his daughter on his arm, to cross over to the church, I shot by him, closely followed by the vet., who was making desperate play with both whip and spurs to close in upon me. I saw all, as it were, through a mist—the country people who were assembled in the churchyard waiting for the clergyman, stood amazed, and the old officer, after remarking to his daughter "that it was the most disgraceful scene he had ever witnessed in his life," led her into the church. A little further on I met the clergyman and his family. And now the mare, as if knowing that she had done all the mischief she cared about, pulled up, and I jumped off just as the vet. rode up and breathlessly inquired, "Why, whatever are you up to, Master Tom?" It was a little while before I could get breath sufficiently to explain myself; and then, to his astonishment, he found that it was no "lark," as he at first imagined it to be.

I dare not turn back till the people were well in church. We then led both our horses home by a cross-country road, which passed the back of my old friend's lodge, where I arrived in about an hour after I had left it—a rather different figure from what I was when I last rode up to his door. The old gentleman had been in a state of great anxiety till I returned. He had gone down to the turnpike-gate to pick up a little news, and had taken care to measure the jump, the tape showing from where the mare bated to where she fell, measuring over the stile, just 23 feet, or only two less than Jack

Russell's noted jump, which he had also witnessed and measured; and this he considered wonderful for a pony. I borrowed a hat and pea-jacket of the old man, and rode home in the evening on a horse of his, leaving the little mare in his hands to see what *he* could make of her, feeling confident in my own mind that *I* had made a very bad day's work with my new purchase.

Of course such an affair as this made a bit of a stir in a little country neighbourhood, where people are dying for the want of something to talk about; and a pretty story they got up about me. "Give a dog a bad name and you hang him," is an old and a true saying; and as "casualty horses" generally prove to be *casualty horses* in more ways than one to their owners, and as there was generally a 'goodish deal of larking going on about us in those days —in which, as in duty bound, I took my part—I was, as the police would say, rather a marked man, and got the credit for many a lark with which I had not the least to do. However, I could not deny this last little freak, which no one was charitable enough to attribute to its right cause—that of accident. Oh, no! it was all planned at old Jackson's! After a champagne breakfast, I had backed myself to clear the turnpike-gate, and reach the village where the old nabob lived, in so many minutes; and the poor vet. (who was as innocent as a child unborn of any foreknowledge that I was even going to ride the little mare on that day) was, as they said, stationed in the lane to see that it was done.

Such was the tale that got bruited about in the morning, and which, of course, reached the ears of the old nabob and his daughter. Little did I know what strictures were passed upon my conduct by all the old gossips in the neighbourhood; and it is perhaps as well I did not. No one was a bit surprised at my leaping the turnpike-stile, for they all said I was just the sort of fellow to do it; but to choose the Sunday! of all days! for such a feat, and just as everybody was going into church—it was disgraceful—it was wicked—it was scarcely to be believed!

In our little market-town we had a nasty little weekly paper, which came out on every Tuesday, under the domestic title of the *Bee*. What resemblance it bore to this industrious little animal I was ever at a loss to imagine, for in a country district, the moderate circulation of a little weekly newspaper could bring, I should fancy, very little honey to the editorial hive; and though I will do it justice to say that in its attacks it displayed quite as much rage and venom as its little namesake, still its stings were so coarse and rude, that they bore far more resemblance to a prog from a pitchfork than the neat sting of a bee. It nevertheless had a wide circulation among the farmers, who look for little in a newspaper save the meets of the hounds and the market intelligence. Now it can be easily believed that when local news was scarce, such an adventure as the one I have described would be regarded as a kind of godsend by the editor of the *Bee*, who had seldom anything more interesting with which to treat his readers than that " our enterprising and spirited townsman, the Landlord of the Red Lion," had started an omnibus to run daily to the neighbouring railway station; or that Squire So-and-So, with his usual splendid munificence, had presented the inhabitants of the town with a new pump; or that Hannah Smith, the wife of a labourer, had, with an equal munificence, presented her husband with twins for the fourth occasion, making the extraordinary number of sixteen children in the space of so many years, all of which are living and doing well;—and such other scraps of local news which could not fail to be highly edifying to any one who had at heart the welfare of the "parterre" over whose flowers this provincial little *Bee* was wont to buzz. Now the editor of the *Bee* had taken a great prejudice against me, for what reason I could never make out (for I was not a "writing chap" then, so no slip of my pen could have offended him). And although I had made up my mind to see my ride noticed in his columns, and doubtless with some little embellishments, I hardly expected that it would form a leading article in the next Tuesday's *Bee*. However, great was my surprise on opening the paper of that day to see a leader of a column and a half in length, headed,

"How Long is this to Last?" describing every particular of my eventful ride (of course carefully concealing the fact, which the editor could have known as well as myself, that my mare had run away with me from my old friend's door), and calling upon the local authorities to take strict and vigorous measures for bringing to justice the offenders in such cases, which were now but too common, and for protecting the lives of her Majesty's subjects, and preventing their being recklessly ridden over on their way to church by a parcel of (shall I finish?) "drunken rough riders and horse-dealers." Such was a specimen of the neat manner in which our *Bee* made its attacks.

This Tuesday was an important day for me. I had been over at my old friend's lodge all the morning, giving the Evening Star what he called a rare "bucketing;" and when I came home I found the paper and a letter lying on my table, and was told that a "gentleman" wished to see me on particular business. I bid the servant show "the gentleman" in, and as I was deep in the leader before referred to, in walked the superintendent of our force of "rural Bobbies," and after the usual commonplace apologies, served me with a summons to appear before the Bench on the following Thursday, to answer the charge of having, *when in a state of intoxication* on the previous Sunday, leaped the turnpike, thus evading the payment of toll, and, galloping along the footpath, endangered the lives of sundry of her Majesty's liege subjects, to wit, the old lady with the pattens, the two Misses Simpkinsons and their young charges, and, worst of all, of the two future editors of the *Bee*. The stinging leader was now accounted for—the two children in the little four-wheeler belonged to no less a personage than the editor.

I cared very little for the summons, as I knew my old friend's evidence would soon clear me; but my "cheek blanched" when I took up the ominous-looking letter, and recognised the coat-of-arms on the seal as belonging to the owner of Chunee Villa. The contents were, like his Indian engagements, which he had so often related to me—sharp, short, and decisive; and as the letter will not occupy a great deal of space, I may as well give the reader the full benefit of it. It ran thus:—

"Chunee Villa, May —, 184—.

"SIR,—[Formerly I was never less than "Dear sir," and occasionally "My dear sir,"]—Allow me to advise you (as a man who knows something of the world) that on the next occasion you ride a race in public, you should choose a fitter day for the performance—a less-crowded course, and a more respectable opponent.

"My poor daughter's nerves received such a shock in witnessing the disgraceful scene of Sunday last, that she has been confined to her room ever since. But she desires me to present her compliments to you, and begs that you will not give yourself any further trouble in looking out for a pony on her account, as we leave this for Cheltenham at the end of the week, where I hope that repose and a complete change of scene will restore her shattered nerves to their former state. This letter requires no answer.

"I am, sir, yours obediently," &c. &c.

It was not long before I was on my way to my old friend's with the paper, letter, and summons in my pocket, to hold a consultation as to our next proceedings. The summons he dismissed very summarily—that would give us very little trouble. The leader in the paper is just what we might have expected from "an ignorant old fool" like the editor; and he returned old Mullagatawny's letter with the remark, "Well, you're scratched for that stake, anyhow." And, considering all the troubles which were gathering round me, I managed to spend a very jolly day, for two or three hard-riding friends—and amongst them Jack Russell himself—looked in to hear the right version of the affair; and twilight was fast closing in before we broke up our little party under the old chestnut tree. The little mare and myself were of course the heroes of the day, and it would have been quite as well for the "Evening Star" if she had kept her jumping accomplishments to herself, for she was saddled and brought out in the afternoon, and, now that we knew that she could jump if she liked, she was put over every kind of fence that the old man's farm afforded. Every one of the party had a mount—no matter now whether she bolted or not. She certainly tried it once, but the iron arms of Jack Russell were too many for her; and he wound up the afternoon's performance by bringing her over the gate into the stable-yard, and triumphantly exclaiming as he slid off her back, when she pulled up, that for her inches he never saw her equal in "lepping." What would the poor consumptive young lady have thought, could she only have seen her little favourite handled as she was this afternoon!

On the Thursday morning I rode over to the magistrates' meeting, with my old friend, whose testimony I felt certain would clear me. The only anxiety he laboured under was that " old Bung " would be chairman on this occasion. I may add, in parenthesis, that "old Bung" was a rich brewer in the town, and possessed of considerable landed property, over which my old friend was continually trespassing with his greyhounds—the only kind of poaching which he cared for—and more than once had been brought up for trespass before this very bench. The magistrates met at twelve, and, after three or four affiliation cases had been disposed of, my charge was called on. I may add that I had no want of counsellors; and, as I entered the court, Jack Russell (whose experience as a defendant in charges before the magistrates was acknowledged to be great) pulled me on one side, and, after whispering to me "that I had no occasion to answer any questions which would criminate myself," he pushed me into the room, bidding me " keep up my head and fight low, for they could not hang me this time." As it was market-day, most of the hard-riding farmers in the district had strolled into court to watch the proceedings on my behalf. The case for the prosecution had evidently been got up with much care, and the weight of evidence against me, as the editor (who was sitting close to the magistrates' clerk to take notes) observed to a friend, was "crushing." Old Giles, the pikeman, the dreadful old lady with the umbrella, the two Miss Simpkinsons, and the nursemaids, were all gathered together in a little group as witnesses against me; and, on looking towards the bench, I not only saw to my dismay that "old Bung" was chairman, but I also saw the owner of Chunee Villa seated on a chair to his right hand. The two other magistrates were, as my old friend whispered to me, " the right sort," and we had nothing to fear from them. After ordering all the witnesses out of court, with as much solemnity as if I was going to be tried for my life, the clerk read the complaint against me, and "old Bung," in a severe tone, asked me what I had to say to it. I merely observed that it would, perhaps, save a great deal of trouble and valuable time if I pleaded guilty to all the charges laid against me, except that of intoxication and having *wilfully* endangered the life of any one. It was altogether an accident on my part, and if they would call my old friend or his stable-lad, the matter could be cleared up at once. After a little consultation they agreed. But this did not suit the old nabob, who was very fond of hearing himself speak; and he rose directly to address a few words to the chairman, who, of course, motioned him to proceed, amidst a dead silence in court. He had just begun, "If your worship will only allow me to say a few words in reference to the—the—the *prisoner at the bar*"—when he was suddenly brought up by a voice in the crowd calling out, "Hold hard, old Mullagatawny! we don't want any drum-head court martials here." The court was convulsed with laughter; the very policemen were obliged to turn their faces away; the clerk pretended to be searching for something among his papers; and the magistrates on the bench could hardly keep their gravity. As for the old major, he grew purple with rage; he could only stammer out the question as to "whether an officer in her Majesty's service was to be so grossly insulted?" when he sat down in his chair, and was seized with such a fit of coughing that we were all fearful he would break a blood-vessel. What he was about to say with reference to the "prisoner at the bar," was thus, unfortunately, lost to the public, for he never put his spoke in the wheel again. The chairman was dreadfully enraged, declared he would clear the court at once, and, if only the policeman would place the offender before him, he would make an example of him. I guessed pretty well who was the offender. My old friend's evidence quite satisfied the bench that I was not to blame in this affair, and I was "discharged with a caution;" much to the chagrin of the editor of the *Bee*, who had already prepared a very pretty little skeleton account of the proceedings, as he fancied and hoped they would be, for the edification of his next week's readers. "Old Bung" suggested that I should be bound over to keep the peace at once to all her Majesty's liege subjects, but the magistrates' clerk thought they could hardly go so far as that, and I left the court, as Mr. Russell observed, without a "stain on my character." But, if she was to be believed, the case terminated quite to the satisfaction of the eldest Miss Simpkinson, who confidentially whispered to a friend, at a little tea-party at old Mrs. Snuffleton's on the same evening, "You can't think, my dear, what a relief it was to my mind when I heard that *the wretched young man had confessed his guilt*. There is something so awful in the thought of having to bear evidence against a fellow creature in a charge of such magnitude; and then the idea of 'kissing' the book in the presence of so many people. I really think, my dear, that I could never have gone through it!"

I am afraid the reader will begin to fancy that I am something like the little mare—very hard to pull up when I have once bolted; so I will crave his patience no longer than just to inform him what became of the young lady and her lac of rupees. As her old father hinted, they proceeded at once to Cheltenham, and three months after I read in the fashionable intelligence of the *Bee* the following paragraph: "At Cheltenham, on the —— inst., the lovely and accomplished daughter of Major ——, late of Chunee Villa, in this county, was united to the Hon. ——, &c." So that prize was lost to me for ever. But if that little paragraph in the *Bee* did cause me any pangs of regret, they all vanished soon after, when I received a letter from a friend, who was hunting down at Leamington in the following spring, and where the lady to whose hand I had once the ambition to aspire was the belle of the season. On the first sheet of the letter was pasted a slip, cut out of a Leamington paper, headed, "Elopement in fashionable life," which informed the world that the Honourable Mrs. ——, daughter of that distinguished Indian officer ——, had a few days previously left her home, &c. It promised further particulars in a future number, and anticipated some employment for the gentlemen of the long robe. My friend was a man of few words, and his only remarks on the affair were contained in two sentences. Above the paragraph he had scrawled "Crumbs of comfort to the afflicted," and under it, " Don't break your heart, old fellow. I fancy the little *bolter* would have just suited her. *I never liked her eye.*" I am far from a vindictive man, but I must say that I read this letter with considerable satisfaction.

My old friend could make nothing of the Evening Star, for she was never to be trusted. He soon chopped her away, and she left our country.

It is quite time, I think, that I returned to Mr. Cox, whom I left standing in the inn yard at Hollerton, about to explain to me how I might, if I wished it, become possessed of the "best fourteen-hander in England."

The secret turned out to be this. A young farmer of his acquaintance (whom I also knew) had brought a pony to Hollerton to run for the cup, which, as Mr. Cox said, would be very hard to beat, for he knew the pony and all about her. The owner was a wild, spendthrift young fellow, who had made away with everything, including two or three good hunters ; and, besides this little pony, possessed scarcely a shilling or a shilling's worth in the world. This pony he had himself bred, and had ridden to hounds ; and, although he had only just taken to racing her, she had won the only two races for which she started. She had now been for a short time in the hands of a trainer, who brought her down and entered her for this cup, paying the entrance money himself ; in fact, the young farmer had no money, either to pay the entrance or the trainer's bill. It seems that they had quarrelled that evening, and the trainer turned round upon him and declared that unless his bill was paid that night he would run the mare as his own next day, keep the cup and stakes if he won them, or else scratch her, and at all events stick to the mare till his bill was paid. The young man was so enraged against the trainer for turning round upon him at the last minute, that he declared to Cox that if he would buy the mare, he should have her with her engagements by paying the trainer's expenses—a little over 20*l.*—and the entrance. His only desire was now to get the mare out of the trainer's hands. I hardly liked to interfere; for in the first place, I always avoided meddling with other men's quarrels, and in the next place, I wondered, if it was such a good thing as Cox represented, why he did not buy the mare himself; but I never liked to see any man put upon, and it did seem here as if this young farmer was hardly being fairly dealt by. I knew something of him, as well as of the trainer; and although I felt certain that I stood very little chance of winning the cup, even were the mare good enough, if I took her out of the trainer's hands just before the race, I felt much inclined to assist the young man. If the mare was only half what Cox said she was, I thought her chances of winning were very good indeed; but then I knew how little reliance I could place on his word. Altogether I was puzzled how to act, for curious cards of this sort often turn up trumps. I thought, however, there could be no harm in hearing a little more about the matter, so I went with Cox back again into the room where he had just left the party sitting.

The trainer, the young farmer, and a few roughish-looking characters sat at a table drinking, and at the time of our entrance the dispute ran high. The trainer was sober and cool; the young man half tipsy and passionate. He was vehemently declaring that he was robbed, for he had backed the mare for the only 10*l.* note he possessed, and the trainer (who, I fancy, knew the mare to be better than the young farmer thought her) appeared to be trying to get her at his own price, of which there seemed every probability, seeing that the young man had neither money nor friends. I could see that the rest of the party, although they said but little, sided with the trainer.

Just as we stepped into the room, the young man declared he would sell the mare to any one; and the trainer stated he was quite willing to deliver her up to anybody who would pay his bill and the entrance. He said almost as much as that he did not fancy there was in the county a fool big enough to do this, seeing that the mare was under his charge with the muzzle set; the key of the stable was in his pocket, and how easy it would be for him to prevent her winning unless he wished it.

I made up my mind at once how to act. I shook hands with the young man and the trainer, and sat down at the table. After a little chat, I asked the young farmer if he would stand to his word. He said yes. I then laid 30*l.* on the table to pay the trainer's bill and the stake, took receipts from both parties, and thus added another very "dark one" to my "string," for I had never seen my new purchase, knew nothing about her, and, although I had the receipts in my pocket, the trainer still had possession of the horse—and possession, we all know, is nine points in the law. I knew there was now only one plan to adopt. The trainer was undoubtedly taken aback, but he did not show it. He merely asked me when I would have the mare delivered; and when I saw him wink at one of the party, whom he told to step out just to find the lad who looked after the mare, I knew it was high time to come to an understanding with him. So I just asked if we could have a few words together, and he directly followed me out into the passage.

I began by saying that it was very hard upon the young fellow obliging him to part with his mare; that I had no intention of trying to win the cup with her now I had bought her, as it would suit my purpose much better to win with the one we had; and that if I did send her, it would be only to cut out the work for our pony. He entered into a long rigmarole, said that the agreement between him and the young farmer was that his bill was to be paid before ten that night, and unless it was so he was to run the mare as his own. I began to think that there might be something in this, because it seemed so natural that the young farmer should fancy that he would be able to find some friend at the races who would lend him the money. Moreover, the trainer did not bluster at all. He said he was quite willing to give the mare up to me directly, told me plainly that she would be very hard to beat if I could only find a boy to ride her, but that he only knew one whom he would trust on her back, and that was his lad. He told me candidly that he had backed her for 10*l.*, at 10 to 1, and he hinted that he did not think it very fair on my part acting as I had done.

I could see that the man really thought the mare would be very near winning; and as I moreover saw that I was in a position where I could hardly help myself, I turned sharp round to him and said, "Now, I'll tell you what I'll do. You shall run the mare just as if she was your own; I shall have nothing to do with her till after the race. If you win, I shall claim the cup, and the stakes you may divide between the young farmer and yourself; and to show how little I think about your mare, I shall bet you 10*l.* our mare beats her."

His answer proved that I had taken the right course. "Done," he said directly. "By ——, sir, you're a gentleman. Now I'll run the mare, and win you the cup; she can do it, but with only one lad on her back, and she shall. And as to your pony beating her, why you never had one in your stable like her."

I had put him a little on his mettle, and this was just what I wanted. I bade him good night, and went to look at the list of entries which were now posted up in the long room of the inn.

Fifteen ponies were entered, and as the money was all down we could reckon on fifteen starters. Among the list I saw the names of cracks from many parts of England. A Cambridge pony and one from Belper, were the favourites; but I was told by many that a little mare from Wiltshire, in whose veins the blood of the renowned "Mat of the Mint" flowed, would win the cup. I casually asked how about The Rejected and Bessy Bedlam—the former our own pony, the latter the new mare in whom I had become so unexpectedly interested. There was a rush at me directly, with offers of 8 to 1 against either of them. I backed Bessy Bedlam for 10*l.* on these odds; and now thought I had invested quite enough on about the wildest and most hazardous speculation I had ever touched in my life.

On turning to leave the room, I met my old friend, who had been, as he said, "searching for me high and low." He had heard that I had been seen in company with "that Joe Cox," and could not rest easy till he had seen me. However, he was glad that he had found me, and we sat down together. I hardly knew how to break my speculation to him, for I could not help thinking I had acted a little rashly; and although if the party were to decamp in the night, taking the mare with them, 50*l.* would cover all my losses, still 50*l.* was a risk, and if I should be done by Joe a second time, I should never hear the end of it. I therefore fidgeted a little in my chair, thinking how I could best open the ball. I have no doubt many of my younger readers will know exactly how I felt, for how few of us who have reached the age of twenty have not had some little matter or other in our time to break to "the governor," and hardly knew how to do it! My old friend was not in a very good humour, he had found the field would be much stronger than he anticipated, and as the Cambridge pony had already beaten The Rejected, and it was considered by most good judges that the little Belper nag could give the Cambridge mare 4lb. and a beating, and as it was whispered that the Wiltshire pony could run away from either of them, he saw little chance of bringing the cup home this time. I told him exactly what I had done. He was not a man of many words, but what he did say were to the purpose. He told me plainly that I was not only born a fool, but that I should die one; and if I went on in this way, the sooner we closed accounts the better. I knew the old man's passion would be of short duration, and I moreover knew that he was a true friend. So I merely observed "this was quite a private matter of my own, and I did not wish him to have any share in it." For the first time in our lives we parted unfriendly. He hopped off on some business of his own, and I went to join the parlour company, to hear Mr. Cox sing "A southerly wind and a cloudy sky," "Tom Moody," and "The death of Nelson," in a style which few, even professionals, could beat. He was in great force on this occasion, and we spent a capital evening.

I did not see my old friend again that night; but about six in the morning I was gratified when I came out into the yard to see him and the trainer in conversation. This proved that the party belonging to my new mare were still in the town. A little farther up the yard I recognised Mr. Cox, holding his head under a pump, the handle of which an ostler was plying most vigorously. When he joined us, his face shone like the rising sun. He confidentially informed us that he had taken *rather* too much brandy-and-water on the preceding evening, but the company was really so excellent that he was a little off his guard. And he further told us that the day's sports were to commence with a match between himself and the notorious Bendigo—who was then barely past his prime—to throw a cricket-ball, kick a football, and hop 100 yards for 10*l*., the best of the three events.

We went then to look at Bessy Bedlam—and she was worth looking at! She had but one eye, and a head like a fiddle, a ewe neck, a goose rump, and a thin rat-tail; but such hind-quarters, chest, and legs, that my old friend swore that "she looked exactly as if she had been built by contract, and that the builder had taken so much time about the legs and quarters, that he was obliged to finish off the top part in a hurry." She had, moreover, a drooping ear on her blind side, and when I looked her over, I felt gratified with one reflection—that if I did not bring the handsomest pony to the post that day, I should at least bring the most remarkable-looking one.

We were next introduced to the jockey; and if the appearance of the mare was striking, that of the lad who was to ride her was no less so. He was about nineteen, but looked just like a little old man of fifty. He was what we might term an "old-man boy," and evidently one of the shrewdest and downiest of his class. He had a strong Jewish cast of countenance, and an enormous hook nose; and when he turned and looked me full in the face to answer a question, I discovered that, like the mare, he also had but one eye: but such an eye! I would not have been an hour in that lad's company for something; for I felt, when that eye was upon me, that the boy could read my inmost thoughts as plainly as if they were written on my face.

On leaving the stable, the old man whispered to me that "at least the whole party were well matched." He rather regretted I had anything to do with such a lot, but considered that I had acted very prudently in trusting implicitly to the trainer; and as to the mare, she was the very sort to be a dead take-in, for all her racing points were good, and he considered her head and tail the best points about her in one respect—for a man who had once seen them would hardly think about looking any further; and yet, he added, "do you see, I never knew a horse that went on either of them." One thing was clear—that if the mare had a coarse, ugly head to carry, she had plenty of strength to carry it with; for although but fourteen hands high, she looked big enough for 12 stone with any hounds in England; and if we could judge from her hind-quarters, her stride must be immense.

At ten, the important ceremony of measuring took place in the inn yard; and it was worth going a hundred miles only to see the little beauties which daintily stepped under the standard that morning. Bessy Bedlam came last, and a roar of laughter announced her appearance. She came lounging up, with her great head almost on a line with her withers, a round blinker over her off-side eye, and her rat-tail sticking out like a postman's horn. The clerk of the course declared that she could never pass under the standard; but she did. I saw that it was rather an anxious time just then with the trainer, who would not now trust her in anybody's hands but his own: he spoke two or three words sharply to her, and she flinched slightly as the standard passed over her withers. My old friend was breathlessly watching the proceedings, but though he made no remark, he gave me the slightest wink out of one corner of his eye, which spoke volumes. The operation had to be repeated three times before the clerk passed her; and then the owner of the Belper mare offered to lay 50*l.* that if he could measure her fairly and alone, she would stand 14.1.

At twelve we proceeded to the racecourse, in a meadow about half a mile from the town. Mr. Cox's match came off first, and ended—as such affairs usually do between such parties—in a wrangle. The Nottingham roughs mustered strong, and proved themselves able proficients in the vulgar tongue; but I will do Mr. Cox the justice to say that neither himself nor his party required any tutors; and the first match of the day seemed to create most amusement among the rough lot which were collected on that little racecourse—and a rougher lot I think I never saw. There was a grand stand, a sort of temporary weather-boarded erection, from which the whole race could be seen; but I borrowed a pony of the trainer that I might watch the start and finish, for the course was in the shape of a horse-shoe. There were lots of waggons for the country-people; the course was in beautiful order, and exceedingly well kept.

At one the bell rang for saddling, and at a quarter past the clerk of the course got the lot to the post. Bessy Bedlam's colours were all black. She seemed to become a great favourite with the crowd, on account of the original appearance of both herself and jockey. As she walked up to the post, I felt sure there was more in her than met the eye—and more than one good judge held the same opinion.

The jockey of Bessy Bedlam managed to get the mare close in to the cords on the near side, for he was anxious to see as much of the horses as he could with his good eye, and he was just as anxious that the mare should not. There he patiently sat till the starter had got them all well in a line, and directly the word to "go" was given, he suddenly seized hold of the mare's off ear, dug both spurs into her sides, and jumped away with the lead as if the race was to be only a furlong. As soon as he had set her well going, he let go of her ear, got his reins together, settled himself in his saddle, and went striding away as if he meant to cut the whole field down before he got to the distance. The secret of the mare was this: She was dangerous in a crowd, and, moreover, would never make an effort if she got shut in by her horses; but if she could jump away from them at first, she took a good deal of catching; and although she seemed to have but one pace, that was a strong one, and one which, as the trainer observed, she would "keep on at for a day." This accounted for his saying that there was but one lad who could ride her. I had heard his last instructions to the jockey as he threw him up into the saddle: "None of your half lengths. Take the lead and keep it the whole way round, and win by as far as ever you can."

Not one of the other jockeys seemed to take the least notice of Bessy Bedlam, as she went sailing along with her head down, gaining at every stride. They sat watching one another, naturally concluding that she had bolted with the lad, and must soon come back to them. But they were reckoning without their host. The long, lurching stride of the one-eyed mare soon began to tell, and long before they had covered a mile the tailing had begun. When they came into the distance, she was at least ten lengths ahead, the boy sitting with his hands down, as quiet as a statue. The Rejected, to my old friend's mortification, had shot her bolt, and only four were now in the race, except the one-eyed mare. The Cambridge and the Belper ponies now came away, and made a last effort to close in with Bessy Bedlam. But it was useless, she neither slackened nor increased her speed, but shot past the post alone, and pulled up as cool as if she had only been taking a common canter.

My old friend was thunderstruck, and so were a good many more; and all declared that they had never seen the Hollerton Cup won in this fashion before.

A hurdle race followed; we got a post entrance, and won this nearly as easily as the cup; and a match for 25*l*. against the Belper mare made her third victory on that day.

When she was led off the course, we could hardly get near her for the crowd, and she went hobbling off, with her head down, after her old style, apparently as ready to begin again as when she first came on to the course in the morning. The trainer was as quiet as the mare, merely observing, "I told you how it would be, sir." And as for the lad, he never spoke a word, but quietly set to work with the mare as soon as he got her into the loose-box, without at all seeming to fancy that he was entitled to any praise for the share which he had borne in the day's performance.

The mare was certainly mine to all intents and purposes, but I had not the heart to take her away from the young farmer now that I saw she was likely to be the means of retrieving his fallen fortunes. I had won the cup, and had picked up a little in bets and stakes. Even my old friend, much as he coveted such a prize, seemed to think that it would be acting badly towards the young farmer if we took her away from him; and, moreover, he observed, we could do nothing unless we had the lad who rode her as well—and he would not have such a boy on his premises for ten times the worth of the mare. So, much to the joy of the trainer and the young farmer, I gave back the mare, took back the money I had paid, and left Hollerton with the inward satisfaction always attendant upon the consciousness of having done a good action, and satisfied with the reflection that without the aid of the one-eyed mare I should certainly never have brought away the Hollerton Cup on this occasion.

For two years after that I often used to see the little mare's name, which, however, was now changed, at the head of the poll amongst the best of company; but it was the last time I ever attended Hollerton Races, and I rarely saw any of that party again, for they all lived on the far side of the country.

THE KEEPER'S TREE.

Most men who lead a country life—whether sportsmen or not—know the sort of tree to which I allude, and the kind of fruit which decorates its branches. There are usually three or four such trees scattered over every large manor, generally on the edge of some spinny, often a lone weird-like ash or small oak, from whose lower branches are suspended skeletons and bodies in every state of decomposition, of all such beasts and birds as come under the denomination of vermin—a word which bears a very extensive signification in the gamekeeper's vocabulary. As the wind sighs through the branches of the old tree, cats, pole-cats, weasels, hawks, owls, crows, magpies, jays, swing to and fro, like so many malefactors hung in chains; and well do I recollect as a boy, when the taste for natural history was just developing itself, with what interest I used to examine the " keeper's tree " which stood at the entrance of a little wood close to our village, to see what rarities I could discover in this miscellaneous and ghastly museum.

The subject may be a stale one to many, and it may have possibly been treated of before; but I have often thought that a chapter on the keeper's tree might prove not only interesting, but useful to many gamekeepers and men who are addicted to the pursuits of a country life, as pointing out in a concise manner what quadrupeds and birds may really be considered vermin by the keeper (because in this case, the innocent often suffer for the guilty), and also shortly to describe the habits and appearance of the different birds of prey, to enable the gamekeeper, who is not generally a scientific naturalist, to say at a glance what species it is that he has shot or trapped. I do not intend to give any instructions respecting the art of trapping or killing vermin in any way. Every gamekeeper who knows his business, knows, probably, far more than I do how this is to be done. I only wish to point out the distinguishing differences between one species and another, and to give him a hint as to what specimens will pay him far better to carry to the nearest bird-stuffer or collector, than to hang up to rot on the branches of his "keeper's tree." But my observations must necessarily be very short. We will first slightly notice the four-footed vermin peculiar to the British Isles, and the list is meagre enough.

There can be no doubt at all that the man who preserves foxes must pay for it by his game; for even supposing, as we are told, that a fox does not molest game and poultry in its own immediate vicinity, still, others from a distance will invade the preserves; and there cannot be a doubt, in my opinion, that the fox is the greatest enemy to the game preserver at all seasons of the year. The English preserves are so well stocked, and, moreover, are so full of rabbits, that the damage done by "Old Charley" is not so apparent; but in our Swedish forests, which swarm with foxes, the damage they do to the game is incalculable. We have good proofs of this in early spring, when the snow first melts. During the winter the black grouse huddle together in small packs, and bury themselves under the snow, leaving little air-holes to breathe through. How long they can lie in this way, or how long they can subsist without food, is, I believe, not rightly known, or whether they leave the hole to return to it; but as soon as the snow melts, we can always see by the large heap of droppings, often more than a peck, where such a hiding-place has been, and, when the ground is clear, the bones and wings of the birds scattered about so many of these burrowing places, prove that they form the principal larders of the hundreds of foxes that prowl about our forests throughout the winter. I do not believe that the capercailly ever burrows in the snow like the black grouse.

In Sweden, during the winter, many thousand foxes are annually shot for the sake of the skin, which is worth about half a guinea;

and as there is no fox-hunting in a country like this, I am always glad to hear when one is killed.

But in England the case is very different; and as every British pack of foxhounds must be regarded (by every one who has his country's interest at heart) as a national benefit in more ways than one, any little damage a fox may do in the preserves or the hen-roost is willingly overlooked, and in our " old country," at least, I should have as soon expected to see a child as a fox suspended from the branches of the " keeper's tree."

There is a great question whether the badger can be ranked among the list of vermin. That they will occasionally destroy young birds is pretty certain, but the habits of this animal are such as to render him a very innocuous enemy to the keeper.

In such districts as they frequent the marten (or, as it is usually called, the marten-cat), is most destructive, not only to game, but to every small bird and animal that comes within its reach. To the cruel bloodthirsty nature of the wolf, the marten adds the stealthy cunning of the cat, and it can creep from branch to branch with a noiseless step, neither the old birds at roost, the young ones in the nest, or even the nimble squirrel, are secure from its attack. In Sweden the forests are full of martens, and the skin is highly valued. I fancy their principal food with us is the squirrel; at least, I know, as soon as the martens come into the forest in the winter, if they are at all numerous, the squirrels disappear. I do not fancy that the marten is at all common in any part of England, but of the two species, the stone or beech marten is certainly the most so. This is not the case in Sweden, for we very rarely hear of a stone-marten being killed with us; whereas a winter never passes but I get four or five fine martens in the woods close to home.

Some naturalists consider that we have but one species of marten, and that the pine-marten is only a variety of the common stone-marten; but this I will not agree to. The principal difference is that the breast of the pine-marten is yellow, that of the stone-marten white. This might be the result of age; but I can prove from young specimens that the breast of the pine-marten is yellow from its birth. Moreover, in the pine-marten the soles of the feet are covered with hair; in the stone-marten they are bare. And the habits and localities frequented by the two are entirely different.

Although I never remember to have seen a marten hanging from the branches of the "keeper's tree," I scarcely ever recollect looking at one of these museums without seeing an old "fumar" or two (as we used to call the pole-cats), and well did they deserve their fate, for I fancy that no animal of its size is more destructive to game than the pole-cat. It has been stated (I know not upon what authority) that sixteen turkeys have been known to be killed by a single polecat in one night.

The polecat resembles the marten-cat, but is smaller. The tail is about five inches shorter, and there is no spot on the breast, either white or yellow, all the underpart being black.

If a keeper should chance to kill a polecat in which the toes are webbed, and the hair of the body dark brown instead of yellow at the bottom, let him preserve it, for this is a rare northern species; but it probably will never be met with in Britain.

The stoat and the weasel may justly be ranked among the keeper's enemies. It is true they are both small, but neither a young hare nor a rabbit is secure from the attacks of either, and I fancy that both are very destructive to the eggs of all kinds of birds.

The weasel is much smaller than the stoat, and the tail is always of the same colour as the rest of the body. In the stoat the tip of the tail is always black.

In Sweden both the weasel and the stoat turn pure white during the winter.

Perháps there is no greater enemy to all kinds of game than the common cat when it once takes to roam; and if a cat is by chance found a quarter of a mile from the village, the keeper is fully justified in knocking him over. A cat has no excuse, for it is always well cared for at home; and if it once turns poacher it is of little or no use for the legitimate purpose of killing rats or mice. I really think some cats, like men, are born poachers. I recollect at home that we had a fat sleek old tabby who lived principally in the parlour on the fat of the land, and took his afternoon's doze in the winter as regularly as any old octogenarian on a cushion provided for him before the parlour fire. Now, he surely had no business to stray away from home—at least, after game. However, one day we missed him, and there was great lamentation, for he was a nice sleek-coated, round, well-fed cat, of a monstrous size, and a general favourite. About a week after his mysterious disappearance I chanced to pass by the keeper's tree, and there hung my old favourite, "grinning a ghastly grin," a warning to all other evil-doers.

These are about all the quadrupeds that the British keeper has to fear, except, perhaps, the lurching cur, and if one of these falls by the keeper's gun (as undoubtedly hundreds do in the course of every year) I suppose he is left to rot in a ditch, for I never recollect seeing a dog in any one of the scores of these museums which I have examined.

Both the squirrel and the hedgehog are accused of stealing eggs: I can't say, for my own part, that ever I caught one in the act of "petty larceny," and I fancy this is a very unusual occurrence.

The list of feathered vermin is more numerous.

The eagle is never very likely to grace the branches of the keeper's tree. This is a bird which is rarely killed in any of the cultivated districts of Great Britain, and if by chance one should fall, the most unscientific keeper would scarcely decorate his own museum with so grand a prize. I need only observe that of the two species peculiar to Britain the golden eagle is the rarest and finest, and may be known at a glance by the legs, which are feathered down to the toes, and the centre half of the tail being at all ages dark brown. The root of the tail in the young bird is white, in the old bird grey. In the white-tailed or sea eagle half of the legs and feet are bare, and the tail in the old bird is white, in the young bird speckled throughout its whole length.

Few keepers are able to distinguish a falcon from a hawk; and the best marks I can give them are, that in the falcons the tail is level, or nearly so, with the closed wings: in the hawks, of which we have but one species common in England (the sparrow-hawk), the tail extends two-thirds of its length beyond the closed wings. In all the falcons, there is a sharp lip in the sides of the upper mandible of the beak, which distinguishes them from any other birds of prey. Moreover, in the falcons, the second wing feather is longest, which is the case with no other of the birds of prey.

The largest of the falcons is the gyrfalcon (we use this as a common name), and without going into a description of the three different species (the Greenland, the Iceland, and the gyrfalcon), I can only say, that if a keeper should chance to kill a white, blue-grey, or white-spotted falcon, about two feet long, any collector will willingly give him a good price for it as a British-killed specimen.

The peregrine-falcon is so rare in Britain that a British-killed specimen should never decorate the branches of the "keeper's tree." The peregrine is about sixteen inches long, with a broad black moustache under the eyes. It is not likely to be confounded with any other falcon except the last, from which, however, it may be known at a glance by the tail, which, instead of being two inches longer, is level with the closed wings. The young bird differs very much in colour from the old, but the tail in both has several dark bars across it.

I cannot arrange the birds in this list scientifically, nor is it necessary. I need only add that in keeper's parlance the term *hawk* is applied to every genus in this family.

The goshawk is larger than the peregrine, and without describing it more minutely I will just say that if a keeper shoots a large hawk, about two feet long, in which the tail extends two-thirds of its whole length beyond the closed wings, he may be certain that this is a goshawk; and if he shoots a smaller hawk, of about one foot in length, in which the tail extends two inches beyond the closed wings, it is the sparrow-hawk.

The goshawk is rare in England, and a very old grey specimen, which I have always found very difficult to obtain even in Sweden, is well worth preserving. In Sweden, where the goshawk abounds,

I fancy that it is, especially in the forests, by far the most destructive of all the birds of prey. I have seen a goshawk strike down a capercailly.

The sparrow-hawk is a quick, spiteful little bird, and in Sweden I have observed them pursue the snipe (often when I have flushed them) more than any other hawk.

Should the keeper fall in with a large brown hawk, not quite so large as the goshawk, but more plump in the body, in which the end of the tail is level with the closed wings, it is a buzzard. Of these we have three British species, two of which, the rough-legged buzzard and the honey buzzard, are rare in Britain.

In the common buzzard the legs are bare, and the tail is dark from the root to the tip.

In the rough-legged buzzard the legs are feathered, and the root of the tail is white. This is very conspicuous when the bird is in the air.

The honey buzzard is rather smaller than either of the two last, and may always be known by the beak, the root of which, instead of being covered with bristles, as in all other birds of prey, is covered with small close-set feathers.

Of the three I consider the rough-legged buzzard far the most destructive to game; and in Lapland, where these birds swarm on the fells, I had good opportunities of seeing their eyries strewed with the remains of ptarmigan. Doubtless both of the others will also strike down game if it comes in their way, but, generally speaking, the buzzard is a dull, sluggish bird, whose principal food is frogs, lizards, snakes, and small animals.

I may here remark that in most of the birds of prey whose breasts are spotted, if the spots are longitudinal, or set end on end, the bird is a young one (but may be two or three years old); if the spots, however, are placed transversely or across, the bird is old, and in full plumage.

The osprey is very rare now in England, and its depredations are principally confined to the river and fish-stews. Still it should always be shot when an opportunity presents itself, for when an osprey has once taken a fancy to a particular pond or stream it never leaves it as long as it is unmolested and the supply of food lasts.

The osprey is a dark-looking hawk, hardly as large as the kite, and may always be known by the white unspotted breast and belly, the blue legs and feet, and the tail, which is fully two inches shorter than the closed wings.

The kite is known to every keeper by the deeply-cloven tail; is not much more destructive to game than the common buzzard.

None of the family are, however, so destructive, so obnoxious to the keeper as the falcons, for their courage and powers of flight are superior to those of any other birds of prey.

We have already noticed the only two large falcons which are known in Britain, but we have still three left—three real little pests, which should never be spared. These are the kestrel, the merlin, and the hobby, and these, with the sparrow-hawk, are the only four small hawks which the British keeper need dread.

The commonest of all is the kestrel, and the male and female are so unlike, that most keepers suppose them to be different species. In the kestrel the tail extends one-fourth of its length beyond the closed wings, and this will distinguish it at once from either of the others. In the female the tail is red-brown, with about ten dark bars across it. In the mail the tail is blue-grey, only with a broad dark tip. The body-colour of the male is deep red; in the female and young birds, red-brown; length about fourteen inches.

The hobby is smaller—*the tail is shorter than the wings*, and in plumage it is not unlike the peregrine; upper parts dark bluish-black, with a small moustache on the cheek, and a white chin. In the old bird the thigh feathers are pale rusty red, unspotted; in the young birds they are covered with dark oblong spots.

There is another species of hobby common on the Continent, very rare in Britain, the orange-legged hobby, which may be known at once from the last one, by the nearly black body colour, the tail being exactly equal in length with the closed wings; the thighs, feet, legs, and under tail coverts are deep red instead of rusty yellow.

The merlin is the smallest of all British hawks, breeds on the ground on the moors in the north of Britain, but is not often seen farther south. The male is light blue on the back, the female is brown. May be known directly from the last by the tail, which extends two inches beyond the closed wings. In all the birds of prey the female is considerably the largest.

The harriers or hunting hawks, as they used to be called in the fen, are principally confined to fens and large open moors, where they may be seen beating the ground with a slow steady flight, as regularly as the best trained pointer. The only one I ever met with among the stubble and turnips has been the common hen harrier, the male and female of which differ so much in plumage that a man even possessing more ornithological knowledge than the generality of keepers might be well excused in considering them distinct species.

The harriers are distinguished from all the other hawks by the round disc of feathers encircling the face (like owls), the long pointed wings, and the long thin legs.

The marsh harrier is the largest, being scarcely smaller than the goshawk, of a dark-brown colour, with a rusty yellow tinge on the head and thighs. Tail scarcely longer than the closed wings.

The male hen harrier is blue grey above, white underneath, with the outer edge of the wings underneath black. The female, or ringtail as it is called, is brown above, rusty yellow beneath; smaller than the last. The tail is much longer than the closed wings.

There is another species which has, I dare say, often been confounded with the last—Montague's harrier. It very much resembles the hen harrier, but is rather smaller. The best distinguishing marks are the tail, and the relative length of the wing feathers. In Montague's harrier the tail is level with the closed wings, and the third wing feather is the longest. In the hen harrier the third and fourth wing feathers are equal, and the tail, as I before observed, is much longer than the closed wings.

I have a great doubt whether an owl of any kind that is met

with in Britain ought ever to be destroyed, for they do but little damage to the game, and incalculable benefit to the agriculturist and farmer, and yet we rarely see "a keeper's tree" without an old owl or two (I do not know why of all birds the owl should always be an "old owl" among our keepers and countrymen) decorating its branches.

There are but two species, however, common in Britain, and both of these are so well known to every keeper and country lad, as to need no description. These are the barn owl and the brown wood owl.

It is true the long-eared owl and the short-eared owl in some districts and at some seasons are not so very rare. Of these the short-eared owl is a summer migrant. Neither of these is so large as the common brown owl. In the long-eared owl the horns or ears on the forehead are very conspicuous. In this species the tail is more than one inch shorter than the closed wings. In the short-eared owl the horns are very short, and the tail is nearly level with the closed wings. In the brown owl it is two inches longer.

The great eagle owl and the snowy owl are neither of them ever likely to grace the branches of a British keeper's tree, and if by chance he should kill the hawk owl, in which the long-pointed tail reaches nearly four inches beyond the wings, or any one of the smaller species, he would, if he did not know exactly what it was himself, be sure, for curiosity's sake at least, to take it to some ornithological friend in his neighbourhood.

The carrion crow, the magpie, and the jay, all come within the list of vermin, and, I believe, these complete my list.

Many foresters and keepers have an idea that woodpeckers do a great deal of harm to the trees by boring them in search of insects. This is not the case, for such insects as the woodpecker seeks after are not found in healthy trees. As soon as ever the woodpecker is seen feeding on a tree stem, it is a sure sign that the tree is sickly, and will soon decay, and the sooner it comes down the better. Sacrifice the tree, but spare the woodpecker, unless, indeed, it is wanted as a specimen.

The Keeper's Tree.

The useless destruction of any animal must be deprecated by all; but if I want a specimen, either for preserving or eating, I feel no scruple in killing it. I don't know that ever I kill a quadruped, bird, fish, or insect wantonly; but the man who wishes to preserve his game, has an undoubted right to destroy any quadruped or bird which is destructive to that game. Every true naturalist must reverence the memory and envy the feelings of the late Mr. Waterton; and were I a rich man, and possessed the opportunities that he did, I would follow his footsteps to the shadow. But if all were to do this, the chain of nature would be totally destroyed. If the stronger animals were all allowed to roam over the face of the world unmolested, the weaker would soon be swept away; and, on the other hand, unless the latter were kept down, the world would soon become uninhabitable. It is all very well for the sentimentalist to tell us that we have no right to take away a life which we cannot restore. This sounds well in theory, but it will not do in practice, for even the most careless observer cannot open a page in the great book of nature without seeing that one universal system of destruction, is hourly carried on, from the lowest to the highest of those creatures who form the brightest pictures in that great book. I cannot exemplify my subject better than by referring the reader to a little woodcut which forms the frontispiece of a small book, *The Boy Hunters*, by Captain Mayne Reid. It is entitled, "The Chain of Destruction," and consists of seven groups. In the first the humming-bird is diving into a flower-bell, behind which the jaws of death are waiting to receive the unconscious bird in the shape of a huge tarantula spider. In the next the tarantula falls a prey to the cameleon, which, in its turn, is destroyed by a scorpion lizard. No sooner is this act in the drama played out, than the lizard is attacked by a snake; this is carried high in air by a swallow-tailed kite, when man, the lord of all, steps in, and, with his rifle, forms the last link in the "chain of destruction." I have looked at this picture times and often, and many a train of suggestive thought has been awakened in my mind by the contemplation of that little woodcut.

THE RABBIT BATTUE.

About the end of 1864, a discussion took place in the columns of *The Field* on the subject of "Battue Shooting," in which the non-contents appeared to have the best of it.

In this discussion I took no part, but I must candidly admit that it did then, and still does, seem rather strange to me that any nobleman or gentleman who goes to a great expense in preserving game, should not be allowed to kill that game in the manner which is most pleasing to himself; and I do not consider that a man like myself, who goes to no expense in game preserving, but is content to wander about over wild, half-preserved ground, and pick up a brace or two of birds and a hare after a hard day's fagging, has any right to tell my Lord this, or the Duke of that, that he is no sportsman, because he rather prefers "a warm corner" in one of his own well-stocked preserves, where he is sure of a shot about every five minutes, to a day's hard work over a rough country, where one shot in the hour is, perhaps, all he can expect.

It is quite another question whether there is the spirit attendant upon the battue that there is upon following a brace of good dogs over a country tolerably supplied with game. I take it that this is entirely a matter of taste. Probably the aristocrat finds quite as much excitement in knocking over his twenty-five brace of "rocketers" in two hours, as I do in bagging my twelve couple of duck or snipe on a Swedish moss in the day. Different men have such different ideas of sport. The salmon-fisher sneers at the punt-fisher; the punt-fisher thinks that the *ne plus ultra* in angling is to kill a two-pound roach with a single hair. The fox-hunter jibes at the thistle-whipper; and the man who has once lived through a fast thing from Crick Gorse, or the Coplow, wonders how any one can call it sport to hunt with the Old Surrey.

The Rabbit Battue.

So it is, so it always will be, and so it ought to be. I, for my part, am quite content to take my sport as I find it, and without tantalizing myself with the idea that many men have better sport than myself, am consoled with the reflection that a great many have worse.

I certainly never did join in one of those lordly battues, for a very good reason—I never had a chance. So I am quite unable to say whether there is any fun or excitement in them or not; but all I can say is this, that if they are only half as jolly as our "rabbit battues" used to be in the old forest of ———, in the days when I could bowl over nine out of ten rabbits, and scarcely see half of them (I should be sorry to back myself to do it now), I only wish some game-preserver would be kind enough to give me a chance of joining in one. But this will most probably never be the case, and even if he did, I very much fear I should not feel half so much at home among the aristocratic breech-loaders as I used to do among a lot of game-keepers and farmers, armed with old-fashioned muzzle-loaders, and some of those of a very primitive description. I am afraid a breech-loader would puzzle me; and I am quite sure I should never like to see myself in "knickerbockers." Besides, every fish had best keep to its own swim. So I much fear I shall die without having the satisfaction of deciding for myself whether these aristocratic battues are so unsportsmanlike as many wish us to believe, and live upon the recollection of the pleasure I have experienced in the only sort of battues which I have ever had the luck to join in, and one of which I will now attempt to describe to the reader.

"We shall want you to help us on Saturday, Master Tom, to kill a few rabbits. You'd better be at my lodge to breakfast by eight; we shall have nobody there but the old lot."

Such was the invitation I received from our head keeper (the keeper who looks after the land in our own parish is always our keeper, although we have not the slightest interest in the game further than that we feed it), as, on his pony, he met me coming out of our gate one afternoon towards the middle of February, and the contract was ratified by—

"Thank you, Mr. Johnson; I shall be very happy to come. Wont you get off and have a glass of ale?"

This was an invitation I was expecting, for I knew that they had begun rabbiting in the forest, and when there was to be a great day I was always sent for. I knew what a "few rabbits" meant —often thirty to forty dozen; and I also knew who the "old lot" would include.

I never could find out exactly whether or not Mr. Johnson claimed the rabbits in our forest as his own peculiar perquisite; but this I know, that I never by any chance called at his lodge (no matter what was the season of the year), but it was sure to be, "Come in and have a glass of ale and a bit of cold rabbit-pie." On one occasion, I recollect finding a bone on my plate, which I was sure did not belong to a rabbit. My host saw it as soon as I did, and I suppose he deemed some explanation necessary, or he would hardly have told me, "Ah, I'm so glad we had that pie to-day, for I shot an old heron down at the pond the other night, and I told the missus we'll try how it eats; for I never tasted one before. What do you think of it?" I thought it tasted wonderfully like pheasant; but this I kept to myself. However, it was in December, when pheasant, as well as heron, is in season.

As soon as the regular season closed, and the "party staying at the hall" had wound up with their last battue, Mr. Johnson appeared to assume a temporary ownership of the forest, and sent round invitations to his friends to come and join him in what he used to call "a day's rabbiting, and a bit of lunch with us in the forest," with quite as much form as my lord had, the month before, invited his more aristocratic friends to a day's pheasant-shooting and dinner on such a day. He found dogs, ammunition, &c., and stood lunch: all we had to do was to kill the rabbits—which he kept.

This was rare policy on his part. Of course these little gatherings were chiefly composed of his lordship's tenants, and gave each one, as it were, a kind of interest in the game on the estate; and although just round us, every farmer was a far better hand in the saddle than with the gun, still they liked a bit of sport in any shape; and these rollickings were looked forward to as little jubilees by every farmer who could shoot; and I really believe if anyone of them had not been invited to the rabbit battue and the rook shooting at the hall, he would have looked upon it as a personal insult. Anyhow, all the others would have supposed that something was wrong between him and Mr. Johnson. Thus, every tenant-farmer on the estate had a kind of indirect interest in preserving the game, and standing well in with the head-keeper.

There is no shrewder judge of human nature than a Yorkshireman; and one winter which I spent in a little village not far from York, I was much amused at the way in which the village tradesmen collected their Christmas bills. About the new year a succession of feasts was held at the sign of the Charles the Twelfth. One evening it was the shoemakers' feast; another night it was the blacksmith's, and so on. Each, in his turn, would invite all his customers in the village to a bread-and-cheese supper and ale; and it was understood that this was the evening he intended to gather toll. Every one came prepared to pay, and not a single customer was ever absent; for, as a jolly old farmer told me, if you did not go the others would think you had not got " the brass ;" and if you went you must pay. So, at a very trifling outlay for bread-and-cheese and " yeal," the tradesman collected his debts punctually without any trouble.

So it was with Mr. Johnson and our farmers. When lunch came on, the past season was sure to be discussed, and it was then a treat to him—casually, as it were—to allude to " that afternoon in Mr. Jones's turnips; my lord often talked about it afterwards" (I believe just then Mr. Jones considered himself a personal friend of his lordship's), or, " My lord said to me, 'We'll shoot over Brown's farm to-morrow; we're always sure to find game, and lots of it there.'" No trouble to preserve game if the keeper only identified himself with the tenants; and this is no difficult matter after all—at least, not if every keeper can " soft sawder" them like Mr. Johnson.

But there was another class of men with whom it was also his interest to ingratiate himself, and, moreover, without whose assistance I am very much afraid Mr. Johnson would never have been able to get all the rabbits he wanted; for our farmers, who had but little time or opportunity for practice (keen as they might be) were no great hands with the gun. There is always, in every village, some "ne'er-do-weel," or other, of a better class than the day labourer—say, for instance, one of the clergyman's five sons, or a young farmer (in a town it is generally a publican or sporting butcher), who seem as if the love for a gun was born in them. These men are the keeper's greatest plagues. He can hardly declare a civil war against them as against the regular poachers; but they require continual watching, and cause the keepers as much anxiety and trouble as all the night poachers put together.

"I tell you what, Master Tom," blurted out Mr. Johnson one day to me (as he burst through a hedge which had hidden him from my view, and caught me in the act of picking up a dead bird out of the ditch, which I had shot on ground where I had a right, but which had unfortunately towered out of bounds), "if there were three such young scamps as you in the parish, I'd give up my place to-morrow." But it was just such scamps as we whom he was right glad to enlist into his rank at a rabbit battue, and depend upon it we were in the best places somewhere in the middle of the line. This post of honour was of course occupied by Mr. Johnson himself; and as the spaniels were never far from him, the two men on his right and left hand were sure to get the best shooting. Besides, when we sat down to lunch we used to come in for our share of the same sauce as the farmers, only served up in a different style—something after this wise.

"I heard a double shot the other afternoon in old Brown's turnips, but I never came down to see, for I said to Joe: 'Oh, it's only Master Tom killing a couple of rabbits, for I'm sure that he will never meddle with the game after his lordship has so kindly given him leave to shoot the rabbits.'" Or, addressing himself to Mr. Simpson (a sporting publican in the neighbouring town, who had a nasty trick of driving a dog-cart along the high road with one old pointer covered up by the apron, and beating any likely field by the road side which he fancied was out of the way of the keepers, and, after one double shot, popping up again into his dog-cart, and driving on a little distance before he repeated the trick), thus: " Somebody told me the other day, that he saw a dog-cart very like Mr. Simpson's drive down the lane over Tillmyre; but I said, ' It's no matter if it was him: he's too much of a gentleman ever to meddle with our game after his lordship has given me such strict orders always to invite him whenever we have a good day's rabbiting.' "

These little bits of flattery saved Mr. Johnson many a hare and partridge. He had, as it were, touched our honour. We were under an obligation to him for a nice day or two's sport, and there would have been something very mean if we had requited his generosity by killing his game.

But civil as he was with us, with the daring poacher it was the *fortiter in re* and nothing else; and no keeper in our county had consigned more of this class to the county gaol than Mr. Johnson.

By eight A.M. on the Saturday morning I was at Mr. Johnson's lodge, and found that a goodly company had already arrived there before me. It was a beautiful hunting morning, and every one of my readers knows, without my telling him, what sort of a morning that is in the middle of February in England; and the more the weather was like hunting, the better it always used to be for our rabbit battues.

Jovial were the greetings, as I gave my pony into Joe's hands—a lathy under-keeper, who was standing outside the door bare-headed (not, however, out of compliment to me), to meet me—and walked into the lodge, which was now filled with game-keepers, farmers (many of them in top-boots, by the way), and one or two of the neighbouring gentlemen, who, according to Mr. Johnson's phraseology, were "of the right sort, and capital shots." Great was the Babel; half a score men talking, eating, laughing, and drinking at once. It was a sort of standing breakfast. There was plenty to cut at; every one helped himself, and ate it how he liked. It was, as we used to say in the olden days at Lord's Ground, when we retired to dinner with the players, a regular "scrabble." All were in high spirits, and everyone seemed as if he had made up his mind to enjoy himself on this day at least.

But, "Now then, gentlemen, it's time to be off!" brought us all to our feet; and "Who wants powder or shot?" "Have you got any caps?" "Shall we take old Pilot to-day, Joe?" "What quarter of the forest shall we beat first?" and such like questions, proved that the real business of the day was about to commence. The forest where we are to begin lies about one mile from the keeper's lodge, and we form a merry group as we walk up the village lane towards it; but one of the party is missing, and the often-repeated question, "I wonder what's got young Tom Hardy to-day?" proves that the missing man is a general favourite; and so he may well be—a proficient in every field sport, a capital shot, and one of our best riders, and, moreover, the life and soul of every village feast and harvest-home for miles round. Just as we are turning into a hand gate which led from the village lane up to the wood, a figure is observed, a few fields distant, working his way, on a grey horse, across country towards us. We recognise him by his white hat, and as he comes sailing over a hedge and double ditch, leading into the field next but one to that in which we are now standing, we can see his gun slung across his back. All eyes are now centred upon this object of attraction, and many are the speculations as to what he's on to-day. "Why, it's the grey colt," exclaims the most far-seeing of the hard-riding lot who are now intently watching how he will come over those rails in the corner, which Tom has purposely ridden out of his line to have a shy at. A balk! But the grey colt is in hands which will stand no nonsense; at the second attempt he charges them gallantly, and, "That's you! Well done, Tom!"—as he lands safely in the large hundred acres of old swarth, in which we are standing—burst from the assembled group, who have for the moment forgotten all about the coming sport while watching the performance of the grey colt.

Tom soon canters up, and after explaining to us, "that, as the colt was a little fresh, and wanted handling, he thought he'd just lark him over from his lodge "—about two miles distant, over as pretty a line of country as one could choose even for a Grand Aristocratic—he slides out of his saddle, and giving the colt to one of the beaters to lead back to the keeper's lodge, joins the party; and we are soon at the edge of the wood, where a wiry young underkeeper is waiting for us at the gate with about six couple of spaniels.

As it is now nine o'clock, we lose no more time, and Mr. Johnson having marshalled his forces, assigns each man his place, and gives us the following brief instructions: " Now mind and keep well in line, gentlemen. No hares! Stop at every shot, and, above all things, take care of the dogs." A very necessary precaution, by the way, seeing that the undergrowth is thick, the dogs close hunters, and the rabbits lie like stones. We muster about sixteen guns, only seven of which, however, are to be depended on. Of course, Mr. Johnson takes the post of honour—the middle place. The best men are to his right and left; and as for the top-boots, who are anxiously asking " Where about in the line they shall be," he merely remarks, that " He does not care a pin, so long as they are at least two gun-shots from him." The beaters are also in the line, for in this fun there was no sneaking down to the bottom of the wood for a favourite stand; every man had as good a chance as his neighbour, for we used to walk in a line right through the forest, kick the rabbits up, with the help of the dogs, and knock them over as best we could. No covert in England could have been so well adapted for this sport. The old oaks stood wide apart; and the undergrowth, which was tolerably open, was formed of hazel bushes and long dead grass.

We had not been five minutes in line before the fun begins. Bang, bang! " Dead, Flora!" then a pause; then bang again on both sides, amidst shouts of " Look to!" " Well killed!" " Well missed you!" as the case may be. The heaviest shooting is of course in the middle of the line, for the spaniels never hunt far from the head keeper, and we, who are pretty near him, get some capital sport. I generally used to have to account for fifty or sixty caps at the end of the day: and, without boasting, I well recollect that nine caps out of ten told a good tale. It used to be beautiful to see Mr. Johnson roll rabbit after rabbit over without hardly ever missing a shot. There was a wonderful knack in this rabbit-shooting. A quick shot did not see his rabbit six times out of ten. "Keep your eye on the grass, and fire well forward," was Johnson's motto: and I am sure that I have seen him pick a rabbit so close out of a dog's mouth (as it were), that it was a miracle how he could miss the dog; and as both rolled over in a confused mass I often thought that "Dead, Prince, dead!" shouted in his husky voice, might apply to the dog as well as the rabbit. But, as he was wont to observe in his blunt way, "If men like us keepers, who always have the gun in their hands, can't shoot, I should like to know who can!"

Thus we go on beating the whole quarter of the forest slowly backwards and forwards, firing on an average, I suppose, two shots in the minute, when we are in motion. We do not waste much time in loading, and sometimes the cannonade runs along the whole line. Now and then the cry of "Mark cock!" puts every one on his mettle, for to kill a cock is the height of every man's ambition; and though our forest was not a very noted one for cocks, we generally used to bring to bag three or four couple in a day's rabbiting.

But our friends the farmers are getting thirsty, and begin to ask if it is not almost lunch-time. The lunch is to meet us at the well-known spot, an old oak in the middle riding, and we begin to draw towards it. Sure enough, as soon as we come in sight of the old tree, there stands the keeper's pony, quietly grazing under it; and Joe, the under-keeper, lying on the grass, keeping ward and watch over the provision-basket and the ale. The party soon settle down; and although every one of us played a tolerable knife and fork at breakfast, we appear to have found our appetites again, for the cold round of beef and rabbit-pie provided from Mr. Johnson's larder very soon began to look small. The ale is from the village ale-house, and a "shilling whip" among the non-professionals pays for this, and leaves a trifle over for the under-keeper. As soon as the serious business of the lunch is over, the short pipes are brought out, and cigar-cases are handed round. I invariably notice that men who are quite unused to cigar-smoking, and who would infinitely prefer a yard of clay, are the last to refuse a cigar when it is once offered to them. I presume there is in their ideas something aristocratic in smoking a cigar; and in general what a sad mess they make of it! Such rolling and wetting, such trouble in lighting! (Has the reader ever had the pleasure of giving a light from his nice even-smoked cigar to a man who is not used to smoking? I have often, and I have inwardly wished my persecutor somewhere else, as he thrusts his cigar-end into mine, puffs three or four huge volumes of smoke right into my face; and if he does not altogether extinguish my cigar, is sure to return it to me in such a dilapidated condition that it is hardly worth smoking again.) Such puffing to set the weed well going! and when it is once alight it generally burns half-way down one side, leaving a long outer crust upon the other. Talk of throwing pearls before swine! I always shudder when I see a first-rate regalia in such hands. Of course, Mr. Johnson, during a thirty years' attendance upon the "swells," as he terms them, has learnt to smoke a cigar as it should be; but it is evident that he does not think smoking improves the shooting, for he significantly remarks, "I like to see the cigars come out. Now I don't care whether you shoot at hares or rabbits."

The hour of lunch is the jolliest of the day. Old jokes, which we have heard over and over again, but which somehow never appear to become stale; anecdotes of feats in the saddle, or with the gun, which we know by heart, now and then interspersed with a quiet bit of "chaff," passing away the time. And as all are on an equality this day, there is no restraint on the conversation. My lord's doings are canvassed just as candidly as those of his meanest tenants; and if any one in the neighbourhood should chance to have a blot on his escutcheon, it is now freely commented on: just as freely are the good points in another man's character applauded. That old oak, in the deep quiet of the forest glade, forms a picturesque and English scene in itself; and if any one wished to sketch a truly British group, here they are ready to hand under the shade of its old branches. Tradition tells us that there are old oaks in the forest which were coeval with the Druids. Certain it is that many of them (and probably the very one under which we are now lying) have often sheltered the bold outlaw, Robin Hood, when he and his merry band were wont to wander at will over these forest glades after a more noble quarry than that which we are this day pursuing. But it seems that even then this forest had lost its guardians, for not so very far from this old oak an upright stone marks the spot to this day where " Stoode ye bocasse tree in which Robin Hoode hyde his bowe and arrowes when pursued by the sheriffe. Blown down in 17—." The bow and arrow has now given place to the fowling-piece, and the red deer now no longer roam in a state of nature over the old forest; but I don't fancy the race of foresters have degenerated, for though the "kirtle of Lincoln green" has been laid aside for the rusty old bit of velveteen, I very much question whether I could not pick half-a-dozen men out of the group now assembled under this old oak who would give the bold outlaw and his resolute followers some trouble if they were once again to appear in the precincts of this chase.

I have always been of Pope's opinion that "the proper study of mankind is man," and I have derived considerable instruction and amusement during my journey through life, in studying the dress, habits, and appearance of my fellow travellers whom I chance to meet on the road. And there is a good deal to study in the group now before me; and the study is not the less pleasing because every man bears the impress of the true Briton unmistakably marked in every feature and appointment. I am not fond of quoting from others, for to say the least of it such a practice betokens a want of ability in one's self; but there is a something so truly national and so full of true British sentiment in the following passage, copied from a little series of sporting sketches entitled " Behind the Bar " (sketches, moreover, which, for true and vivid descriptions, can never be beaten), that I cannot help borrowing it, believing fully it will find

The Rabbit Battue. 241

a response in the breast of every English reader: " I like the round-cropped bullet-head that one never sees out of our own little island. I like the fresh healthy colour that deepens instead of fading with age; and the burly, thick-set form, square and substantial as a tower, deriving its solid proportions from a good English ancestry, 'men of mould,' since the days of Robin Hood, and the vigour from good English beef and floods of nut-brown ale. These are the sort of men that kept the greenwood in merry Nottinghamshire, and bore back the chivalry of Europe at Agincourt, Cressy, and Poitiers; these are the sort of men that would turn the tide of an invasion. To-day handling the rifle as deftly as their fathers did the bow, yet impatient, somewhat, of long bowls at five or six hundred yards, and longing withal to get to close quarters, and try conclusions with the bayonet. When it comes to clash of steel, depend upon it the 'weakest will go to the wall.' "

I have often thought that if our French neighbours should ever be rash enough to throw a body of their far-famed Zouaves on to our coast, how a band of British gamekeepers, active resolute men, armed with rifles, in the pride of manly strength, would bear them down, especially if it came to clubbing distance. How easy is it to pick every keeper out of this group! The muscular form, the resolute and determined, but frank, open countenance, the firm, but respectful bearing, and, moreover, the true cut of the workman about every one of them, all tell their own tale; while the well-worn, usefully-built fustian shooting-coat, and breeches and gaiters, form an appropriate sporting costume, such as one never sees out of England. I don't know how it is, but a real, well-built English shooting-coat seems a Chinese puzzle to a foreigner. What a contrast to the group now before us would a lot of swarthy, bearded French *chasseurs* form! each with a huge French horn slung across his back, his *couteau de chasse* by his side, his nondescript cap, his long coat with no pockets, and his embroidered game-bag, in which are stuffed all his shooting paraphernalia in one confused mass! Or, worse still, a group of blowsy, fat German *jägers*, each with his long pipe, and his broad, pasty-coloured face, looking exactly as if he had been sat upon! I am not a prejudiced man, and I believe that just as good a heart can beat under one sort of coat as another, but I do like to see a man's dress fitted for his occupation. I must confess to a leaning towards the old sporting dress of some twenty-five years since, and I can hardly fancy a greater burlesque than to see the burly form and features of my old friend Mr. Johnson disfigured in a pork-pie hat, knickerbockers, red stockings and moustaches.

But we have still two hours' more work before us, and we again form in line. The afternoon's shooting much resembles that of the morning, save that the men's voices are a little louder, and the guns seem to go a little quicker. By four we have beaten back to the gate, where we began in the morning, by the side of which all the dead rabbits are collected. We have had a very good day's sport, about fifty-seven dozen rabbits and three and a half couple of cocks, Mr. Johnson scored the highest—eighty-two rabbits and two cocks, out of eighty-seven shots. The seven best men average about sixty each, and no man scores less than a dozen. Each man takes a couple or so of rabbits home with him (for the missus, if he has one); the under-keepers are left behind to paunch the remainder; and we all walk back to Mr. Johnson's lodge just to "have a crust of bread and cheese and a glass of ale," and to light a cigar to smoke on our road home.

Here the next day's fixture is planned, and as we ride home in the deepening twilight of the chill February evening, we think what a void this life would be if it was not for occasional little gatherings like the present, and how foolish is the cuckoo cry of the leveller that no one but the wealthy aristocrat can enjoy the sports of the field!

MY LAST DAY IN THE FEN.

> "At evening, o'er the sullen fen,
> The bittern's boom came far."

THE dull haze of a November evening was fast closing in over the landscape as I drove down the North Bank from Peterborough, now many years since, on my last visit to the Crowland fen. The starlings had settled down to roost on the large reed beds with which the wide expanse of flat, uncultivated country around was studded; and, save the monotonous call of the restless peewits dashing round and round over their night's camping-place, and the occasional quacking of a pair of ducks as they rose from their splashy feeding-grounds, a total silence reigned over all. The heavy mist was rising fast, obscuring the few landmarks visible by daylight in this dreary waste; and it was with no little satisfaction that I hailed a glimmering light shining murkily through the window of the solitary public-house half-way down the Bank, which was to be my head-quarters for the night, preparatory to the last day's snipe shooting I should probably ever enjoy in a spot endeared to me by so many fond recollections.

At that day *the fen* was *the fen*. The many thousand acres, ay, miles, of low, marshy ground extending along the east coasts of Norfolk, Cambridge, and Lincolnshire, afforded *then* excellent sport to the wildfowl-shooter, a wide field for the naturalist, and a home to a half-amphibious class of men, as an old writer quaintly observes, "of a rugged and uncivilized temper, envying others whom they call upland men, and usually walking about on a sort of stilts, and who keep to the business of grazing (qy. geese), fishing and fowling."

It was to one of these "ancient fossils" that my visit was

intended, and right glad was I when I pulled up at the door of his rude hostel, and, giving my horse in charge of an antediluvian ostler, whose whole appearance was in perfect keeping with the locality, I made my way into the kitchen of the inn (the bar-parlour of this sporting snuggery), attracted by the blazing light on the open hearth, contrasting well with the gloomy landscape I was leaving outside. A glance round the room at once discovered the owner's calling, and another at the chimney-corner showed me the owner himself. Two or three lumbering, huge punt-guns, all upon the flint-and-steel principle, hung from the rafters; a crazy hand-gun for stopping the cripples stood in one corner; while sprits, stalking-poles, and setting-sticks, nets of every variety, and huge water-boots were stowed away wherever space could be found for them. Seated in a venerable arm-chair (of which he seemed to form part and parcel) sat our friend the host, touching up the lock of an old duck-gun; and a smile played over his withered features as he rose to welcome me. A small group of fen "bankers"—not of the Lombard-street genus, but rough hirsute navvies, in red nightcaps, mud-stained frocks, worsteds, and highlows—who were seated round a small deal table, deep in the mysteries of "High, low, jack, and the game," made way for me with a rough but genuine civility; and "Come, wont you drink with us, master," carried with it a well-meant and hearty welcome.

The king of the fen gunners now stood before me, nearly seventy years of age, short, but compactly built, his old weather-beaten face something resembling the colour of the turf sods that lay on his hearth. The few scant silvery locks combed over his wrinkled forehead plainly told that he had reached the period of years usually allotted to man; yet the active motion, the spare, erect figure, and above all the bright grey eye, also as plainly told that the hand of time had dealt lightly with him. Bred in the fen, his whole life had been spent in its solitudes, and his whole little world centred in this rude spot. Rarely, indeed, did he visit the haunts of his fellow men, except when the autumn floods drove the birds into the uplands, and he made certain periodical trips up the river with his punt and big gun. Scarcely cognisant of what was going on in the outer world, he was nevertheless perfectly at home in his own peculiar district; and, rich in lowland lore, a rare fund of reliable information regarding the fauna of the fen, the results of more than half a century's experience, flowed glibly from the lips of one who had probably never opened a book in his life. Our supper was soon ready and heartily enjoyed, and the evening glided by in converse with the old man, and in listening to the anecdotes which poured in on all sides; for as soon as the navvies knew what was the purport of my visit, each one had something extraordinary to relate respecting the fishing or shooting in this locality.

I shall never forget on a previous occasion being camped in this very public with a friend from the North, now, perhaps, one of the best ornithologists that not only England, but Europe can boast. It was in the spring, and we had come down to explore the fen, and to see if we could obtain nests of the bearded tit, hen harrier, &c. As usual, a lot of these navvies were billeted in our hostel, and they listened with evident interest to the cross-examination which the old gunner underwent respecting his knowledge of the habits of the fen-birds, &c. Next morning, about breakfast-time, I heard an unwonted stir outside the house, and the clattering of heavy highlows and a confused murmur of voices told us something was up. Presently the door burst open, and a gang of about a dozen elbowed their way into the room. One was elected spokesman, and, holding up a handkerchief which evidently contained, in his estimation, a treasure of some kind or other, he accosted my friend with, "Now, then, Old Curossity, we've got something for you." It is needless to say that "Old Curossity" was soon on his legs, and after many injunctions to be very careful, the handkerchief was opened, and a hedgehog crawled out on the floor! The scene at that moment was a rich study for Leech; and I can hardly say which was the most striking—the triumphant air with which the navvies regarded their treasure, or the blank look of disappointment which suddenly overspread the countenance of my friend. I dared not look at either, but busied myself with my breakfast. However, "Old Curossity" was too old a collector to show his disappointment, especially when he felt that a good-natured motive had prompted the gift; so, thanking them cordially for their present, and ordering a gallon of ale to be instantly distributed among the lot, he dismissed them, after strongly impressing upon their minds that he did not want any more such animals unless they should happen to fall in with one *perfectly white*. His mind, however, was not at rest throughout the day, and he frequently expressed his fears that on our return we might find another group awaiting our arrival, with some other such specimen; and, as he truly observed, "I should not mind if they came single, but when they come in such droves a gallon of ale hardly furnishes a mouthful each."

After that night of sound repose, which no one enjoys better than the sportsman, I was up betimes. The weather had cleared, the wind blew gently from the west, and it was the day of all others for snipe-shooting. To describe the day's sport would be superfluous, one day's snipe-shooting so much resembles another. The splashing through the reed-beds and marshy meadows; the jumps of the fen ditches; the "scape" of the rising snipe; the "Well killed, master," of the guide when a good shot was made—are familiar to every sportsman. Suffice it to say that I never had a better day in the fen than my last. Nine and a half couples of snipe, three mallard, five teal, was the bag; and the last shot that I fired in the fen I can remember as if it was but yesterday, for we had nearly reached home, and as I was climbing over a gate two mallard rose from a fen-dyke close to me, and I made a good wind-up by killing them right and left. There is nearly always something of melancholy associated in this life with the reflection that "this is the last," and as the echoes of my gun died away in the distance I thought of the many solitary and happy rambles I had enjoyed in this spot; and it was with a feeling of depression, heightened by the gloom of the evening, that I bade adieu to my old friend and turned my horse's head homewards. That

I should ever see him again I much doubted; but that the old place should ever be drained, and a railway carried into the heart of the fen, was past my belief. The old duck-man has long since been gathered to his fathers, and it is possible even that the "Old Cross Guns" or "Dog and Doublet," has been whitewashed up and shines forth in cockneyfied array as the "Railway Hotel."

It is now so long since I set a foot on the fen that I hardly know what changes have been effected in this region by the march of improvement and cultivation; but I will proceed to make a few remarks on this district as it was in my day; and I suppose even now something remains to remind us of what was once the true fen. And although a railway whistle is now heard in districts where twenty years back the wild cry of the curlew was borne over the breezy wold, and corn now waves on the site of Whittlesea Mere, there must, I suppose, be still an odd corner or two which will yet hold a snipe, and localities even now where the bearded tit and swallow-tail butterfly are still to be met with. I know no district in England so favourable to the pursuits of the shooter as this used to be. If we seek the wild moorlands of Scotland, or our more northern counties, we shall perhaps enjoy better and more exciting sport; and in the well-preserved stubbles and coverts of midland and southern England we can always make sure of a heavier bag than in the fen. But if, as the old song has it, "'Tis variety gives constant life to the chase," a day in the fen is worth a dozen in the inclosures; and the man who happily combines the naturalist with the sportsman, and thinks the face of nature never looks so bright as when in her own original dress, rude as that dress may be, will testify to the pleasure which he has experienced whenever he falls in with a district isolated as it were from the rest of the world, and where he can follow his favourite pursuits alone and unmolested. I suppose it is the force of early association, but I well know, as regards myself, that in every foreign country which I have traversed since I left England, I cared little for the well-stocked districts, but have always felt the greatest delight when wandering alone by the wild sea-beach, or plashing through the reed beds in some lonely morass where probably no human foot had ever trodden before.

But to return to our more immediate subject. In 1635, as we find by Hayward's Survey, the fen lands in the counties of Norfolk, Cambridge, Huntingdon, and Lincoln extended over above 300,000 acres, of which the Great Bedford Level formed the principal part. The general character of the fen is a rich peaty soil, in many places marshy, covered with bushes and coarse grass, intersected with dykes, whose banks are fringed with reeds and aquatic plants. There are several lakes or meres in the fens, the principal of which in my day was Whittlesea Mere, the most extensive southern lake in England, lying about three miles from Stilton, on the Great North Road. And in bygone days before the railway era, when this road was the pride of coachmen, the traveller on the mail during the summer was struck with the beauty of the lowland landscape which burst upon his view beyond Stilton, the quiet waters of the mere glistening in the rays of the morning sun just rising over the fens. This mere was about nine miles in circumference, covering about 1600 acres, lying in a hollow, surrounded by the high lands of Whittlesea, Yaxley, and Stilton. The water was shallow and pretty uniform throughout, rarely exceeding five feet in depth. It was surrounded by fens; and though many acres were yearly drained, still thousands of acres retained their original character. Of course the reclaimed lands, a rich alluvial soil, carried capital crops. Nowhere have I seen such coleseed as in the fen; and I have heard of new land growing ten quarters of wheat to the acre. On such farms the holders must do well; and a very substantial class were the fen farmers of my day, and I only trust they still continue so. The mere, as well as the fen dykes, abounded in fish, principally of the coarser kinds, perch, pike, eels, &c.; and I recollect we used to take a fish here that went by the name of the eel-pout, but whether it was the burbolt or not, I am not able to say. I have had many an excellent day's sport with floating trimmers on the mere, but I never caught any out-of-the-way sized

My Last Day in the Fen. 249

fish; 14lb. was about the largest I ever took, although I saw one taken of above 35lb., and one eel, the largest I ever saw in my life, weighing 6lb. I recollect, when quite a boy, the mere being *blown dry*. Yes, the water was actually blown out of the mere by, I think, a strong easterly wind. But whichever quarter the wind came from, the result was that the bottom of the mere lay nearly dry, and it was then that " the mighty wonders of the deep" were brought to light. Eels, bream, tench, and pike of an immense size, were taken out of the holes by the neighbouring fishermen, who launched their gunning-punts on rollers, and then slid them over the muddy bottom. It must have been a curious scene. It was graphically described to me in after years by old Cole, of Holme (who in my day rented the fishing of the mere), and I recollect he told me that he was almost frightened at times on seeing a hole filled with large bream and eels struggling and splashing, the eels ravenously fixing on the large bream as if they would devour them. So immense was the quantity of fish which died in the mud, that for days a pestilential vapour hung over the mere, and so great was the destruction that the fishery of the mere had never to my day recovered itself. But another great source of profit in this region consisted of the extensive reed-banks that fringed the borders of the mere. Hundreds and hundreds of acres were yearly cut and carried away for the purposes of thatching; and I know no prettier landscape than a view of the mere in its icy winter coat, the fringe of reeds glistening in the white hoar frost.

Every naturalist can well suppose how rich such a district must have been, and to many a botanist, entomologist, and ornithologist, this was in my day as sacred ground. The swallow-tail and other rare butterflies were often common enough here, and the drawers of my egg-cabinet can even to this day boast of many treasures taken in the fen. The kite and common buzzard bred then in Holme and Alconbury woods, close by; the harriers on the fen itself; and the water rail, the spotted crake, and many other aquatic birds, among the reeds and coarse herbage, which afforded them a secluded, and except to the prying eye of the collector, a secure retreat. The ruff and reeve were never common in this fen, but farther down in the Thorny fen many couples were annually taken and fattened for the table. But one of the prettiest of all the little fen birds, was the bearded tit (*Parus biarmicus*), which bred in the reed-beds near the mere; and so eagerly were the birds and nests sought after by our collectors, that every year it was becoming more rare, and by this time, like many other of our rarer species, is probably extinct. It was called in the fens the bell-ringer, from its clear musical little note; and I have many a time watched with pleasure the graceful and airy motions of a family of these birds flitting among the reeds after each other, in the manner of a long-tailed tit down a tall hedgerow, or balancing themselves on the reeds, their bell-like note ringing through the clear winter air. They remained in the fen during the whole year; and were it not that the gunner was forbidden to shoot among the reeds in the winter, on account of the damage the shot would do, they would probably have all been shot out long before my day. Another curious and interesting object in the fauna of the fen was the immense flights of starlings which nightly visited the mere at the close of autumn to roost upon the reeds. They appeared to come in from all quarters, and I have observed hundreds of these birds passing over, heading for the fen many miles distant, at the close of an October day. Thousands would settle on one spot, and the damage they would do in one night was incalculable. One of the fishermen who rented part of the reeds has told me that he has had an acre broken down in one night; and the pounds of powder that were shot away in the big swivel guns every evening to drive them off is past all belief. The guns were rarely shotted, or I am certain on many evenings might have equalled Colonel Hawker's famous "starling shot."

But it was at the fall of the year that hundreds of aquatic birds of different species, driven down from northern climes, resorted to the fen for shelter; and it was then that the duck-shooters and decoy-men reaped a rich harvest. Till the autumn floods set in the birds kept in the fens; but, as soon as the upland meadows were flooded, they dispersed over the country, and betook themselves to favourite feeding grounds far away from the mere; and of course the punt-shooters followed them up. The low meadows up country were then a favourite resort for fowl, and Warmington Sulk and Perry Hurn were household words in the vocabularies of the wildfowl-shooters; and how well can I, even now, recollect a winter scene in this neighbourhood!

The November flood has set in, all the meadows are flooded, in many places one foot deep, and the muddy, turbid stream of the Nene warns us that there is still much water to come down. A trip of ducks has just passed upwards, and the deep-measured cackle of a flight of wild geese, high in air above our heads, falls musically on the ear. We strain our eyes over the waste of waters to watch them gradually disappear, when, skimming over the surface of the floods, a solitary figure bears in sight, which we at once recognise as one of our friends the duck-men. At first he is standing erect, spritting his punt along in the shallow water, when all at once he shifts his position, for he has caught sight of a small flock of birds feeding on the edge of the flood; and now it is an interesting sight to see the cautious way he works up to them. Lying flat in the bottom of the punt, his legs stretched out behind on each side to steady it, a small stalking stick in either hand, he gradually and noiselessly approaches the unconscious fowl, which go on feeding, little aware of the enemy that is drifting down upon them. As long as they keep their position all is right, but as soon as one rises on the water and shakes his wings, and the rest of the birds draw together, it is plain they suspect danger. If the gunner is not yet within shot, now is the time for his greatest caution; however, he quietly drifts down to within about a hundred yards—the cover is thrown off the lock of the gun, a bright flash, a loud report, the boat flies back many yards through the water, and two pair of half-birds (as they call the pochards here) and a pair of ducks are lying breast upwards on the water. The dead birds are collected, the punt is drawn up on to a bank, the big gun sponged out and loaded, and, after scanning the horizon with his eagle-eye, he proceeds in search of another trip of fowl.

Considering the rudeness of the tackle, it is wonderful with what accuracy these fellows shot. The guns were always of the rudest description, and I never saw a swivel of any kind used in this fen. The gun just lay flat in the boat, the muzzle protruding a few inches, and the line of aim was regulated by the man reclining to the right or left of the boat, according to the distance that the fowl are from him. The end of the butt was padded, and when it went off, the shooter let it fly under his right arm, and woe to his shoulder if by chance it resisted the recoil. The powder in use was the common blasting powder, the shot No. 2, the wadding oaken or coarse fen grass; charge, about three ounces of powder to one pound of shot. It is best to approach fowl up-wind or sideways; next to impossible to get them down-wind. When the birds were well in, punt-shooting used not to be such a bad game. Even in this district, I have known a gunner to shoot 5*l*. worth of fowl in one trip. The prices here used generally to be 4*s*. for a pair of whole birds; 2*s*. 6*d*. for pochards or widgeon. But, after all, the life of a wildfowl-shooter, when he has to depend upon it for a subsistence, is hard and precarious—to say nothing of the exposure to weather. The risk of shooting in these crank punts, with the tackle these fenmen generally use, is not little. I recollect one poor fellow, who was out flight-shooting in these meadows, breaking his collar-bone with the recoil of the gun, and having to lie all night in the bottom of his boat till daylight (being unable to steer his punt), exposed to the bitter inclemency of a drizzling December night; and more than once I have known of a gunner being frozen in at night, and having to wade home through a mile of shallow ice. I knew one or two amateurs who sported punt-guns here, but they made sad bungling work of it; and all that I ever heard of their doing was frightening up the fowl from men who could have killed them. In my day there were several decoys in these fens, but I believe Skelton was the largest. They used to begin working them about six weeks before Christmas, and continued until four weeks after. Five-and-twenty years ago, the decoy-men, however, were complaining of the scarcity of fowl, so I should suppose at the present day the trade cannot be worth following.

The principal ducks in this fen were the common wild duck, the pochard, widgeon, and teal, now and then a few golden-eye, and I have killed an occasional pintail and shoveller.

It is the opinion of many antiquarians that at the time of the Romans this fen-land was one vast forest, and old De la Prynne even supposes that the fall of the trees was the proximate cause of the formation of the turf and soil, which accumulated by degrees around the fallen trees, till additions year after year produced the fen-land as we now see it. Certainly old trunks are occasionally dug up in this and many other of the fens. Probably, in the days of bold Robin Hood, Rockingham Forest, which now comes within twenty miles of the fen, extended much farther; and I well recollect a friend of mine, when digging out for a boat-house by the side of the Nene, finding, about four feet below the surface, a curious old buckhorn-hafted knife, and a single horn of a *red* deer (not a fallow), doubtless left there centuries before by some of the merry outlaws who then roamed at will over the forest of Rockingham and merry Sherwood. As it is, there was but one tree of any magnitude standing in the Holme fen at my day, and this was a huge willow on the western bank of the mere, which had evidently braved the blasts of centuries.

Following a familiar train of ideas, the mind instinctively wanders back from the scenes of our own time to the days of yore, when

"Unheeded was the Manton by the partridge and the quail,
And o'er each lazy inland mere were wild ducks wont to sail."

But although the boom of the modern punt even then never broke the stillness of the fen, the sports of the field were probably then carried on with as much zest as at the present day, and the "Heighlo-la-la-leup!" of the falconer cheered his well-trained falcon on to the quarry. Many a gay cavalcade of knights and ladies gay, whose bones have long since crumbled into dust, then rode forth with falcon on wrist from the portals of many an ancient hall in the neighbourhood for a day's heron-hawking in the fens. It was merry days in old England then. Vast must have been the extent of fen land when Ethelwold was king, and the monastery of Crowland (whose ruins still form a bold memento of the days that are past), was founded. Many are the traditions of genii and kelpies inhabiting the fens at that time; and the benighted traveller has trembled in his lonely journey over the dark, dank fen, as the sullen boom of the bittern shook the night air, or the deep, solemn note of the curfew bell from the distant abbey of Crowland, borne upon the night breeze across the dreary flat, fell upon his startled ear. Benumbed with cold, his senses bewildered with fear, how many a one has sunk in hopeless despair upon that damp, cold bed, from which few have ever risen again alive; or misled by the treacherous flickering light of the "Will-o'-the-Wisp," dancing "in murky night o'er fen and lake," has wandered out of his track, and, floundering on through bog and mire, has found a grave in the dark pool, and the last despairing shriek of the dying man sinking below the surface was carried on the night breeze over the dreary marshes, where there was no one to hear it.

The fen must have, indeed, been a favoured region in the days of old William of Malmesbury, if his quaint account of the Isle of Ely in his time is at all correct; for he describes it as "the very picture of paradise, a wonderful solitary and retired place, fit for monks, as making them mindful of heavenly things, and more mortified to things below. It is a prodigy to see a woman here, but when a man comes he is welcomed like an angel; so that we may truly call this isle a lodge of chastity, a harbour of honesty, and a school of divine philosophy." As for chastity and honesty, I guess the fen-men now are about on a par with their upland neighbours; but I must say I think if I condemned myself to do penance, and mortify my flesh to things below, I should not take up my residence in the fen; for harder riders, better shots, and a more jovial, rollicking set than the fen farmers of my day it would be hard to meet with. The welcome, certainly, is as hearty as of yore; but I fear the bright eyes of some of the fen women of the present day would upset the theory, and play sad havoc with the ascetic maxims of even so rigid a disciplinarian as William himself.

I recollect in my time the question of ever being able to drain the mere was a point often under discussion, and although many enterprising minds never for a moment doubted the practicability of such a scheme, others of surer dispositions shook their heads, and appeared to think with Camden, "that it is the safest plan to follow the oracle's advice in the like case, and not to venture too far where Heaven has put a stop." But had old Camden lived till the go-ahead nineteenth century, his opinion might probably have changed; and I can fancy the venerable historian would open his eyes widely were he to wake up from his long sleep (after the manner of "Nimrod's" old gentleman in the Quicksilver mail) and find himself some fine morning whisked into Whittlesea in a quick train, and his trance broken by the civil request of the green-coated guard, "Whittlesea, gentlemen; tickets, if you please."

As a matter of national benefit, there can be no doubt of immense advantages to be derived by bringing this waste land into cultivation. But looking upon it with the eye of a sportsman or naturalist, I must say I always feel regret when I see these wild districts reclaimed; for so little now remains to prove to us the original state of our island, and there are now so few spots in England where the sportsman or naturalist can wander free and unmolested away from the busy haunts of men, and look upon nature in her original state. To a cosmopolite like myself, this matters little, for, happily, there are many other countries where I can always pitch my tent in the forest or on the moor, with but little chance of annoying my next neighbour. But let the sport be what it may in a foreign land, it still wants the charm of home association to complete it; for, although I have killed more snipe in one day in Northern Europe than I could, perhaps, bag in England in a week, and more wildfowl in one evening's flight-shooting in Australia than I could well carry home, I have never felt half the true pleasure in the sport that I used to do when wandering in bygone days with no one but my old guide in the wild solitude of the Crowland fen.

DID YOU EVER DRIVE A JIBBER DOWN TO A FIGHT?

READER, have you ever driven a jibbing horse? The chances are that you have. Well, is not it pleasant?—especially if you have a woman by your side, and the horse goes through the performance, as he generally does, in a crowded thoroughfare or in the market square of a country town, when the footpaths are thronged with passengers. I have always remarked that a rank jibber, as if proud of his accomplishments, invariably chooses a place for the display of the pantomime where there are plenty of spectators; and on this account, jibbing, although one of the most annoying, is perhaps one of the least dangerous of all vices, for assistance is nearly always at hand, and there appear to be in every town a particular class of men who are always on the look-out to assist on such occasions. Where they come from it would be hard to say. You scarcely ever see them about the streets; but so sure as a mishap of any kind happens with a horse, three or four baggy-breeched fellows, generally bareheaded, with gaiters buttoned up in front, and long-sleeved waistcoats, are on the spot in an instant; and while the eager spectators stand gazing at a respectful distance—every one suggesting some plan of relief, which not one of them has either the skill or pluck to execute—these fellows push their way through the crowd, pounce on the horse at once, as if he was their peculiar prey, and, no matter what the nature of the accident, go to work to set things right, with a coolness and dexterity perfectly marvellous. You will see such fellows hanging about stable-yards, and you are sure to meet with them at the taps of coaching inns; but yon rarely see them beyond the precincts of the yard itself, save on occasions like those above mentioned, or else when a brake turns into the street with an awkward young horse coupled up alongside of a steady old near-wheeler. You then behold them in all their glory; and no aristocrat, as he leans back in his well-appointed barouche, enjoys his park ride more than these fellows seem now to enjoy themselves, perched on and about the brake in all the dishabille of the stable-yard, ready for any emergency.

Well, we will suppose all this is familiar to you. You have probably more than once been started by the powerful assistance of three or four such fellows, one at each wheel, and another at the head of the horse, who will persist in backing your gig into a linendraper's shop-window.

But did you ever drive a jibber down to a fight?

I dare say not. I, however, have; and I will describe a little adventure of the kind which once happened to me—a good many years ago, but still not so long as to be entirely forgotten. Do not, however, be shocked! it is the drive down, and not the fight, which I am about to describe.

In the year 1842, a prize-fight was fixed to come off in Cambridgeshire, on a common called Melbourne Heath, between two worthies—the one a black man, named Sambo Sutton; the other, a copper-coloured individual from the antipodes, the champion of Australia, who rejoiced in the aboriginal *sobriquet* of Bungaree; and I received the following laconic note from head-quarters a few days previous:—"Littlebury, Oct. 25, ten A.M. Be in time." I was then about twenty miles to the east of Cambridge, so on the afternoon of the 24th I rode over to the old town, intending to hire a fresh horse to ride down to the fight on the next day, and have my own horse fresh to take me home again in the evening. These were the days when the prize-ring was hardly at so low an ebb as it is at present; and special trains were not then chartered for the occasion to convey the company stealthily down to the meeting, but all who wished to see the performance had due notice of the time and place, and travelled down as best they could—in gigs, cabs, go-carts, or on horseback, making no more secret or mystery of their mission than if they were going to a race or a fair.

I reached old Alma Mater about eight P.M., and as I was a perfect stranger in the good old town I asked the first policeman I chanced to meet whether he could recommend me to a snug little second-rate sporting inn where I could put up for the night, and hire a horse for the next day? He at once directed me to a little inn in Trumpington-street, which he said was just the sort of house to suit me, kept by a landlord of the right sort, where he told me I could hire a horse, and, moreover, hear all the news respecting the next day's proceedings. On riding into the inn-yard I met the landlord, and found him just what the policeman had described. He knew all about the fight; agreed directly to let me have a saddle-horse for the morning; and said he would have gone down himself, but the Newmarket October Meeting was then on, and he was anxious to be there. After seeing my horse located in a very snug loose box, I turned to go into the inn with the landlord, who, on leaving the stable, bid the ostler be sure and have the "Capten's dog-cart" all clean and neat in the morning, as the "Capten" was going to drive him down to the races in it. The "Capten's dog-cart," however, as the reader will presently see, was destined for a journey of quite another kind on the morrow.

I found every room in the little inn crowded with racing men. The day's racing at Newmarket, of course, formed the sole topic of conversation; and during the whole of my tea, disjointed sentences, such as "collared him at the bushes," "came away from him over the flat," "give him three pound and a beating," floated on my ear. After tea I lit a cigar, proposing to myself to have a stroll round the old town; but just as I was walking out of the gateway of the inn, I ran against two men, both of whom I well knew, one being no less a personage than the "Capten," the proprietor of the dog-cart then standing in the yard. "Halloa! what are *you* doing here? Come in and have a glass of brandy-and-water. I have not seen you for an age," was his cheery greeting; and while I follow him back again to the snug little bar-parlour I will introduce him to the reader.

The " Capten" was a jolly, handsome-looking fellow of about forty, always dressed in a scrupulously neat, sporting style, and who managed to make an income of about 500*l.* per year out of his wits, and a little annuity of 250*l.*, which he used to tell us had been left him by a maiden aunt, a lock of whose hair he always wore in an enormous brooch, encircled by a gold horse-shoe. He was never "Capten" with us—always plain Harry; but on every racecourse, and at the principal sporting inn in every town from Hereford to Newcastle, he was known as the "Capten," and nothing else. What right he had to the title none of us ever cared to inquire. He was a true cosmopolite—a perfect citizen of the world; and his whole year was spent in travelling throughout England, from one race meeting to another. In the winter, steeple-chasing claimed his attention; and I think I can safely answer for it that I never went on to a racecourse or steeple-chase ground, at that day, without seeing the " Capten's" handsome face and portly form, seated generally in a low four-wheeler, drawn by a perfect cob, surrounded by a little mob of knowing fellows, who were either convulsed with laughter at some anecdote he was relating, or else deferentially listening to his opinion on passing events. Where he lived, or if he had any home at all, I never knew. His letters always used to be addressed to Craven-street, in the Strand; but although I have called there a score of times, I was never lucky enough to find the " Capten" at home. It is needless to say that a man leading such a life as he did, was tolerably wide-awake; and though he never betted heavily, he put on quietly and safely his " little fivers," as he used to term them, and at a little bit of three-card loo had scarcely an equal. He certainly was one of the jolliest fellows in England, and the best of company; but there are spots even on the disc of the sun, and so it is hardly to be supposed the " Capten's" character was stainless, and his worst faults were a hasty temper, selfishness, and egotism. " What's the good of having friends unless you make use of them?" was the motto which he never failed to act up to. No man had a better opinion of himself. "If *I say so*, it *was* so!" used to be his invariable answer, if by chance he had been describing a race to you, and you happened to hint that one of the very jockeys who had ridden in it had given you quite a different version of the affair just before. He used to boast (what I believe was true) that he could travel to every race meeting in England without spending a shilling for "the wear and tear of his teeth;" and as, to use an expression of his own, he was "no bread and cheese man," this was a matter of some little consequence to him. There was not a town in England which owned a racecourse where the "Capten" had not a friend in some sporting farmer in the immediate neighbourhood; and as he could sing a good song, tell the best of stories, and as his presence always shed a cheerful ray of light upon any company, he was welcome wherever he came. He rarely stayed in a town, and would have made no exception in this instance; but he had to meet a man in Cambridge that night to settle some money matters with, so had driven up expressly from Newmarket after the day's racing was over.

I soon told him what my errand was, and directly he found out I had hired a horse, he proposed that, instead of my riding down, as I intended, we should put it into his new dog-cart (which, by the way, he had just taken for a bad debt), he would be coachman, and we would toddle down to Littlebury to breakfast, as comfortable as could be—see the fight, and return to Cambridge in the afternoon. There was nothing coming off at Newmarket next day which he cared about seeing; moreover, a day's rest, as he said, would do his cob no harm, and besides which, he had a great desire to see the "mill" as he termed it. I had not the least objection to make to the proposed arrangement: in fact, his company was a treat at all times; and as he knew a great deal more both of sporting men and sporting life than I did, I felt rather flattered by his patronage than otherwise.

I went down soon after to the stable to see my horse suppered-up, and to tell the ostler the arrangements for the morning; besides, to know if he had any objection to substitute the dog-cart for the saddle. "In course I've no objection," said the man, "if the Capten hasn't; but although the horse you're going to have to-morrow is an out-and-out saddle horse, I'd hardly trust him myself in harness. However, if the Capten's made his mind up, there's nothing to be said; but I should recommend you if you do mean driving down, to take a saddle that you may 'ride and tie' home—(I fancy I see the Capten at this game!" added the fellow with a grin)—"and a 'sack' to bring the new dog-cart back in."

"Why, what's the matter with the horse?" I asked; "is he a bolter!" "Oh, not by no means; he'll never run away with you in harnish! you'll only be lucky if you get him along, for a ranker jibber I never put between the shafts!" And the fellow wound up by giving me a bit of most sensible advice, holding me all the while fast by the button, and speaking in a slow and distinct tone. "If you're determined upon letting the Capten drive you down, mind that he stands all repairs. If you risk the horse, let him risk the cart. I'm not much afeerd of harm coming to the hoss, but I would not give much for the shafts of the new dog-cart if he do take to jibbing as I have seen him. My word! I fancy I see the Capten if he do begin! Well, he must be a hawful man sure*ly* to think of taking a beautiful new dog-cart like that" (we were standing just against it) "down to a fight of all places, with a hoss of which he knows nought! Why, it was only this afternoon he almost blew my head off because a little scratch come on one of the panels!"

I went back to the Capten, and told him exactly as the ostler had told me; but he was then in his third glass of brandy-and-water, and not in the humour for being dissuaded from any project on which he had set his mind. If that was all the matter with the horse, he did not care. He never yet saw the jibber which he could not shove along; and as the landlord, who was drinking with him, did not give the horse half so bad a character as the man had done, he willingly agreed to stand all repairs if anything happened to the dog-cart; and we arranged to start at eight next morning.

The Capten was certainly an excellent whip, and if he prided himself upon one accomplishment more than other, it was in screwing an awkward horse in and out of a crowd. He was too heavy for violent horse exercise; but if it had been possible to follow hounds in his four-wheeler, I'll warrant he would have seen as much of a run as any man. The old hackney coachman's remark to the swell, " Ah ! you look like a coachman, but you drive like a *gentleman*," would certainly not have applied to him; for when he was on the box he not only looked a workman, but he was one.

About eight next morning we were in the yard, and the jibber put to. Let the horse be what he might, he certainly was a very showy-looking one; and when the Capten, cigar in mouth, had mounted the new dog-cart in all the pride of a neat drab coat and a horse-rug artistically wrapped round his knees, I could not help fancying that a more sporting turn-out would hardly leave Cambridge that morning. I asked the ostler quietly how about the " saddle and the sack ?" but he seemed overawed in the Capten's presence, and never said a word. I jumped up into the cart beside the Capten; the man led us out of the gateway, and we rattled up Trumpington-street at about nine miles an hour, without the slightest attempt at jibbing on the horse's part. It seemed as if he really knew he had a man behind him who would stand no nonsense; and we were soon clear of the town, and bowling along the smooth turnpike-road as gaily as you please. The morning was fine, the air pure and bracing, the Capten was in high spirits, and I fancy felt a little proud in showing me how well he could handle a horse respecting whom I had hinted my fears on the preceding evening. He was evidently, however, quite prepared, for he kept the horse well up to the collar ; and if ever he showed the least symptoms of shirking, down came the double thong across his quarters, with, " Oh ! you would, would you ? you brute !" In fact, he never gave the horse time to think about playing any tricks; he was evidently bent upon showing him that his master was behind him, and this he did with a vengeance. I now began to feel quite at my ease, and fancied that the jibbing existed only in the musty brain of the old ostler, who had invented the tale for some purpose or other best known to himself.

The horse bowled us down to Littlebury without a mistake, and we pulled up in front of the inn, amidst a crowd of vehicles of every description; and as the Capten threw his whip to an ostler who had caught hold of the horse's head, he triumphantly turned round to me, with, "It's no use a jibber trying it on with me, I never give him time to begin." This inn was the head-quarters of the "fancy" on the present occasion. The black man was staying in the house, and the fight was to come off on a common some six or eight miles distant. Every one of the motley group assembled in and about the inn seemed to know the Capten, and the Capten seemed to know every one of them. The black was a tremendous favourite; his blue-and-white colours were round every neck, and I fancy they would have laid two to one on him; and, according to the Capten, who generally went with the swim, it was like coining money to back him. I knew the black, but I had never seen the Australian; and although I fancied, like the rest, that Sambo must win, I bore in mind the old motto that a battle's never won till it's lost, and did not deem it prudent either to lay or take the odds till I saw the men in the ring.

After a scrambling breakfast—or lunch, for it was eleven before we sat down—we all started for the common, and I dare say the throng of vehicles standing about the inn had now swelled to above a hundred. Our horse had been taken out to feed, and the dog-cart stood in the yard. Whether he was rather disgusted at the sharp practice of the early part of the morning, I cannot say, but, certain it is, when we got up into the dog-cart again, the horse began to show temper, and, much to the discomfiture of the Capten, he refused to stir an inch. However, there was plenty of help at hand, and we were shoved out into the road amidst the cheers of the bystanders, with lots of advice how to manage the horse on the road, all which, however, the Capten treated with supreme contempt. This little incident did not improve his temper, and, as there always appears to be a kind of secret sympathy between a horse and his driver, the horse's temper seemed to go too. We had hardly got him well out of the sight of the inn, before he shut up again, and I dare say he did this five-and-twenty times in the first four miles. But it would tire the reader's patience out to describe that drive. There is, moreover, something so monotonous in jibbing —the same thing over and over again. Carriages, gigs, dog-carts kept passing us, and every one who drove by had some little bit of consolation to offer to us. The Capten's temper and patience—never great at the best of times—soon became fairly exhausted. The doubled thong was now never still—behind the collar, before the collar, over the ears, across the flank; in fact, he now seemed bent upon acting up to the old Irishman's advice to his son in a row, "Wherever you see a head, hit at it." I hardly know which came in for the greatest share of abuse, the horse, the ostler, or myself. "If it hadn't been for me, he'd never have thought of coming. He might have been quietly down at Newmarket, instead of exposing himself in this manner before so many men who knew him;" and as for the poor ostler, if he could only have heard half the epithets which were showered upon his head for putting such a brute in harness, he might truly have said that the Capten was, indeed, " a hawful man."

There was only one plan to keep us going, and that was, directly the horse stopped, for one to jump down, get to his head, lead him on a bit, when he would start and take us on a little way before he stopped again; and I was thus kept in very good exercise, continually hopping out of that dog-cart. Beyond the annoyance of the thing, we suffered little inconvenience just then, for we had lots of time before us. The road was wide, and although a good many vehicles were driving to the same point as ourselves, there was plenty of room to pass us.

I may add that, notwithstanding all the horse's good behaviour in the morning, I had not forgotten the ostler's warning, and I tried at Littlebury if I could not hire another horse, instead of this to take us on. But there was not one to be had for love or money. We had nothing, therefore, to do but to go on, and make as good a fight of it as we could. The Capten was obstinate, and swore he would not be beat; so, by dint of double-thonging and leading, we managed to come into the road which ran across the common, as it were, horizontally with us. Now, on this road was a continuous stream of carriages of every description, perhaps a mile long, all heading to our right, and we just cut the road about the middle of the line. They were not so closely packed as to leave any difficulty for us to fall in; but when we were in, the cart just behind us, in which sat four of about the biggest roughs I have ever seen, was far too close to be pleasant. The Capten, to my surprise, was now very quiet; in fact, he was meditating, and if I had only known what a master-stroke of policy he was just then revolving in his mind to cut the whole concern, I should not have been surprised at his silence. It was not long before the horse stopped again, which, of course, brought up all directly behind us; and if the chaff and advice which we received on our starting from Littlebury was severe, they were classical compared with the taunts and epithets which were now showered upon us. I was out of the cart in an instant, to start the horse; and this performance had to be repeated about once in every five minutes. However, everything in this life must have an end, and on looking ahead I saw the cart which was heading the procession suddenly turn from the road on to the common, followed by all the rest. This cart contained no less a personage than the commissary of the P.R. (described in *All the Year Round* in the notice of the Farnborough fight in 1860, as a sage of hoary and venerable aspect") with the important material, the ropes and stakes. He drove a little way on to the common, where he proceeded to pitch the ring.

We had now not much farther to go, and I began to wonder inwardly to myself what the Capten would do with the horse and cart, for it seemed to me perfect madness to take them to the side of a crowded ring; and the only house that I could see was a lone red-brick house at the further end of the common, about one mile and a half distant. But I need have been under no apprehension on the Capten's account, for we no sooner came to where the first cart had turned off (at which point the horse again resolutely shut up) than the Capten began to groan as if he were seized with a sudden fit of the cholera.

"Oh! this dreadful cramp! Just catch hold of the reins and let me jump out and shake my leg a bit or I shall go mad!"

I was taken completely off my guard, seized hold of the reins, the Capten jumped down (certainly, for a man with a violent fit of the cramp on him, he was wonderfully active), and disappeared among the gigs and carts, which were just forming in one dense mass by the roadside. He certainly did "shake his leg" to some purpose, for I never saw him again.

I sat wondering what would be the next move, when I was roughly told, in language more emphatic than polite, not to block up the road, but to move on one way or the other; and, as I would rather miss the fight altogether than tackle that horse single-handed in such a rough mob, I jumped down and led him out of the way of farther mischief. That I must now lose the fight I felt certain, because, as I was answerable for the horse, I must get him somewhere in safety, and there was nothing for it but to try and reach the red-brick house in the distance; and, as it was less trouble to walk altogether and lead the horse, than to keep jumping up and down from the dog-cart, I led him the whole way, and found to my relief, when I arrived at the house that it was a roadside inn.

My feelings just then "could be better imagined than described." To be put to the expense and trouble of coming so far merely to lose the fight, and, moreover, to be done so cleverly by the Capten, who, I felt certain, would not forget to tell it to his friends at the ring-side, was too much to be borne (at least patiently), and I was in no very amiable humour when I led the horse into the inn-yard, and gave him in charge of an ostler. My savage reply to the man's civil question as to what he should give him—"An ounce ball through his head if I had my way"—caused the man to stare open-mouthed at me. I fancy he regarded me as a lunatic; and it was not till I explained to him all the circumstances of the case, that he appeared to be fully at his ease.

"Well, sir, that *is* annoying," remarked the good-natured fellow as he proceeded to take the horse out of harness. "But I'll tell you what you do. You see that four-wheeler there? Well, master's going to drive a few friends down to the fight in it hisself, and I shouldn't wonder, as you aint a very big 'un, if he would not give you a lift as well. You'd better go and speak to him; you'll find him indoors."

"Yes," I said, "that's all very well, but I expect the fight'll be half over by this, for the stakes were pitched before I left."

"Oh, no," replied the fellow coolly, as he led the horse up the yard; "the fight's not begun yet." And I went into the inn.

It was one of those rambling old roadside inns—a house of accommodation for the large waggons which in that day used to come up from all parts of the country to London, and for the droves of cattle on their way up to Smithfield Market. Although there doubtless was a parlour, I walked straight into the large, clean, bricked kitchen, before the fire of which a jovial-looking man, half gamekeeper, half farmer, was standing in his shirt-sleeves, smoking a pipe; and I at once took him to be the landlord. There were three or four other men in the room, one of whom bore the unmistakable impress of the prize-fighter (but I did not know him); while seated by the fire was a man whose countenance I could not then catch, swathed in a rough white great-coat, a fur cap on his head, and a flaming yellow-and-white handkerchief round his neck, and whom, at the first glance, I took to be a poacher. I immediately opened the ball by ordering "glasses all round," and then told the landlord exactly my position. After a hearty laugh at my expense, he said I need be under no apprehension of losing the fight, for although, if I liked, I had lots of time to run back to the ring, if I chose to wait I might willingly "hang on" his four-wheeler; and adding, "Depend upon it, sir, we mean to see it," he turned away to brew the brandy-and-water, which was the liquor selected by the company. I must confess I was altogether puzzled by the cool way in which they all seemed to be taking matters; and I ventured to remark to the rough gentleman by the fire, that if we did mean to go, I thought it was about time we left: when he gruffly replied, "Oh, there's lots of time! they wont fight till I get there." "And why not?" I asked, determined to get at the bottom of the mystery, which his answer solved at once, "Because I'm Bungaree."

Here was a piece of luck! Chance had brought me to the Australian's head-quarters; and, notwithstanding the trick which the Capten had served me, I was now in a better position than himself, for I was comfortably under shelter by the side of a good fire (no bad thing even in England on a day towards the end of October), in company with one of the principal actors in the day's performance, while he was standing on that bleak common—no doubt, fuming and fretting at the non-appearance of the Australian.

Presently Dick Curtis came in. Now Dick had been my preceptor in the " noble art" of self-defence, and, of course, I knew him well. He was going to second Bungaree, of whom, however, he did not appear to think much. He whispered to me to buy one of his colours, as it would encourage him; and this I willingly did, especially as I was about to have the honour of escorting him to the ring—and, moreover, I determined now to back him for all the money I had about me.

Soon after we all left the house. The landlord's four-wheeler was as accommodating as a patent portmanteau, for it managed to stow away seven of us, with a little squeezing. We all sported the flaming yellow-and-white, and our carriage must almost have resembled a huge moving bed of full-blown crocuses.

We were soon at the ring, and we pulled up amid a perfect hurricane of abuse and rough language from the mob, who had for the last hour been anxiously awaiting the arrival of the Australian, whom they began to fear would not dare to show. In fact, even bets had been laid that there would be no fight. The backers of the black, and their name appeared to be legion—for I saw very few "crocuses" sported round that ring-side—talked of claiming forfeit; but Mr. Curtis knew a trick worth two of that, so merely referred them to the articles—and, quickly pushing his way through the excited mob, the Australian tossed his cap into the ring, and followed it himself, attended by his seconds.

I soon met the Capten, in company with two or three friends, all sporting the black man's colours. I knew he was a pretty cool hand, but I must own I was rather surprised when he asked me in a bullying tone what I meant by serving him such a trick as driving away from him in the manner I had done, and telling me he should hold me answerable for the new dog-cart. I was not just then in the humour for any nonsense, and I plainly told him where I had left the cart, and when he wanted it he might go and see after it himself. The dispute between us would have waxed high, but we were stopped by poor Tom Spring, who asked, "What are you *boys* quarrelling about?" and suggested that if we could not settle our dispute in any other way, we had better step into the ring after the black and the Australian had left it. The Capten soon cooled down, and in a tone of irony begged to know what I was doing with that handkerchief round my neck, adding that he supposed, now I had mounted the Australian's colours, I was game enough to back him for a "tenner." I told him I had no objection, and almost before the words were out of my mouth, he laid me 10*l*. to 5*l*. on the black. Hardly was the bet closed before a quiet, downy-looking, long-faced gentleman, who was with him, remarked in the most polite manner, that although himself quite a stranger to the Capten's young friend, as I seemed bent upon losing my money, I might as well let *him* have a little as any one else. To use a Yankee phrase, I was then about "as savage as a meat-axe," and the drawling tone and supercilious air of the Capten's long-faced friend did not improve my temper, so I directly took his 20*l*. to 10*l*. All the bets were staked in Spring's hands, and the fight began.

Now don't let the reader be the least afraid that I am about to treat him with an account of the fight after the fashion of the sensation articles in the morning papers of the present day—telling him how the blows sounded like "dead thuds on raw meat," and such other interesting details which render a prize-fight far more disgusting upon paper than in the ring itself. Suffice it to say, I think that I never did see so bad a fighter as the Australian. He had not the slightest chance with the black man, who, to use an expressive simile of the Capten's, "walked round him like a cooper round a tub," and hit him just when and where he pleased, without the slightest return. The Capten was in esctacies; and his long-faced friend, who was of a much less demonstrative temperament, mildly expressed his regret that I should have been so unfortunate as to risk my money on so bad a man, but at the same time politely offered to accommodate me now with 30*l.* to 10*l.* if I wished it. I had one solitary ten-pound note and a few shillings, and was just in the humour for any rash act; so I handed it over at once to Spring who was standing close behind us, and it was covered in an instant by three new crisp ten-pound notes, which the long-faced gentleman seemed to be holding all ready in his hand. As he gave the money to Tom Spring, I heard him tell him to stand where he was for a few minutes, as he would not have to hold the money long; and I moreover heard the Capten whisper to him, "Mind, I go you halves!"

It is a good old motto that a great deal of harm arises from doing things in too much of a hurry; and if the long-faced gent had not been so desperately eager to close my bet, he would have saved himself 30*l.* I don't think the fight had lasted more than twenty minutes, and the black's partisans were already shouting to him to go in and win. It really seemed now as if there would be very little trouble to do this, and he went hopping up to Bungaree in his usual dancing-master fashion, as "The Life" would term it, "to put the final polish on him." But the Australian, like one of his native snakes, was scotched, but not killed, and he met the black with a tremendous blow on the throat, which sent him off his legs just like a nine-pin. No pen can describe the hubbub and excitement which arose round the ring at this unexpected change in the aspect of affairs. Several of the black's friends pushed their way to his corner to offer advice to his seconds. He never, however, could shake off the effects of that blow. The Australian, now determined to make hay while the sun shone, never gave him a moment's rest, but paid back with good interest all the rough usage he had received in the early part of the contest; and after fighting perhaps half an hour longer, the black was reluctantly taken from the ring by his seconds, who deemed it cruelty to persevere any longer with a beaten man. The Australian was thus unexpectedly declared the winner; your humble servant was a richer man by 60*l*., and I never won any money with so much pleasure in my life. There was a second fight, in which, however, very few appeared to be interested, and most of us prepared to leave the ring as soon as the first affair was over.

The Capten was never a very good loser at any time, but on this occasion he lost with worse grace than usual. I generally was an easy-tempered fellow, and as I had won his money, I stood his growling for some time pretty well. But at length, when he bade me in a tone of command, go back to the inn at once and fetch the dog-cart to him, while he stayed to see the second fight, I told him plainly I was going back by another road, and unless he chose to walk back to the inn with me, he might get home as best he could. A young swell who was standing close by, however, directly offered him a seat back to Cambridge on his drag, which he willingly accepted; and politely informing me that I could now drive to the devil if I chose, he turned his back on me, and walked away in company with his new friend. I soon found Spring and got the bets, and then started on foot for the inn where the dog-cart was standing. Where they took the Australian to I don't know; but he did not go back to the inn which he had left in the morning; and I saw him no more.

The Capten had already paid pretty well for the shabby trick he had served me in the morning, but I had not done with him yet. I had made up my mind not to bring his dog-cart home for him, so when I got back to the inn I borrowed a saddle and bridle of the ostler (the landlord had not got home—I suppose he was stopping to see the second fight), and, bidding him take care of the dog-cart till a man came from Cambridge with the saddle and bridle, on a horse to fetch it, I left the inn to return on horseback. I may add that one of the springs of the dog-cart was sprung, and a goodish deal of paint, as well as the Capten's crest, was scratched off the hind panel. Whatever faults the horse might possess in harness, he was certainly, to use the ostler's words, " an out-and-out saddle hoss." I took a quiet cross-country cut to Littlebury, and thus avoided the crowded road over the common; and as I cantered along the grass by the side of the lane, I kept picturing to myself the Capten's rage when he found out the trick I was playing him. As I passed by the inn at Littlebury, the drag stood at the door. The party were inside, doubtless "washing out their throats," and it is hardly necessary to say that I did not go in to join them, for I was most anxious to get back to Cambridge as soon as I could, and not the least anxious to face the Capten in his present humour; so I just cantered quietly by, without any one observing me, and never pulled up till I reached the town.

It was good daylight when I arrived and delivered up the jibber into the ostler's hands. "So you've come back in a saddle after all—and whatever have you done with the Capten?" asked the man, as he carefully examined the horse all over to see if he could find a blemish on him. Luckily he was as sound as when he left the yard in the morning. I told him all that had happened, where I had left the cart, and bade him give my compliments to the Capten, and tell him he could have it whenever he chose to send back the bridle and saddle and pay the expenses. The man seemed very unwilling to undertake the job. "But whatever will the Capten say to all this? Why, it will cost him a matter of about $3l.$ to get the cart home!" and he began totting up on his fingers the different terms—"$2l.$ $2s.$ for a harness hoss (and lucky if he gets one for that in the race week), a crown for the man, a crown for the ostler; and then you say there's a spring broke and a panel scratched—let alone the money you've won on him. No! I really do think I never dare tell him all. Can't you just step in, and write a bit of a note?" and as the poor fellow did seem in awful dread of the Capten, I went into the bar and wrote as short a note as I could, telling where the cart was left. I may add, that although the Capten could never deny himself a single gratification, he always had an eye to the main chance, and never threw a shilling away where he could save it, and this the ostler well knew. This ostler, like many others of his class, was a bit of a wag: and there was something inimitable in the manner in which he mimicked the Capten's rage when he was supposed to receive my note. I was now in a terrible fidget to get away, for I would not have had the Capten walk into the yard just then for a trifle. So I mounted my horse directly, and it was not until I had left the old town some miles behind me that I pulled up at a little roadside inn to get my dinner, which I now began to want, having eaten nothing since morning. I think I never enjoyed a beefsteak so much in my life; and I did not hurry, for I knew the Capten was safe enough in Cambridge, and not likely to walk into this little parlour and spoil my meal.

I got home that night, and for several days after rather nervously looked over my letters before I opened them, in case I should recognise the Capten's bold superscription on the outside of one. But, strange to say, I never received a line from him, and I did not see him again till, on going into the starting-field at the next "Newport Pagnall," I spied the identical dog-cart and the Capten's broad back just in front of me. I thought it best to take the bull by the horns, so I rode up and hailed him. I will do him justice to say, that although a passionate, he was not a vindictive man; and, moreover, as luck would have it, he had made a capital little book on the race which was just coming off. He greeted me in his usual cordial manner, and merely remarking that I had served him out very cleverly for the trick he had played me, and that the repairs and expenses had cost him nearly 5*l*., wound up by assuring me that no power on earth should ever induce him again to drive a jibber down to a fight.

THE LEATHER PLATER.

"While knowing postilions his pedigree trace,
Tell his dam won that sweepstakes, his sire won that race,
And what matches he won to the ostlers count o'er,
As they loiter their time at some hedge alehouse door."

It was the evening after the Hollerton Steeple-chase—a dull, drizzly, dark night in March—that I pulled up at the door of the Chequers (a little roadside coaching inn, just half-way between the steeple-chase course and our place) to wash my horse's mouth out with a pailful of gruel, and my own with a glass of hot brandy-and-water—of both which we stood "very much in need," to use the words of old Louis Philippe when he bolted from France, and, landing an outcast at a small inn on the English coast, gave orders to the landlord to procure him a new suit of clothes.

I had ridden twenty miles over to the race in the morning, and had never been off the horse's back save for an hour the whole day, and, except a hasty snack at the race lunch, had not broken my fast since breakfast. We had run in the day's steeple-chase a four-year-old, who had never been out before, but who had promised great things in his home trials; and although the field was strong, we went in for the odd chance, and fancied it possible that he might pull the race off for us. But it was not to be. He could only manage to finish fourth, and probably would not even have secured that place if a good many of the horses that started had not been put *hors de combat* before they reached the distance flag.

We had one of our best professional steeple-chase jockeys up, and when I paid him, as he gave me back the jacket and cap after the race, I had the satisfaction of hearing his opinion of the horse delivered in the following candid terms:—that "of all the brutes he ever did ride, our horse was the worst. As for galloping, he'd be d——d if he could not kick his hat as fast; and as for leaping, he'd bring a thirteen-hand pony which would pound him any day;" adding, that "if we had any more like him at home, the sooner we cut their throats the better." He ironically thanked me for a very pleasant ride, and went off to the jockeys' tent to dress for the hurdle race, for which they were just then clearing the course.

Now it is true the horse had been beaten, but he did not cut up quite so badly as Tom made it out, for he had finished fourth with three of the best horses in England before him; but then Tom was known to be as energetic in his language as in his riding, and when excited his discourse (to use the phrase of a late great dignitary in our church) was wont to be "more pagan than parliamentary." A better little fellow than Tom never lived, but he had evidently never studied old Talleyrand's maxim, that "speech was given us to conceal our thoughts."

However, there was no help for it now. I had suffered the mortification of seeing the horse beaten, but I was not obliged to stay and hear him abused; so, giving orders to our head lad to bring the horse on to the Chequers that night, where I would wait for him I left the course, and did not even stay to see my energetic little friend win the hurdle race on a screw of his own, which he always kept bottled up for such occasions, and which he had appropriately christened "Flatcatcher."

I know nothing in this world more cheering than, when tired, disappointed, and hungry, on a dark rainy evening, to see the bright ray of light which suddenly blazes across the road from the un-shuttered window of a road-side inn—especially if it is one which we are in the habit of "using." All our troubles and disasters are forgotten, and vanish before that blaze of light like the mist before the morning sun. We are sure of a hearty welcome (for, say what they may of hospitality, there is no welcome so sincere as one which is paid for) and a snug haven for the night, and we put nobody out of their way by our arrival. Our horse seems to know all this as well as ourselves, for, pricking up his ears, he breaks out into a sharper trot as soon as he sees the well-known signal. The old ostler has heard us coming, and stands by the water-trough with his lantern held above his head to endeavour to make us out before we reach the door; and when we do pull up, he takes our horse with the cordial greeting, "Oh, it's you, is it, master? What, you're on the old mare to night? I thought I knew her trot. Glad to see you, sir. Gently, old gal, we'll soon have you all right. You won't go any further to-night, sir? I'll take care of the old mare." And he leads her round to the stables as we walk in to the well-lighted passage, and turn into the snug little parlour, where we have spent many a pleasant hour before. No occasion for us to go round to the stable to see that our mare has her fair allowance; we can safely trust old Sam. And we feel just as confident that in half an hour she will be rubbed dry, revelling in a snug loose box with straw up to her knees, and anxiously waiting for the pail of gruel which the old ostler will be mixing for her at the kitchen fire, as that we shall be comfortably seated before a blazing coal fire, with a heel on each hob, watching the pretty waiting-maid laying the cloth for our supper, and contentedly listening, every time the door opens, to the hissing of the half-pound of rump-steak which is grilling for us on the kitchen fire.

The Chequers was an excellent type of a country roadside inn, as we used to see them some five-and-twenty years ago; and its landlord, old John Harrison, the very man to rule over such an hostelry. He had for nearly a quarter of a century driven one of the London coaches up and down this road, till, weary of so long a servitude, he married the buxom cook up at the Hall and settled down as landlord of the Chequers. Three or four of our coaches used to change here; and those coachmen who did not change seldom passed his door without pulling up on some excuse or other—but in reality to have a word with old John and taste his old ale, which was as much renowned all down that road as himself. The railways, of course, have taken away much of the romance of road-travelling, and probably these little road-side inns are now hard to find; but I suppose even now there must be nooks and corners in the far country, beyond the screech and whistle of the engine, where one or other is still to be met with, whose jovial landlord can remember the day when half a dozen London coaches passed by his door, and when ten miles an hour, including stoppages, used to be considered good going.

Every man has some favourite hobby of his own which he is never tired of riding, and my old friend John Harrison's hobby was a singular one. Of course it was "horsey"—that was natural. And yet I never heard that he bought a horse in his life; in fact, he would not even horse a single stage of any one of the coaches which changed at his own stables. But there was not a horse, either in the hands of a gentleman or a farmer, within a radius of ten miles from the Chequers, of which he did not know the value and capabilities; not a horse in the hunt that he did not appear to know as much about as the man who rode him; not a colt was ever foaled in the neighbourhood but he had the pedigree of both dam and sire at his fingers' ends; and not a horse was for sale in his part of the country that old John had not mentally appraised, and whose buying and selling value he could not tell you to a five-pound note. He had a good deal of leisure and time on his hands, for, except the smoking and talking part of the business, his wife managed the indoor concerns, and he was continually poking about the country on a punchy, wall-eyed, weight-carrying old cob (John rode sixteen *stun*, as he pronounced it) looking in at all the farm-houses—where he was an especial favourite—just to see what sort of a colt the last which the old mare threw was likely to turn out; or up at the Hall stables, where his brother was stud groom, to see how the horses were getting on. In fact, he seemed to have the key of every stable in that part of the country; he used to be here, there, and everywhere—and no telling, when you were riding about the little lanes for which our country was noted, but old John and the wall-eyed cob might turn up. His memory was remarkable; he never forgot a horse when he had once seen it, and was certainly an extraordinary judge of horseflesh, insomuch that he became quite notorious; and the Chequers at length became a sort of a registry office for all the horses which were for sale in the neighbourhood. Lucky for the seller if John passed a favourable verdict on his horse as he sat in solemn conclave smoking his pipe on an evening among the parlour company at the Chequers. And if old John once "crabbed" a horse, the sooner he was sent up to Tattersall's or Aldridge's for unreserved sale, the better; for if the fact once got wind, no one on this country side would have looked at him.

John no sooner heard that it was I who had ridden up, than he came waddling into the parlour to hear all the particulars of the day's racing. Bad news travels fast, and although I had left the course within an hour after the race, the intelligence of our horse's defeat had already reached the Chequers. "Sorry to hear the colt," for with some men who know when a horse was foaled he remains a colt for an indefinite period, "got beat to-day," was his greeting as he shook my hand, and "Excuse me, sir, but I think you made a mistake this time—put him into rather too good company. He did not come of a fast sort. Lots of staying and jumping blood in him, but neither dam or sire had ever pace. I knew them both well. Hope you did not get hit very hard, sir," was his oracular disquisition, after I had sketched him the leading features of the race. Then telling me that he would come in and have a bit of chat with me as soon as I had done my supper, he toddled out of the room, evidently fully impressed with the idea that it was the "colt's" lack of pace, and nothing else, that had lost us the race. It appears that Tom, who rode him, thought so too; but then he did not express his opinion quite so mildly.

After supper old John again appeared, bearing in two smoking tumblers of hot brandy-and-water and pipes (*his* "treat," as he observed), and drawing our chairs into the fire, we proceeded to talk over the day's racing, and to canvass the merits and demerits of every horse in the neighbourhood. The fund of horsey lore which the old man possessed was extraordinary.

Towards the close of our *tête-à-tête*, and when I was getting rather yawning—for a man who has been on horseback all day tires at length, even of talking about horses, that most prolific of all sources of conversation—old John observed, that "he thought he knew of a colt which would just suit me, if I could only buy him right."

"Do you?" I carelessly answered; "and where is that?"

The fact is, he had just woke me up out of a brown study, in which I was engaged in drawing up a mental balance-sheet—a kind of profit and loss account between the brown horse and myself—and trying to calculate how many horses it would take to ruin a man of my means, if he was in the habit of bringing them out over and over again to be beaten, as I was just then doing.

"You know Shark's Lodge, up at Holliwell?" inquired he.

"Oh, yes, near the gibbet, where our hounds often meet."

"Well, do you know old Jack Radford, who lives up there?"

"I've seen the old beggar, but I can't say I know much of him; nor do I want, if all I hear is true, for they tell me a rougher, surlier old customer never breathed."

"Yes, he is certainly not very polished, but old Jack's a good sort at bottom, for all that. I've known him many years before ever he came into this country, and I never knew him tell a lie or put a friend in the hole in his life. Now he's got a two-year-old bay colt—will be three this grass—by Mulatto out of his old black mare Plover, that will make a galloper some day or other, or I'm out in my reckoning. Now you take my advice—get rid of this one; he'll only lose you heaps of money. He'll never be fast enough for a steeple-chase, but is just the very horse to carry Charley, the first whip; and he's a good-looking one too. They'll give you all the money you ask for him up at the stables; I've had a little conversation with my brother on the subject. And you take and buy old Jack Radford's colt, and go into leather plating at once. He's as near thorough-bred as Eclipse—for, though the old mare has got a stain, there's not many besides old Jack and myself can tell you where it lies—yet he'll always be a half-bred 'un, and nothing else; and you'll be able to run him for any half-bred stakes in England, when and where you please." He then launched out into a description of the colt, given with the most wonderful accuracy, and after that gave me the performances and pedigree of the old mare Plover in full, pointing out to me exactly where the stain lay, which gave her, as he expressed it, "the long hairs in her pasterns." As he warmed with his subject, I could not help gazing in silent admiration on that wonderful old man, whose head could not only carry a description of some scores of horses, but even their pedigrees in full; and I was just promising him that I would certainly ride over and look at Jack Radford's colt, when our lad came up with the beaten horse, and we both went out to look at him and see him done up for the night; so Mr. Radford's two-year-old was forgotten for that evening. But as I bade old John good-bye next morning, he strictly enjoined me to ride over soon and look at the colt, adding impressively, "Now mind what I say. If you don't buy him the day will come when you'll blame yourself for not taking my word. If you can get him under one hundred he's cheap; but mind, it's no use trying to beat the old man down, for he always asks what he means to take, and nothing else." And, giving me a sly poke in the ribs, he added, with the knowingest wink out of his keen little grey left eye, "There's a *filly* indoors worth double the money, if you could only get her at the price;" and so we parted.

The village of Holliwell was perhaps one of the ugliest and dirtiest in England; and the only redeeming quality which it possessed was, that Holliwell Hangers, one of the best coverts and surest finds in our hunt, lay within its precincts. I don't believe, unless it was to meet the hounds at "Holliwell Gibbet," that any stranger would ever have found his way into this village from one year's end to the other. It was a long, straggling village, situate on the borders of Holliwell Openfield,—a large, unenclosed tract of some thousands of acres of stiff clay ground, and coarse, spongy, undrained grass land, in which the holdings were divided from each other by broad, deep ditches (big enough to hold a man and horse very comfortably), with rotten banks, choked up with briars, coarse grass, and all such other rubbish as a good farmer will never willingly see on his farm.

There was not a tree of any size in the whole parish, excepting the wood, which lay about half a mile on the other side of the village, and a few old elms which stood close into the church, and served in some degree to shelter the parsonage from the biting east wind, which, when it did blow, seemed to expend all its fury upon Holliwell. The village consisted of one long, straggling street, from the wretched hovels on each side of which hang-dog, poaching-looking scoundrels, with the eternal short black pipe in their mouths, and slatternly half-dressed women, would peer out upon the stranger with sullen scowling looks, without ever offering him the slightest recognition of civility which the English labourer usually bestows on his betters. In fact, the village of Holliwell bore the worst repute of any village round us—a nest of sheep-stealers and poachers; and I cannot describe the Holliwell villagers better than in the words of poor Tom Hood:

> "The women—the wretches had soiled and marr'd,
> Whatever to womanly nature belongs.
> For the marriage tie they had no regard;
> And as for drinking, they drank so hard
> That they drank their flat-irons, pokers, and tongs.
> The men, they fought and gambled at fairs,
> And poached, and did not respect grey hairs;
> Stole linen, money, plate, poultry, and corses,
> And broke in houses as well as horses;
> Unfolded folds to kill their own mutton,
> And would sell their own mothers and wives for a button.
> But, not to repeat the deeds they did—
> Backsliding, in spite of each moral skid—
> If all was true that fell from the tongue,
> There was not a villager, old or young,
> But deserved to be whipt, imprisoned, or hung,
> Or sent on those travels which nobody hurries
> To publish at Colburn's, or Longman's, or Murray's."

Of course there was one public-house in the village—" The Five Bells," kept by the village blacksmith, a bloated, blear-eyed, tun-bellied old sinner (in every sense of the word), who was never seen with either coat or hat on, whose highlows were always unlaced, his breeches unbuttoned at the knee, and whose principal occupation appeared to consist in drinking his own ale and smoking a long pipe in the winter by his kitchen fire; in the summer, on the bench in front of his old shanty. Half-way down the street was a kind of dissenting chapel, a little Zion, where an ignorant Chartist shoemaker was wont to expound the Scriptures to a congregation as ignorant and radical as himself, in a style which bordered both on heresy and blasphemy.

The clergyman who looked after the religious welfare of the poor district was a hard-riding, roystering divine of the old school, whose principal boast was " that he was born in the same year with the ' Game Chicken,' and that they were the same weight to a pound;" whose breed of game fowls was unrivalled; who was a capital shot; who could give you the winner and duration of every prize-fight which had taken place during the last thirty years; who could tell you without hesitation the winner of every Derby and Leger since the commencement; and whose sole library consisted of the *Racing Calendar* from the beginning, and some odd volumes of the old *Sporting Magazine*. I attended this old clergyman's sale after his decease, and a more unclerical miscellany I never before saw exposed at any auction. Not that he was altogether a bad clergyman; but, living in such a wild, out-of-the-way place, among such parishioners, he was hardly likely to be any other than what he was. His charity was unbounded; and when any of his sick parishioners chose to send for him, he was ever ready to attend at the dying man's bedside; and although the words of consolation which fell from his lips were uttered in strong language, they were well suited to the rough ears which heard them. His discourses from the pulpit were, however, beautiful; his voice and delivery first-rate; and old Stephen, our huntsman, who once happened to ride over to Holliwell one Sunday morning to see about a young hound at walk, chanced to stroll into the church while the old clergyman was delivering his sermon, and he ever after used to declare that it was worth riding fifty miles only to hear old parson T—— " rally it out" from the pulpit.

The whole village wore a wild and desolate appearance; and even the summer's sun failed to shed any beauty on the bleak, cheerless landscape round Holliwell. In the autumn and winter the roads leading to and from the village were almost impassable; and as to the Openfield—except just in the very height of summer, the water stood in pools in all the rushy furrows and low places; and if by chance a fox broke away from the Hangers across the Openfield, it was "bellows to mend" with a good many before they had got even to the end of it; for a bit of more dangerous or deeper riding was not to be met with in our hunt. But, strange to say, on the other side the Hangers a splendid rich, enclosed, agricultural and hunting country stretched away for miles, and some of the best runs with our hounds were from Holliwell Hangers. Whichever side of the wood the fox broke from, there was sure to be a burning scent; and I have seen the hounds fly over the Holliwell Openfield "heads up and sterns down," and go right away from the horses, which were floundering and squashing, in many places knee-deep, after them. Holliwell Openfield was a noted place for plovers, and thousands of plover eggs were yearly sent away from this spot to the London markets; and if by chance you lost your way coming home from hunting, and wandered after nightfall across this desolate place, the melancholy, never-ceasing cry of the peewit, and the scape of the snipe, as it rose under your horse's very nose, soon told that you were in Holliwell Openfield. But that the land was not altogether incapable of carrying crops, if only properly managed, was proved by the fact that when this Openfield was enclosed and drained some years after the date of my tale, and a new race of men succeeded the original tenants of the soil, not a parish in the country grew better or larger crops of wheat to the acre than this. But at the time I speak of the Openfield was unenclosed, not an acre of it drained, and the land was in the hands of the poorest and slovenliest farmers in England. The best and most laconic description which I ever heard of Holliwell was given by Charley, our first whip, to a gentleman who asked him what place this was as they rode through the village with the hounds one evening after hunting. "Well, I should say it was the last that the Lord built, and the first he forsook."

The words Holliwell Gibbet also gave an awful significance to the place, and told a fearful tale of about as horrid and cold-blooded a deed as was ever perpetrated. The cross-tree of the gibbet had been down for some years, but the old post still remained. The lone cottage by the edge of the wood where the dreadful murder was committed had long since tumbled to decay; but there were old men still alive in the village who well remembered that Sunday afternoon when the young sailor, who had been absent from his home for years, made his appearance once again at Holliwell, and was seen to enter his poor old father's cottage. He had always been a wild reckless youth from his earliest boyhood, and from the day he ran away to sea, a beardless boy, he had never been heard of till he again made his appearance at Holliwell, a weathen-beaten, black-whiskered man. Yet, with all his faults, the old father loved that boy dearly, and wild as he had been—wild as he even still might be —the old man's morning and evening prayer was, that his reprobate son would come back—that he might see him once more, and bless him before he died; and the son did come back, and the old father saw him, and for the last time. The old man owned a little bit of land on the common, kept a cow or two, a few sheep and geese, and even in this wild spot, by a life of hard work and privation, had managed to scrape together a few pounds. These he kept concealed in an old box under his bed; and it was this paltry sum that doubtless cost the old man his life. Towards nightfall the son left the hovel, and next morning the old man was not seen hobbling about the common on his stick, as was his usual wont. A labourer, who by chance passed the cottage soon after daybreak next morning, was horrified at seeing a pool of stagnant blood which had welled its way under the door, and settled in a deep red clot on the stone before it. He broke open the door at once, and there lay the old man stiff and dead on the floor, the back of his head broken in with a hatchet, and his throat cut from ear to ear. The box was open, but no money in it. It is rarely that a murderer does not leave some trace behind him which inevitably leads to his detection, and the young sailor, in the confusion of the moment, had dropped his tobacco-box, which lay by his old father's head, a damning evidence of the son's guilt. The police in those days might not have been so quick as they now are, but they were as sure. The young sailor was traced to Liverpool, where he was taken on board a brig loading for South America, brought back, tried, convicted, and executed, and after that hung in chains in front of the poor old father's cottage, on the green where he had so often played in childish innocence, but which he had now desecrated by the blackest crime of which man can be guilty. Many years have passed away since that deed of blood was perpetrated, but as long as the old gibbet-post stands, the remembrance of it will ever cast a blight over Holliwell.

But barren and uncultivated as the whole district just round the village might be, and rough and uncouth as were its inhabitants, there was not a more desolate spot or a more neglected farm in the whole parish than "Shark's Lodge;" and old Jack Radford, who lived there, was probably the roughest and most uncultivated old fellow in the whole village. The lodge stood so lonely, on a rising ground, without a hill to shelter it from the howling blast; and around it lay the farm of six hundred acres, which, as Charley the whip—who had taken a dreadful spite against Holliwell and all that belonged to it—again observed, might, perhaps, on a dry season, "carry fifty grasshoppers to the acre."

But even up at that desolate lodge were two treasures which one would have little dreamt of seeking in so wild a spot—the old black mare Plover, who was acknowledged by all who had seen her go, some twelve or fifteen years back, to have been the very best hunter that was ever ridden to our hounds, and who was now as good as a fifty-pound annuity to her old owner; and Annie Radford, the old man's daughter ("the filly indoors," to whom John Harrison had alluded), one of the finest women in England, and who was soon afterwards destined to wear a coronet of her own winning. Who or what old Jack Radford originally was I do not believe a man in our parts, save John Harrison, knew, nor did any one care much to inquire. He had migrated to Holliwell from the Yorkshire Wolds some eighteen years before, bringing with him the black mare Plover, then in her prime, and his little daughter Annie, a child of about a year old. It was soon evident to the hard-riding crew, amongst whom he had so promiscuously dropped, that the old man (for although he was scarcely fifty when he came to Holliwell, he looked full sixty, and was never known from the first by any other name than "Old Jack Radford") was as deep in the mysteries of horseflesh as the best of them; and his greatest detractors (for, strange to say, not a man in the hunt or a farmer in the neighbourhood ever liked him from the first) could not help owning that a better seat or hands on a horse they never saw, and that Jack Radford on Plover was harder to beat than any man and horse in the hunt. He owned but one hunter, and consequently rarely showed with the hounds; but he always picked the best meets when he did show, and never went home from a run without having done something to be talked about. The old man's day was before my time, and I never saw him out; but I have been told that it was a treat to see him leading the field over our stiffest country—the old man, with his jockey seat and hands down, sitting as still as if he were part and parcel of his horse, his countenance grim as death, and the old mare stealing along with a low, lurching stride, taking every fence in her line without a mistake and apparently without any exertion. The day was never too long or the country too stiff for old Jack Radford and Plover. But he never boasted or talked about either his own deeds or those of his favourite mare; he was one of the most surly, taciturn men that ever lived, and if he did answer a question, it was in so rough and uncivil a manner that one hardly cared to risk a second rebuff. As years wore on, his manners became even ruder and more unpolished; the old man began to get a little stiff in his joints, and it was really a relief to the whole hunt when at length he turned the old mare up, and was no longer seen at the covert-side. Various were the surmises as to what serious crime was weighing on old Jack Radford's mind, and rendered him so gloomy and taciturn; and Charley, the whip, who was the wit of the kennel, declared "that he must have sold his soul to the devil, or he never dare ride in the reckless manner which he did; or, if the pair of them were really mortal, they must be Dick Turpin and old Black Bess come to life again." From the day he turned the old mare up he became more testy and misanthropical, rarely went off his own farm, was never seen at market, and, if a butcher did want to buy any of his stock he must come to Shark's Lodge himself for that purpose. Now, the old man's farm was not quite so bad as Charley represented it. It was a decent, rough, grazing farm, consisting of large pastures, divided from each other by deep, broad ditches—a capital one for breeding horses on and pasturing young colts. It is true that the land in many places was in very wretched condition, and the herbage coarse and rough; still, in parts, the bottom was good, and many prime beasts were really grazed at Shark's Lodge. There was very little arable land, and as the grazing land was principally fed down by rough colts and bullocks taken in at tack, the old man farmed his land with very little trouble and at very little expense.

I had never exchanged a word, good, bad or indifferent, with the old man, and had never seen either the old mare Plover, or the "filly indoors," though I had heard both of them rapturously spoken of. As for calling at the lodge, no one would ever dream of this, except upon the most urgent business; for, by all accounts, old Radford was more likely to slam the door in your face than ask you to walk in. He was, moreover, a particularly ugly old fellow, with a cadaverous-looking, hatchet-shaped face, cold, bleak, grey eyes, and large projecting front teeth like a rabbit; and Charley used to tell a good tale, that a sailor, who was on the tramp down to Liverpool, happened one day to call at the lodge to ask for a bit of bread. Old Radford spied him from the window, and, bustling to the door, opened it, and bid the man be off, without even giving him a chance of asking for what he wanted. The man went his way out; in less than a quarter of an hour he returned. Old Jack met him again on the threshold, and, holding the door half ajar, went on at the sailor with "Did not I tell you five minutes ago that I never gave anything to vagrants?" "Oh, yes," said the man; "but I did not come to you to beg for anything; I only came back to tell you something I forgot when I was here just now." Old Radford's curiosity was aroused, and still holding the knob of the door in his hand, he asked the man what it was. "Well," said the sailor, "I've been all over the world, and among all kinds of people, but I never before in my life did see such an ugly old —— as you are. I thought you might like to know it. Good-morning, master." Old Cleaver, the butcher, who happened to be in the parlour settling for some beasts, heard the conversation, and he did not forget to retail so good a joke.

The time had now arrived when I must either beard the lion in his den—must pay a visit to Shark's Lodge, see old Jack Radford, and have a look at the "bay colt out of Plover,"—or run the risk of forfeiting the respect of my esteemed friend John Harrison for ever. I had, through his instrumentality, sold my brown horse for eighty guineas to the stables up at the Hall—not, however, for the use of Charley, the first whip: the master taking a fancy to him, he at once went into his private stables, carried him for nearly ten years with the hounds, and never gave him a fall. He always declared that he was the safest as well as the cheapest horse he ever rode. Well, one afternoon, very early in April, I left the hounds running a ringing fox up and down The Hangers, and rode up to Holliwell village. I did not choose to ride up direct to Shark's Lodge, because I felt pretty certain that I should have to tie my horse up to the garden rails while I went in; so I rode up to the Five Bells—where, as the sign-board boasted, there was "excellent accommodation for man and beast." The old blacksmith led my horse into a rude but very warm stable—for it was a thatched hovel, with every crevice and air-hole stopped up with straw; and, throwing an old sack over his loins, I gave him a feed of corn and made him as comfortable as circumstances would allow. I was rather surprised to see that my horse was not the only occupant of the shed, for a large, slashing, bang-tailed black horse, with a peculiarly neat hunting saddle and martingale still on him (the girths having been slackened), was going in at a feed of corn with apparent relish. I did not, however, take much notice of this, for I naturally concluded that he belonged to some one or other who had been out that day with the hounds, and had called to refresh himself and his horse at the Five Bells on his road home from hunting.

I followed the landlord into the house, and in passing through the kitchen, where I stopped to order a rasher or two of bacon and some poached eggs, I had time to observe the company who sat smoking round the fire—and a more villanous lot of scoundrels I never clapped eyes on. Poacher and sheepstealer were as unmistakably branded on every countenance as if the words had been seared in with a red-hot iron. In fact, every man in that kitchen was of the same stamp, and belonged to a set of ruffians who would stick at nothing where plunder was concerned; a set of miscreants—

"Who did not care a ——
For the law or the new police,
And would scruple but little in killing the lamb
If they fancied they wanted the fleece."

And as I looked at the blackened rafters and the dingy old settle by the fireside, I thought if they could only speak, what nice tales of desperate deeds, and deeds of villany which had been planned in that old kitchen, they could tell us of.

The old blacksmith showed me into the parlour—a dull, dark, dirty little room, the walls of which were decorated with rudely-drawn, highly-coloured scriptural pictures, among the most extraordinary of which was old Noah coming out of the ark in *top boots*. It is very strange—and I never could make out why—but I have invariably remarked that you always see scriptural pieces suspended from the walls of rooms where you would least expect to find them. Fancy that old blacksmith leaving his kitchen company, whose conversation was made up of the most blasphemous oaths and dark allusions to the most desperate crimes, and going into his parlour to gaze upon a representation of our first parents in their original innocence, or the birth of the infant Saviour! In this room, before the fire, with his chair on the tilt and his feet cocked up on each side of the grate, in true Yankee fashion, sat the owner of the black horse, smoking a cigar and drinking a tumbler of thick, muddy-coloured brandy-and-water. We looked each other over at the same moment. It was not a long survey—something like the glance which a detective throws over a chap whom he fancies "is wanted;" but that survey, short as it might be, was sufficient instinctively to tell each of us that the other was "a party concerned about horses," and, with a touch of the freemasonry which characterizes the craft, he drew his chair a little on one side to make room for me at the fire (for April at Holliwell was like February in any other part of the county), and glancing at my dirty top boots and splashed appearance, he opened the ball with " Any sport to-day, sir ?" I sat down by the fire, informed him what we had done, and a desultory conversation on horses, hunters, and the like took place, during which I had a good opportunity of taking stock of my new acquaintance. He was a peculiarly neat, dapper, good-looking little fellow, with an eye and beak like an eagle's; crisp curly hair and whiskers, both neatly trimmed, as if the singeing-lamp had been slightly passed over them, and both sparingly powdered with grey; wiry, but slightly built, and whose riding-weight out of the saddle would not much exceed nine stone. He was dressed in the orthodox sporting style of the day, long-waisted pepper-and-salt single-breasted cutaway, looped up in front with two fox's teeth ; long-waistcoat to match ; tight-fitting drab trowsers, roomy in the seat but tight at the bottom, stitched and strapped all over in a most mysterious fashion ; and remarkably neat round-toed Wellingtons. His scarf was white worsted with black-currant spots, fixed in front with a large plain gold horse-shoe pin. His *very* straight-brimmed hat stood on the table, and a plain Molucca hunting cross and a pair of well-worn dog-skin gloves lay by its side. There was no mistake about this man ; the stable, and nothing but the stable, was his vocation; but whether he was a steeple-chase rider, a swell horse-dealer, kidman (I could tell somehow or other that he was not a regular horse-dealer), or stud-groom, I could not for the life of me guess. I could see at once he was not a gentleman; and he certainly did not belong to the hard-riding crew of blackcoats that followed our hounds. He was a stranger; and I could never call to mind having seen him out in our country. He had clearly not been out with the hounds that day—the drab trowsers and Wellingtons plainly told that; but who or what he was, or what possible business such a dapper little man could have in the frowsy old parlour of the Five Bells at Holliwell, was a mystery which I was most anxious to solve. He had hardly a speck of dirt on his well-polished Wellingtons. I ventured to remark this; and his reply soon told me all about the man and his business. "Well," he said, "in general I do manage to ride pretty clean; but the roads were good enough till I came over the north road and got into this God-forgotten country."

"Have you ridden far?" I asked.

"Oh, about fifteen miles, from —— (mentioning our county town, where there were cavalry barracks). The fact is *my chap* was out with your hounds about a fortnight ago, and he heard of a colt in this very place which they told him was a well-bred 'un, and he thought it might make a charger, and, perhaps, win our Cavalry Cup in the autumn, so he sent me over to look at him. My name's Turner, his stud-groom."

"And who is *your chap?*" I inquired.

"Oh, Captain C., of the ——," he answered: "you must have seen him out with your hounds."

I certainly had seen the captain out with our hounds; and, moreover, I owed him a bit of a grudge for a little circumstance which took place a short time before—no doubt on the very day that he had heard of "the bay colt out of Plover." The captain and I were *riding at* each other, and, as far as our horses went, we were pretty equally matched; but, as for riding, I could not hold a candle to the captain, who was one of the crack gentlemen jocks of the day. We had got a little out of our line, and found ourselves alone in a large grass pasture surrounded by a bullfinch, through no part of which any horse in the world could possibly force his way. There were but two really practicable places in the whole line of fence—the gate over which we had come into the field, and four stiffish rails in the corner, under a haystack, out of it. I knew this field well, for I had once been pounded here before. The captain had the gate first, and, without turning to see me come over, he sent his horse on at a thundering pace down a straight dry ride, evidently meaning to have the bullfinch at the bottom. As soon as I was over the gate I slanted my horse to the right for the rails in the corner, as I knew that was the only way out of the field. Of course by this I lost ground, but I was not half-way across the field before I saw the captain take a pull at his horse: he was now evidently watching me, and I fancy, even at that distance, did not half like the looks of the bullfinch which stared him in the face. I went hand-over-hand at the rails, which the captain had now spied, and turning his horse towards me, we raced down to them. The old swarth was sound, and capital galloping. I got to them first, and catching my horse tight by the head, was just beginning to drive at them, when he suddenly shied at a boy who at that very minute rose from the bottom of the haystack, where he had been lying. The horse, however, could not balk the rails altogether, but he rose too near, and breasting them, we came over into the next field all in a heap; and as I lay on my back—to use a favourite phrase of my poor old friend Tom Heycock—" I had an excellent opportunity of seeing the sun, moon, and stars in full illumination." The horse was a good deal shaken, for I was up first. I was not stunned, although very " dizzy like ;" for I remember as I lay the captain cleared the rails gallantly to my right, and his derisive laugh as he went sailing on to catch the hounds, which were now turning again towards us, did not improve my temper, which was already rather ruffled by the fall. I picked myself together as well as I could, and got the horse on his legs; he was so lame in the shoulder that he could scarcely go. Luckily we were close to a farm lodge, and I knew the farmer who lived there well, so I led my horse up, left him there, rode home on an old pony I borrowed of him, and sent a man next morning to bring home my horse. I owed the captain one for his civility; and the thought immediately flashed across my mind that I could not get rid of my obligation in a better way than by buying the " bay colt by Plover" over his head if it were possible.

So I asked the groom rather anxiously, but as unconcernedly as I could, " Have you seen the colt?"

" Yes, and I never in my life saw such an old ruffian as the farmer who owns him," was the reply.

" What did you think of the colt—did you buy him?" was my next question.

" Well, he's not a bad like colt," answered the groom, taking a long pull at his cigar; " and he looks all over like galloping; stands on rather short legs, but covers a deal of ground; looks like flying with about nine stone up, but he'll never carry my chap; he rides eleven stone, and is about as hard on a horse as a man can be. Besides, the colt is a little light below the knee. However, he's good enough to win our cup, even with the captain up, among the lot of muffs he'll have to meet; and even if he can't do that he'll make a sweet park hack or a ladies' horse,—and my chap knows where to place him if it comes to that. It won't be the first one we've given away from our stud to a favourite."

" Well, but did you buy him?" I again asked, waiting anxiously for his reply.

" Why, no, I have not bought him yet. The fact is, the old chap as owns him wants eighty for him, and it seems the captain knows that. So he just gives me a cheque for that sum, and tells me to buy the colt if I liked him. Now, it's not very likely I mean to buy without standing in; but as for getting a ten-pound note out of this pig-headed old clodhopper, that's no go. I showed him the cheque, and told him very plainly that the sale of the colt was in my hands, and that if I gave up the cheque I should expect ten pounds out of it from him when the colt was delivered. If my chap had never heard anything about the price I could have made a good thing of it, for the colt looks a hundred and fifty all over; and, what's more, he's worth it, too," added the groom, viciously poking the dead coals on the top of the fire with the toe of his boot.

"What did the old chap say when you asked him for the tenner back?" I then inquired.

"Why, I thought he'd have pitched into me with a hayfork he had in his hand. He just walked out of the box, held the door in hand till I had followed him out, then locked it, and walked up to the house without saying another word—never asking me in, nor even so much as bidding me good-day. I never did see such an old ruffian in all my life. I wonder whether they breed them all like him in these parts; and yet the old boy knows a horse well, too," added the groom apologetically—as if that circumstance would cover a multitude of sins.

"What shall you do now?" I next asked.

"Why, I shall call on my road home and buy the colt, and see if I can work anything out of the old fellow. I must have the colt, for my chap seems to have set his mind on him. I'll just wait an hour to let the old boy get over his temper; but I must be out of this one-eyed place by daylight, so that I can get on to the north road before the sun goes down."

It was now two o'clock. I had learned all I wanted to know, and it struck me rather forcibly that unless the groom looked pretty sharp, the bay colt by Plover was not very likely ever to carry one of the captain's favourites as a park hack.

Our conversation was now interrupted by the entrance of my poached eggs and bacon. While I was discussing them my friend sat by the fire cursing things in general, especially our country and the state of the roads; wondering whoever could have been fool enough to think of placing a village where Holliwell stood; and anathematizing all masters who interfered in the buying of their horses without first consulting their stud-grooms. "What the devil is the use of a man having a stud-groom," he fiercely asked me, "if he knows as much about a horse himself?"

Of course I never hinted that I was on the same errand as he was, and as soon as ever I had bolted my dinner I rose, and, bidding him good-by, saying that I had a tired horse and a longish way to ride home, I walked into the yard, jumped on to my horse, and rode straight up to Shark's Lodge.

Old Radford was leaning over the garden-gate as I rode up, looking about as vicious as ever I saw a man in my life. I knew my customer, so determined to be as rough with him as I was sure he would be with me.

As I pulled up at the gate his first shot was not encouraging.

"Now, what do *youre* want?" (in broad Yorkshire.)

"I want to see old Jack Radford," I roared out at the top of my voice. I have invariably found that nothing discomposes these sort of customers so much as shouting at them.

"And what do you want with 'old Jack Radford?' as you call him."

"I want to see him," I again shouted.

"Well, you can see him now, for I'm old Jack Radford; but I aint deaf."

"Oh, you're old Jack Radford, are you? I should not have thought it. Well, I want to buy your bay colt;" and I jumped off my horse, and proceeded to tie him up by the bridle to the garden-gate.

Had I treated the old man with deference and civility I should probably never have seen the colt; but he now seemed to regard me as one of his own kidney, and opened the garden-gate with "What are you doing now—do you think we aint got no stabling here?" I thereupon led the horse through, and followed the old fellow to the stables, which were at the bottom of the garden, and were the only part of the premises that seemed to be in tolerable repair.

As soon as I had tied my horse up, the old man threw open the door of the loose-box, and our bargain was closed in less than three minutes, after this fashion—

"Now, there's the colt."

I did not care to look him over; I meant buying. I knew old John Harrison would not deceive me, and I had not forgotten what the stud-groom had said about his value. So I merely asked, " What's his price ?"

" Eighty," was the curt reply.

" Guineas or pounds ?"

" It was guineas last winter, but I'll take pounds now. I've got another coming on, and one's as much as I can look after now."

" I'll have him," I said. " I suppose you warrant him ?"

" Yes; he's never had anything the matter with him in his life that I know on."

We left the stable without another word; and this is how the bay colt out of Plover became mine at exactly the same price I had got for my brown horse.

On the road up to the house—for the old fellow was obliged to ask me in to settle—I told him I supposed it would do if I gave him ten pounds to bind the bargain, and left my cheque for the remainder, which I would cash the next day when the colt was delivered. He was perfectly satisfied. We had now reached the back door, and he pushed me into his kitchen, with " Never mind your boots," seeing that I was looking about for a scraper or mat to rub them on. We walked through the kitchen into the little parlour beyond, in which sat two persons who deserve a passing notice. The one was a slim, handsome, pale-faced young man of about twenty, who sat propped up by pillows in an easy-chair before the fire, his head bandaged up, and his right arm in splints and a sling. The other was a girl about nineteen, who was sitting working at a small table by the window. The room was neat and clean enough, giving evidence of a woman's care; the furniture massive, old-fashioned, and simple; and the only ornaments in the room were a vase filled with violets, primroses, and snowdrops on the table, and a portrait of old Plover suspended over the mantel-piece. An open piano stood at the end of the room. All these I took in at a glance.

The old man introduced me thus: "Here, Annie, here's a —I do believe he was very nearly saying gentleman, but he checked himself—*party* as has come and bought the bay colt."

"Has he?" quietly remarked the girl, in a tone that indicated neither interest nor surprise; and, rising from her seat, she made me a kind of half-bow, half-curtsey, in a style which I never saw beaten amongst the highest-bred ones, and drawing herself up to her full height, regarded me with a fixed stare, so steady, so long, and so searching, that I was almost tempted to ask her if she thought she should know me if she saw me again—when the old man turned to the door, and calling to her with a rude, "Here, gal," she followed him, and swept out of the room with the air of a Mrs. Siddons.

Whether or not she would have known me again was of little moment; but I'll swear that only from the parting glimpse which I obtained of that woman, I should have known her again among a thousand. The first glance of Annie Radford left an impression upon my mind which years could not eradicate. I was so taken by surprise—so thunderstruck with her surpassing beauty, which flashed so suddenly upon me—that for the moment I forgot where I was, and stood vacantly gazing at the door out of which she had just passed, as if I fancied I could see her through it; and I was only aroused from my reverie by the sick man asking me, in a faint, mild tone, "So, you've bought our bay colt, have you, sir?"

I am not an adept at describing female beauty; and I very much question whether any pen, however good, could do justice to Annie Radford. Tall and exquisitely formed, with a rich, clear olive complexion, dark as that of any Spaniard; large, full, languishing blue eyes, and hair as black and glossy as the raven's wing. Her features were as regular and as faultless as her form; and there was a look of determination about her beautiful mouth and her sharp, clearly-chiselled chin, which said that if once she got the upper hand of a man, she would be very likely to keep it, and a proud, haughty bearing about the whole woman, which plainly told that she would be able to hold her own among any company. Her hair was simply parted on each side of her temples, and plaited behind in a long, thin braid, which reached nearly down to her waist. A little bunch of snowdrops was carelessly stuck in on one side of her temples, as if by their pure white contrast to set off the deep purple gloss of her hair. She was dressed in a plain black silk dress, the bodice of which fitted tightly over a magnificent bust, that any sculptor might have longed to model; and a kind of small black velvet mantilla was thrown loosely over beautiful shoulders.

A horsey old friend of ours used to observe that if he was in the habit of buying women, as he did his horses, and was not quite certain about their pedigrees, he should look only for three points, which would be certain to indicate their breeding—the ear, the ankle, and the hand. He did not put the least faith in the face. for, as he said, you just as often saw a pretty face on a dairy-maid as a duchess; but the small ear, the long tapering hand, and the clean, well-turned ankle, were only to be met with among the "high-bred ones." These three points were perfection in Annie Radford, for I criticised them all pretty closely when she returned to the parlour shortly after, bringing in a tray, on which was set out a very nice little lunch. The hand and ankle were both superb, but they were nothing in comparison to her beautiful little ear. It was so pink and transparent that it reminded one of a delicate little pink shell. I know this simile is a very stale one, but I can find no better. I fancy that I have read somewhere that our great great-grandmothers—who, by the way, appear to have been for the most part arrant coquettes—were in the habit of presenting the tips of their ears for their favourites to kiss. Had Annie only lived in those days, how the old powdered pig-tailed beaux would have contested for a kiss at that delicate little ear! I certainly never had seen that girl's equal before. As we sat at lunch, I looked first at old Radford, then at Annie: I could not see the slightest resemblance between them in any one respect; and I mentally offered to lay 100 to 20 that old Jack Radford was no more Annie's father than that he was mine. I should have won if I had laid, for not long after I learnt both their histories from John Harrison, who appearer to have known old Jack some twenty years before, when he kept a small roadside inn, somewhere up in Yorkshire, and Harrison drove one of the north country coaches that changed at his door; and I will tell the tale as it was told to me.

Annie's mother, the only child of one of the oldest and proudest houses in the county, when a lovely girl of eighteen, eloped from her father's house with a man whom she dearly loved—her inferior in birth, it was true, but her equal in every other respect—whose only fault consisted in his poverty. Six weeks after their marriage, they both wrote to the father, praying for his forgiveness. That father was a stern, unforgiving old man, and the reply he wrote to his daughter's letter was, that as she had made her bed, so might she lie upon it; and, enclosing a cheque for one hundred pounds, told her that he had now done with her for ever, and that the letter he was now writing, was the last communication he would hold with her in this world. And he kept his word. Two more letters which the daughter wrote to him were returned unopened, and the poor girl had not the heart to write another. Her husband, who had unfortunately been brought up to no profession, but who had been maintained by an old uncle, who was believed to be rich, now applied to that uncle for assistance. He was a great speculator in railways, and such like. Just at that time a panic occurred among all the speculators in England. Shares fell, the old man became a bankrupt, and was obliged to retire to the continent, where he lived for a few years upon a slender pittance doled out to him by his creditors.

After they were married, the young couple went up to London, where the husband managed to eke out a slender subsistence, sometimes as amanuensis, sometimes as contributor to the daily papers. The poor girl was devotedly attached to her husband, and although the privations which she had to undergo were such as she had been little used to, she never complained. Two years after the marriage little Annie was born, and six months after her birth, the poor father, who had never been a strong man, and who was ill fitted to stand against the troubles which pressed so heavily on him, died. The poor girl—for she was scarcely anything else—was thus thrown upon the wide world without a friend to assist her, and almost penniless. She resolved once more to seek her father, and endeavour to enlist his sympathies—if not for herself, at least on behalf of her infant daughter. She travelled down into Yorkshire by the very coach which Harrison drove.

Old Jack Radford, who had been a groom in her father's stables for nearly twenty years, had left the service, and, marrying an old female servant at the Hall, who had nursed Annie's mother in her infancy, had taken the little roadside inn which he then kept. The only faults that could be brought against Jack Radford were his ugliness, his short crusty temper towards men (no man, however, could be kinder with his horses, and many a vicious savage brute which had been turned out of the breaker's hands as incurable, succumbed to his gentle treatment), and his rude, uncultivated manners, which even a five-and-twenty years' servitude and connexion with gentlemen could not tone down. He had been brought up in a racing-stable—so there is little wonder that he could ride; and, when we add that he was a thorough-bred Yorkshireman, we need hardly say that he was a consummate judge of a horse. He was as good a groom as ever strapped a horse, as honest as the day, and a trusty, faithful, and attached servant in his own rough way. His public was just six miles from the Hall gates, and here the poor girl alighted with her little daughter, one dark, cheerless November evening. She had not the courage to go straight to her father's door. It is needless to say that she was received as a daughter both by Jack Radford and his wife, who had both known her from her childhood.

The next morning Jack took a letter from her up to the Hall. He did not see the old father; but in about half-an-hour he received an answer, which he was commissioned to deliver to the poor girl. He rode home with a light heart, for, from what he could gather in the servants' hall, he was led to believe that the old man was becoming more reconciled to his daughter. He delivered the letter himself into the poor girl's hands, and, with the freedom of an old domestic, remained in the room while she read it. But had he only guessed the contents of that unnatural letter, he would not have delivered it for untold gold; for it was filled with the most bitter invectives and unkind reproaches, and there was not one single sentence in it which carried the slightest ray of hope to the poor girl's blighted heart. But she read every sentence of it from end to end, and, although her eyes were dimmed with tears, not one word in that fatal letter escaped them. When she had finished it, she stood for some moments with compressed lips and heaving bosom, motionless as a statue, gazing on little Annie, who was lying fast asleep on the bed, when all at once the letter dropped from her hand, and lifting her beautiful eyes to heaven, she uttered this simple and heartfelt prayer: "O God, protect my little Annie, for I have no power to help her!" and sank upon the bed in a swoon. And God heard her prayer, for her child's protector stood there by her side; and that simple, honest groom vowed at the moment that if anything happened to the mother, he would be a father to the child, and he religiously kept his vow.

Nobody liked Jack Radford; his appearance was unprepossessing, his manner repulsive, and no one cared to probe beneath that rude surface. Had any one done so, he would have found as kind and true a heart as ever beat, and a religious probity of feeling which would have done honour to the noblest in the land.

The swoon was succeeded by the most violent hysterics, which lasted for some time, when suddenly she became tranquil. But it was only the lull that precedes the coming storm. Radford and his wife stood by the bedside watching her, when all of a sudden they perceived that the pillow on which her fair cheek rested was saturated with blood. In the violence of her paroxysms the poor girl had burst a blood-vessel. No human power could stay that welling tide, and in less than ten minutes the young mother lay a corpse by the side of her infant daughter.

Radford immediately galloped over to the Hall that he might himself break the sad intelligence to the father. He sent up word to the old man that he wished to speak to him on the most important business, and the answer which he received was that he might send up any message he had to deliver by the footman. Jack's patience was now fairly exhausted, and bursting out with, "Then tell the old man that dear Miss Annie (Annie was also the mother's name) is now lying dead up at my house;" and, wiping away a tear which trickled down his rugged cheek—the first he had ever been known to shed—he left the servants' hall, and went round to the stables for his horse.

The servant went upstairs and delivered the message exactly in Radford's own words. When he entered the study, the old father was walking to and fro, a rigid, gloomy frown spread over his whole countenance, and his breast torn with the fiercest of all human conflicts—a struggle between affection and pride. It is probable that in a short time nature would have asserted her sway, and the old man would have eventually become reconciled to his daughter; but his pride would not allow him to make the concession too freely —and behold the results! When the man delivered the message, he watched the old father's countenance anxiously, to see what would be the effect of it; but he watched in vain, for not a muscle of that iron face moved—not the slightest change came over those gloomy features. He stopped in his walk, looked the servant full in the face, and the only remark he made was in a tone of thunder, "Send Radford up to me." Radford had not left the stables, and in five minutes was closeted with the old father in his study. The interview was a brief one, and all that Radford said when he returned to the servants' hall was this, "I always thought that the old man had the hardest nerve of any man in the county, but I never *knew* it before to-day."

That evening the body was conveyed over to the Hall in a hearse; a few days after it was buried in the family vault, and the dark hatchment frowned over the massive old doorway at the Hall. The last time that hatchment was up was when his poor child's mother had died in giving her birth. Since then his wife had lived to him in the image of his daughter. She was now lost to him for ever, and his own cursed pride had made him what he now was, and must remain to the end of his life—a broken-hearted, childless, and lonely old man. The little orphan was left in charge of Radford's wife. From the day that his daughter's corpse entered the Hall until the day of the funeral, the old father never left his study by day, and was seen by no one save the servant who carried him up his solitary meals. But at nightfall he would steal to the room where his dead daughter lay, and sit for hours gazing on those calm, lovely features, whose beauty even the hand of death had no power to mar. He and Radford were the only mourners who attended the funeral; and as they walked after the corpse to the little village church (for he would have no vain display), Jack could scarcely believe it possible that six short days could have wrought so great a change in any man. Instead of the tall, great, iron-framed man, which he was but a week ago, he was now only a shattered, tottering wreck of his former self, and the agony of mind which he had suffered during that period, appeared to have added twenty years to his life. After the funeral, he called Radford into the study, and warning him that it was the last time that his daughter's name should ever pass his lips, gave him a cheque for three thousand pounds. With one thousand of this Jack was to leave the neighbourhood, taking the little Annie with him, and settle on a farm in a distant county; the other two thousand were to be invested, and the interest applied towards the maintenance of the child till she came of age, when the principal was to be paid over to her. No persuasion could ever induce him to see his dead daughter's child.

Jack happened to hear of this farm at Holliwell, and as he was always of a reserved misanthropical turn, the locality just suited him. He took it on a twenty-one years' lease, renewable at the end of the term, and left Yorkshire at once with his wife and little Annie. He had no children of his own, and therefore took a double pleasure and pride in the rearing of his little ward. His old master, at the time Jack lived with him, was one of the hardest and boldest men across country, but he never saw the hounds again after his daughter's death. The day before Radford left he sent for him and gave him the choice of two of the best horses in his stable. Radford chose an old brood mare and the black mare Plover, then rising four years old.

The old father did not long survive his daughter, although he never by deed or word gave the slightest outward indication that remorse for his past conduct was silently wearing him out. The canker was gnawing at his heart, and in less than twelve months the family vault received another guest, and the old man slept side by side with his once loved daughter. Had he but listened to the voice of affection instead of that of pride, both father and daughter would still have been alive and happy, and the close of the old man's life might have been cheered by the love and kindness of a child, who, save by an imprudent marriage—how coldly and devoid of all affection does this hacknied phrase sound—had never given him an hour's uneasiness in her life. The estates were strictly entailed, and as the old man had always lived pretty well up to his income, he left but little personal property. All he had he bequeathed to his nephew, a captain in the Royal Navy, who succeeded to the estates.

Radford never had any communication with this gentleman; and the sad tale of Annie's mother, like other events in this world, by degrees became forgotten. Neither Radford nor his wife ever breathed the slightest hint to Annie that she was anything but their own daughter, and the little girl, in whose veins some of the best and oldest blood in England flowed, grew up and thrived in the rude district to which she had been transported under the fostering care of the old groom and his wife, as wild and unrestrained as any one of the colts which roamed over its rugged pastures. Had she been their own daughter, the worthy old couple could not have treated her more kindly. No one was allowed even to say an unkind word to Annie, who did exactly as she pleased at the Lodge. Old Radford's wife died when Annie was twelve years of age, and the old man, who determined scrupulously to fulfil the sacred trust which he had undertaken, took little Annie up to London, and placed her at one of the best ladies' boarding-schools which he could

x

find. It was a sorrowful day both for the old man and the girl when she left the Lodge, and her letters, which she used regularly to write once a month, plainly showed that she pined after her rude country home. She, however, soon became more reconciled. She was a girl of extraordinary parts; no task was too hard for her to master, for she possessed a spirit of determination which could surmount every obstacle. Years passed quickly on; her term of schooling had expired, and she returned once more to the freedom of a country life, which she had never forgotten. Old Radford met the coach which brought her home, and he could scarcely believe that the splendid, handsomely-dressed young woman who sprang out of it with the light step of a fawn was his "little Annie," whom he remembered only as a rompish, curly-haired little girl, whose sole delight was in playing with the old Newfoundland dog Nero, or scampering over the common on a pony as wild and untutored as herself.

Annie had been home from school some time previous to the day on which I saw her first, and although only nineteen, her face and figure had fully ripened into all the charms of mature womanhood. We have not quite done with Annie yet; but as the reader may probably like to change the subject for a while, we will return to the invalid who sat by the fire, and who had broken my reverie by the simple question, "So, you've bought our bay colt, have you, sir?"

To the invalid's inquiry whether I had bought the bay colt, I replied "Yes;" and drawing a chair close to the fire, I seated myself by his side.

"And what do you mean doing with him, sir?" asked the young man.

"Well, I did think of giving him a summer's run, getting him fit by autumn, riding him a bit with the hounds, and, if his pace is pretty good, putting him into a steeple-chase or hurdle-race. His breed ought to pull him through."

"Yes, he's well bred enough, if it comes to that; and if he only turns out as good as the old mare, you need not be afraid of anything on this country side. But I'll tell you what," observed the young man, shifting himself uneasily in his chair, "I've had the schooling of that colt, and a sweeter colt I never wish to ride—a lady could ride him in a pack-thread (I directly thought of the captain and his favourites). He's got lots of pace, and can fly for a mile and a half with about nine stone on his back, and I don't think there are many half-bred uns that can live with him at that distance. He's certain to make a hurdle-racer, for that's just his distance, and he can take a hurdle almost in his stride. He's as quick on his legs as a cat. But somehow or other I don't think that he'll ever make a steeple-chaser, for whenever I put him at a big fence he rises just as if his fore-legs were tied. I've got to thank him for this," observed the youth, pointing to his bandaged arm. "I will, however, say one thing—it's the only fall he's ever given me. But it was a rum un. However, it was perhaps more my fault than his, for it was a gate he fell at, and he was nearly pumped before he came to it. Still, I never fancy he'll have substance enough for a steeple-chaser, and if I was you, sir, I'd keep him for hurdle-racing or the flat. However, I dare say you know best, for I don't suppose you'd have bought him if you did not know what to do with him," and the sick man leaned back in his chair as if the exertion of speaking was too much for him.

"I wonder you never sold him before, for he's a very taking colt," I observed, after a pause.

"Did you look at his near hock?" he asked.

"No," I replied; "I did not care much to examine the colt very closely. I bought him entirely on old John Robinson's recommendation, and I'm quite sure that he'd never deceive me."

"No, that I'm sure he never would," observed the young man; "but, as I was a-saying, that hock has always 'crabbed' the colt. We could have sold him for a hundred and twenty in the autumn, but Mr. Hawthorn—you know him, sir, the veterinary surgeon—refused to pass him, that hock looks so curby; but take my word, sir, there's nothing in it. He was foaled just so, and I've always remarked that these sort of hocks stand the longest, if the colt is foaled with them. No; if he should ever spring a curb it wont be in that hock, you may lay your life."

Our conversation was interrupted by the appearance of Annie with our lunch.

Directly she had set this out, she proceeded to make the invalid comfortable by adjusting his pillows, and by other little attentions, which she performed with all the dexterity and care of a professional nurse, and when she affectionately patted him on the head after she had finished, saying "Poor Frank!" as she did so, I regarded it as *une affaire finie* between the two, and for the moment felt quite jealous of the poor sick rough-rider.

But had I known all, I should have been much more inclined to pity than to envy that young man; for the pain of body which he was then suffering was nothing compared to the agony of his mind, devoured as it just then was with the heartburning passion for a girl whom his instinct told him was as heartless a coquette as ever lived, and whom he yet could not help loving. It appeared that he was in some distant manner connected with old Radford, and, like Annie, was an orphan; but, unlike her, a penniless one. The old man had given him a home at the Lodge, and in return he looked after the horses, broke in the colts, and made himself generally useful about those hundred and one odd jobs which are always to be done in every stable, although perhaps not absolutely necessary, and which never seem to fall into the regular routine of any man's business in the yard. We used to call such fellows in my day "odd men." Frank had been well brought up; his father had been a respectable Yorkshire farmer; he had received a tolerable education, but the taste for horses which was inherent in him led him to choose the life which he was now leading. He had been at the Lodge two years before Annie returned home from school; and up to that time there was not a more careless or lighter-hearted young fellow in the county. He was an exceedingly fresh, clean-looking, handsome young fellow; a capital rider, with an excellent nerve and pluck; and during the season could always manage to earn fifteen shillings to a pound per day by riding young horses to the hounds.

He was also a nice weight, a very tolerable race-rider considering the practice he got, and had won more than one steeple-chase in our county.

To be under the same roof with Annie Radford and not to love her was an impossibility; and as the young rough-rider never dreamt that there was any difference in their positions, and, moreover, as he felt confident that he could always fight his way in the world, and considered that what little property old Radford had saved would eventually become Annie's, he did not deem it in the least preposterous to aspire to her hand. It is true that she had received a superior education, but at home she took the entire management of the house; and although she felt that a drawing-room was her proper place, she never gave herself airs. The consequence was, that Frank soon fell desperately in love with Annie; and the worst of all was, that the girl encouraged his passion, well knowing at the time that she never meant to marry him, but merely to indulge that passion as a passing whim. He consulted with the old father, who neither favoured nor discouraged his suit, merely telling him that Annie might do exactly as she pleased, for that she was quite able to take care of herself—and so she was, as the sequel will prove.

It was impossible for a girl to be so surpassingly beautiful as Annie without knowing it herself, and the flatteries which she had received from her schoolfellows, among whom she was unanimously voted the belle, had influenced her mind; while a compliment which had been paid her by a foolish old fellow in London, who told her that "she was handsome enough to be a countess," was never forgotten. From that time she had made up her mind "to fly at high game;" and while she was playing fast-and-loose with the poor horsebreaker, she was only biding her time and waiting quietly for the fulfilment of the old gentleman's compliment; and she brought it about in this manner—and as we shall only see Annie on the stage once more, we may as well anticipate a little and finish up with her history.

Now, counts and lords do not usually go poking about into such out-of-the-way places as Holliwell to seek their mates; and Annie instinctively felt that the first act to be played out in the drama was to leave the old Lodge, and come out into the world and show herself. Although a heartless coquette, Annie was an affectionate girl where she took a liking; and it was not without a pang that she made up her mind to quit the old Lodge for ever. Rough as old Jack Radford might be, he had been always kind to her. He was in her firm belief her father; and, as Sam Slick says, "this is a large word when it's spelt in big letters." She had, moreover, conceived a romantic affection for the wild district in which she had been reared; and had it not been for her ambition and love of admiration, would, no doubt, very willingly have taken Frank for a husband—although the odds are that she would soon have broken his heart afterwards. However, she felt that she had a destiny to fulfil, and she set about her task just as we should expect a woman of her determined character would do.

One evening, about a week after the day on which I had bought the bay colt, Annie and the young rough-rider were sitting by the fire alone. Old Radford, who was rather unwell, had retired to bed early. The young man sat, as usual, propped up in his chair, and Annie sat on an ottoman at his feet, her beautiful head resting on his knee. He had been pleading for her love with more than usual earnestness, and the girl, whose manner towards him appeared of late to have undergone a complete change, treated him with more genuine affection on that evening than she had ever done before. One of her hands was clasped in his, and as she looked up into his face her countenance was tinged with a tender melancholy, and there was a softened expression of pity in her deep blue eye. Beautiful as he had always thought her, she never appeared in his eyes half so beautiful as on that sad evening. They sat thus for perhaps ten minutes without speaking a word, when she suddenly rose, and gently disengaging her hand from his, she kissed him on the forehead and bade him good-night in these words, which he never afterwards forgot: " Good-by, Frank; God bless you! You'll never forget your poor Annie." She gave him no chance for a reply, but hurriedly left the parlour. This was the last time he ever saw her as Annie Radford.

She went straight up to her bedroom, where she had already packed up a small trunk; wrote a hasty note to old Radford, which she left upon the table, and in which she told him that she was going up to London to get a situation as governess, and could not trust herself to say good-by, but that he would soon hear from her again, and then went down to the kitchen to wake up the farm servant whom she had engaged to wait upon her. Poor Frank was tossing uneasily on his feverish bed; old Radford was snoring in his ancient four-poster; the whole house was still—and at ten she silently stole out at the back door, accompanied by the lad who carried her trunk and Nero, the Newfoundland dog, who never left his favourite mistress's side. They took a short cut across the fields into the lane which led up to the north road, about four miles distant, and by the top of which one of the night coaches up to London would pass about twelve o'clock.

The night was still and fine, the moon was riding high in the clear blue heavens, and even the bleak cheerless tract round Holliwell wore a mild and mellow aspect under the soft influence of her silvery rays. But the wayward girl heeded not this. She felt a choking sensation at her breast, her breath came quick, and her heart throbbed as though it would burst from its confinement; but she neither stopped nor turned till they came to the top of a little hill on the farther edge of old Radford's farm, from which she must take her last look at the old Lodge, or see it no more. Here she stopped, and turning round, gazed earnestly for some minutes on the wide open prospect which lay stretched out below her. Every distant object was nearly as visible as by day, and as her eye wandered vacantly over the little village which now lay so quietly at her feet, the memories of her early childhood rushed with full force across her mind. But there was one well-known spot endeared to her by a thousand fond recollections, upon which her dimmed eyes rested longer than upon any other; it was the old farm Lodge, where the only true friends she had ever possessed in this world resided. Her eyes seemed riveted upon the old house, which the bright rays of the moon had now brought out into full relief, and which she was now leaving for ever.

> She saw the white cottage, the garden she made,
> And she thought of the lover, forsaken, betrayed!

Her resolution all at once gave way, and her long-pent-up feelings found relief in a violent burst of tears.

But her courage soon returned, and again she nerved herself for the task she had undertaken. They reached the north road in good time, and had to wait a little while under the sign-post before the rattling of wheels and the cheery twang of the horn (for the turnpike was just ahead) announced the approach of the old Highflyer.

"Any room inside?" shouted the lad, as the coach pulled up.

"Plenty," was the laconic reply of the jolly old guard, as he swung himself down from his perch behind to open the coach door. "Here, jump in, miss;" for the old fellow, who was not insensible to the charms of a pretty face, had already made out, by the aid of the moon's rays, that she was both young and "exceedingly fair to look upon," and, as he afterwards observed to the coachman, "evidently belonged to a better sort."

"How far are you going with us, miss?"

"To London," was the reply given in a thick choking voice, which was not lost upon the shrewd old guard, who remarked it to the coachman at the next change, adding that he should not be a bit surprised if it was a "helopement;" and throughout the whole journey Annie was always alluded to as "that mysterious party we took up at the Holliwell way-post."

Her little portmanteau was flung into the hind boot. As she bade good-by to the poor farm servant she slipped a sovereign into his hand. She patted Nero on the head, inwardly wondering whether the old dog would soon forget her. The guard scrambled up again into his seat; and with an "All right, Jem," and another twang of the horn, the Highflyer rolled on and bore Annie away from the home of her childhood, which she was destined never to see again.

Annie had the coach pretty well to herself all the way up to London, and her gloomy reveries (for she was far from happy) were only disturbed at the different changes, when the kind old guard, who had constituted himself a sort of father protector during the journey, would thrust his jolly mottled face in at the coach window just to inquire how she was "getting on;" to remark that the nights were uncommon cold for the season of the year, and to ask if she would not "get out to take a little refreshment." But her heart was too full to allow of her swallowing a mouthful, and she gently and civilly repulsed all the old gentleman's little advances at familiarity. However, about eight in the morning they stopped to breakfast, and here, as she peremptorily refused to alight, the guard took upon himself to bring her out a cup of tea and some toast, and observing that her eyes were red with weeping, he felt it his duty to say a word or two to comfort her.

"Come, cheer up, miss; you'll see the old folks at home once more if you live, I dare say."

This the old fellow considered a very shrewd diplomatic speech; for he now fancied she must drop some chance word or another which would unravel the mystery which he had been puzzling himself throughout the whole night to solve, perched as he was in solitary state on his old backgammon board; for they had but two passengers besides Annie, and these were both in front.

But the shaft missed its mark. She replied not a word to his kindly-meant observations, but merely thanked him for all his little attentions to her, and this with a smile so gloomy, and yet so sweetly sad, that the old man afterwards declared that the High-flyer had never carried such a passenger since he had been guard on her.

If, however, he had been struck by her surprising beauty when seen only imperfectly by the light of the moon, how much more was he astonished now, when it burst upon him in all the full blaze of daylight. He could talk of nothing else when he went back to the inn to get his own breakfast, and it was not long before the coach door again opened, and the new coachman (one of the greatest swells of that road), apologizing for disturbing her, proceeded to ransack the whole inside of the coach under pretence of seeking for a small brown-paper parcel—which it is needless to say he was unable to find.

Now this coachman was far younger and less plethoric than the old guard, and was, moreover, considered to be the best judge of a woman and a horse down the road; and the glowing eulogy he passed on Annie's charms so raised the curiosity of the pretty barmaid that she stepped across to the coach to ask the lady inside if she would not just step upstairs "to wash her hands and straighten her hair a bit"—an offer which Annie at once accepted.

When she came downstairs again all traces of sorrow had disappeared from her countenance; the cold water had added a brighter glow to her beautiful features; and she looked so fresh and blooming as she sailed majestically across the bar passage, that every one instinctively did her homage. Even " Old Ginger," the oldest, surliest, and ugliest horsekeeper in the yard, raised his battered cap to her as he met her coming down the steps; and the portly landlord himself bustled to the coach door to open it and hand her in—a thing which he had never been known to do before in his life.

In the afternoon the coach rolled over the London stones. By five the old Highflyer had "shot her rubbish" at the White Horse in Fetter Lane, and the guard and coachman were seated in the Magpie and Stump over the way, discussing their pipes and brandy-and-water and their mysterious passenger at the same time.

Annie had plenty of money, for every half-year old Radford used scrupulously to pay over to her the interest of her funded property, and for which he invariably took her receipt. Living in the private retired manner which they did up at the Lodge, Annie had but few wants and fewer opportunities of spending her money; and except among the poor villagers (and it was a sad day for them when she left), she hardly spent a ten-pound note in the year. Out of her two years' allowance she had saved nearly one hundred pounds, which she brought up to London with her. Now avarice was not one of Annie's faults, and she had not lived long enough in the world to have learned the true value of money. She considered it was only so much dross, which was meant to be spent; and the sooner it was got rid of the sooner the trouble was over. A more liberal, open-hearted girl did not exist. Every coachman who drove her that night received a half-guinea tip as he presented himself at the coach door, with a civil touch of the hat and "I leave you here, miss;" and a sovereign to the old guard, and thanks for all his kindness, given in her sweetest manner, quite confirmed the old man in the opinion he had formed respecting her. He shook her hand with all the familiarity of an "old friend of the family," and bidding her, if ever she wanted a friend in London, to be sure and find out old Ned Simpson, the guard of the Highflyer, he wished her a most cordial good-by, and turned away, remarking to the coachman who stood waiting for him, that "If that 'ere gal isn't a countess, she only ought to be."

The sentence fell on Annie's ear—that word had been uppermost in her thoughts for the last two years—and she felt as if there was something prophetic in the old guard's speech.

She followed the chambermaid upstairs, and after changing her dress, ordered a cab and drove at once to the house of her friend the schoolmistress at Kensington. Annie had always been a favourite with every one at the school, and as the servant opened the door to the cabman's knock, she gave a little scream of delight as she called out, "Why, if here isn't Miss Annie come back!" As usual, she paid the cabman double his fare, who, as he thanked her, gallantly observed, that if she wished it, he'd wait two hours and drive back for nothing, only for the sake of having so handsome a fare. Annie walked straight up to her former preceptress's parlour. The greeting was cordial on both sides, and Annie's cheeks flushed with haughty pride as the old lady held her at arm's length, that she might scan her features well, and wound up her survey by exclaiming, "Why, I declare that you are looking more beautiful than ever, child."

Annie soon unfolded her errand to her old friend, who knew of just the very situation to suit her. A lady down in Hampshire wanted a governess for her two little daughters. She wrote off by that night's post, a favourable answer was received, and in a week Annie was installed at Woodbine Cottage, one of the sweetest spots in Hampshire, as governess to two little girls, who soon learned to love her as an elder sister. Here Annie remained for six months, and was treated with such uniform kindness by all, that she might perhaps have almost forgotten the destiny she had left home to fulfil, and been content to remain at the cottage—at any rate till the education of her young charges was completed—had not a little circumstance taken place which led to the accomplishment of her fate.

The lady, who was a widow, had gone away for a few days to visit a neighbouring friend, leaving Annie at home; during the lady's absence the cottage was honoured with a visit from her nephew, a good-looking fellow enough, but one of those shallow-brained fools who think that every woman they see must be at once struck with them, and, in fact, whose whole life passes without a single idea, save that of flirting with and saying smart things to every pretty girl they meet. Of course he was immediately struck with Annie's beauty, and commenced a flirtation with her from the very first evening they met. To this sort of thing Annie made not the slightest objection; his manner was sufficiently respectful—that was enough for her; and at a quiet bit of playful badinage and persiflage she was fully his match. But his manner became more familiar. He was one of that mean, low, spiritless class, who consider that a poor governess, because she is a friendly dependent, is "fair game," and must feel flattered by the attentions of any one whose circumstances happened to be better than her own. He, however, did not know Annie yet; but he soon found out his mistake. He considered himself very lucky in having met with so handsome a companion as Annie to dispel the gloom of a dull country house, and he was continually following her about. This rather bored her, but at the same time amused her. One morning she was sitting alone in the drawing-room, painting in water-colours, in which art she was a proficient. Her hanger-on was not long before he found her out, and, drawing his chair close to her, commenced a violent flirtation. As long as he confined himself to this all was well; but emboldened by Annie's submission, he proceeded to freedoms which he would never have dared to attempt with any female had he not fancied that she was unprotected. Annie's hot blood was up—she rose from her seat, looked him fixedly in the face for some seconds, then taking up the glass of dirty water in which she was cleaning her brushes, coolly dashed it into his face, and left the room without saying a word.

Annie went to her bedchamber and wrote a note, in which, after thanking the lady for all the kindness she had received since she had been at the cottage, she told her that circumstances compelled her to leave the situation without a moment's notice. She referred the lady to her nephew for an explanation, and wound up by saying that, although she was aware by leaving thus abruptly she had forfeited all claims to any salary which might be due to her, still, if the lady chose to pay, she begged that she would hand it over to her nephew, in order to purchase him a new white waistcoat, in place of the one which she was afraid she had spoilt, when giving him his last lesson in painting.

She then packed up her trunk, got one of the outdoor servants to carry it to the railway station, not half-a-mile distant, and in less than an hour was on her road back to London.

Half-way between the cottage and London was a little refreshment station, hardly in the style of the Swindon or Wolverton station, but still a very neat little room where half-a-dozen nymphs served out hot soups, buns, porter, &c., to those hungry and thirsty railway travellers who required them. These girls were chosen principally for their good looks, and when Annie pushed her way up to the counter for a plate of soup she took a critical survey of the beauties behind it, and saw at a glance that not one could hold a candle to her on the score of good looks. A thought at once struck her that it would be capital fun to have such employment for a short time. She made up her mind at once, and asked if she could speak to the station-master. She was shown into a small room at the bottom of the station. The station-master, quite surprised at seeing such a visitor enter his little room, rose to salute her with an obeisance such as he might have used towards Majesty itself, but he was still more surprised when he heard upon what errand she had come. He was just then in want of a hand, one of his syrens having left him the day before, and he had not yet been able to supply her place. He would have eagerly jumped at Annie's offer, for such a girl behind his counter would be a treasure to him. But he was a cautious, shrewd old fellow, and of course must learn who and what Annie was, and what she had been. Annie directly gave him a reference to the lady whom she had just left. The station-master knew her well; and it was agreed that Annie should remain at the station till replies were received to the two notes which they wrote her that night.

The next post brought satisfactory answers. The lady wrote most kindly to Annie, said she was very sorry to part with her; reprobated her nephew's conduct severely, considered that Annie's conduct was just what it should have been, enclosed her a cheque for a whole year's salary, and wound up by telling her that if she wanted a situation again she knew where to apply.

Annie was at once installed behind the counter, and was unanimously voted queen of the bevy of beauties that served there. The first basin of soup she was asked for was by her late admirer, who pushed his way to the bar to have a "chaff," as he expressed it, with the girls. He had little idea that it was Annie who would serve him, but he recognised her at once; and when she demurely asked him "how he would have it?" he was fairly nonplussed, and throwing a shilling down upon the counter, turned away without tasting the soup.

Now it so happened that about eight miles down the line was Beechwood Hall, where resided an old Sir Somebody Something, a great officer and a K.C.B. He had served in India, in Africa, and through the whole of the Peninsular campaign; had distinguished himself upon many occasions; and, on leaving the service, his country could do no less than confer a baronetcy and a pension on the brave old warrior, who then hung up his "toasting-fork," and retired to pass the close of a stormy life in the quiet solitudes of Beechwood. He had been terribly battered in the wars, had lost an arm, and suffered considerably from a bullet which had lodged in the thigh, and which no doctor could extract. The old man had often great trouble to get about at all, and always went lame. He was a cheery, hearty old cock, as tough as pinwire; had a very aristocratic appearance and bearing, with a noble old head as white as snow; and, notwithstanding his infirmities, looked and fancied himself ten years younger than he really was. Now, this old K.C.B. was enormously rich, and only wanted one thing—which was a wife. Not that he would have had much trouble to procure one if he had only set about the task in earnest—for money can procure this luxury as well as any other: but he went very little into company, and knew well that if any woman in his rank of life should deign to bestow her hand upon him, it would be for the sake of his money and nothing else, Many match-making mothers would gladly have sacrificed their daughters, and many scheming daughters would have gladly sacrificed themselves, and vowed at the altar "to love, honour, and obey" this old ruin of a man, merely for the sake of his property and status in society; and this he well knew. His was a solitary, cheerless life, and he began to feel the want of some one to nurse and comfort him.

The old baronet was one of the directors of this line, and the principal business and pleasure of his life was to ride up and down it. He always travelled in his own carriage, which was fitted up most comfortably. Here he could lie at his ease, read, smoke, or sleep, just as it pleased him. The incidents of the journey amused him, and half his days were spent on the railroad. Of course he was as well known down the line as any one of the drivers. He never stopped at the station without having a plate of soup brought out to him, for it was too great an exertion for him to get out of his carriage and hobble to the refreshment-room; and as it was well known that the old man in his young days had been a devoted admirer of the fair sex, the prettiest girl in the station always tripped across the platform with the old K.C.B.'s mulligatawny. He was a liberal-hearted, generous old fellow, and the presents he gave away among these girls amounted to a considerable yearly sum. The Spanish was the style of beauty which the old gentleman most admired; and even now, when in company with any of his old comrades, he used enthusiastically to dwell upon the conquests he had made among the dark-eyed "donnas" in Madrid, Seville, and other of the cities of sunny Spain, when campaigning with the "Iron Duke."

On the very day after Annie had been installed as queen of the ceremonies at the Resborough Refreshment Rooms, the twelve o'clock train brought up the old K.C.B.; and his very respectable-looking valet, who always travelled with him, came into the room to order his soup. He saw at a glance that Annie's was a new face, and moreover that such a face had never been seen at that counter before. She had heard a little about the old officer already from the other girls, some of whom had boasted of the presents they had received from him, so she was not at all unwilling to carry out his soup on a neat little tray. The old officer fairly started when the valet opened the carriage-door, and Annie handed him in his tray. Visions of the sunny South flitted across his memory, and the images of stately flashing-eyed donnas appeared on the tablet of his mind with all the freshness of yesterday.

Annie handed him his soup, adjusted his couch, spoke to him so kindly and tenderly, and, in fact, played her part so well that the old man declared to his valet that he had never seen such a girl in England before; and every time he saw her the more he liked her. He was up and down the line now more often than before, and no one ever brought him his soup but Annie. On her sixth visit to the carriage she came back with a splendid diamond ring on her finger. This was not, however, the ring she was playing for; a plain gold ring without a gem would suit her much better. She never showed the ring to the other girls, who, however, had begun "to chaff" her about her conquest.

In less than a month the baronet invited her to his house, and not being troubled with any false notions of propriety, Annie went. The old officer was a fine honourable old man, and he at once, in the most delicate terms, proposed to marry her. He never hinted in the slightest at the disparity of rank that there was between them. He plainly told her that he would probably be a sad burden to her during his life, but that he should not live long, and that if she could only cheer and comfort his declining days, he should in return leave her every shilling he possessed. He had not a relative in the world, and could and would do exactly as he pleased.

Annie did not take long to consider. "Better be an old man's darling than a young man's slave," she thought. She accepted his offer; left the station at once; they were married by special licence off-hand; and although she had not attained to the rank of a countess, she had married a baronet, a distinguished and brave old officer, whose property was immense. She did her duty faithfully to her decrepit old husband, who in return denied her nothing.

Annie well befitted the station to which she had been elevated, and had she been born a lady in her own right, she could not have been a greater ornament to the peerage.

"There, thank goodness, we've done with Miss Annie," I fancy I hear the reader exclaim; "and now, perhaps, we shall have a little more about the Leather Plater." And for this purpose we must go back for about nine months, and return again to the little parlour at Shark's Lodge.

As soon as lunch was over, and I had settled with old Radford for the colt, I left. I was not particularly anxious to wait till Mr. Turner arrived. Just, however, as I turned out of the end of the lane, which led from the Lodge into the bridle-road across the Openfield, I saw that gentleman picking his way up the dirty lane to the Lodge from the village. "Too late, my friend," I thought;

and, as I considered that I had bought the colt rather out of the fire, I at once christened him "Chance."

He was delivered next day, and two days after I had a *levée* of hard-riding friends in the neighbourhood to look at him. Many had heard of him, some had seen him; but Mr. Hawthorn's verdict on that queer-looking near hock had spoilt his sale, and no one dare venture on him, although more than one fancied him very much. It is always good fun to hear the criticisms which are passed on a new purchase, especially if you have not taken the counsel of the criticisers beforehand. Nothing is so easy as to find fault. "He stands on very short legs," observed one. "That hock will never stand; I'd draw the iron over it at once if he were mine," observed a second. "He'll never have substance enough to carry your weight across our country. He may make a galloper for a mile, but if he should not, he'll never bring you twenty pounds," said a third; and so on.

Jack Russell was the only one of them who did not try to put me out of conceit with him. He never gave an opinion hastily, especially about a horse; and all he said was, "Bring him up to my Lodge to-morrow morning, and after that, I'll tell you what I think of the colt."

Accordingly, I took him up in the morning, and the colt underwent an hour's trial in the hands of a man who was never deceived in what a horse could do or ought to do. He galloped him, he cantered him; he put him over every sort of fence to be found on his farm, and when he took him back to the stable, observed to me, "You've got something a little better there than you're aware of, old fellow; and you can give my respectful compliments to Frank, and tell him it was his hands, and not the colt's fore-legs, that were tied, for I could lift that colt over any fence that it's fair to ride a horse at."

He proposed to take the entire management of the colt off my hands—keep him and train him, on the condition that I did not interfere in the least with him; and, in return, I was to allow him to stand in half the winnings of the next year. To this I agreed.

The colt furnished a good deal that summer, and by the next winter had grown into a very slashing bloodlike, *multum in parvo* horse, showing a deal of breeding. He had all the splendid blood-like symmetry of his sire, but his head was the counterpart of old Plover's, very wide under the cheek bones, and heavy in the jowl, which gave him rather a coarse appearance. By the end of December Jack had found out exactly what he could do, and although like the rest, he always stuck to it that hurdle-racing would turn out his *forte*, he proposed that we should send him for the Hollerton in March, and declared that—although it was ten years since he had put on a silk jacket—on this first occasion he would ride the colt himself.

"Oh! I see they've entered that Holliwell colt for the Hollerton Steeple-chase," observed Captain —— to Mr. Turner, as he entered the stable one morning early in March, with the list of entries for that race in his hand. "It was a d—d stupid blunder of yours letting that colt slip."

"Well, I don't know," answered Mr. Turner, who, although he had never ceased inwardly to regret the mistake he had made, did not care to own it. "He'd never have carried your weight, sir; and as for winning the Hollerton, why they might just as well send a man in boots."

"I wont say that," thoughtfully observed the captain. "I see Jack Russell names him, and, what's more, *rides* him. This looks like mischief, for that old fox does not often make a mistake. However, how's our mare getting on?"

"Oh, first-rate sir; don't you be a bit afraid, sir; she'll beat that colt easy enough, especially as the country is likely to be this year. I don't say our mare will win, but you may lay every shilling you can get on at evens that she beats the Plover colt in their places." And this was given with such a certainty that the captain determined to act on the advice, which he did, and Jack Russell found himself 50*l*. richer by the venture.

A fine morning in the end of March, and white flags were again flying over four miles of the deep, stiffly-enclosed country around

Hollerton. The course was heavy, the fences large, the brook swollen, and I inwardly felt that if our young horse could come up well this day we had little to fear for his future. It was a weight-for-age race. The first favourite, an old steeple-chaser, the hero of a hundred fights, with my energetic friend Tom up, had to give our colt 21 lb.; and the captain's mare gave us 14 lb. The rest of the field were either untried or very moderate. Seventeen came to the post. The captain jumped off with the lead, close followed by the favourite, our horse lying well up. Although Jack Russell had not ridden in a race for so long, it was quite evident that he had not forgotten his jockeyship, and before they had cleared the sixth fence Tom saw it, and from that point he watched the colt and no other horse in the race. The brook put eight out of the race, and three more fell at the posts and rails beyond it. Among these was our horse, and breaking away from Jack, he galloped down to the bottom of the field before he was caught, and brought back. The six other horses went on, Tom and the captain leading. This fall lost us the race, but it also told us what a treasure we had got in the bay colt out of Plover. He lost three fields before Jack had mounted and set him going again, and there was not a mile and a half left. But now his wonderful speed showed itself. Before seven fences more were cleared he was well up with his horses. He passed these one after the other; he left the captain in the large meadow next to the winning field, collared Tom at the last fence, and ran him a slashing race home, which he lost only by about two lengths. It was a very exciting race, and the air resounded with shouts of "Crimson wins!" "Green and white wins!" the latter being rather the most popular colour, as our horse was bred in the county.

Tom was now so satisfied with the colt's speed that he declared if we would enter him for the hurdle-race he'd ride him for us for nothing. This offer was gladly accepted. There was a strong field, and the old "long-headed dun," who had been kept for it, was a hot favourite. Tom declared that this time "he'd reduce the matter to a certainty." He went off at tremendous score, was never headed, and won the first heat (just one mile), with the dun second; the captain again third on a fresh horse. These were the only three that went for the next heat, and they came in again in the same order, Tom making running throughout. The young horse had now "won his spurs," and we were offered two hundred for him on the course, which we refused.

There were "sounds of revelry" that night at the Chequers, to which all our party adjourned after the races; and old John Harrison was more oracular than ever.

After the race Tom advised us to keep the young horse only for hurdle-racing or the flat, and added that he did not think just then there were many half-bred horses in England could beat him; and so it turned out, for we had a very merry summer, all over the country, picking up all the little county stakes for which we chose to enter him. We did not fly at any high game the first year: but when Jack Russell and myself came to divide the profits of that year's racing, we were both very well satisfied with the result. I may add, that Frank, the young rough-rider, rode the colt for us three or four times, and in his second season we engaged him for our regular jockey.

The captain was more vexed with his defeat in the hurdle-race than in the steeple-chase. He had always felt a little sore at my buying the colt out of his hands, and the first time we met we had a word or two on the subject. We were both of us a little "peppery," and the result of the interview was that he matched his mare, which had run third in the hurdle-race, against our young horse—one mile and a half over the flat, for 50*l.* a side, at 10 st. each. He very much wanted to get the match on with "owners up," but as I knew this would be as much as giving the race away, I declined on these terms, and he conceded the point. The match was to come off over Hollerton Race-course in six weeks, and we engaged Tom to ride for us, as Frank was hardly within 5 lb. of the captain in race riding. But even with Tom up I was giving away great odds. The captain's mare was thorough-bred, there was no "long hair in her pasterns," and she had won more than one good race over the flat in good company. She was just a year older than our colt and stood exactly two inches higher. I therefore did not display much skill in match-making when I matched our young horse at even weights against his, and more than one friend told me so pretty plainly. However, as the race was p.p., and all the money down, there was nothing to do but to run it out. John Harrison had a capital exercising and training ground in some large old meadows close by the Chequers, where many hunters used to stand during the winter, for three good packs could be reached from this little inn; and about a month before the race we sent the colt to stand at the Chequers, and take his exercise under Frank's care. Both horses were in good hunting condition, so they required little more than to be kept in good wind; for, obedient to an old principle, which was time-renowned in our county, whether in hunting or steeple-chasing we always liked to run our horses above their weight, and we never drew them fine.

It was a singular thing, but our horse had not stood at the Chequers more than a fortnight when Mr. Turner also brought the captain's mare over to finish her exercise on these very meadows, and to be in the neighbourhood of the course on which the match was to come off.

Now he had never fairly got over his little pique against me, and he had always been most anxious, as he expressed it, "to square accounts with me for buying the colt out of his hands." I'll do Mr. Turner the credit to say that he was what old Doctor Johnson so much liked, " a good hater," and he had formed a very masterly plan for putting " our party in the hole," of which, however, even his own master, the captain, was kept entirely in the dark. It was scarcely likely that he and Frank should be under the same roof without becoming acquainted, and although they did not exercise their horses exactly together, still they both watched each other pretty closely, and it took no long time for a man of Mr. Turner's experience to see that, even if I had made the match right, and had received the proper allowance of weight, there would have been no certainty in it; but as the conditions now stood, they had fully a stone the best of us, and the match was almost reduced to a certainty for the captain. This was a pleasing reflection for the stud-groom, as he leant against the door-post of the Chequers in the evening smoking one of the captain's best cigars, at four guineas a pound; but he was not satisfied with this, he wanted to "have the boot on the other leg," and to try and make us believe that ours was the best horse. For this very reason he brought his mare to stand at the Chequers, and after "sounding" Frank—whom he found, to use a favourite expression of his own, "as green as a radish top"—he proposed one evening, after stable hours, that they should have a spin together for a mile and a half next morning in ten-pound saddles. There was scarcely a pound difference between the weight of the two men. Mr. Turner, who was candour itself with Frank, and who had attained a sort of influence over the young man, had not much difficulty in the task. As he observed, the trial could do no harm; the money was all down; the match must come off; if the trial was ridden fairly the best horse would win, and this would be the case in the match. He fancied his mare must win, and she was sure to be a great favourite, for "all the mess-room money would be on her." If she beat our horse in the trial, it would give us a very good line to go by, and might save us many pounds; but if our horse could win the trial, it would be like coining money to back him.

Of course it was Mr. Turner's meaning that our horse should win the trial, and yet he meant that both horses should do all they knew, and that, as far as riding went, everything should appear to be on the square; and, moreover, he wanted it to get wind that our horse had beat the mare in a private trial. So, in the evening, he confided to old John Harrison and two or three more friends that the trial was to come off next morning, quite privately, the consequence of which was that it was watched by more than a dozen eager eyes, and in twenty-four hours the news spread half over the county and up at the barracks that our horse had beaten the mare in a trial by half-a-dozen lengths.

Although the match was not a heavy one, it created much inte rest in our county. There was always a great deal of jealousy in our hunt between the military and the civilian, and every member of the hunt felt that the honour of the county was at stake, and the match was looked forward to with no little interest. Of course the captain's mare was the favourite among the ladies and the swells, while our horse represented the farmers and hard-riding division of the neighbourhood. So old John Harrison was taken into confidence, and he apparently fell into the trap at once, observing that it was a capital thing for them all, such a chance did not often turn up, and that if they did not make the most of it, they had no one to blame but themselves.

But though the stud-groom had not much difficulty in hoodwinking Frank, it was quite another thing with the old Yorkshire coachman, who instinctively felt, as he afterwards expressed it, that "some deep dodge was up, though he could not, for the life of him, get to the bottom of it." He had watched both horses closely at exercise, on the old wall-eyed cob, and, although they had never been put together, he had seen enough to convince him that at even weights the match was a certainty all one way. The captain's mare was a great, slashing thorough-bred—rising six, and had beaten many good fields before this day. She looked nearly as big again as our young horse, who was always a little light-timbered, although very fast. Old John felt confident that this trial was proposed merely for the purpose of throwing the dust in our eyes in some way or other, and he moreover felt that he was not in Mr. Turner's full confidence, and his Yorkshire pride was hurt at this. He felt quite sure that Turner knew the mare was the best; in fact, that worthy had told him as much, and he was certain that the stud-groom was playing some deep game to suit his own purposes. If only you can once set a Yorkshireman's curiosity or suspicions on the *qui vive* about anything in horses, he will work out the trail as surely as any London detective. Old John determined himself to supply the missing links in the chain of evidence. He therefore watched the trial closely when it came off next morning; he saw that it was fairly run out from end to end; that both men and horses did their best, and that our horse beat the captain's mare by two lengths. His private opinion on the result can, however, best be gathered from the following note which I received two days after the trial.

It was headed "private and confidential," and sent express, and ran thus:—

"The Chequers, Wednesday Morning.

"DEAR SIR,—Turner gammoned your lad to try your young horse against his mare on Monday morning at even weights, and 'I stood in.' I saw the trial, and watched both horses very closely. They both did all they knew, there's no mistake about that, and your horse won by a couple of lengths. They rode in ten-pound saddles, which I weighed, as well as both the men. Now I know that this running was not correct, for at even weights I am sure the mare can beat the horse when she pleases. I am certain that Turner has put the double on your lad. I fancy, mind, although I can't prove it, that he managed somehow or other to slip in a stone of dead weight, and if this was the case the running was about correct. I am confident that Turner got up this trial for no other purpose than to make your horse a favourite; for, instead of keeping the trial dark, he talked about it to everybody, and it's known all over the country. I was at Hollerton market yesterday, and they were all talking about it. They made the young horse first favourite, and I quietly took 50 to 40 and stood the mare, and you take my advice and do the same, for at even weight she'll win, in spite of all the trials.

"Yours obediently,
"JOHN HARRISON."

It turned out afterwards, just as old John supposed, that Turner, when saddling for the trial, managed to slip in a stone of dead weight unseen by any one, and this brought the horses together. The match came off. Tom made a waiting race of it, and the captain won; but instead of putting us in the hole, as Mr. Turner intended, the trial was a capital thing for us, for we got all our money quietly on the mare by commission, and, although beaten, we won more on this match than on any other race the horse ever ran for.

Tom felt, however, so confident that ten pounds would bring the horse and mare together, that directly after the first race he challenged the captain to run over again that afternoon for 50*l.*, the horse receiving ten pounds' allowance. To this the captain, who was rather flushed with his first victory, agreed. In this race Tom changed his tactics, made all the running, and won very cleverly. A good deal of the mess-room money came back to us in the second match.

We sent the horse into Tom's stables, who now generally rode for us, and the next year Chance ran in eleven races and won nine.

We ran him next summer down in Hampshire in a hurdle-race— two-mile heats. He won the first in a canter, and as we were walking him up and down the course between the first and second heats, we were all surprised by the approach of a most gorgeous flunkey, who, politely touching his cockaded and silver-laced hat, addressed me in the following extraordinary and mysterious speech:—" *Her ladyship's* compliments, and would feel much obliged by our bringing Chance up to her carriage that *she might pat him.*" I was walking just then by the side of the horse (whom a lad was leading), in company with Tom, the jockey, and Bob M., the betting man, the rudest and noisiest of his class. We were naturally all very much surprised at such a strange request, and Bob blurted out—

"What the devil does the fellow mean? Why, he must be drunk."

I shall never forget the air of offended dignity with which the footman drew himself up as he answered Bob, "Excuse me, sir, no more drunk than you are;" and taking me a little aside, he explained the mystery by saying in an under-tone, "Lady ——, Miss Annie Radford *as* was, sir."

Now, I had heard that Annie was either married to, or under the protection of, some old nob or other, who was old enough to be her father (of course the latter version of her history was accepted as the truth by this charitable world), but I had not the least idea that she was living close by the town where these races were held, and just as little did I imagine that the Lady ——, who headed the list of lady-patronesses for the race ball in the evening, was my old acquaintance, "Annie Radford *as* was." I told the lad directly to lead the horse over to the other side of the course, and followed him with the servant, leaving Tom and the betting-man staring

after us in blank amazement, and both declared that they had never seen "such a go on a race-course before." Tom, in addtion, bade the footman present his respectful compliments to her ladyship, and say that "if she wished to *pat the jockey* as well as the horse, she had only to send for him, and he'd step over directly;" to which free-and-easy speech the man only replied by a more supercilious stare.

As we were walking across the course, I took the liberty of asking the flunkey if "it was all on the square." He affected not to understand me, so I asked him plainly if Annie was really married. He appeared to be quite offended at my presuming to doubt in fact, and replied with his grandest air, "Married, sir, yes, by special licence; I had the honour of assisting at the ceremony." In what manner he assisted, however, he did not explain.

We had now arrived at the rails on the other side of the course, and there, in an open barouche, drawn by a splendid pair of greys sat Lady —— (*née* Annie Radford), by far the handsomest and best-dressed woman on that course. A battered, grey-haired old ruin of a man, her husband, sat by her side. Her greeting was most cordial.

"Oh, Mr. ——, perhaps you don't remember me." (Oh, did not I? I felt quite angry with the old K.C.B. for looking so supremely happy in the possession of such a treasure, and inwardly vowed, that if I had the making of the laws, it should be felony at least for an old man above sixty to marry a blooming young girl of twenty). "I saw the name of your horse on the card, and that's the reason I drove over to the races to-day. I watched you leading the colt Chance up and down the course. I knew him again directly, and I could not help sending for him that I might just pat him once again for the sake of 'auld lang syne.'" A melancholy shade passed over her beautiful features as she said this; but it vanished in an instant, and, turning towards the old fossil, who was leaning back in the carriage, with his leg cocked up on a sort of gouty prop, she introduced me to "Sir ——, my husband," with a particular stress on the last word, and shot a coquettish half look of triumph at me, as much as to say, "You see that I've done what I always said I would."

I was not in the best of tempers just then, and I had never quite forgotten Miss Annie's conduct towards poor Frank, who was as decent and worthy a young fellow as ever lived, so I " countered on her " in this fashion : " I'm so glad to find that your ladyship," with a slight stress on the word, "still remembers some of us in the old county. If I had not thought that you had quite forgotten him, I would certainly have brought Frank over as well as the horse. He's waiting for me in the jockey's tent." I watched her keenly as I said this, but I would have given worlds to have recalled the speech as soon as I had uttered it, for her face wore such an expression of bitter anguish, as she leaned over the side of the carriage and asked me, in a low, plaintive tone, " Is it generous of you, Mr. ———, thus to remind me of the only event in my past life upon which I can never look back without shame ?"

The old officer was most affable, and politely asked me to stay and take lunch, which the servants were just then unpacking. We could not get the horse near to the carriage on account of the rails, so " her ladyship " begged me to hand her out and escort her to him, which I did; and I really think he knew her again as she passed her delicate, lavender-kidded hand over his soft nose and sleek shiny neck. She asked me, in an under-tone, if I had seen her old father lately, and, unfastening a splendid brooch, in which was braided a lock of her raven hair, along with one of her husband's, she begged me, as a particular favour, to ride over when I came home, and give it to him with " his little Annie's love." She had already written to old Jack a long letter announcing her marriage, not one word of which did the old man believe. However, on the very day that she came of age, he appeared at the Hall, and, to the surprise of both Annie and her husband, related to them her full history. He had kept a strict account of every shilling which he had disbursed for her, and handed over the credentials for the two thousand which had been invested in his name. Not a shilling of this, however, would Annie touch, and she cheerfully gave it up to the old man who had so faithfully performed the trust which he had undertaken, and proved himself so kind a father to the orphan girl.

It would be tedious to follow the career of the leather-plater through the four subsequent years that we owned him. He won most of the stakes which he ran for, but the expenses took a good deal of the profits, and as these half-bred stakes are never very large when they come to be divided, but a small share fell to each of us that were part owners of Chance. Still we had a good deal of fun with him, and the man who does not possess the means of owning a good thorough-bred racer, will find, perhaps, as much pleasure and excitement, at a far less cost, by running a good leather-plater. What generally licks him, however, is this—he is apt to think too much of his cock-tail, and run him in company which he finds too late are "a leetle" too good for him.

The last race in which we ran our leather-plater was his most unlucky one. It was a hurdle-race in Nottinghamshire, and as complaints had been made the year before that the hurdles were not stiff enough, the stewards were determined that there should be no mistake this year. They put them up 4 ft. 6 in. high, supported by stiff posts driven into the ground, and strong bars were mortised into the tops of them throughout their whole length. Chance won the first heat easily without a mistake, and only one horse went against him for the second. This was a farmer's horse, ridden by his owner, and it was a guinea to a shilling on Chance. A friend of mine, who was certainly one of the most unlucky betters out, was on the stand, and as our horse cleared the hurdles opposite, and went on with the lead, pulling double, the young farmer being hard at work with his horse some fifty lengths behind, my friend observed that it was the hollowest thing he ever saw, and offered 50*l.* to 10*s.* on Chance. A sleek bookmaker, who stood by his side, took him up at once, and booked the bet with this terse remark, "Mind, Mr. ——, it's the odds and not the horse that tempts me." They had to come once more round, and win just below the stand. The race was two-mile heats, and I really think that our horse would have distanced the farmer if he had stood the race out; but in coming over the flight of hurdles next above the stand, he slipped, breasted the top rail, rolled over, and broke his near hind-leg just below the hock as short as a carrot. He rolled over Tom, who was a good deal shaken, and of course his Chance was out; and the young farmer, whose horse also fell at the same flight of hurdles, but without receiving any damage, managed to struggle in alone, and walked over at his leisure for the third heat. It was with great difficulty that we got the horse up, and he was in such dreadful pain that a gun was sent for, and we had him shot on the spot. It was a sad loss for us; we had refused two hundred for him many times, and I think, had he won this race, we should have got two hundred and fifty for him. Thus ended the career of poor Chance, in his day one of the best leather-platers in England.

Let me, in concluding this tale, make one remark. These little sporting sketches are intended for the amusement, and not for the instruction, of the reader, who is requested to read them as he would a novel or any other work of fiction, and not as plain matter-of-fact. Although the principal incidents in every one of these sporting sketches took place much as they are here described, I have not confined myself to plain matter-of-fact, but have coloured simple details to make them read the better, and, for obvious reasons, have mystified names and localities.

THE POACHER.

"Donald Caird can wire a maukin,
Kens the wiles o' dun deer stalken,
Leisters kippers, maks a shift
To shoot the muir fowl in a drift;
Water-bailiffs, watchers, keepers,
He can wake while ye are sleepers;
Nor for bounty or reward,
Dare ye mell wi' Donald Caird."

It was a dull evening in the beginning of December, now many years since, that I had to lead a "beaten horse" home for about twelve miles, after one of the best runs, perhaps, ever known with our hounds. I recollect not only that day, but that season well. We had not a day's frost to stop the hunting until long after Christmas. The scent had lain breast high, the hounds had been running like wildfire, and the men going like mad up to this; and those whose studs were short, and yet who liked to see as much of the fun as possible, began to wish for a little frost to give our nags a fortnight's rest. This was a peculiar season. In every hunt there are certain crack meets—coverts which are sure finds; and the man who can only hunt twice a week fixes his days according to the advertisement in the county paper, and saves his horses for those fixtures where he can make sure of a run. But this year the foxes appeared to be scattered all over the country. They kept turning up in all sorts of unaccountable places. Hedge-rows, turnip-fields, belts of plantations which we never thought of drawing, all seemed to hold a flying fox; and some of our best runs this year were from coverts to which, in ordinary seasons, no man (except the most inveterate sportsmen who have plenty of horses at command, and who deem it a bounden duty, as it were, to appear at every covert side during the season) ever thought of sending a horse on. There are some such men in every hunt, men who appear to be as regularly attached to the hounds as the servants of the establishment; and if by chance one of these well-known faces is missed from any covert-side, the question immediately passes from mouth to mouth, "I wonder where So-and-so is to-day; I hope there's nothing the matter at home."

But this year no man liked, if he could help it, to miss a single meet, for there were no blank days; every run seemed to be better than the last; and whenever I met the hounds on the Saturday or the Wednesday (the two days in the week which best suited the "short-handed" men in our hunt), the first question invariably used to be, "Did you hear what a rattling thing we had on the Monday or Thursday?"—the day which I had missed. I only owned two horses, and I could not manage more than two days a week comfortably: in fact, this was rather too much in a season like the one I am describing; but up to this, I had got on very well. We had three "crackers" in November, all of which I had seen; but the meets had hitherto been rather wide of us, and the "run of the season" had yet to come. However, at last the long-wished for announcement—"Saturday: Findon Toll-bar"—appeared in the county paper, and every man who read that paragraph knew that his work was cut out for him on the Saturday. There was not a man in our hunt who would not sooner miss his dinner for a week than a Findon Toll-bar meet; and a Findon-gorse fox generally gave us something to talk about for months after. We had had a goodish thing on the Wednesday, over perhaps as good, but quite a different sort of country from the Findon. The hounds had never yet this season met at Findon; but as this was always a Saturday's meet, and I had been expecting that it would soon come, I had been saving the grey (my best horse) as much as I could, and always riding him on the Saturdays.

I was at breakfast on Thursday when the paper arrived, and five minutes after was in the stable to tell the glad news to the groom.

The Poacher.

The man had just brought in the grey from exercise, and, almost before I spoke to him, I was met with the unwelcome tidings that " he could not think whatever was the matter with the old grey; he was quite off his feed, had been coughing all the morning, and did not seem to have half got over last Saturday." The horse certainly looked dull. Before night the vet. had visited him, and next morning influenza had set in, which, as his medical adviser predicted, would probably keep him in the stable for a month at the very least. What was to be done now? To miss a Findon Toll-bar meet was out of the question; and, although he had done his work well on the Wednesday, there was nothing for it but the brown. He was a rare constitutioned horse. It was, however, hardly fair play to bring him again out so soon; but I could not help it unless I missed this meet altogether. As the Scotch say truly, " 'Tis indeed a bad cause which we cannot excuse to ourselves;" and although I could see that he wanted rest, and felt it was a shame to press upon good nature, still I reasoned with myself thus. " That we could not be long without a frost, which was generally due about this time, when both horses would have plenty of rest. After all, I need not do anything more than just see the find; and if I sent the horse on the night before, I might even have a mile or two with them without distressing him, and pull up when I liked." Pretty reasoning this! Why, I would as soon have chopped my right hand off as have pulled up in a Findon-gorse run while the horse had a leg to stand upon. And as for just seeing the meet, I would rather have stayed at home altogether than see a fox break from this covert and sit still to watch the hounds running over the finest country perhaps in the world. Still, I was not doing exactly right, and felt rather ill at ease the whole morning; but it often happens that in this life the lucky card turns up at the last moment, when we least expect it.

Findon was nearly twelve miles from us, and I was in the stable making all the final arrangements with the groom to take the horse on in the afternoon, when a ragged urchin came up with a message that " Muster Russell " wanted to see me up at the lodge directly.

I asked the boy whether he knew what he wanted, but all I could get out of him was, that "Master was ill in bed, and wanted to see me *summut* about a horse." I rode over directly, bidding my man wait till I returned. The lodge was not two miles distant, and on my arrival I found my friend Mr. Russell, or Jack Russell, as we all called him, propped up in bed ; his jolly rubicund face set off to advantage by a clean, white, high tasselled nightcap, his right arm bandaged in splints, resting on a pillow ; his countenance the very picture of despair.

"Why, whatever is up now, Jack?" was my first question, when he bade me sit down by his bedside, and listen to his tale of woe.

Jack Russell was one of the hardest-riding farmers in our hunt, and always in the first flight. He rode his horses to sell ; and cared little what sort of a harvest he got, so long as only the hunting season was open. Now, this year he had a magnificent four-year old, which he had bought at Horncastle, and in which Jack (who was seldom deceived in the points of a horse) saw, as he termed it, a little fortune. He had never yet shown the horse the hounds—he had quietly been bottled up at the lodge, taking his lessons over the farm under his owner's able tuition. But Jack had intended that he was soon to "come out," and he had been anxiously waiting for this Findon Toll-bar meet, when he meant, as he termed it, to "have a cut at every hard rider in the hunt" with him. No horse could promise better—a splendid fencer, with a good turn of speed ; as temperate as the oldest hunter in the field, and of a make and shape that were sure to strike the eye at once. The long-wished-for day had come at last, and on the Thursday, at Bramley market, Jack confided to his friends "that something was coming to Findon-gorse on the Saturday which was worth looking at." Jack was a jovial sort of fellow, and was always about the last to leave the farmer's ordinary at the Red Lion ; on this occasion he sat a little longer than usual. The price of wheat was up, the farmers were in high spirits, and the astonishing sport which our hounds had shown this season, was, of course, the leading topic of conversation among a company, every man of whom was either a breeder or a hard rider. Jack acknowledged to me that when he got into his gig to leave, he was a "little gone," but nothing to signify; however, somehow or other he managed to upset the gig, about two miles from his own door, and hobbled home on foot with a broken collar-bone and his right arm fractured. Now, all his projects of showing this brown colt to the swells at Findon-gorse were quite thrown over, and, as he told me, the pain of the accident was nothing, but the disappointment about the horse had kept him awake the whole night. Towards morning he had dozed off, and in a feverish dream had seen me, as plain as daylight, ride this colt over the gate out of his farmyard. He interpreted this as an omen. The destiny of the brown colt was clearly in my hands, and, as it was impossible for him to leave his sick bed, would I do him the favour of riding the colt at Findon-gorse instead of him? If I would he'd never forget it.

Would I do him the favour! Why, I would almost have given him 10*l.* for such a mount on such a day under the present circumstances; but of course I did not tell him that. I was very willing to ride the horse if he fancied I could do it justice, but I could not help owning that it was a great responsibility. And supposing anything should happen to the horse?

Oh! he'd stand all risk. Never mind the horse's neck, or my own, if it came to that. So long as I rode the horse straight and well, he did not care what happened; but if I tried to shirk, he'd never forgive me. Above all, I was to *ride at* young Tom Hardy; and if only I could beat him over the Findon country, the brown was as good as sold. But to beat Tom Hardy was easier said than done.

I sat by that bedside for half-an-hour, receiving a long instruction from a man who had ridden to hounds ever since he was ten years old, who for the last twenty years had been one of our crack riders, and who had always sold his horses for longer prices than any man in our hunt. In fact, "I got him of Jack Russell!" would apply to nearly all the best horses in our county.

He kept continually harping on this string, "Whatever you do,

beat Tom Hardy;" and his last remark on bidding me good-by
was, "Two hundred is his price—guineas, mind ; and if you can
sell him for me, you shall never want a mount this season."

He agreed to send the horse on that afternoon, and I left him to
fret and fidget on a sick bed, while I was picturing to myself in
imagination how I would hop over the splashed blackthorns and
stiff post-and-rails in the Findon country, now I was sure that I had
got a mount on a horse which could do it.

I will not occupy too much space in a description of this day's
run ; suffice it to say that it was the " run of the season." We found
our fox directly the hounds were thrown into the gorse—a regular
"silver-grey flyer." He headed straight for Waverley Wood,
eight miles without a check, over the cream of our country. Every
man meant going that day, and more than half took his own line
and kept it. We crossed the Findon brook twice, but as it was early
in the run, the cold water proved a stopper to but very few. Tom
Hardy was riding a grey, so he was good to make out. As I had
not got his length, I did not deem it prudent to take liberties with
him at starting, and for the first four miles he led us; but the rest of
us were close behind him, ready to come when we were wanted ;
and I never remember in my life seeing so even a field, or one, to
use a racing phrase, which appeared to be so well handicapped. Out
of about a hundred men who went away with the fox, I do not believe we lost thirty between Findon and Waverley Wood. For
nearly the whole eight miles we rode in a line, every man in his
place, and if a man and horse did come down, they were up again
and in their places like magic. Each seemed to feel that the pace
was too good, and the run likely to last too long, to take any liberties with our horses ; and every one, if he could only keep his place,
felt satisfied. The hounds were in view the whole run up to
Waverley Wood, and as every man silently watched his neighbour,
he inwardly wondered when the pace would begin to tell. Before
we got to the wood, it was " bellows to mend" with some of us,
and the tailing began. About fifty men, however, were well up

with the hounds when the fox dashed in—the brown colt and Tom Hardy both in good places.

Waverley Wood was full of foxes; and after dwelling in it for about a quarter of an hour—which gave time for the stragglers to come up, and allowed us to pull our horses a bit together—the hounds went away with a fresh fox, who took us as straight as a crow could fly for about seven miles, over a country, if anything, deeper and stiffer than the last: and they pulled him down in Leyton Openfield (then just inclosed), after giving us such a dance among the new stiff doubles as few of us who saw the end of that run ever forgot. I always hated doubles—I don't know why, but I always "funked" them, and this day I shirked them; but I jumped four stiff new gates (certainly not very high ones) in a line across the open field without a mistake; and this performance sold the horse. I could not beat Tom Hardy, but I "tied him." I got a pad to take home to Jack Russell, who was highly delighted when he heard from a friend how well the horse had gone.

He kept his word, and gave me three or four mounts that season; and I dare say I could have had more if I had wished; but he had picked up a hard-pulling, impetuous young chestnut, who rushed his fences like a bull: he christened it "Kangaroo," and he fancied it would be good enough to win the Findon in the spring. I don't believe Jack cared much about riding him himself, but was always glad to give me a mount on Kangaroo when I chose to ask for it. I sometimes fancied he would make a nice horse, for he had lots of speed, and could jump when he pleased. I could scarcely, if I had wished, have kept count how many falls that horse gave me, suffice it to say I considered myself very lucky if I got less than two in a day (and as I had the honour of schooling him for the Findon, I was on him during the winter perhaps two days a week), whenever I rode the celebrated Kangaroo (and he did become a celebrated horse after). But one day the hounds cast up suddenly in a lane, which I could not see for the hedge, and the chestnut, who had got the bit between his teeth, carried me through a stiff bulfinch right into the middle of them. The lecture I received from the huntsman had such an effect upon me, that I turned the horse's head, and rode him about four miles home in cool blood, straight as a pigeon to Jack Russell's lodge, and I never rode him to hounds again. The old huntsman's sermon was preached quite as much at Mr. Russell as myself, but he was incorrigible. He only regretted I was not two stone heavier to steady the horse, whom he always declared in time would be one of the best with our hounds, and he was right; but he was so pleased with the after-piece, that he thought nothing of the trick that the chestnut had served me in the lane.

It was on the evening after this famous run that I was leading Mr. Russell's horse home to our village, picking my way as best I could, through deep, muddy, cross-country lanes and by-roads, one of which a surly old countryman would persist in telling me led to *nowhere*. Leyton Openfield was a very out-of-the-way place, and the inhabitants of the dirty little village a very primitive lot. At last, however, I found my way into a country which I knew, and the sun was just sinking as I crossed the turnpike-road and struck into a by-lane which led about two miles down to our village. Somehow or other, now I had "got the key" of Jack Russell's stable, I did not seem to feel half so anxious about a frost, and I was rather glad to mark a heavy bank of clouds rising in the west as the sun set, which to my mind bespoke wind and rain rather than frost. The wood-pigeons had just finished their evening meal off the turnips, and were dropping down to roost on the tall oaks in a spinney to my right. The sheep were folded for the night, and a dead silence so peculiar to a winter evening reigned over all. Just as I got into the lane I heard a double shot in a stubble field by the side of the road, and a little further on I saw the head keeper's pony tied to a gate. He was coming up the field as I passed; and as the gamekeeper is rather an important personage in every rural district, especially as he looked over all our village, I stopped to have a chat with him. Of course I gave him a very accurate description of the run, not forgetting my share in the performance; and he asked me if I would be kind enough to leave a couple of brace of birds for him at the Parsonage as I rode by, for it would save him the trouble of riding down to the village himself—adding, "I must get home as soon as I can, for we expect 'your gang' over to-night, and I want to be ready for them." We then parted. I must not trouble the reader with a slight description of our village and our head keeper, and explain what the latter meant when he alluded to "your gang."

Our village lay in the heart of, perhaps, the very strictest preserved county in England at that day. It was a pretty little village enough; the forest came up within a mile of it one side, while a stiff inclosed rich agricultural country stretched for miles and miles around it on the other. The forest land was full of pheasants, hares, and rabbits, while the open country swarmed with partridges. The whole district for miles around belonged to the Duke of B., one of our strictest game preservers; and his head keeper, Johnson, was the very type of his calling—a stout, heavy, muscular, middle-aged man, able-bodied and resolute; the terror of all the poachers round us, for he looked upon them as the rankest of vermin, and if he could have had his own way, would, I believe, have hung them up on the branches of his "keeper's tree" with as little remorse as polecats or weasels. As I said before, our village was a small one, and I suppose scarcely contained two hundred inhabitants; but it was a nest of poachers, and Johnson used to reckon that on any night we could turn out a gang of half a score of the most determined poachers in the county—men who were well versed in all the minutiæ of the trade; who could snare a hare in an open furrow as well as in a smeuse; who could silently sweep off covey after covey of birds in a night in the very heart of the manor; who could clear the home preserves close up to the keeper's lodge without firing a shot; but who would at times muster in a gang, armed with guns, and, laying aside all secrecy, march through the forest and nail the pheasants at perch like so many barn-door fowls. Every one of these poachers was a marked man, and every one in the village well knew how he obtained his livelihood during the winter months; but they were always civil and respectful enough to us, and somehow or other none of us who had no game to preserve seemed to think that poaching was a very grave offence. It is true they did the farmers in our village but little service, for just before the hay harvest they all used to migrate into distant counties where labourers were scarcer than with us, and wages higher, and they did not return till the bean harvest was over. During the winter it was very rarely that any one of them did a steady day's work: they were always ready for any little odd job which turned up, but could never settle down to regular work, and their whole days appeared to be spent lounging about the beershop and the blacksmith's forge (the usual winter resort of all the vagabonds in the parish), and three nights out of the seven most probably in the woods, so it was scarcely likely they would be much fit for work by day. Of course we had in the village one of the greatest curses of that day, a higgler, and his cart carried away all the poached game and stolen poultry to a distant market, generally to the guards of the London coaches on the North road, who were always ready purchasers. I am not at all for granting too much licence to a police force, but I must say I think that it was an excellent measure, and one which gave the greatest death-blow to poaching, when the law allowed the police the power to apprehend and search any suspected person or vehicle and seize any game which was found upon them. At this time the police had no such power, in fact, our only protectors in the country were the old parish constables, and they were about as much use as the old London " Charlies."

Of course there was a leader to our gang, and he was a man in every respect fitted for the post. He was the son of the old higgler before alluded to, and a more ruffianly-looking fellow it would have been hard to find. His name was Hammerton—Bill Hammerton, and he was known among his associates, in fact nearly all over the county, by the nickname of " Sloppy." He was at this time a little over thirty years of age, a stout, thickset fellow, standing about 5 feet 9 inches, and weighing 13 stone. A more desperate character did not exist, and, unless rumour grossly lied, far darker charges than poaching could be laid to his charge. But although he had been imprisoned three or four times for snaring, he had always as yet been lucky enough to escape being taken in any night affray; and this was the more singular, for he was always at the head of his gang and in the thickest of the fray in the night encounters which were then so frequently taking place between the gamekeepers and poachers. He was a noted fighter, and the champion of our county. Scarcely a village feast or country fair for miles around us but this Bill Hammerton was engaged in a pugilistic contest, and I never heard that he was beaten. He was a true type of the ruffianly Englishman, combining the strength of an ox with the pluck of a bulldog; and one could not help thinking, as one looked at his ugly but resolute and determined features, what a soldier that man would have made if he had been properly trained.

Now, the head keeper, Johnson, who was himself as brave as a lion, would have given any money to capture Hammerton in a night row, for a price was set upon his head, and if he was only taken the gang would, in all probability be broken up. But he had never yet been lucky enough.

The others of the gang were common farm-labourers, who could not withstand the fascinations of this desperate trade; and, say what we will, there must be some fascination in poaching more than in any other crime, for I have known men follow it who, barring the excitement, had no other earthly inducement. For instance, we had once a helper in our stables, who lodged and slept in the house. Now, this man had as good a place as a servant could wish, and wanted nothing. But he was a confirmed poacher, and used to steal out at night and join the village gang whenever an onslaught was meditated on one of the best preserves. We never suspected him, for he was always at his work in the morning. But one morning he was missing altogether. There had been a desperate battle in a wood not two miles from us, and I recollect well that I sat on our garden-wall and counted nearly one hundred shots fired about eleven o'clock, before the keepers came up. The battle was a sharp one, but the keepers, as usual, got the best of it. Three poachers were taken; the rest escaped, and among them our helper. His hat, however, had been knocked off in the *mêlée*, and the head keeper secured it. He read the man's name in it, and next morning rode over to see if we could identify it. There was, of course, no trouble to do this. The man never came back to us, nor did we hear of him again till one evening, about two years after, I pulled up on the box of the old Regulator, at the Three Cups in Aldersgate-street. To my surprise, I recognised in the slovenly cad that came out to stand at the horses' heads (for we only stopped there a few minutes) our quondam stableman. I offered to take him back, for he was a rare good man with horses; but he would not come into the country again, and I never heard anything more of him.

It was nearly dark before I reached the village, and there was something cheery in the ruddy blaze of light which shot across the road from the blacksmith's forge, and the clang of his hammer, as I approached it. I stopped and called the man out, for I wanted to speak to him about "four removes" next morning; and as I looked in through the open door, I saw the shop was full, as usual, and I recognised four or five of the poachers whom I knew well. One was just unscrewing a short gun-barrel, which he thrust into his pocket as I pulled up. He was a very civil, decent young fellow, and came out to hold my horse while I spoke to the blacksmith. He was followed by a little half-starved lurching cur, which never left his heels, and which, as a mute dog for driving hares into the nets, was invaluable to the gang. As I got on my horse, he asked me in a low tone if I wanted a hare or a brace of "long-tails" in the morning; and I told him "they had better look out, for that Johnson was expecting them." He laughed, and said "they knew it, but that they wanted game that night, and game they would have." This was the last conversation I ever had with that poor fellow, for he was dead before morning. Of course Bill Hammerton was in the shop, apparently engaged in heating some wire at the blacksmith's fire, no doubt for snares.

The Poacher. 347

It was a curious thing, but whenever any great poaching visit was planned to a favourite preserve, our keepers always seemed to know of it beforehand, and to be prepared. In fact sometimes, out of sheer bravado, the poachers would send word to say that they were coming on such a night, and hoped the keepers would meet them like men.

Now on this night there was to be a grand "gathering of the clans" to sweep the home preserves before the Christmas battues began. Four gangs from four different villages had agreed to meet at the old "trysting place," a gravel pit by the side of the forest. Twenty of the best men with guns were to be told off to shoot the pheasants in the home woods, and the rest were quietly to net hares and rabbits in the forest. The poachers reckoned that they should muster about thirty-five men, which they did. As I said before, Johnson was prepared for them; but with all his watchers he could not reckon on more than eight men, so he applied for help to the head keeper of the Earl of D., whose preserves joined. Now on this estate every labourer was obliged to take his turn at night watching, so he had no difficulty in borrowing twelve men for this occasion (in fact it was a common cause with the keepers, for if the poachers had swept our woods first, they would certainly on another night have gone on to the next estate); and the earl's head keeper, as resolute a fellow as Johnson, agreed to head them, just for the fun of the thing. Johnson's men were never allowed any other weapons besides sticks (each had a handkerchief tied round his hat to distinguish him—a rather useful precaution in a night affray, where the rule used to be, wherever you see a head hit at it), but Johnson himself used a singular but far more effective weapon, a stout hayfork, about three feet long in the shaft, "a tolloch over the head from which (I use his own expressive phrase) would bring the strongest man down on his knees like a bullock." I saw this identical hayfork at his house a few days after this battle, and the tines were bent crooked over Bill Hammerton's head. The keepers of the Earl of D. always fought with short dog-spears. The keepers on this night mustered about twenty, the poachers about thirty-five men. These seemed long odds, but still they were in favour of the keepers, for " thrice is he armed that hath his quarrel just." Besides, as Johnson once observed to me, " Bless you! when you come really to tackle a poacher, he's very little good. He's never got anything in him but gin and tobacco. They don't, perhaps, get a good meal of meat once in a week;" which I dare say was about true.

By ten the poachers had mustered in the gravel-pit by the side of a lane, close to the forest where the netting was to commence. The keepers, who were not up to the trick of their dividing, went down to one of the home-preserves, nearly a mile from the gravel-pit, where they fancied the general attack would be made. But they went to the wrong spot, for they waited on this post nearly half-an-hour without hearing a sound, and they almost began to think that the poachers had given up the thought of coming that night, when a double shot was fired in the wood closest to our village, more than a mile from where they were watching. This shot was fired about half-past ten, and I was standing in the stable-yard talking with Jem. We both heard it, and he observed, " That's only a plant to draw the keepers down ; it's not that wood they mean to work to-night." In a little time after we counted five more shots, and then all was still. I may add, that it was just the very night of all others that our poachers loved. I never could fancy that the man who wrote the old popular poaching song of " My delight on a shiny night at a season of the year," knew much about real poaching, as our chaps never went out at the full moon for any great attack. A dark, gusty, blowing night, with the moon certainly not older than twelve days, was the night they generally chose; or a moon three-quarters old, if the night was all right, was nearly as good, only it always rose so late. On this night there would probably have been rather too much moon if the sky had been clear, but heavy clouds drifted across the stormy sky, and the wind was blowing fresh from the south-west. The consequence was, that the reports of the guns were carried plain enough down to our village, which lay to leeward of the wood; but the keepers, who were to the windward, never heard them, so that the *ruse*, although well planned, entirely failed.

At about eleven, however, the general attack began. I may add that Hammerton was to head the shooting party, and the young man whom I spoke to in the blacksmith's shop headed the netters. The poachers had gone to a home preserve, full of pheasants, which on account of the storm, were perching low. This wood lay rather to the windward of the keepers, so they heard the shots, but only indistinctly—at first a dropping fire, but soon four or five to the minute all over the wood. "By G—!" said Johnson, "they're in the home wood. Come on, my lads! or they'll clear it before we get there." And off the keepers started in the direction of the guns. But the road was rough, and the moon gave little light. It was not easy running, and it was half-an-hour before they reached the wood. After the first twenty minutes the fire slackened, and by the time they got up the poachers were beating a retreat to join their comrades, who were netting in another covert, about half-a-mile distant. It was excellently planned. Hammerton got all his men off but three, who lay hidden with the game in a ditch, by the very side of which the keepers passed in full pursuit without discovering them. It was very unlucky for Johnson that old Sailor (his favourite night-dog) had staked himself the day before in jumping over a dead fence with a pheasant in his mouth, and was obliged to be left at home, or these three men and their booty would have been secured. As it was, they lay quiet till the keepers had passed, and then ran home as fast as they could under a load of about fifty of Johnson's finest pheasants—which had, perhaps, cost nearly $1l.$ each to fatten. The men reached the village safely; the old higgler's cart was got under way at once; by five in the morning they were on the top of one of the night-coaches, and the same night were in London.

It had been planned beforehand that directly the firing ceased, the poachers who were netting were to assemble under a large oak well known to every one of them, and wait till the Hammerton

party joined them. He rightly guessed that the keepers would
come down in a body to the guns, and if they could only get a
quarter of an hour or twenty minutes' good shooting, his stratagem
was to leave off and retreat quickly upon the netting party, so that,
in case of an attack, the forces would not be divided. And it was
even possible that the keepers would remain searching the wood
where they had heard the firing, and in this case they would escape
with all their booty, and without bloodshed. It was a very near thing,
and, had the keepers come up five minutes later, the poachers
might have escaped. They had got clear of the wood, and were
keeping well under the hedgerows out of sight; but the crashing of
a dead fence as they sprang over it caught the quick ear of Johnson,
and he halloaed his men on like a pack of fox-hounds. But they
were more blown than the poachers, and although when they once
got on the trail they never left it, the poachers reached the wood
more than five minutes in advance. As soon as they got safe into
the wood, a long but low whistle warned them where their comrades were standing; and in a few minutes more the whole party
were drawn up under the old oak, breathlessly waiting the coming
of the keepers. Johnson was pretty certain that the poachers had
entered the wood, but he did not exactly know where. The old
oak was perhaps five hundred yards in the depth of the forest, and
as the poachers stood as mute and silent as statues beneath its
shades, the keepers were completely at fault. Had the poachers
been content to carry with them a part of the hares and rabbits
which they had already secured, and silently retreated, in all probability they would have got clear off; but they wished to save their
nets, which were worth ten or fifteen pounds, and they stood still,
thinking that the keepers might overlook them in the gloom of the
forest. Blue lights and rockets were not, I think, invented then—
at least I never heard of our keepers using them; but what I most
wondered at was, that not one even carried a dark lantern in his
pocket. Johnson was fairly puzzled. He dared not divide his men,
for he knew the poachers were strong, although not aware of their
actual numbers, and he thought it worse than useless to try to follow

up their trail through the wood, now that he had nothing to guide him. He called up his men to hold a consultation as to what was best to be done; and this was lucky, for it allowed them to gather breath for what was coming.

The old oak under which the poachers were gathered stood in a forest clearing, with, perhaps, open grass for a hundred yards round it on all sides. The keepers were standing consulting in the thick wood within two hundred yards of the tree, little thinking how near they were to the poachers. They would probably have turned back, when all of a sudden the heavy clouds drifting away from the face of the moon, she shone out in all her glory. Only for a few minutes ; but those few minutes enabled the keepers to see the poachers; and Johnson's shout of triumph, " Here they are! close in, my lads !" warned them that nothing was left for them but to stand up and fight like men. All their faces were blackened, and many of them disfigured with red patches, and they formed a wild group when their uncouth figures and the old dead tree were suddenly brought into bold relief by the moon's shimmering rays. The keepers dashed into the open space, but the poachers presented a formidable front, for those who had guns were ranged in a line—every muzzle presented to them. They drew back, and rather hesitated, and Johnson's challenge of " Come, my men—no nonsense ! we know you all, so you'd better give it up !" was met by a derisive cheer from the poachers, who bade them come on if they dared. Johnson's blood was up. He had recognised his old enemy, Hammerton, in the crowd, and he was determined to have him or die in the attempt. Heedless of all consequences, he rushed in at him, and the keepers, instead of showing a front line, followed him in Indian file, and the attack was so sudden that only two guns were fired, one charge wounding a keeper in the thigh. " No firing ! buttends, my lads !" roared out Hammerton, as he sprung aside and aimed a heavy blow at Johnson's head with the butt-end of his gun ; but the hayfork stood the keeper in good need, for he skilfully parried a blow which would probably have dashed his brains out if it had reached him, and, recovering himself, he brought Hammerton to the ground with a swinging round-handed hit on the side of the head. The poacher fell, and the keeper, who was overbalanced by the force of his own blow, fell on him. Hammerton was not even stunned, and he seized Johnson like a bulldog by the throat, and these two strong men rolled over and over on the grass, in a mortal embrace, snarling and tearing at each other like two fierce dogs, sometimes the one above, sometimes the other. Meanwhile the battle was raging fiercely all around; now and then a crashing blow from a gun-stock would bring a keeper to the ground, but the short dog-spears did dreadful service. The men were strictly ordered only to use them as sticks, and not to stab with them, but more than one poacher fell with a dog-spear in his side. It is singular that during the whole of the battle only three guns were fired; but this is accounted for by the fact that only five of the poachers had any ammunition left; and if the keepers had known that only five out of the twenty guns which were pointed at them were loaded, they would not have hesitated an instant about rushing in. It was a curious fact that in this hand-to-hand fight, even when their blood was up, the poachers seemed to have a repugnance at firing upon the keepers, who had no guns; for as one of them who escaped told me afterwards, that although his gun was loaded during the whole time, he did not seem to feel to dare to fire it, but only fought with the butt-end.

The battle was too fierce to last long, and in five minutes the poachers beat a retreat, leaving seven prisoners and all their nets, hares, and rabbits, in the hands of the keepers. Poor Johnson was in rather an awkward case. He could not rise, for he could not shake Hammerton off, who was as strong a man as himself. By a desperate struggle, the poacher got above the keeper, and dashing his head against the ground, which partially stunned him, he sprang to his feet, and, giving Johnson one settler by a tremendous kick under the ear, he plunged into the thickest of the forest, and, favoured by the night and the confusion of the moment, escaped. It was some little time before Johnson could rise, and his first expression, as he stared wildly round him, "D—n him! I'll have him yet," proved how sorry he felt for the loss of the prize which he considered so fairly within his grasp. Several of the keepers had broken heads, but none were seriously hurt except the man who was shot in the thigh, and one of the young watchers who gave chase to a poacher for some hundred yards into the forest. The poacher, finding himself sorely pressed, suddenly threw himself down—the watcher tumbled over him, and, before he could rise, was stunned by a blow from the poacher's bludgeon, who then made his escape. The prisoners, with their booty, were marched off to Johnson's lodge, and next morning were taken before a neighbouring magistrate, and committed for trial to the next assizes.

When the keepers mustered, one was missing—the young watcher who had followed the poacher into the wood. In vain his comrades shouted—in vain the shrill whistle which every one of them carried at night, sounded through the wood. No answer was returned, and they were obliged to leave the forest without him, rightly judging that he would turn up before morning; and so he did, but not till daylight, when he staggered up to the head keeper's lodge, pale as death, sick and faint; his head and face covered with blood, and wearing altogether so ghastly an appearance that the other keepers scarcely knew him. The poacher had left him stunned and disabled, and it was probably a long time before he came to himself. When he woke up, all was quiet in the wood; and he then knew that his comrades had left him, and he must find his way home as he best could. His keeper's instinct soon put him in the right path, and partly by walking, partly by crawling on all-fours, he managed to find his way to the edge of the covert. The night was now as dark as pitch, for the moon had gone down. He was staggering along a narrow ride in the forest, when his foot struck against something that lay across the path, and he stumbled over the dead body of the young poacher who had headed the netting party. He had been stabbed in the side with a dog-spear, but had run as far as his strength could carry him, till he fell dead from internal hemorrhage. His poor little dog kept watch over the body,

and was endeavouring by all the mute eloquence he possessed, by
licking his hands and face, pulling at his coat, to wake up his dead
master—but in vain. The poor fellow was buried in our churchyard, and of all the mourners that followed him to the grave, not
one deplored his loss more deeply than that ragged little half-starved
cur. The keeper fell over the dead body, and for some time lay
side by side with the corpse. He was already faint with pain and
loss of blood; and when his hand came in contact with that cold
face, and dabbled in the pool of blood which surrounded the dead
poacher, it was more than he could stand—he fainted away. The
night breeze swept in hollow gusts through the dead trees, and the
dismal hoot of the owl echoed mournfully through the forest
glade; but the two sleepers heard nothing, and it was not till daylight glimmered in the east that the watcher woke, and the grey
twilight of the drear winter's morning revealed to him the ghastly
features of the dead man who had been his companion through the
night upon that damp, chill bed on which they had both fallen.

The young poacher's sad death caused no little sensation among
our simple villagers, and I remember a melancholy ballad was made
by some rustic poet on the events of that fatal night. It was a
standard song at our harvest-homes for years after. I do not recollect it now—nor, if I did, should I inflict a repetition of it upon the
reader; but the refrain ran thus:

> "The keepers heard us fire a gun,
> And to the spot did quickly run,
> And swore before the rising sun
> That one of us should die."

The whole occurrences of that eventful night were faithfully
described, and the song was sung in a melancholy, drawling tone,
so peculiar to a country harvest-home or in the forecastle of a ship.
And strange to say, many years after, when I had nearly forgotten
not only the song itself, but all the circumstances upon which it
was founded, I was standing on the forecastle of the good barque
Blackheath, one fine calm night, in the middle watch, south of the
equator, watching the rippling waves as they sparkled under our

cutwater, and now and then gazing upwards with solemn admiration at the Southern Cross and the other beautiful constellations which spangled the deep blue sky—all was silent as the grave, when suddenly one of the lookouts, who was sitting on the foot of the bowsprit began, in a low but not unmusical voice, the first stanza of that melancholy ditty. I have heard it observed that nothing recals the scenes of youth and home to the wanderer's mind so much as hearing the songs of his earlier days in a foreign land; and never shall I forget how vividly the occurrences which I have just described rushed across my mind when I heard this old song crooned out in that "lone, lone sea." I was some thousand miles away from the spot: but the old village, the forest, and the very oak under which the battle took place, stood as plain before me as the bowsprit of that ship. I could see Johnson and Hammerton, as it were, locked together on the ground in deadly conflict, and I could well picture to myself the tableau of the watcher, the dead poacher, and the dog lying together in the forest glade.

The poachers were tried at the next assizes, but their sentence was not so heavy as we expected it would have been. In fact, the circumstance of the young poacher being killed by the dog-spear, and on which the counsel for the defence dwelt eloquently, served, I think, to influence both judge and jury. The gang was broken up, and although poaching was carried on on a small scale, we rarely heard afterwards in our woods of any serious battles which before that night were so constantly taking place between the keepers and the poachers.

Hammerton escaped the vigilance of the police for two years, notwithstanding a reward was offered for his apprehension, and he was a well-known character in our parts. I will here narrate a curious circumstance. A description of his person was inserted in the notices, and we did not think it would be very difficult to identify a man who was peculiarly marked by a large mole on one cheek. But, strange to say, there was not one in the parish (except his most intimate friends, and, of course, they would not help us) who could positively swear on which cheek this mole stood. Some were certain that it was on the right, others on the left; but no one would swear positively, and this mark of identity was useless. He absconded into a western county, and fell in with a character as desperate as himself—one "Bristol Jack," a low, coping horse-dealer. They worked together for some time; and not being very particular how they obtained their horses, they soon got into trouble, and were committed to Exeter gaol for horse-stealing. A notice was sent down to us that one of these men was most probably the man we wanted. A constable went down to identify Hammerton at his trial. He was acquitted of horse-stealing, but on leaving the dock was arrested on a poaching warrant by our constable and brought back. Our assizes were held the following week. He was tried, and found guilty; but his sentence was a light one—two years' imprisonment. The words, "No firing, my lads—use your butt-ends," which he shouted to his gang when the keepers attacked them, probably saved him from a heavier sentence.

We had now got rid certainly of the worst of our gang, and for a while our village was altered for the better; and Johnson's mind was at rest. I have no doubt a little snaring and netting went on, but the gang seemed to be broken up, and the deeds of violence which had been committed during Hammerton's reign had become almost a matter of history, and served now merely to furnish conversation among the rustics at the beer-house and the blacksmith's shop. However, time sped on. Hammerton's two years were up; and one afternoon, as Johnson was riding home from our village, he met his old enemy walking into it, in better "working condition," as he told his friends, than ever he had been in his life. Hammerton politely bade the keeper "Good afternoon," thanked him for his kindness, and told him he would never forget it—words which bore an awful significance when uttered by as great a ruffian as ever breathed. Johnson, however, was not a man to be frightened by words; and merely telling the poacher that he had better not let him get hold of him again, rode on. Hammerton certainly did not forget Johnson's kindness to him, but took a very early opportunity of repaying the obligation. It was in August when he returned, so there was nothing to be done in his line just then. He found his gang disorganized, and many of them settled down into steady labourers; but there were two or three lawless spirits who were too far gone ever to settle down steadily, and they welcomed their old captain back, and longed for the dark winter nights to come once again.

Except a little fowl-stealing, we had, however, nothing to complain of now; but it was quite evident that Hammerton was organizing another gang for the winter, and at Johnson's request his band of night-watchers was doubled. There would assuredly have been some roughish work this winter if Hammerton could only have kept himself quiet for a few months; but he was longing to be revenged upon Johnson, and this revenge he determined to gratify on the first occasion. But this was not an easy task. Johnson very rarely went out without his gun; and " old Sailor," who seldom left his heels, was as good, and perhaps better, than any one man.

Our village feast was in the beginning of October, and on the Monday afternoon he rode over to spend the afternoon with his brother, a farmer in our place. He had neither gun nor dog with him. I looked in to smoke a pipe with them in the afternoon, and talk over the season. About five, Johnson left. On his road home, half way between our village and his lodge, was a small spinny, which lay one field from the road; and just as he passed a double shot was fired, apparently in this spinny. It took him a very few minutes to tie his pony to the gate, and run down the ditch under cover of the hedge, to see what was up; and when he reached the coppice a decently-dressed man, quite a stranger to him, was standing loading his gun, about twenty yards in the wood. The man never attempted to escape, and his reply to Johnson's challenge, " Now, who the —— are you, and where's your certificate ?" was, " You'd better come and see." Johnson was scrambling over the hedge into the spinny, when suddenly another man sprang up from the ditch behind him (he had been covered up under a heap of ferns), and in less time than it takes to write it the keeper was

knocked senseless into the ditch by a blow on the back of the head
from the butt-end of a gun-stock. It was but the work of a few
seconds; but even in those few seconds he had time before the blow
fell to recognise the brutal features of Hammerton. The attack
had been all planned beforehand. The poachers watched Johnson
down to the feast, and knew about what time he would come back.
Hammerton lay hidden, and the other poacher fired the double
shot when he saw Johnson ride up the lane, to draw him down to
Hammerton's hiding-place. The stratagem succeeded well; and,
but for the special interference of Providence, murder would most
assuredly have been added to the "bead-roll" of Hammerton's
iniquities. But, as good luck would have it, three farm labourers,
on their way to the village feast, came over the hedge at the end of
the spinny at the very moment, or the keeper never would have
lived to tell the tale; for Hammerton was standing over him with
his gun raised to give him the *coup de grâce*, when a sharp exclamation from the man in the wood caused him to turn round, and he
saw the three labourers getting over the fence not fifty yards from
him. The second blow fell harmless. He dashed at once through
the hedge into the spinny, and made his escape with his comrade on
the other side of it. The labourers, had, however, seen him, but
no one dared to follow him, and they turned their attention to the
apparently lifeless keeper. The youngest and most active of the
three galloped down to the village on the keeper's pony, to tell the
news; the other two carried the body up to the road; and in less
than half-an-hour Johnson's brother drove up in a tax-cart, and
took him to his lodge. Although his skull was dreadfully fractured,
he was not dead; but brain fever set in, and for weeks his life
hung upon a thread. A strong constitution, however, pulled him
through; and, although he never was the same man again, he still
kept his place as head keeper, but under strict injunctions that he
never again went out to watch at night.

It was not likely that such a desperate attack in broad daylight
should pass unnoticed. A hundred pounds reward was now offered
by Johnson's master for Hammerton's apprehension; and, as a good

London detective was set on his trail, he did not long escape. He was apprehended in London, tried at our next assizes, and sentence of death recorded against him. The other man was never taken; and Hammerton's sullen remark that he "never would split upon a pal, even if the halter was round his neck," gave the police very little hopes of obtaining any information from him. Hammerton was transported for life. After serving in a convict gang for some years, he obtained a ticket of leave; and when the diggings first broke out, like many others of his stamp, had an extraordinary run of luck. But his eyesight failed him, and he set up a weather-boarded lodging-house and sly grog-shop on Forest Creek. A young man from the same village, who was working on the Creek, chanced one afternoon to go in, and, as no one else was in the shanty, he got into conversation with a hairy, purblind old ruffian, who was smoking his pipe on a log. One question an "old hand" invariably asks you as soon as you begin to talk with him is, " And what part of the old country do you come out of?"—and the young digger found himself unexpectedly a guest of a man from the same village as himself—a man whom he had never seen, but of whom he had often heard, and a man, moreover, who appeared to feel very little remorse for the crimes he had committed, for he told the digger his only regret was that "he could not get his b—— eyes back again and return home, in which case he would be as bad as ever he had been."

There are many such men in the bush and on the diggings—ruffians on whose faces the "overseer's brand" (a broken nose) is indelibly imprinted—men of whom, on looking at their brutal, hardened countenances, you are tempted to ask yourself "Could such a man ever have been a baby?"—men whose chief delight seems to be to compare notes and growl out their deeds of villany in their peculiar colonial slang, as they smoke their short pipes on an evening in the log-hut or round the camp-fire. I have sat and listened scores of times to their conversations, but I do not believe I ever in a single instance heard one such man utter a sentence of regret for his past life.

We have now done with Mr. William Hammerton; and probably the reader is by this quite as tired of him as myself.

The gang was now completely broken up, and we rarely after this heard of any very serious affrays between the keepers and poachers in our woods; but a very lawless set still existed among our villagers, who had always been noted as the worst characters in the county, and they took to a new trade, that of sheep-stealing. But we soon put a stopper on this game. However little the farmers might care when they heard that every pheasant had been cleared off in such a wood, or on such a night, they did not much like to hear, morning after morning, that Farmer Smith, or old Roberts up at the Lodge, had lost another sheep on the previous night; and as the sheep-stealers began to get more daring, a consultation was held as to what was best to be done. Now, the English farmers take some rousing, but when once fairly roused, they generally prove themselves men of action and decision. So an association was formed at once, about fifty members were enrolled from our village and those in the neighbourhood, nearly a hundred pounds were subscribed, and one fine morning a man (a London dealer) walked up to Mr. Jack Russell's lodge, leading a brace of perhaps the handsomest black-and-tan bloodhounds that were ever seen. In the afternoon, a long-winded, lathy young fellow, who got his living by rat-catching, was started with a drag (a sheep's head), with instructions to run it through two villages next to ours, come back, and walk into our beershop, and there sit till the hounds came up. We gave him two hours' law, and then laid the hounds on. It was a treat to see them hit off his scent from the farmyard. The scent was a hot one, and they followed him yard for yard, but in couples, through all his doublings and dodgings; and he had scarcely been seated in the beershop half-an-hour, before the deep bay of the hounds, as they dashed up to the door, told us that he was there.

The little beershop, as usual, was filled with poachers and sheep-stealers, and great was their astonishment when the door burst open, and the dealer led the two hounds in, coupled up; and greater still when the rat-catcher, who had jumped up on to the table, threw them down the sheep's head out of the pocket of his greasy old shooting-jacket, and delivered himself up as though in custody. It was a capital play. I could have picked every sheep-stealer out of that group, merely by watching their countenances at that moment.

The hounds were stationed at Russell's; he was appointed huntsman, and the rat-catcher ran the drag twice a week during the winter. The news soon spread far and wide, and for three or four months none of our farmers lost a single sheep. But one Saturday night, when the ewes were lambing, in March, a fat ewe was taken out of Jack Russell's own flock. The loss was discovered in the morning about five. There was a nasty little hoar-frost on the ground, and the scent had got very cold. But the hounds were laid on directly, and after a slow run of two hours, they took us to a village nearly six miles distant, inhabited, if possible, by as bad a lot as our own. They picked the scent up steadily step by step, to the door of a cottage which they would not leave. Mr. Russell did not stop to inquire whether he had any right or not to enter the house without a warrant, but kicked the door open at once. Two men sat at breakfast, with plates of sheep's liver before them (no doubt the property of Mr. Russell), and in the corner of the house lay the skin of the sheep just taken off. We secured this, and the next day the men were apprehended. They confessed, and were transported for seven years.

We never lost a sheep after this; but we kept the hounds on, and running these drags became such a fashionable amusement among our hard-riding farmers that we always ran them on by-days when the hounds were not out. We often used to have from twenty to thirty well-mounted men at our meets, and, as Russell always picked a stiff line of country, whenever there was a good scent our drag hunts were more like steeple-chases than anything else. This just suited the men who lived round us at that time (I often wonder what sort of a lot live there now), and especially Jack Russell, who was always making some young one up for the hounds; and in this kind of hunting, as he observed, you never need be afraid of heading your fox or riding over the hounds.

Times have doubtless much altered since my day, and probably now poaching is not carried on to the extent which it used to be then; but I have not the least exaggerated, in the previous description, how it used to be with us some five-and-twenty years ago. I could not help remarking in Australia that nine-tenths of the old convicts, according to their own confession, had been sent out for breaches of the game laws; and, if such was the case, it does indeed seem as if there was some peculiar charm in the poacher's life. I am not one of those, however, who defend the poacher, as many do, on this plea; and it would be just as absurd to argue that game in a preserved state is *feræ naturæ*, and as much one man's property as another. I have heard many use this argument, but I fancy now we see things in a different light, and I consider the man who walks into a preserve at night to shoot a pheasant is as much guilty of a robbery as the man who breaks into a hen-house to steal poultry, or into a sheep-fold to steal a sheep.

Moreover, that man must possess a good share of hardihood of the wrong sort who can wander about a forest in the dead of the night, very often at the risk of his life, engaged in a pursuit which he knows to be unlawful; and depend upon it such a man has gone through the worst of the training to render him fit for any other deed of rapine or bloodshed. In my younger days, I had good opportunities of studying the habits of real desperate poachers, and I am certain that such men would have just as soon stolen a horse or a sheep as a hare or a pheasant, if the risk had been no greater; and the reason why we seldom suffered any depredations at the hands of our gang was, that they acted upon the same principle as the fox, who is said seldom to molest game or poultry in the immediate neighbourhood of his own earth.

ON GUN ACCIDENTS.

It is a curious fact, but one which daily experience proves to be true, that in ordinary life we generally find the most serious warnings pass unheeded; and it always appears, when we hear or read of any of the numerous accidents which are so constantly happening through the incautious use of fire-arms, that if the very commonest precaution had been used, the accident would never have occurred. Strange to say, these accidents are not confined merely to the young and inexperienced—for during my career I have seen quite as many, if not serious accidents, still, hairbreadth escapes, happen from guns in the hands of old sportsmen who were well accustomed to their use, as in those of the young and thoughtless; and whenever I look back upon the accidents and hairbreadth escapes which have come under my personal notice (and these have not been few), it appears almost certain that not a single one would have taken place if the merest caution had been observed. It seems that neither remonstrance nor experience will ever teach men to be as cautious with guns as they ought to be; and any invention which tends to lessen the chance, or altogether prevent the possibility, of an accident happening with a gun, must be regarded as a great boon, not only to every sportsman, but to mankind at large.

A perusal of some excellent remarks in the *Field* newspaper on the breech-loader dictated this chapter; and if the invention had no other recommendation than its safe manner of loading, and the ease and quickness with which the cartridge can be removed, for safety sake, when the gun is put away, or about to be carried in a gig, boat, or on horseback, these alone would warrant every prudent man in adopting it.

Experience has painfully taught us that a common percussion-gun, when loaded, can hardly ever be considered perfectly safe from exploding, in whatever way it is carried or wherever it is placed. As to carrying the hammer down upon the cap, I would just as soon see the gun at full-cock, for about nine-tenths of the casualties which I have witnessed have arisen from the hammer being slightly elevated and then falling down again upon the cap. This is in a great measure prevented by a plan I have seen adopted in many of Rigby's guns—and I dare say those of other makers—which is, where the *sear* has three catches into the tumbler, the first one when the cock is scarcely raised one-eighth of an inch from the nipple. Were this plan generally adopted, I am certain one-half of the accidents which have arisen from percussion-guns would have been avoided. I notice that this is the plan adopted with foreign makers pretty generally, and I really believe that on this account we do not hear of accidents arising from guns in any country so frequently as in England. Were I a father, and about to put a muzzle-loading percussion-gun into the hands of my son, the lock should be on this principle and no other; and he should be taught as his first lesson invariably to carry his gun with the hammer at rest just off the nipple. In such a position it is next to impossible for an accident to happen unless the locks break inside; for if the hammer is suddenly and accidentally drawn back (unless the trigger is pressed at the same time), it must either come up to half-cock, or the *sear* will fall again into the third notch of the tumbler instead of allowing the hammer to fall on the cap; and even if the hammer of such a lock is suddenly drawn back when resting on the nipple, the chances are that it will certainly come back so far as to allow the *sear* to fall into the lowest notch, and the hammer will not strike on to the cap.

Even at half-cock—which we must all acknowledge is the safest way of carrying a common percussion-gun, the risk of explosion is not altogether avoided; for we all know that very often a slight blow will explode a cap, and I suppose (although I never knew a case in point) that if the *sear* were to suddenly snap, through any flaw in the steel, the hammer would fall down and explode the cap. Even when the cap is removed, a loaded gun is not safe. The foil-lined caps are certainly safer than those in which the percussion powder is only pasted into the top of the cap without any covering; but I have known two instances myself of the gun firing through a little of the detonating powder being left loose on the top of the nipple after the cap had been removed.

Now these casualties may not altogether be avoided by the breech-loading system, but two prolific causes of the accidents which are so frequently happening with the old muzzle-loader are altogether done away with by the new plan of loading. I of course allude to the risk of one barrel in a double gun going off while the sportsman is ramming down the charge in the other barrel, and to the chance of the gun bursting through the wadding slipping up in the barrel and leaving a vacuum between it and the charge. I will be bound to say that there are very few men who have shot much, who have not more than once in their lives, when loading a double gun in a hurry, been horrified at discovering that they have been hammering down the left-hand charge, for instance, with the right-hand lock at full cock. Now this can never happen with a breech-loader.

If admonitions and warnings are to be regarded, and will serve to render a man careful in the use of a gun, no one ought to be more so than myself; for I have not only witnessed serious accidents happen from firearms, but I have had some awfully narrow escapes myself. I do not believe I am more careless than the generality of sportsmen, and I ought to know how to use and handle a gun, if practice can teach it; and yet I am certain not a year passes but I can look back at the end of it, and call to mind one, if not more, narrow escapes which, because I escaped, I thought nothing of, but which, if I had not escaped, would have cost me the loss of a limb, if not of my life. I believe a man who is in the constant habit of shooting by himself is, in general, far more reckless and careless with his gun than the man who is accustomed to shoot in company. It is true that the solitary sportsman has only to look out for himself, and does not risk the life of another by his carelessness; but it is also true that he does not run half the risk which that man does who shoots in company: and I have now become so accustomed to be out alone, that I always shoot nervously in a party. No power on earth will ever now induce me to go out in a boat, if there is more than one gun in it. I have just said no man, perhaps, has had more serious warnings than myself, and I speak the truth. I have had guns go off in my hand, when I least expected it; and though I have escaped myself, had another man been with me, I perhaps should have had a human life to answer for. I had a habit in the bush (where one is of necessity required to have a loaded gun in the hut or tent) of setting my gun at the head of my bed (instead of, as I always do now, laying it on the bed during the day), to be ready to catch up at a moment's notice. Three or four times, when I have been taking it up quickly for a snap shot outside the tent, the gun has gone off by the hammer catching the edge of the bed. I was one dark night in England coming home from pheasant-shooting on a fidgety mare. I got off to pick up a glow-worm which was shining by the road side, and, in getting on again, somehow or other, the gun went off in my left hand, and the charge must have passed pretty close to my head, for my hat was blown off. I was both deaf and blind for some time after, and my face, when I got home (the mare ran away, and never stopped till she pulled up at my own gate), was as black as a powder-monkey's. Now these casualties, as well as a dozen more which I could mention, were certainly caused by the hammer resting on the nipple.

I once recollect crawling on to some black duck through a rough tussocky plain in Australia, wriggling along, like a snake, close to the ground, pulling my gun after me—when bang off it went, and the charge ploughed up the ground just by my cheek. Now I was certain in this case the hammer was down upon the nipple. In these instances I have had no one to blame but myself. However, more than once has my life been placed in jeopardy through guns in the hands of others; and once I had so narrow an escape from certain death that, at the risk of tiring my readers, I must relate it.

When kangarooing in Australia, there was a little patch of swamp oak, two or three feet high, in a meadow close to which some kangaroo used to come and feed every night, about a mile from our tent. Besides our party there was another tent about three miles from us, occupied by two shooting American backwoodsmen, who never drove the kangaroo, and when the drove came up murdered them by wholesale with charges of buck shot, but always stalked them in the bush, and killed them in a sportsmanlike manner with long rifles. It is needless to say that they were both first-rate shots, and I have seen them cut a pigeon's head off with a single ball when sitting on a tree at a distance of fifty or sixty paces. Although the bush where we camped was as free to one as another, as each party had lots of kangaroo within a short distance of home (this was before they were shot out in the Western Port district), by a kind of tacit consent we made a rule never hardly to go on each other's beat. Now this patch of scrub was in our territory, and I never expected meeting one of these Canadians there, especially at night. I had often seen the kangaroo feeding here in the twilight, and one evening determined to "lurch" one if possible. It was moonlight, but hazy, and the moon gave a sickly uncertain light. I went down quietly by myself through the forest, and got within, perhaps, a hundred and fifty yards of the kangaroo, which I could indistinctly see feeding by the edge of the scrub. I then began to creep. I was dressed all in grey, with a kangaroo-skin cap on (this colour I fancy best for all night shooting); and as I kept occasionally cautiously lifting up my head while creeping through the scrub, to peep if the kangaroo were quiet, I have no doubt, at a little distance off in that indistinct light, I could well be mistaken for a kangaroo myself. I had not crept far, however, before the kangaroo either heard or winded me; and the deep, measured "thump, thump" of their tails upon the ground as they started off was very unpleasant music to my ear. But the click of the lock of a backwoodsman's rifle would have sounded far more unpleasant, could I have heard it just then. I sprang up to see if I could get a snap shot, but they had gone out of distance.

Just as I was turning to walk home, I was challenged by a deep voice—

"Is that you, —— ?" and a figure rose out of the scrub where it had been hidden.

It was one of the Canadians! We stared at one another for a while, as if each were an apparition.

"Waall, my bully, I guess you never was nearer —— than you've been for the last five minutes. I've had my rifle three times up to my shoulder, but I took it down again because I could not get a clear pull at your head!"

It seems that the backwoodsman knew of these kangaroo as well as myself, and had planted himself in the scrub for a shot before I got down. But he had not seen the kangaroo at all. I had crept down on the other side (little expecting any one was near me) so quietly that he never heard me till I got into the scrub. His attention was then altogether directed to my movements. He took me to be a kangaroo coming right towards him. I was rather too far from him for him to make me out distinctly, and as I never kept my head long above the scrub, he never had time to get a clear shot; but a few more steps would have sealed my fate, for I was gradually coming well within shot, and in fact, as he told me afterwards, had I only raised my head on the last occasion instead of springing right up, he should probably have pulled, for he was getting tired of waiting—and I should never have lived to tell the tale. It is not every man who can boast that he has been within range of the muzzle of a backwoodsman's rifle pointed well on him, and escaped as I did. We went back to our tent to supper, and both agreed that stalking kangaroo at night was " hardly safe."

But the darkest day in my life was when I saw perhaps my dearest friend (for we were both then just at the age when true and indelible friendships are formed) shot dead within two yards of me by his own rifle, as he was pitching it over the gate to another of the party to catch. The rifle, we all fancied, exploded in the air, for the bullet went in at the front of his throat and came out at the back of his neck; and had he been struck down by lightning, his death could not have been more instantaneous. I say we all fancied that the rifle exploded in the air, for the man to whom it was thrown did not catch it, and the rifle fell on the ground; and although we all heard the report, and saw the young man fall, not one of us could, at the coroner's inquest, give any satisfactory evidence how the strange accident happened. I was sitting across a gate leading into a lane from a meadow which we had just crossed; the three others stood in the lane, having got through the hedge, and my friend was alone in the meadow. When I last saw him alive he was just uncocking the rifle, and I heard him distinctly call out to one in the lane to look out and catch it. I stooped my head as the rifle passed me in the air, and the same moment I heard the report and saw the young man fall dead. We supposed he must have taken the rifle by the end of the barrel, and pitched it but-end first. It was, perhaps, not surprising that an accident should have happened on this occasion, as our party consisted of five young fellows under twenty-one, with three guns and one rifle amongst us. I had no gun, for I had come down the North-road on one of the London coaches, and the party had walked across to meet me. It seems often as if these accidents were predetermined by Providence, and that no human foresight can prevent them, for in this case there were but four bullets. While the party were waiting at the roadside for me they had shot three bullets into an ash tree, and the last one was in the rifle. They wanted me to fire this, and make a diamond on the tree; but I wished to try my hand at a crow or a magpie, and I carried the rifle till we came to the meadow where he was shot, when I gave it back to him. Now, had I fired away the last bullet as the others wished me, this poor young man would not at least have been shot by his own rifle. It happened just before Christmas, and it is easy to guess what a gloom such a sad occurrence shed over a quiet country family at this joyous season.

B B

Without being anything of a fatalist, it seems hard to doubt that the finger of an All-wise Providence directs even the minutest actions in the life of man, and that although it is the duty of every Christian to use all human caution to guard against accidents, it is pretty clear to me at least that the most important events in our career through life are predestined, and that no human power can change their course. It is with no irreligious feeling that I say this; on the contrary, such a belief teaches us that we are all in the hands of a Higher Power, that we are totally helpless of ourselves, and that we have no right, either to be too much elated by prosperity, or bowed down by adversity, in this life. But I am writing to amuse, not to sermonize my readers. If, as I fancy, it was plain that the hand of Providence guided the bullet which struck my young friend dead in the prime of youth and strength, another little circumstance which happened to me, a short time after, as clearly proves that the same High Power is constantly at work in our behalf, and that many an accident which no human foresight could have prevented was, for some wise purpose or other, turned aside, but by a higher influence than our own. The circumstance which I am about to relate appears almost too miraculous to be true: I have often been doubted when I have told the fact in company, (for it is as true a *fact* as ever I wrote), and I shall therefore not feel the least offended if any one doubts it. It was this:—

I had one afternoon, many years ago, come home from partridge-shooting. I had just fired off both barrels of my gun at a covey of birds in a bit of turnips, not three hundred yards from the house, and I therefore did not see the least danger in setting the gun in a corner of the kitchen, while I went up to get ready for dinner. I had not fired a dozen shots the whole day, so did not care to clean my gun, which I found standing next morning, apparently untouched, in the corner where I had left it. Directly I took it up, a fat old cook, who was always terribly frightened at the sight of a gun, began to scream and run away; so, thinking that I would have a lark with her, I put on two caps, and foolishly presenting the gun, snapped them off to frighten her. I will not say that I aimed straight at the old lady's head, nor will I say I did not—anyhow I fancy if the gun had gone off, the whole charge would have passed through her like a bullet. The explosion of the caps, however, frightened the whole party in the kitchen nearly as much as if the gun had gone off, and boy-like I walked out immensely pleased. But my feelings soon changed, when I began to load in the yard. I rammed down the powder in the left barrel all right, but when I came to the right-hand one I could not apparently get the wadding well down. I drew it, shook out the powder, and then found that the right-hand barrel was loaded; *and it went off directly I tried it again with another cap!* I attribute the first missfire to the powder not being well rammed home, for paper had been used as wadding; but by my ramming down the second charge of powder I had shaken the first charge well down into the chamber. I did not go back into the house, but walked directly to the stable, when the mystery was soon explained. It turned out that the groom, who had ammunition himself, but no gun, had taken my gun early in the morning and loaded it to shoot an "old steernel," as he called it, which frequented our pigeon house. These country chaps have an absurd idea that starlings suck the pigeons' eggs, and kill the young birds. He could not, however, get a shot, and set the gun again in the corner without saying a word to any one, having first taken the precaution of removing the cap. This fancied precaution, however, nearly cost a human life, for had the cap been on the gun, I should of course have seen when I took it up that somebody had loaded it, and I should not have attempted any practical joking with it. Now had I shot this woman it would have caused me the regret of a whole life, and, although it might have been quite inadvertently on my part, I should have at least been guilty of wilful homicide, for nothing can excuse a man, who has no wish for the gun to go off, in pointing it deliberately at a fellow-creature, even if he fancies that he is certain in his own mind the gun is not loaded. I felt quite convinced that this gun was unloaded, and yet how I was deceived!

One thing certainly is clear, that no mode of ignition can be more dangerous than the common percussion system with the sidelock, and when loaded from the muzzle the chance of accident is doubled. Moreover, the system of loading from the powder-flask is very objectionable, for it can easily happen that a spark may remain in the barrel, which will ignite the charge when poured in—the flash communicates with the flask, which bursts in the hand. A friend of mine in Australia lost a thumb and three fingers by this very thing; and another, a gamekeeper, in England, whom I knew well, had his thumb and forefinger blown off the right hand by the left-hand barrel of his gun going off while he was loading the right. Had he been loading the left-hand barrel, his whole hand would probably have been carried away. Now he was a careful man, and his left-hand hammer was down on the nipple; but a spaniel jumped up and pawed the gun while he was loading, and caused the accident which might have cost him his life. Now neither of these accidents could possibly have happened with a breech-loader.

A gun is, however, never half so dangerous as when in a boat or a gig. Twice have I been within an ace of being shot through the head by a gun going off accidentally in a boat, and I will never now go out shooting ducks if there are two guns in the same boat. One of the most melancholy accidents I ever knew happened here about three years ago, to a poor young fellow, an officer, who had only left the river duck-shooting an hour before, to drive his two sisters home in a little carriage. He was standing behind the carriage, and shoved his gun in, but-end downwards, between the two girls, the muzzle pointing to his own head. The gun went off, and literally blew his head away.

It seems clear that every one of these accidents or escapes could have been avoided if proper caution had been used; but, nevertheless, they did all happen (it is nothing to our purpose whether they were caused by negligence or not), and I therefore again repeat that any invention which renders it impossible that such accidents can happen must be regarded as a blessing to mankind. It is not enough to say, "Oh, such-and-such an accident could have been easily prevented, if proper caution had been used." But show me the man who is always on his guard, and you will show me a being that has never yet existed. The fact is, a gun is certainly the most dangerous weapon a man handles; and a gun accident happens always instantaneously, and without the slightest warning, and is, moreover, if not fatal, sure to carry away a limb. Most other accidents are, in some little degree, foreshadowed, and time is given often for escape; but not so with firearms. And when we consider that weapons from which a serious accident can result in half-a-dozen different ways are continually in the hands of one half of the male population in every civilized land, the only wonder to me is that we do not hear of ten times more accidents happening than we do now.

We do not so often hear of an accident, at least in England, happening from the bursting of a gun-barrel; but in Sweden—where every blacksmith is also a gunsmith after his own fashion, and a barrel is never proved—the case is different. Some years ago one of my fellows had a gun burst in his hand; and when he went into the Carlstad Hospital to have the wound dressed, the surgeon told him that this was (I think) the sixth accident of the same kind that had come before him within the last month. It was in the spring, when the capercally were playing, and every peasant is a poacher, and all sorts of old spouts are brought into use. In this case there was no wonder at the gun bursting, for when I examined the barrel after the accident, I found that the breech plug was not screwed in, but just shoved in like a cork; and I fancy this was the case with many others of these homespun barrels.

I have had four guns burst in my hand—the one a gingerbread German walking-stick thing, in which the charge lay half way up the barrel. I could never discover where the barrel flew to; the stick remained in my hand. The three others were good English twist, and they did not fly, but only opened and bulged. I met with no accident. I knew well how all these three barrels burst. One was stuffed up with snow, the other with mud, which had accidentally come into the muzzle; in the other, the wadding in the right-hand barrel had risen. Now any one would wonder how it was possible that three such accidents could happen with guns in the hands of a man who was well accustomed to them; and so do I now, as I sit in my chair and write this; but they did happen, and I would not lay 5 to 1 that a similar accident might not happen to me to-morrow if I were to go struggling through the snow in our forests in the excitement of following up any game. Some men are by nature more prudent and cautious than others, and to such men there is less chance of accidents of any kind happening; but not one man in a thousand is by nature careful enough to warrant him saying that no gun accident can ever happen to him.

I have seen three or four awful smashes in Australia with the two-penny twist brummagem barrels that are sent out into the colonies, when stock, lock, and barrel have all disappeared. One happened at my tent door with a gun which a mate of mine had that very afternoon bought for a 10*l.* note, against my advice. In fact, it was so palpable a "duffer" that no one but a fool would have trusted himself at either end of it. The barrel burst close to the breech. Both locks were carried away (one flew into my tent), and, strange to say, the man who fired it was uninjured. He held the gun with his left hand stretched about ten inches up the barrel, which I cannot help thinking is after all the safest way of holding a gun when firing.

As I before observed, the common powder-flask is far from safe when loading; but one would, at least think that there would not be much danger of the flask exploding in the pocket. But it does not appear that this is always so certain, for I once saw a very curious thing happen in Australia—where, however, strange and unaccountable things are always taking place. Three of us were out quail-shooting on a blazing hot day, and as the birds were plentiful and lay like stones, the shooting had been heavy. When we sat down to lunch, we all took out our flasks to take stock of our ammunition. On shaking his flask up and down to see how near it was empty, one of the party fancied he heard something rattle inside it. Upon unscrewing the top, to his surprise he found three lucifer matches in the flask loose among the powder. How they got there, not one of us could form the least idea; but there they were, for I saw them taken out myself, and I shall never forget the *sang-froid* with which the man coolly lighted one of the matches at his short pipe right over the open powder-flask, just to see if it " would go;" and having ascertained this important fact, he tersely remarked: " Ah, that shows my time is not come yet."

Any one who reads the foregoing chapter of accidents will, I expect, think that I have either grossly exaggerated, or else have certainly seen much more than other men; but neither of these is the case. I could mention a score more narrow escapes if I wished, which had happened either to myself or to other men in my presence; and I have no doubt that if any one of my readers, who, like myself, has shot hard for thirty years, were to reckon up all the accidents he had witnessed or narrowly escaped, it would be seen that others have had quite as many narrow escapes as myself with guns.

I will merely add that this chapter of hair-breadth escapes is not intended as a *sensation* article. I have not exaggerated a single fact, nor is a single statement contained in this narration untrue. I wrote it merely to put young sportsmen on their guard, and to prove how easily an accident may happen from a gun, be the cause carelessness or what it may.

A gun now-a-days is in the hands of as many men and boys as an umbrella or a walking-stick, and in nine cases out of ten is handled and tossed about in quite as careless a manner.

When this letter first appeared in the columns of *The Field*, one correspondent informed us that he had read it with astonishment, and probably both might also have added, with incredulity; another, with amusement; but both joined issue on one point, that the escapes and accidents therein described were the results of " gross and unpardonable negligence." I was seriously thinking of confessing myself to the readers of *The Field* as a man in whose hands a gun could hardly be safely trusted, but luckily just before I went to confessional, I received a letter from a very old friend of mine, a gamekeeper, who told me he had read my chapter with great interest, and that if he chose he could narrate quite as many narrow escapes. Now, probably, this man had had double the experience, perhaps ten times that, of the two *Field* correspondents who sneered at my list of escapes—so I was perfectly satisfied that if casualties with guns are always to be attributed to carelessness, there was at least one man living who was as careless as myself.

Probably many men may have shot for years without either an accident or an escape; but I do not think such men have any right altogether to attribute this circumstance to their great care and caution when handling guns, for I have no doubt that if they did but know it, many times the muzzle of their guns have been in a position (though perhaps only for a moment) when a discharge would have cost them a life or a limb. I do not for a moment deny that a naturally careful man is much fitter to be trusted with a gun than a careless one; but no one can say that a gun is always safe even in the hands of the most cautious and experienced—for I again repeat it, that no mortal can be on his guard at all times; and a man, when out shooting, will often altogether forget even that he has a gun in his hand, and at such times it is impossible for any one to say that an accident might not have happened had Providence so willed it.

ON THE ENCOURAGEMENT OF MANLY AND ATHLETIC EXERCISES,

SUCH AS SPARRING; AND A FEW REMARKS IN DEFENCE OF THE MUCH-ABUSED CUSTOM OF BRITISH BOXING.

I.

"Why should scholars bend for ever
　Over Livy's pictured tome,
Why ponder o'er the terse with lore
　Of ancient pagan Rome?
Why sigh to view the chariots
　Career 'midst dust and spray,
Why long for oil and canvass
　Of an ancient circus day?

II.

"Ye artists, take Apelles' pencil,
　'Twas a sight to woo the chisel
Of a Phidias, when each Roman
　Chose to die before he'd " mizzle."
When the Latian tens of thousands,
　Sat and gloried in the "foight,"
At the clashing of the cestus,
　At the glancing of the quoit.

III.

"Oh, then there were no crosses,
　When a man once dared to peel,
No lyings down to compromise,
　No turnings on the heel.

Each loved the slip of palm-tree,
  Far more than sordid gold,
Each loved the crown of parsley,
  In the ruddy days of old.

IV.

"Then men retained their sinew,
  And their giant strength of limb,
Till old age made them totter,
  And their eagle vision dim ;
Then men could hit out gallantly,
  Though verging on four-score.
There were no cigars and brandy,
  In the ruddy days of yore."

IN the end of 1864, a discussion took place in the columns of *The Field* on the advantage which would accrue to all who feel a pride in those manly and athletic exercises which are so characteristic of the youth of Great Britain (and of those of no other country under the sun), by the institution of sparring clubs in all our large towns, where the members could keep themselves select, and practise an exercise which is so peculiarly British, and, perhaps, one of the best and most useful going—that of sparring with the gloves. The suggestion, as might have been expected, when emanating in the columns of so manly and straightforward a paper as *The Field*, met with general approval, and many of its readers who were utterly opposed to *boxing*, advocated the practice of *sparring* with the gloves. Of course I took a part in the discussion, but unfortunately my zeal carried me a little beyond bounds, and the transition from the sparring-room to the twenty-four foot roped-ring was so natural and easy, that my letter not only advocated strenuously the benefits which would accrue to every young man from becoming a proficient in the art of sparring, but I even had the audacity and hardihood (and it does require some little amount of courage in these days of refinement to say a word in favour of a custom which is fashionably designated as disgusting and brutalizing) to enter into a defence of the much abused system of fair British boxing.

This letter drew down upon my head a tremendous philippic from one of the old school, like myself, but no friend to the ring, in which he stated that letters such as mine should never be admitted into a paper like *The Field*; and after a column's abuse of the prize-ring, and all who had anything to do with it, he wound up by observing, that it was a disgrace to the country that prize-fighting was not made criminal like cock-fighting and bull-baiting.

Of course I was bound to defend my position as best I could; and as I still adhere to my original opinion, and am not the least ashamed of repeating anything I have ever yet written in the defence of the practice of fair British boxing, properly carried out, I trust I shall be excused if I recapitulate in these little Sporting Sketches what I then wrote, merely observing, that I am far from expecting that all my readers will be of the same opinion as myself; and as every one can see by reading the heading of this chapter upon what subject it treats, no one is obliged to read it unless he pleases, but can skip it and go on to the next. I shall, however, hope that it will interest some. It is needless here to quote my opponent's letter at full length, but I must at starting set forth the gist of his arguments and observations, because my reply to them forms the groundwork of this present article.

He first begged to know what I was asking for, and how far I should wish to go?

He told us that he was old enough to recollect the time when cock-fighting and bull-baiting had as many advocates as the ring has now, adding that the same innate cruelty of our nature is at the root of all these barbarous amusements.

He then asked me, did I wish those days to return when (quoting my words in a previous letter) "the rules of fair fighting, as exemplified in the prize-ring, became, as it were, the law of the land," when a dispute had to be settled by an appeal to the *arms?*

Did I wish milling to return? or would I, while *gentlemen* are content to settle their disputes amicably, or by an appeal to law courts, encourage those whose passions are fierce to have recourse to violence?

He asked me did I wish to contend that the British youth of the present day are not as manly and well bred as in the days of Mendoza or Beau Brummel, or when Horace Walpole with other members of the aristocracy used to attend executions?

He stated that it was all clap-trap to say that the rabble who crowd to see a fight between two navvies, go to see fair-play, or to admire manly pluck, or skilful science, "It is the untamed savage within us." And he moreover stated, that he himself had seen bloody fights enough at fairs and races, attracted to them by a strange fascination, when "he knew he was not in the right place;" and he further added, that the attraction to all such sights (executions, prize-fights, and women endangering their lives on the tight-rope) is the same feeling of morbid excitement.

He asked why the arguments in favour of fostering a pugnacious principle among boys at school should not equally apply to girls. He tells us of "Saturnalian epochs" which used to take place at his school half a century ago, *just before* the holidays, when the little boys were urged on to fight by the big ones.

And he wound up his letter with this monstrous remark, "If prize-fighting is the manly British pastime that it is represented, why do not our noblemen and gentlemen put themselves upon an equality with the players as they do in other sports? If they did, and a few of them were knocked into the other world, the ring would soon be put down." Why, he might just as well say that every "gentleman" should be obliged to serve in the ranks as a private soldier.

This was his case, and this is my reply.

I am asked how far I would go, and what am I asking for? I am asking for the opponents of the ring to state their case fairly—not to support it by false arguments—and I want no clap-traps to be used on either side. I would go thus far and no farther. I would do all that lay in my power once again to restore the British prize-ring to the position it held in the days when Crib and Spring were champions, and when those scenes of brutality, violence, and intimidation which are the characteristics of prize-battles at the present day (and which have alone brought the prize-ring to the low position it now holds) were unknown. I would wish no more.

I do not consider that a combat between two parties who are free agents and rational beings, who can begin when they please, leave off when they please—in fact, have no occasion to begin at all unless they do please—can even by the most ingenious sophistry be placed in the same category as the baiting of bulls and other dumb animals. I am no advocate myself for dog-fighting, because I am sorry to see such faithful, generous, and useful animals put to so bad a purpose; but I am not here going to defend or condemn it. I see nothing in cock-fighting a bit more cruel or barbarous than many other of our field sports; and if the same "innate cruelty of our nature" is at the bottom of all, the motive that leads me to see an execution, a prize-fight, a cock-fight, a horse-race, or a steeple-chase, must be the same; and hunting, shooting, and angling must, if we are consistent, and argue only on these grounds, be placed in schedule A, as well as prize-fighting.

I do most sincerely wish to see those times return (if they have ever departed from our countrymen, which I much doubt), when the rules of fair fighting, as exemplified in the prize-ring, became, as it were, the law of the land; when a dispute had to be settled by an appeal to *arms;* and by *arms,* be it clearly understood, that I mean such only as nature has provided man with.

It is in my opinion, one of the best features of the age we live in that duelling is abolished, and I trust it will never be revived; and I hope I may yet live *to see* the day when flogging in the army will be put a stop to. I will allow that it is an open question, but, for my part, I should be happy to see capital punishment abolished in all civilized nations.

Some *gentlemen* may be inclined to settle their disputes amicably or by an appeal to the courts of law—two very excellent plans, but hardly to be adopted I fear in all cases. We must, I suppose, allow something for the difference of habit and feeling, acquired by education, between the higher and lower classes. Disputes between gentlemen do not in general commence with any violence, and one gentleman can reason with another, which would be of little use with a rough after he had sent forth the fierce British challenge, bidding you "stand up fairly and fight like a man."

I deny altogether that to settle a quarrel by an appeal to *arms* (as I understand the term) is (quoting the words of my opponent) "the most unfair and cowardly that human ingenuity can devise." The weak is not, as he says, always necessarily at the mercy of the strong, for how often do we see a big bully soundly thrashed by a man of half his size.

Although I am not going to set myself up as champion for the morals of the members of the British P.R., I will say this, that I have known many of them, and some pretty intimately, from old Tom Crib down to Jem Mace, and, take them as a class, they have invariably been quiet and well-behaved men, and in general far superior to men of the same rank in life following different occupations.

I have no wish to see members of our aristocracy in the habit of attending executions, and I will never for a single moment allow that the attraction to such a sight is "the same feeling of morbid excitement" which draws a man to the side of the prize-ring. There doubtless are some brutes in the world who would gloat over any sight of refined cruelty, but it would be the grossest libel upon some of the kindest and best-hearted men I ever had the pleasure of knowing to say that this was the feeling which attracted them (where I have often seen them, and where they were not ashamed of being seen themselves) to the side of the prize-ring. If this argument holds good, it will, of course, apply to myself as well as any other man. Now, I have seen one execution in my life, at Horsemonger-lane, and I would not see another for a large sum of money. Through the influence of the Under-Sheriff, I was admitted into the gaol, and stood close to the poor wretch when the drop fell. I have seen many and many a good prize-battle since, and all I can say is, that I wish I was going to see another, conducted after the old style, to-morrow. But the "feeling of morbid excitement" never drew me again to the foot of the scaffold, although I had plenty of subsequent opportunities of witnessing executions if I had pleased; but I always made a point of seeing a good prize-fight whenever I had a chance. It speaks, I fancy, very poorly for a man's moral courage when he acknowledges that he has seen "bloody fights enough at fairs and races," attracted to them by a strange fascination, when "he knew he was out of place."

As to the practice of fighting at schools, I have lately read that the boys at our large schools are more refined than they were—"much above that sort of thing now," and that the custom is discontinued; and this has been quoted as an instance that the present age is becoming more polished, and that pugilism is on the decline.

I know little of the habits of school-boys now-a-days. My school-days (so grossly misnamed by some as the happiest days of one's life) have left no single remembrance in my breast save that of utter repugnance. It is probable that the proprietary schools of the present day may turn out more "genteel young men" than the schools of some thirty years ago. Still I should be very sorry to allow that school-boys ought to set the fashions of the age; and just as sorry should I be to acknowledge that a single lesson which I learnt at school (save reading, writing, and arithmetic) was worthy to be remembered in after life.

A greater set of tyrants and bullies than the bigger boys were I never hope to meet again, and as was natural with slaves, the younger lads during their novitiate were a parcel of unprincipled little sneaks, whose sole aim was to curry favour with their tyrants at the expense of their comrades, and pass the days of their slavery (for no slavery could be more abject and pitiful than that of a fag to a bullying master) as best they might, cheered by the sole reflection that when the time came, they would pay off the debt they were incurring with full interest, which they never failed to do when they rose to be masters; and I fancy this is much about the same at large schools of the present day. Fagging, bullying, fighting, and flogging had full licence at the public school where I was "dragged up." As for bullying and fagging, of course, these two systems have left nothing but the most unpleasant recollections on my mind, especially as I had not the pleasure of staying there long enough to enjoy a little reign of tyranny myself. I had my share of fighting, and came off sometimes the winner, sometimes the loser; but the severest thrashing I ever got in a fair stand-up fight left nothing more than a transient feeling of (what shall I say?) disappointment in my mind, certainly, nothing like malice against my conqueror, whereas feelings of revenge at the treatment I received from the bigger bullies of the school rankled in my breast years after I had left it. As to the flogging part of the business, that has certainly left its remembrance, and one not easily effaced, for, like Mr. Foker in "Pendennis," I sometimes dream even now "that the doctor is walking into me." I can certainly not uphold the Saturnalian epochs alluded to in my opponent's letter, but I fancy these must have been very harmless battles, if, as he says, the master always allowed them to take place just before the holidays, for, although a father may jokingly ask his son when he comes home at Christmas, "Well, Charley, how many boys have you thrashed this half?" I can scarcely fancy that an anxious mother would be particularly well pleased at seeing a young son come home with a black eye, especially if she knew that this academical polish was reserved to the end of the half, so that there might be no mistake about the lad carrying his brand home with him. This, however, is neither here nor there, for I feel pretty certain that battles at school, if fairly and manfully conducted, never did the boys who fought the slightest harm in after life.

If all disputes between gentlemen can be so easily settled amicably, or by appeal to law courts, how is it that disputes between nations cannot be settled in the same way? When the time arrives that standing armies can be safely dispensed with, then will I at once retract every sentence I have written—every syllable I have uttered in defence of the prize-ring; but as long as it is absolutely necessary for every nation to keep up bands of paid and trained fighting men, who are bound to take the field armed with deadly weapons, against they know not who, and in a cause of which

Manly and Athletic Exercises.

notably they understand little, and for which they care less, I do again repeat that it is sheer nonsense to raise such an outcry against the prize-ring. What a deal of inconsistency and humbug there is in this world. We glory in the account of a victory which is probably gained at the expense of thousands, but pretend to be shocked at the description of a fair stand-up fight between two men, armed with no other weapons than those provided by nature, and even the use of which is modified and restricted, so that not once in a hundred times can any fatal accident result, and neither of whom is in general a bit the worse a fortnight after the fight than he was before it. One of the favourite arguments with the opponents of the prize-ring is this, that the common prize-fighter has no animosity against his opponent? Why, therefore, should he punish him? Does it not seem that this remark will equally apply to the red-coated prize-fighter?

Prize-fighting is peculiarly a British institution, and one of which no real Englishman need be ashamed. When it is properly carried out on the continent, of course, where the words "fair play" are unknown, the practice is stigmatized as brutal and disgusting, and the British nation branded as blood-thirsty blackguards. This all looks very well upon paper, and would sound all the better if I could see that our continental neigbours were a bit more honourable, manly, or less brutal and blood-thirsty than ourselves. I have now been in many European countries, but I never was in one yet where the lower orders had not some national method of settling disputes other than by arbitration or appeal to law courts. The French sabot, the Italian stiletto, the Yankee German hug, are just as common in their peculiar districts as the fair knock-down blow of the Englishman, and yet we have no outcry against all these. It is only the unfortunate practice of British boxing, which after all said and done is the manliest and less cruel of all, that is stigmatized. We must all allow that, whatever the national mode of fighting, the one which is least likely to sacrifice human life is the one most worthy of being adopted. That the naked fist is the most harmless no one can deny, and the moderation and fair play exhibited in prize-battles render them by far the least dangerous combats in which men can engage. Moreover, in whatever foreign land can a man cry enough when he is beaten, and where but in England will the bystanders, to a man, see that both parties in a casual encounter have fair play? It is most unfair to condemn an institution because it is badly managed, and I think that the greatest proof that there must be good in the British prize-ring lies in this fact—that in no other country in which the practice of boxing is unknown do we ever see the rules of fair play which are, as it were, so characteristic of the good Englishman, the least regarded in the settlement of those unavoidable quarrels and disputes which must and will be daily occurring as long as man is man. And why is this? Because the rules of fair fighting exemplified in the ring became, as it were, a part of the law of the land, when a dispute must be settled by an appeal to arms; and the pluck and manly forbearance of the good British boxer was not only admired but imitated by his countrymen. Let foreigners abroad, and let who will at home, abuse the prize-ring as an arena fit for nothing but blackguards and ruffians, no one can, however, deny the fact that if a man—whether he be an Englishman or a foreigner—happens to come into a row in England, he may chance to get a good licking, but in nine cases out of ten not a man will lay a hand upon him save his opponent. As soon as ever he pleases to acknowledge himself beaten the fight is stopped, and every bystander, although all may be total strangers to him will see that at least he has fair play. There is something so truly British in the words "Give him fair play," that one would almost think they were one of the earliest lessons of a true Englishman's childhood. I do not mean to say there are not exceptions to the rule. We have brutes and ruffians in England as elsewhere, and perhaps a brutal Englishman is the greatest brute under the sun; but, thank God! these men are not to be taken as types of our national character.

Far different is the case when a man, especially if he be a stranger, gets into a row in a foreign country. The words "fair play," as we understand them, are scarcely to be found in any foreign vocabulary. Such a thing as a fair stand-up fight is scarcely known out of England; and when a man is lying defenceless at his opponent's feet, then is the time (anywhere but in England) to punish him. Still, however, I should care little, if I had only one man to deal with, how he fought—whether he kicked me on the side of my head with his sabot, after the manner of our volatile and polite neighbours across the Channel; whether he tried the German-Yankee hug, or came at me with a swinging round open-handed blow on the ear, as is the fashion in Sweden—so long as he came at me alone, and we were left to settle our little passage of arms without interference; for I will back any good man possessing a knowledge of sparring to lick a rough, even at his own game, by straight knock-down blows. But when foreigners fight, they scarcely ever let two men fairly fight it out. Three or four will set on one; and it is very little use a poor fellow crying out that he has had enough, with two or three men on him, not one of whom has the slightest idea of fair play. I am not contending that an Englishman is to expect that every man with whom he falls out must be obliged to fight after English fashion. I do not complain of the foreigner's method of fighting when no deadly weapons are used. Like the brutes (and man is little better than a brute when his worst passions are roused), different men have different tactics; but still, whatever his mode of fighting, there should at least be that generous impulse implanted in the breast of every man which will forbid him to trample on a fallen foe, and that honest manly feeling which will not allow him to use a knife or any other weapon against an unarmed adversary.

It is for this reason that I always have upheld, and always will uphold as far as lies in my power, the fair and manly custom of British boxing—not solely because it teaches men a less brutal and better mode of fighting, but because it implants in the breast of every man who has witnessed a prize-fight fairly conducted, a system of manly forbearance, and a detestation of that cowardly practice of striking a fallen foe, or setting two men upon one like wild beasts.

Moreover, in what other country is the knife held in such universal detestation as in England; and God grant that the opponents of fair British boxing may not be over-zealous in the cause, and while putting down an old English custom, introduce among their countrymen this along with other foreign fashions! I am truly glad to say that the knife is certainly going out of use in Sweden, but it is not easy to teach old dogs new tricks; and we seldom hear of a fair or any other meeting of peasants even now without the knife being drawn as soon as they get drunk. The fact is this, the fist is the Englishman's weapon, the knife is the foreigner's—and which is the best? I recollect once hearing a foreign gentleman vehemently declaiming against the brutality of the English prize-ring, and ten minutes after uttering the following sentence respecting a man who had made himself obnoxious: "Oh, he had better not go out after dark." Fancy such a speech coming from the lips of Jem Mace or Tom King.

Times and the manners of men certainly change as centuries roll round, and the savage customs of our forefathers give way to the march of intellect and civilization. Witness the deadly combats of the Scandinavian "Bält spannare," when the two naked combatants, armed with knives, were strapped together so that there could be no flinching from the cold steel, and the battle rarely ceased till one or other of them fell dead from his wounds. Those barbarous practices have, however, passed away and the best memento of them which we now possess is Malin's beautiful bronze statue, as large as life, of the old Swedish "Bält spannare." This is now set up in the park opposite the theatre in Gothenburg, and a more beautiful piece of statuary I never beheld. The two struggling forms locked together in mortal conflict; the savage determined expression depicted in the countenances of the two gladiators, for whom there is no retreat; and the distended muscles, are all so true and natural, that one almost expects, while gazing on this splendid work of art, to see the two naked figures start into life, and a real instead of an imaginary battle take place. I remember that I was in Gothenburg the day it was put up, and naturally stopped to look at it. A few people were grouped around it, and among them I observed a crew of Bohus Land fishermen. Every one had his case-knife by his side, and, as I watched their stern determined countenances while they silently criticised this statue, I felt pretty certain that the spirit of the old "Bält spannare" had not entirely died out, but that if a man unhappily came in collision with this crew, the case-knife at their sides would prove their readiest weapon. By a curious coincidence, on returning to the town I saw exposed in a shop window a picture of the boxing match which had just taken place in England between Tom King and Jem Mace. On pushing my way through the crowd to have a look at it, I found the full crew of an English brig admiring it, and it sounded cheery in a foreign land to hear these manly fellows' remarks upon the battle. Now each of these sailors had his clasp-knife by his side, but, nevertheless, I felt pretty certain that if I did chance to get into a row with one of them his knife would never be drawn against my naked fist, and though very probably I should receive a good licking, I should be sure at least of a fair even-handed fight, and that his mates would never interfere even if I did get the best of it, as long as I fought fairly. And it is my firm belief that this manly feeling is in a great degree owing to the usages of the British prize-ring, properly conducted, and, moreover, that it will in a great measure die out among our lower classes when the prize-ring is put down, and the race of good old English boxers becomes extinct.

I do not consider that I am myself a bit more cruel or evil disposed than my neighbours, although I do uphold the cause of fair British boxing, looking upon the practice as I do as a necessary evil. Once for all I will say this: I regard fighting and quarrelling of every kind as a breach of the moral law, and as a social evil; and if all would obey the Divine commandment, that man should love his neighbour as himself, we could dispense with many other institutions besides the prize-ring which the conduct of man towards his brother has now rendered absolutely necessary, not only to protect his property, but his very life. If man had retained his original innocence, neither the prize-ring nor many other customs equally culpable, would require supporters or opponents. But as long as the nature of man remains as man himself has perverted it; as long as I see the unmistakable curse of Cain branded on so many countenances; as long as I meet with ruffians among the lower classes of every land in which I travel; as long as I see that the quarrels and disputes which daily arise between men of refinement and education are conducted with quite as much spite and malice, and are marked with every feature, except, perhaps, the bloodshed, which characterizes a street fight between two of the most ruffianly blackguards in London—so long will I uphold the fair practice of British boxing, as teaching the lower classes especially the most natural and least brutal way of settling those disputes which can neither be arranged amicably or by appeal to the courts of law, and these are far more numerous than many of us suppose. Change our nature altogether, and then will I respect my opponent's doctrine; but this, I fear, is not going to be done all at once, seeing that it has remained much about the same for some thousands of years, and vices of all descriptions flourish as luxuriantly in the nineteenth century as of yore. I do not, however, for one moment wish to contend that it does absolutely follow that the prize-ring must flourish in order to keep up the true pluck and bottom of the British nation; but this I will say, that the rules of fair play as exemplified in a boxing match fairly conducted must and ever will set a good example to the lower classes, and teach them a far more humane and manly method of settling those disputes which are of daily occurrence than any foreign nation can boast.

Depend upon it, if boxing is done away with the savage disposition of the mob will remain unchanged, and some other mode of settling disputes among the lower classes will be soon adopted. It is all stuff to talk about amicable settlements and courts of law to men who do not possess the better feelings dependent on birth and education. When their worst passions are roused, let any opponent of fair British boxing with the naked fist suggest a better plan for the settlement of all such disputes as cannot be amicably arranged, and I will cheerfully bow to his decision. But as I feel certain that no one will be able to do so, and as I also feel quite as certain that some other redress than that afforded by the courts of law will be sought for by the lower classes, I once again, and for the last time, contend that fair British boxing is the best recourse, and that as long as the prize-ring exists, boxing matches will generally be conducted in a fair and manly spirit. It is rarely that any national custom is put down without a foreign one usurping its place, and trifling as any such innovations may appear, they nevertheless point significantly to departing nationality.

One thing is certain, that this is not the time to interfere in the least with any custom, rude as it may be, which has the slightest tendency to keep up the true old national British spirit among our lower classes. The fact may not be apparent to those "gentlemen of England who live at home at ease," but men like myself who reside abroad cannot shut their eyes to the fact of the grossest jealousy with which Great Britain and all her doings are regarded by all foreigners, and I say it in full confidence that I am speaking the truth, that she has not one true friend in any foreign nation, nor is there, I fancy, a single country in the world (although they may not perhaps own it), but would rejoice to see her involved in a war which might ultimately prove her downfall. "Why does not England help the Poles?" "Why does not England help the Danes?" was in everybody's mouth in the north of Europe during these late disturbances. All honour to our good Queen and her advisers, that we were not drawn into that struggle, and I trust that we may always steer as clear of interfering between foreign powers. It is probably on this account that the English have lost great caste on the continent, but whatever the cause, one thing is clear, that the name of an Englishman certainly does not now carry the *prestige* in any foreign country which it did twenty-five years ago.

This, however, I care little about, and as long as Britons are but true to themselves, I have little fear for the old " red, white, and blue." But the day may not be so very far distant when England may have to hold her own in another great struggle, and depend upon it, then she must trust solely to herself, and the chief actors in the scene will have to be chosen from the very men who take most interest in those sports which it has of late become the fashion to cry down.

Whatever changes may have taken place, I have never said or even fancied that the British youth of the present day are a bit less manly than they were in the days when I was young. I certainly do think that we ape our neighbours across the Channel rather too much, and I could perhaps point out more than one change since my young days, which I do not think has benefited us in the least. But I have every confidence that the heart of "Young England" is still in the right place; and, even if prize-fighting does die away, we have cricket, hunting, rowing, steeple-chasing, and many other sports left, and, as far as I can see, quite as good a breed of young fellows as ever we had to carry them on.

If public opinion has so strongly set in against prize-fighting, it seems far better that it should be altogether done away with than kept up by the feeble balances which now uphold it. And in conclusion I will remark, that it appears to me perfectly unaccountable if there is such a strong feeling against the prize-ring in England, as many pretend, that boxing matches are not decidedly put a stop to at once. They must either be legal or illegal; if they are legal, it seems a great shame that they should be interfered with—and if they are really illegal, it is a disgrace to all who have anything to do with the administration of justice in the land that they are not put down. The arm of the British law generally proves itself strong enough to suppress any public nuisance or offence against the laws; and no good Englishman ever attempts to interfere with the administration of justice when the law is put in force for the real welfare of the subject. There was little or no trouble in putting a stop to bull-baiting and dog-fighting, and if the prize-ring has not more stanch admirers among all classes, it would be just as easy to put a stop to boxing. But I most emphatically deny that such is the case; and with the recollection of the fight between King and Heenan, and Heenan and Sayers, fresh in my mind, I feel confident that if we had as good men in the ring as we had thirty years ago, and if prize-fights were still conducted as fairly and honourably as in those days, that boxing would still be as popular as ever, and that it is owing solely to the misconduct of the men themselves connected with the ring, and to no reaction of true British feeling, that the prize-ring has been brought to its present low position.

THE WRECK.

A Sketch from Australian Bush-Life in 1853.

The traveller who has made an Australian voyage in a crowded passenger-ship will well remember the feelings of joy which he experienced when the bluff headlands of South Australia first burst upon the view—a rugged, iron-bound coast, whose rocky mountains rise perpendicularly from the sea, and against whose bases the rude waves of the Pacific have lashed in wild fury for ages; the summits clad with huge forests of iron and stringy bark, whose solitudes, but a few years since, were unbroken save by the loud, shrill coo-ee of the native, or the dismal howl of the dingo. A couple of days' coasting, and the Heads are in sight, and, passing through a narrow and dangerous inlet, little more than one English mile in breadth, the good ship rides safely in Port Philip Bay, one of the most beautiful in the world. This magnificent land-locked bay, which more resembles a large inland lake than anything else, is about forty miles in length, and perhaps twenty across; and, as the emigrant gazes for the first time upon the landscape of singular and novel beauty by which he is on all sides surrounded, the vicissitudes and hardships of the past voyage are forgotten, and any regrets which he may have felt on leaving the land of his birth, perhaps for ever, fade away as he contemplates the smiling aspect which the new country of his adoption wears upon its first introduction.

As the ship proceeds further up the bay, the country gradually opens upon the view, and, till Geelong is reached, nothing is seen but low beaches, faced towards the sea with stunted honeysuckles and gum-trees, or belts of mangrove scrub. After passing Geelong, Mount Elisa dimly rises in the background behind the Geelong plains; Melbourne and Sandridge indistinctly loom in sight, while the Dandenong ranges, rising proudly to the north, stand out in bold relief against a cloudless southern sky—the whole scene forming as bold a panorama of nature as the eye ever gazed upon.

Should the vessel stand in towards the larboard shore, the long flat beach from Geelong to Williamstown will be plainly seen—a belt of stunted honeysuckles, faced by a dense wall of mangrove scrub and banks of black, sun-dried seaweed, the accumulation of ages, shutting out the interior landscape from the view. Behind these honeysuckles is another belt of scattered gum-trees, extending along the whole coast, perhaps a mile in breadth, having far more the appearance of an English park than the primeval forests which are met with on the Western-Port side of the bay; while the whole country beyond is one vast arid, stony plain, over which the weary traveller may plod for miles and miles without a tree to shelter him from the fierce rays of the burning sun, his sole companions the solitary wild turkey, or the little plover of the plains, whose long melancholy cry—in perfect unison with the wild regions which it frequents—is the only sound which breaks upon a solitude painful in its intensity.

Concealed in this nest of honeysuckles, a little south of Williamstown, is a large swamp, in my day called Langhorne Swamp—a rough, tussocky marsh of perhaps two thousand acres, covered with rushes two feet high, and studded by lagoons of different sizes, which, affording capital breeding-ground, were the nightly resort of the hundreds of wild-fowl of all descriptions, which by day rode leisurely on the placid waters of the bay, or lined the banks of seaweed which fringed the coast.

This swamp was divided from the neighbouring station by a creek, bearing the ominous but well-earned name of Skeleton Creek, being filled with weather-bleached skeletons of cattle; for in summer, when the burning sun had dried up all the water on the plains, this, like most other Australian creeks, was nothing more than a succession of muddy water-holes; and the poor beasts, half-maddened with heat and thirst, would heedlessly venture on the treacherous bottom, which, yielding to every step, at last sucked them in, and held them as securely as a vice. Retreat was impossible, and the poor creatures, exhausted by vain struggling, would fall on their sides, never to rise again, and suffer the most horrible of all imaginable deaths; lingering often for days, tantalized by the sight of the water which, although within a few feet of their noses, it was impossible for them to reach; the rays of the sun shooting down upon the brain, as though concentrated in the focus of a burning glass; myriads of huge blowflies depositing living maggots in their eyes, ears, and noses, and, before death came as a welcome relief, their bodies becoming one living mass of corruption. Talk of the horrors of a living grave! I cannot imagine any death half so dreadful as this; and yet the stockman who had missed a bullock off the run would carelessly ride by, and, if it was not one of "our brand," would leave the wretched animal to linger on, without either trying to extricate it or killing it out of its misery.

In the year 1853, there stood in the belt of gum-trees that skirted this coast, and about half a mile from the sea, a large tent, which was well known to every Melbourne duck-shooter as the "grass-cutters' tent," and many a beaten sportsman has gladly hailed the thin blue smoke of this camp-fire, curling among the old gum-trees, for then he well knew his toils for that day were over, and he was sure to find food and shelter for the night—a rude shelter, it is true, but a welcome one.

Let me introduce the reader to this tent—and how vividly does my mind recal the scene! The sun has sunk fiery red behind Mount Elisa, the deep gloom of night (which sets in here as soon as ever the sun dips below the western horizon) hangs over the forest like a dreary pall, and the bright blaze of the log fire in front of the tent shines like a meteor in the waste of darkness, rendering every object for a hundred yards around as visible as by day. Five or six figures are grouped around the fire, chatting, smoking, or resting after their day's labour. These are the grass-cutters, the inmates of the tent, who are employed on the swamp cutting grass for the Melbourne brick-makers. A stranger coming suddenly upon this group would be puzzled at first to guess their occupation or station in life. They might be smugglers—a supposition which the situation of their tent well favoured; or they might even be bush-rangers, who had pitched upon this wild spot as a camping place. Two of them are unmistakably sailors, whose profession can be detected at a glance; but what the rest may be it is more difficult to say. The old cabbage-tree hat, the blue jumper, and the moleskin trousers bespeak the working-man, but it is plain this is not the station they were born for, and, although almost every other sentence they utter is garnished by some strange oath or colonial slang, it is certain that better things might be expected from their lips.

It was in the early days of the diggings, and men of every country, of every station in society, had swelled the ranks of adventurers that flocked to this new Eldorado. All, however, were not successful on the gold-fields; and as some means of subsistence must be found, and light places in Melbourne were eagerly snapped up by such men as really either could not or dared not face the bush on their own account, many a young man of high birth and good education found himself in a situation which a year before he little dreamt ever of filling. To their credit I will say that they most of them took well to the new life, and I have had many proofs in Australia that "an ounce of blood is worth a pound of flesh" in the struggle through life as well as on the race-course. It was very difficult at that time to say who was who in the bush. I recollect on one station where I was camped, a clergyman of the Church of England was hut-keeper to a lot of Sydney sheep-shearers; and stopping one day on the road to accost the younger son of a lord whom I had known at home, but who was then seated on a stone-heap, industriously breaking stones at so much per yard, he told me that he was in rare company, for his next neighbour was nephew to a bishop. These were, indeed, strange times, and such as I fancy we are hardly likely to see again;

and I strongly recommend the curious reader to consult Lewis's
" Victoria in 1853," a book containing an account of the manners
of a people and country which is faithful and true, but will probably,
by any one who has not witnessed the scenes which he describes, be
looked upon as an exaggerated romance.

Still, coarse as may be the dress, and rough as may be the exterior of the men under observation, there is all the frank hearty
manner of the real bushman about them; and as one watches them
one insensibly feels that although out of place in this rude spot,
there are men among the group whose manners would not disgrace
the best drawing-room in England.

But there are two men sitting on a log together who deserve a
passing notice. The tight, well-knit, spare forms, the jack-boots,
and the long, heavy stock-whips wound round their bodies, all
bespeak the stock-rider, even were not their two horses standing
close by, tied up to a small honeysuckle. These two answer to the
names of Jack and George, and are evidently mates, bound by that
indissoluble tie which is perhaps nowhere felt so strongly as in the
bush. But, though sworn friends, there is little resemblance
between the two men. There is nothing very striking about the
appearance of Jack: he is a little, merry-looking fellow, with a
bright, twinkling eye, and evidently a "light-hearted hoss," one
who would confidently penetrate the wildest part of the colony on
his favourite stock-horse, encumbered with no other baggage save a
pair of hobbles, an opossum rug, his quart pot, a little tea, sugar,
flour, tobacco, and matches. He is an old hand, and evidently an
old stock-rider. The other is a man of altogether different stamp.
Far younger, muscular, and strongly built, it is nevertheless quite
clear that he has not the wear and tear of his mate; and as he
stoops down to pick up a coal to light his short, black pipe, the
fitful blaze of the fire lights up a countenance in which intellect
and good-nature struggle for the mastery—and I think, take it all
in all, I never looked upon a much handsomer or finer face. There
was something about the very air and appearance of this young man
which bespoke good breeding, although he was not a whit less

colonial than his comrade, and his remarks proved that this was not his first night in the bush by many hundreds. He had been lucky on the diggings and made a little fortune, and was on the point of returning home to his friends in England, whom he had never seen or heard of for years; and, to pass the time and keep out of the town till the ship sailed, he was living with his old friend Jack, a stock-man on a neighbouring station. The evening wore on, and a desultory conversation—about as intellectual as one generally hears around a camp-fire, in which Jack (who was principal spokesman on all occasions) was engaged in a fierce argument with one of the grass-cutters, as to whether the "kiddy" or the "cove" could drive a laden bullock-dray best out of the bush—was stopped by the abrupt inquiry from his younger mate as to whether he was going to sit there yarning all night. Five minutes afterwards, the clattering of their horses' hoofs, at that sling canter peculiar to the stock-rider, had died away in the distance, and all was soon silent in the grass-cutters' tent.

Like most men who landed in Australia at this time, I had a turn on the diggings, but luck was against me. I came down to Melbourne without a shilling, and for a month or six weeks knocked about the town, living as best I could, sometimes *lumping* on board a ship, sometimes at one thing, sometimes another. I well recollect I lodged at this time in a little, low sailors' boarding-house in Bourke-street, the landlord of which, although an "old hand," was a capital fellow, and behaved most kindly to me. Two curious things happened during my connexion with "Dan." I was one of the company in his back parlour when the Escort robbery, if not planned, was at least talked over nearly a month before it happened, and I well recollect Dan's prophetic words: "It will never do, my lads. It will take six men for the job, and where will you find six men in the colony who will stick together where money is concerned?" The other was this: Dan had saved a little money on the diggings and in his boarding-house, and resolved to return to England by, I think, the *Madagascar*. He offered me a passage home with him if I would accept it, which, however, I declined. As the ship lay in the bay, one, if not two, of the Escort robbers were taken off her. What became of the ill-fated vessel no one ever knew; it is certain she never reached home, and whether she foundered among the icebergs south of the Horn, or was seized by the crew and scuttled (for she had a large cargo of gold on board), is, I believe, a mystery to this day.

Coming down Melbourne one afternoon, heartily sick of my colonial prospects, I happened to meet a man I had known in the old country. He had hired this swamp for the purpose of cutting grass, and as he wanted some one to go down for a short time and overlook the work, I gladly accepted the job—more especially as I had heard the duck-shooting there so highly spoken of.

It was not a bad billet. I had little to do but walk about the swamp with my gun, count the bundles of grass as they were cut, sell them to the draymen, and pay the men who cut them. In fact, I was what we used to call in the old coaching-yards " odd man " on the swamp, and, although I believe I was looked upon by the grass-cutters themselves as a regular " loafer," I had a very jolly life of it. The men who worked for us were principally runaway sailors, who had left their ships in the bay, and were glad enough to lie hid in our tent till the search for them was over and they had earned a few pounds to take them on to the diggings. In fact, any one who wanted an odd job, found his way down to the swamp; and some strange acquaintances I formed there.

It was the morning after the night I allude to (I think the 28th of October), that I was out on the coast at daybreak, to get a good morning shot at the wild-fowl, which used to assemble and sit in hundreds on the seaweed banks to rest after their night's feeding. The wind was blowing a heavy gale from the south, and the usually quiet bay was a sheet of foam, which came dashing in as wave after wave rolled on to the beach. While walking along the seaweed, I chanced to spy a Dutch cheese, which had been washed up above high-water mark; presently another, and another, till at length I came to a broken box half filled with cheeses, and many other articles, "too numerous to mention," as the auctioneers say, lay strewed about. I secured my prizes, hiding them in the mangrove scrub, and hastened back to the tent to give the intelligence that there must have been a wreck on the Heads, and no telling if this south storm continued to blow, what might be washed up. After breakfast, we all turned out, and on going down to the beach, a singular sight presented itself. The coast, the whole length of our station, and probably for miles beyond, was strewed with articles of every description—wax candles, nuts, cheeses, boots, books—in fact, everything that constitutes a general cargo was there. The storm was unabated, and package after package, barrel after barrel, was washed in on the crest of the waves. That there had been an awful wreck on the coast was certain. It turned out that a large ship, the *Ontario*, laden with a general cargo from Liverpool, had struck on the Heads and just gone to pieces; and the wind blowing right on to the Geelong coast, the principal part of her cargo was washed up there. The news spread like wildfire, and every one on the station left work for "wrecking." At last the larger and heavier articles began to make their appearance, and hogshead after hogshead of port wine, gin, and brandy came rolling in one after the other, like so many porpoises. The dry goods were little cared for as soon as the barrels reached the shore; and as more than one barrel was tapped on the beach before it could be taken up, a scene of wild, lawless confusion ensued, such as I never witnessed before, and trust I never may witness again. We were all suddenly transformed into a brutal, selfish, greedy crew of wreckers—battles took place over more than one hogshead, and no one on that day could say, "I am better than my neighbour." I don't know how many hogsheads of liquor were secured, but I recollect that three fell to our share, which were carried upon bullock-drays in triumph to our tent, where they stood against the door for any one to taste who passed by. The brandy lasted the longest, and would have lasted much longer but that an old fellow, who had

had many a previous tasting-order, called at the tent one night when we were all in bed and requested a dram. I did not turn out, but told him where he could find a pannikin, and went to sleep. On going out the next morning, the old boy was lying on the ground insensibly drunk by the side of the barrel he had upset, and, as he had forgotten to put the spigot in, the liquor had all run out and fairly deluged him. I wonder he was not smothered. It reminded me of the lay brother in Tom Ingoldsby's admirable legend of the " Lay of St. Dunstan."

Any one who has spent a year in the bush about that time, can well fancy what a scene that station presented as long as the spirits lasted; and what impressed me most of all was, not a single Custom-house officer or policeman made his appearance during the whole time of the wreck. All work was at a standstill; the men's huts were filled with brandy, which was handed round in pannikins like water. There is no telling what valuables are yet to be found in that scrub, so many were the articles "planted," to be called for on a future occasion, and the hider entirely forgot where he had hidden them. One thing is quite clear, that if the cargo had been altogether a dry one more than one man would have made his fortune, for some thousand pounds' worth of things must have been washed ashore.

How long the wild revelry would have lasted it is quite impossible to say, had not a circumstance happened on about the sixth day which at last brought our lot to their senses, and checked, if it did not entirely quell, the riot, which had now reached its height. It was on the Thursday morning, and the wrecking was over. Only by chance was a stray article now washed up, and the beach was so fairly combed by roughs from Melbourne that we had almost given up looking out. The elder of the stockmen had been our constant companion during the wreck, and the busiest of the busy among the wreckers, but I had never seen George during the whole time. He was a very quiet man, and rather avoided than sought our company. However, on the Thursday morning they both rode up to the tent, and we all went down to the beach to pick up some nuts, which were scattered along the whole coast just like gravel. For some days we had not seen a hogshead come in, but on this morning it seemed to be fated that, just as we got down to the beach, the last cask of gin should come tumbling in. Three Melbourne roughs disputed possession, but our party was too strong for them, and we rolled it above high-water mark. If we had but known that death lay in that cask, we might not have been so eager to secure it. We had neither gimlet nor pannikin, so it was tapped with a knife; and as there was a beautiful spring of cold water close by, in a kind of grotto we used to call "the Smugglers' Cave," we filled a cabbage-tree hat, and mixing some gin therein, retired to the shelter of the cave to rest till the heat of the day was over. Most of us slept, and when I woke the sun was getting low. As it was my turn to cook for the week, I returned to the tent to get supper ready, leaving the rest of the party sleeping. I waited for a couple of hours, but as none came home I went to a neighbouring hut to see if they were there, and I shall not easily forget the scene that hut presented. A bucket of brandy, with a pannikin floating about in it, stood in the middle of the floor; and a rough fellow, the master of the ceremonies, lay on his bunk, yelling out, "Drink mates, drink! We don't get a wreck every week." The hut was filled with strange-looking fellows in every degree of intoxication—squabbling, quarrelling, swearing; and such was the din and uproar that we none of us heard a horse gallop up to the door, which suddenly opened, and Jack, with a face as pale as death, leant against the door-post. Every one seemed sobered by this sudden apparition, for all instinctively felt that something was wrong. It was some little time before he could speak, but at last he stammered out, "Is there a sober man among you?" It was curious to hear the different answers to this (as they all considered it then) insulting question, and every one seemed prepared to take his oath in the most solemn manner that he, at least, was perfectly sober. But I could hardly notice this, for my heart felt sick and faint, as I knew that something dreadful had occurred. " What is it, Jack ?" at last asked one of the soberest of the party, going up to him. " I've killed poor George !" was the answer, and he sank down upon a bench; the very picture of misery and despair. "Where's the body?" I directly asked. " On your bed in the tent," was the reply. We could make nothing more out of him; so jumping on his horse, which stood outside, I galloped back to the tent, about half-a-mile distant, to see what really had happened.

Had I needed proof that something dreadful had taken place, the melancholy looks of our poor old bulldog, who was chained at the entrance of the tent, would have furnished it. In general, when I came home, I had the greatest difficulty in getting into the tent, for the old fellow was so glad to see me, and always testified his joy by the most uncouth antics and caresses. Now, however, the case was different. He uttered no bark of welcome as I rode up, but sat half in and half out of the tent, every now and then looking in with a mournfulness of countenance that was almost reproachful. The poor dog had been neglected during the last week, and now his sad looks seemed to say, as plainly as words could speak, " Come in and see the end of it." My heart fairly misgave me, and I would have given worlds to turn back and avoid the ghastly object which I knew lay awaiting me in the tent. There was, however, nothing for it but to go in; and pushing by the old dog, who followed me as far as his chain would allow, I went up to the bed, and if I was prepared for a dreadful sight, that which then met my eyes was far more horrid than anything I had anticipated. The man was not dead, but lay on his back, his head in a pool of blood. His glassy eyes intently fixed on me as I entered, blood and froth bubbling up between the lips of his half-opened mouth, as with both hands he convulsively clutched the opossum rug which covered my bed. His forehead appeared to be literally split open, and at the first glance it seemed as if I could see right into his head. I raised him a little, and taking off my neck-cloth bound it on the crown and tied it under the chin, for it really appeared to me as if the top of his head would come off. He uttered not a sound, not even a groan; and were it not that his eyes and lips seemed to move a little, and the blood came from his mouth at regular intervals of respiration, I should have fancied him dead. I could do nothing alone, so galloped back to the hut, to send one of the party for the nearest doctor, and then returned to the tent to keep solitary watch over the dying man.

It was one of those lovely evenings so peculiar to the Australian spring: the sun was sinking fast, and his evening rays, as they shot into that solitary tent, fell full upon eyes which never would behold their light again. The air was laden with the perfume of the gum blossoms; flocks of little green paroquets were gaily chirping in every tree; the rosellas dashed by me in all their wild freedom, and the forest re-echoed to their glad screams of joy. All seemed happy on that sad evening, save man.

I found poor Jack stupified, still sitting on the bench where I had left him. We questioned him as to the cause of the accident: it was this. He and George had agreed to race home from the beach; they had almost reached the tent, when George's horse, swerving, carried him under a honeysuckle, a branch of which struck him on the forehead, and dashed him from his horse. He never spoke again. His comrade picked him up and laid him insensible on the bed. This was the whole of the sad story.

As I neared the tent on my return, the long dismal howl of the old bulldog struck mournfully on my ear. I loosed him from his chain—he crept into the tent and laid himself down by the side of the dying man's bed (they had always been friends), and he never ceased his watch till the corpse was carried out. Poor George was just as I had left him; he neither moved nor uttered a groan. His eyes were still wide open, and, though apparently fixed upon vacancy, seemed to follow me about the tent wherever I moved. This might have been fancy, but certainly he did not appear to be sensible. I dared not move him, for I thought perhaps that might hasten death. I poured some cold tea into his mouth, but he could not swallow it, and, save for a faint gurgling in his throat, I could hardly tell whether he was dead or alive. I sat down upon a box at the foot of the bed, and though I tried to keep my eyes off that ghastly countenance it was in vain—there seemed some strange fascination in those staring eyes and blood-stained cheeks. Never did time seem so long as when I sat by that death-bed waiting for the doctor; none of my mates came home, and I really thought that dreadful evening would never end. At length up galloped the doctor: a regular colonial one—"short, sharp, and decisive"— no time to waste in useless words. He gave one quick glance at the poor fellow, felt his pulse, pulled his head about a little, and then, turning to me, said in one rapid sentence, " My word, it's a bad job; I hope you chaps won't get into any mess about it. How did it happen? well, no matter. You see I can do no good here— can't find a new head for him. He'll die in a few hours, and, unless you wish him to die in your bunk, you'd better get him out of the tent as soon as possible;" and, springing on his horse, he galloped off as suddenly as he had come. He told me, however, before leaving, that the poor fellow would lie perfectly quiet till death was at hand, when he would struggle and want water, which would be a sure sign that he had not many minutes to live. These words were fulfilled to the letter: he died about two in the morning, never having uttered a word since the accident, and in his last moments appeared to suffer dreadful agony.

My mates came home late in the evening, so that I was not alone when he died; and next day we got a bullock-dray and carried the body into the wool-shed, where we laid it on trestles till a coffin could be made. Of course this sad event threw a damper over all, for poor George was a general favourite. The coffin was made that day, and as the wool-shed was full of rats and native cats, two of us sat up all night with the body. Next morning a cart was hired to convey it to Williamstown for burial, and about half-a-dozen of his friends followed on horseback, each with a crape band round his cabbage-tree hat. It was curious to hear the different remarks as the body was lifted into the cart. The sailors, of course, monopolized this job, and "That's you," " End on end," " Gently does it," "Cant him a little over," would have sounded strangely in the ears of a professional undertaker.

I did not go to the funeral, for I could not get a horse. Moreover, I wanted to put the tent a little to rights; and as soon as I had shut the paddock-gates after the mournful procession, I wended my way slowly back to the tent, accompanied by the two sailors. The first thing I did was to cut the blood-stained branch off the honeysuckle which caused his death; and I have it now, a memento of the sad event.

Death is a solemn subject at all times, and his presence is felt equally in the palace as in the cottage; but never more deeply than when he invades a small circle of men who are in a manner isolated from the rest of the world, and whose sole dependence is upon each other. The bushman has in general few friends, but these few are bound to him by far stronger ties than the word friendship generally conveys: and when one of the party is snatched away, his form is missed at every turn. In the bush, at the camp fire, in my wanderings over the lonely swamp, the dead man had often been my only companion, and his cheery laugh still seemed to ring in my ears; and where was he now? No; a man must seek the solitude of a bush tent to know the real meaning of the word "mate."

Night fell, and none of the funeral party had returned, and about eleven, tired of watching, I threw myself in my clothes down upon the bed which had so lately been occupied by a corpse. At daybreak a man from the hut, who was coming to fetch wood out of the paddock, called at the tent, and told me that a horse and dray were standing at the paddock fence. I went to fetch them home, and found three horses with empty saddles behind the dray. As soon as breakfast was ready, the first of the mourners appeared. He had lost his horse on the plains, and had come home on foot;

he could not tell where he had lost his mates; he knew that they left Williamstown together, and that is all he recollected. His description of the funeral was graphic in the extreme.

They reached the churchyard in good order, and had to wait nearly an hour for the clergyman; the man who officiated as clerk was in such a state of inebriation that he could scarcely read the responses, and the only spectators were a few diggers, who were walking off the previous night's excesses, and had wandered into the churchyard as they recognised a friend in one of the mourners. However, "ashes to ashes" closed the sad service, and poor George, hurried from a scene of boisterous excitement, was left quietly in that bleak-looking little churchyard, many thousand miles away from his native village. Little did his friends at home, who had waited so long "with the sickening anxiety of hope deferred," for tidings of the absentee, think that the autumnal sun of the 6th of November was shining on his new-made grave.

As soon as the funeral was over, his friends mounted their horses to return home. It was a sore trial to pass by "Old Jennings's" without just calling in for a "nobbler," and to talk over the dead man; but they had made up their minds for once to leave the town respectably. And so they would have done, if they had not been obliged to pass the house of the subtlest of all tempters, one Paddy Connor. This old fellow was a kind of cattle-dealer, a personal friend of the deceased, and was, as he said, "far too much affected at his death to be present at the funeral." This did not, however, prevent him watching for the funeral procession as it passed his house on the road home, and he stopped them, "just to inquire whether they had given poor George a dacent burial." The old man was not a bad sort, although a rough one; and as he stood upon his door-step, he proposed that the whole party "should shed one tear to the memory of the poor deceased." He had but one idea of mourning for a departed friend; and a bottle of rum was brought out. The tear having been shed, the old man solemnly observed, " Poor George! he was such a good sort, don't you think we ought to shed just one tear more?" A table was accordingly set out in the road (his was a lone house just on the edge of the plains), a gallon of rum was put on it, the horses were tied to the garden rails, and the whole party dismounted to mourn for the dead man after the old Irishman's peculiar fashion. How long the carouse lasted, I suppose no one can tell; but the horse—more sensible than the men—walked away with the dray across the plains, and not one of the mourners can tell how he followed it home.

Poor George! it was the cursed drink that killed him, and it even followed him to the grave. The clerk who assisted at the funeral service was far from sober, and not a mourner could ride home from the funeral. Sad that a country so blest by Providence in all other respects, should be tyrannized over by those two greatest of all human curses—the thirst after gold and drink.

And now let no reader think that this sketch is intended as a burlesque—the facts happened exactly as I have stated them; and this little story is intended only to show to quiet stay-at-homes the state of society in Australia in the earlier days of the diggings. It has probably now altered! George's death is no solitary instance, but it was the only one of the kind I ever witnessed; and although I dare say hundreds of men have seen far more distressing accidents, I can only say that this one left upon my mind an impression which can never be obliterated.

Very soon after the funeral I left this station and went down into the Western Port country kangarooing, where I remained for three years. When I left Australia in 1859, our ship lay off Williamstown, and one day I thought I would have a last look at the poor fellow's grave. I well knew where to find it; and there it lay just as it was left after the funeral, save that the little mound which marked his last resting-place was entirely overgrown with wild marsh-mallow—a sure sign that he had died amongst strangers. As I left it, I could not help thinking that there were probably some afar off who would have given much to see that rude grave but for a few minutes, as I had done; and as I closed the churchyard gate behind me, Haynes Bayly's beautiful lines came into my mind—

> "He should have died in his own loved land,
>   With friends and kindred near him,
> Not have withered thus, on a foreign strand,
>   With no thought save of Heaven to cheer him.
> But what recks it now? Is his sleep less sound,
>   In the port where the wild wave swept him,
> Than if home's green turf his grave had bound,
>   Or the friends he loved had wept him?"

THE AUSTRALIAN BUSH.

It was sensibly remarked by the editor of the *Scotsman*, when reviewing my little "Bush Wanderings," that every civilized society produces an annual percentage of men who care nothing for what they consider the "molly-coddle" comforts of civilization. Leaving their brothers to wear fine linen, broadcloth, and patent boots—to fare sumptuously every day, and sleep in curtained "four-posters," under the protection of policemen, these "born vagabonds" rush forth to hard fare and hard work, and risk of life and limb in the prairie or the backwoods, the bush or the diggings—"anywhere, anywhere out of the world" of prim respectability which chokes them. "Society" revenges herself for the contempt with which these rovers treat her, by calling them "ne'er-do-wells," "scapegraces," and other names expressive of slight esteem. It must be owned, however, that "though poor in pelf," as they for the most part continue, they are so rich in experiences that they make far more entertaining company than decorous stay-at-homes—when you can get hold of them bodily during one of their rare, brief visits to the world of newspapers or proprieties. How correct is all this!

Perhaps no country on the face of the globe sends forth so many of these "born vagabonds" as Great Britain. It is true that, as as far as the limits of civilization extend—in the settled districts of the world, if we may be allowed the term—we meet with adventurers of every European country, scattered here and there, engaged in the all-engrossing pursuit of money-making. Their quarry, however, is man: where the game is thickest, there, of course, is the best chance of securing their prey; and as long as we keep in such fellowship there is little difference between one country and another.

But if we seek the wild forest or the rugged fell, the wide prairie or the silent bush—far away from the human herds—we shall see the world as the Almighty has really planned it; and here we can revel in all the luxuriance of untamed nature, with no other companionship than the wild animals who roam in fancied security over feeding grounds rarely trodden by any human foot save that of men as wild and savage as themselves.

It is such scenes that have a peculiar charm for the hardy, adventurous Englishman; and, no matter how distant, or how inaccessible the land—no matter what hardships or dangers he must undergo before he can reach it—there we find him adapting his habits to those of the rude people among whom he has voluntarily exiled himself, and willingly relinquishing all that, in the opinion of many, alone makes life worth living for—purely to gratify a love of danger and adventure.

The Bush—what a magic is there in those two simple words to any one who has spent a few years in its wild solitudes! and what remembrances will they conjure up in his mind of that vast tract of wide-spreading, gloomy-foliaged forest, impenetrable scrub, sandy heath; swamps dotted with the yellow-blossomed swamp oak; lily-covered lagoons, creeks, water-holes, and chains of ponds bristling with rushes and fringed with tea-tree scrub; sun-baked plains, and deep, dank gullies, lighted up only by the yellow cones of the honey-suckle or the light feathery foliage of the magnificent fern-tree! Add to this the quaint beasts, the brilliant birds, ever-buzzing insects, and remarkable-looking reptiles which meet the eye at every step, the pure salubrity of its climate, and, above all, the careless contentment of a life passed in such a spot, where a man has no other care than to provide his daily bread from a larder so liberally spread out before him; and where the thousand petty vexations of civilized life, and the thousand wants which the artificial state of man has now rendered indispensable to his very existence, are never felt.

And yet I have heard some men stigmatize such a life as dull and monotonous.

The Australian Bush.

Dull, is it? when the fairest pages of the noblest book that ever was written, and written, too, by a hand that never yet erred—the great Book of Nature, which a man may study for his life and yet scarcely master a single chapter—is continually lying open before us!

Monotonous, is it? when every season brings some fresh pursuit, every day some fresh charm, and every hour its own particular occupation!

No! let the man who is sated with the enjoyments of fashionable life—which, indeed, we may with some justice call monotonous—or him who has been crushed and broken by the rude conflicts with the world—try such a life for a few years; and if he does not return again to the haunts of civilization, at the end of his probation, a wiser and a better man, all I can say is, there is no help for him.

And now let us see how the year is spent in the Australian bush; and any reader who follows me to the end of my chapter, if he only be a naturalist or a sportsman, will agree with me that a bush life is neither dull nor monotonous. But he must bear in mind that I am not about to describe the life of a squatter, who rules like a baron of old over a run miles in extent, coining money every year where he has no opportunity of spending, save when, with his cattle or his wool, he makes periodical visits down to Sydney or Melbourne from the up-country. Nor of the stock-rider, whose life is spent on horseback, galloping over the bush, looking up his master's cattle; whose sole talk is of bullocks, and whose only study is the different brands of the neighbouring station-masters, and the cultivating a kind of knowledge, which to him seems intuitive, that of singling out at a glance a stray bullock from the largest mob. Nor of the shepherd, who lazily follows his flock from sunrise to sunset in all weathers, and whose life is one calm tame monotony, each day so precisely like its predecessor, that it must be hard for him often to remember how the weeks steal on. Nor of the hut-keeper, the easiest worked, and, generally speaking, the most discontented man on the station. Nor of the bullock-driver—that most useful of all bush servants, the true pioneer into the heart of this wild country; who, undeterred by difficulties, wends his solitary way through ranges, traverses bogs, and crosses creeks with no other guide than his own unerring instinct; who looks upon his bullocks as his only friends and companions, and with whom he keeps up a continual running discourse as he walks by their side, to relieve the monotony of his tedious journey, in a jargon which, if it were not for the oaths with which it is interlarded, would be perfectly unintelligible to the stranger (but every word of which the great, gaunt, spectral animals that compose his team appear to understand as well as himself)—for of the Australian bullock-driver it may with justice be observed that in the use and abuse of expletives, in the number, variety, and intensity of his oaths and maledictions, from the most childish imprecations to the most daring and appalling blasphemy, "none but himself can be his parallel." I allude to none of these, but to him who—following

> The wish, which ages have not yet subdued,
> Of man to have no master save his mood—

pitches his tent in just such a spot as he fancies will suit his purpose, and gains his living (it may not, perhaps, always be an easy one, but it is always an independent one) solely by his gun—either shooting game for the nearest market, or collecting birds and animal skins for sale. I spent five such years myself, and truly happy years they were; and to any one who may feel inclined to follow my steps, the perusal of what I am now writing will, I trust, prove both useful and interesting.

And, by way of preface, I may add that, although the bush in which I camped is no longer bush, but probably the site of some flourishing township in embryo, and the little cockatoo settler—the greatest pest to the real bushman—has built his rude shanty on his small allotment in the heart of that forest, the bush still retains its primeval character if we wander further into the country; and although I believe a railway now runs up from Melbourne to the Murray, a distance of upwards of two hundred miles, this is nothing in a land like Australia. All we have to do is, instead of Melbourne, to take the terminus of the railway as our starting-point, and a few miles' journey from thence will bring us into a bush and scrub far wider, and offering far better attractions both to the naturalist and sportsman than the Melbourne district ever did in its best of days.

The proper number for a good bush party is three; but, strange to say, although two men can and do live together in perfect harmony and goodwill for years, we rarely see three stick together long in Australia. If, however, three good men in the same station of life—men who are, perhaps, neither labourers nor men of business, but who can handle a gun and do not mind roughing it so long as they are free—set out on a few years of such a life in real earnest, I am certain they would never regret it; and I do not know whether they would not make as much at it as many a man in town who, to all appearance, is holding a good and lucrative situation; for, although the profit may not be great, the expenses are small, and, if it were not for "the bursts" which are almost sure to occur when a bushman visits town with the hard earnings of perhaps a twelvemonth in his pocket, he might always save a little money.

Well, we will suppose the party—whether it consists of two or three—to be on their camping ground by the end of March, with a good tent properly pitched, and a good stock of ammunition. It will be always as well to camp within a mile or so of a station, for the blacks are always more civilized in such a district; and, moreover, for the convenience of buying a little flour, tobacco, tea, sugar, and salt (which are the only provisions really necessary in a bush tent, for meat the party must provide with their own guns), whenever they run short. Flour, &c., is, of course, considerably dearer in the bush, but it is better to take the chance of buying it up-country (and it is always to be obtained at some station or another) than bringing it up from town. The end of March is the best time to get settled, for the summer heat is over, the winter rains have not yet set in, and the roads are good. In the winter, the plains up the

country are many of them under water, and not to be traversed.
Moreover, the kangaroo are just now coming into season, and
will afford a good supply of meat for the tent during the winter,
even if the party are camped out of reach of a market where they
can sell them.

Kangaroo-shooting will occupy them till the end of September,
and if they are shooting for the market they will do nothing else,
except duck-shooting, during the winter months. If not shooting
for the market, one good shot with the rifle will be able to kill quite
as many as are required for home consumption; but if the party is
camped within reach of a market, the kangaroo must then be shot
by driving them up to the shooters stationed in a line across the
forest, or caught in snares. For either of these purposes a horse will
be required, both for driving or bringing the bodies home; and as
such a horse will always pick up his own living around the tent, he
will cost nothing more than the original outlay and a pair of hobbles.
An old crawler, good enough for this purpose, can be bought at
any station up-country for perhaps a five-pound note.

The most useful dog for all the bush game—quail, snipe, and
duck—will be a steady, close-hunting retriever. A good bull-terrier
to guard the tent and tree opossums, cats and squirrels, will also
drive the kangaroo. As dogs in the bush get their own living, by
opossums, which you shoot for them, and then throw on the camp
fire whole to warm through, the more you have about the tent the
better.

Next in relation to the bushman's mate stands his dog, and it
would be very difficult to say what is the most general breed of dogs
one meets with in the bush. Every bushman brings a dog or two
up with him of such breed as he fancies best; and as there is no
care bestowed in crossing them they breed indiscriminately, and it
would puzzle a good dog-fancier to distinguish one breed from another. But mongrels as they are, these bush-dogs are not to be despised; for, although self-taught, nature seems to supply the place
of education, and their natural instinct appears to be much more
highly developed than among the fuller-broken and truer-bred

dogs of the old country. No one knows what a true companion the dog is, and what a friend and servant he can become to man, except he who has passed some years in a bush tent with no other companion.

But if the reader is desirous of knowing more about the chase of the kangaroo and field sports of Australia than I have space for here, I will refer him to my little *Bush Wanderings*, which, although " I say it that shouldn't," contains a better and truer account of bush life and sporting in Victoria than any I have ever yet seen. The price is moderate, only 2s. 6d., and the publisher is Warne. I shall deem no apology necessary if I make a few quotations from that little volume in the course of this chapter.

While on the subject of kangaroo-hunting and books, I cannot help telling the reader perhaps the greatest sell I ever had in my life.

Just after I came home from Australia, I noticed an advertisement in the paper, of a little work entitled " The Kangaroo Hunters," by A. Bowman. "Bowman, Bowman!" I called to my mind all the old kangaroo-hunters I had previously known in Victoria—and I fancied I knew all in that district—but no such name as Bowman could I recollect. "However," thought I, " it may be on ' t'other side ;' anyhow I'll have 3s. worth ;" so the first large book shop I came to in London, I went in and purchased the coveted treasure. " You'll find it very useful to you if you're going out there, sir," was the comment of the prim shopkeeper, as he wrapped up my book. I, however, was not going out there ; I had already served my apprenticeship ; but I hailed the little book as an old friend, and longed to travel through its pages, and once again in imagination to hold sweet commune with old companions and familiar scenes. I recollect I turned in early that night in order thoroughly to enjoy the anticipated treat ; for if ever I have a difficult passage to master, or happen to get hold of a book of more than ordinary interest, I like to study it at my ease in my bed. My little book was neatly got up, with pretty illustrations ; but the very first picture which I turned to gave me a little bit of an " eye-opener," and raised my suspicions. It was

E E

that of a kangaroo being strangled by a boa-constrictor more than twice as long as itself. Now, as I certainly never myself saw a snake in Australia more than about six feet long, and never even heard, among all the marvels which are related round a camp fire, of one longer than ten feet—(this was a bullock-driver's measure); and as he had just before been telling us that once when crossing a plain on the Sydney side with his bullock-dray, he saw a patch of grass on one side of the road rustling as if it was alive with something, for at least *six* acres, and on going to the spot he found that it was a colony of snakes gathered together, disporting hither and thither in the long grass—(I wonder the lie did not choke him)—I hardly placed much reliance on his ten-foot snake;—and as I believe the only species of boa peculiar to Australia is a very diminutive fellow, I dipped further into the volume, and the next picture, entitled "A Fight with a Kangaroo,"—representing two striplings of lads, perhaps fourteen years old, the one actually engaged in wrestling with an old man kangaroo, a regular boomer, while the other was attacking him with a case-knife behind—settled the matter in my mind at once. Why, the strongest bushman that ever lived would have stood no chance whatever if the kangaroo once could *put the hug on him* in the manner he is doing to the lad in the picture. I was, I must confess, rather startled at this; and then I did what I ought to have done before I threw away my 3*s*.— turned to the title-page, and found that the book was written by " a lady!" who tells us in her preface that " in order to stimulate the spirit of inquiry in youth, she is encouraged to continue to supply the young with books which do not profess to be true, although they are composed of truths." My wig!—what a sell! Well, as I had bought my book, I thought I might as well read it through; and I found that the title of the book was as great a fiction as the book itself; for instead of enlightening us as to the chase of the kangaroo, it contains the fancied adventures of an emigrant family who were cast away somewhere or other on the Australian coast, and got bushed; and, after wandering pretty well all over the colony, encountering hardships which it was a real mercy they escaped, turned up, as all heroes of romance generally do, " all right at last."

I got through my book and fell asleep. I recollect I dreamt all night of kangaroo, and fancied I was engaged in a deadly struggle with an "old man," which all at once, like the stag of Saint Hubert, assumed a beautiful female form, and I suddenly woke with the last four lines of Peter Pindar's Razor-Seller on the tip of my tongue :

> 'Not think they'd shave!' quoth Hodge, with wondering eyes,
> And voice not much unlike an Indian yell,
> 'What were they made for then, you knave?' he cries.
> 'Made,' quoth the fellow with a smile, 'to sell!'

"And what did you do with the book?" perhaps it may be asked.

Why I cut it into little square pieces, and put it away. It might come in handy for—wrapping specimens in. But to return to my immediate subject.

If the party are shooting the kangaroo for sale, they will, perhaps, require about twenty-five per week, and these, sold at the tent, will average about 3*s*. each without the skins, which will be worth perhaps 1*l*. 1*s*. per dozen. So the weekly returns during the kangaroo season will be something like 5*l*. to be divided between the party, besides ducks. No man's rations in a bush-tent ought to cost more than 12*s*. per week, so, after expenses are paid, there ought always to remain a small margin for profit. Four days will be occupied in shooting the kangaroo, and they will have two days for rest, and to do all "odd chores" in ; or, if they are collecting bird skins, in shooting and skinning their specimens.

The kangaroo must always be skinned as soon as they are brought home, and hung up out of reach of the dogs, and they will then keep a long time.

The Sunday is always a day of rest in the bush tents, and any one who is so inclined can spend the Sabbath in the bush quite as devoutly as at home; and one thing I have remarked in my intercourse with the rough fellows that one often meets in the bush (even among the old hands, many of whom could not probably read a sentence, and who, it is needless to say, make no pretensions to good-breeding or gentility), that I never heard religion made a jest of; nor did I ever find, as is too often the case with the lower classes at home, especially if it should chance—which, although probably seldom happening in England, is of daily occurrence in the colony—that a gentleman is reduced to the level of the working man, that his better manners or birth are thrown in his teeth. I have, on the contrary, always found that a man (and there were, unfortunately, but few) who neither drank nor swore, and spent the Sunday in a proper manner, was always looked upon with respect by his rough bush associates, for they always seemed to have an idea that such a man could be trusted, and his advice and assistance relied on, in cases of difficulty and emergency.

It will be very odd if, wherever the party may be camped, they are not in the neighbourhood of some swamp or creek which swarms with duck, and the man who, like myself, prefers a night's flight-shooting to almost any other sport, will find this country one peculiarly adapted to his pursuit.

Of all field sports in the colony, I think I did like a good night's flight-shooting the best. There is a charm in this silent, solitary sport which I could never find in any other. When seated well in the shade, by the side of some favourite feeding-ground, with the moon just on the wane, all is still, save the occasional cry of some night-bird, as it rises from the neighbouring swamp, or the whistle of the wings of a pair of ducks, as they pass overhead, and the croaking of hundreds of small frogs in concert, the deep clock of the bull-frog joining, as it were, in bass accompaniment. The slight ripple of the clear water dances in the moon's silvery rays, when all at once "whish," a splash in the water, and a sharp " quack, quack, quack, quack," warns the shooter that a black duck has pitched, and the concert of frogs is hushed in an instant. This is soon joined by others, and having risen on the water three or four times to shake their feathers, and chased each other about for a few minutes, they settle down to feed. Now is a moment of breathless suspense to the shooter; the gun is quietly raised, but the birds at first are too far, or not well packed; however, at length he gets three or four in a line, and the heavy boom of the gun breaks the stillness of night, reverberating over the swamp with a hundred echoes. It may be that some scores of birds were feeding on the lagoon out of sight, which now rise like a clap of thunder, and the air is disturbed by the wings and the cries of the birds as they fly round the shooter's head. His quick ear can well distinguish the different birds by their varied call-notes—the soft, musical whoop of the black swan, the sharp, loud quack of the black duck, the hoarse croak of the mountain-duck, the snort of the shoveller, and the shrill call of the teal, are all familiar to him; and as he gathers up his dead birds, he hears the ducks pitching again in various parts of the lagoon, giving him promise of a goodly harvest by morning. When the dead birds are collected, the pipe is lit, the gun charged, and he quietly settles himself down in his rushy screen for another shot. The early part of the evening is best for this sport: the birds leave the feeding-grounds about midnight, often go out to sea, if the lagoon is on the coast, and return again a little before daybreak, when they often pack on the bank of the lagoon. So, in punt-shooting, the evening and the morning shots are those upon which the shooter principally depends. Where the birds are feeding well upon ground which has been but little disturbed, flight-shooting is the best and surest game of any with a shoulder-gun, and there is some little difference between flight-shooting out here and at home, where the shooter has to sit for hours, often in sleet and drizzling rain, his teeth chattering, and his fingers so cold that he can scarcely pull the trigger. Here a good pea-jacket will keep the shooter warm on the coldest night, and though I have occasionally used gloves, I never really wanted them. The best seasons for flight-shooting are the autumn and early winter. In the months of March and April, 1858, my old mate killed upwards of a hundred couple of birds, principally black duck, at night, with his own gun, in one small water-hole close to the coast. This is the only kind of shooting in the colony for which a man really requires water-boots. As the birds generally feed in shallow water, he fetches the dead ones out himself, and he may often have to sit for hours on a tussock of rushes, up to his knees in water. Cording's india-rubber water-proofs are the best I ever used for this work; they are warm, perfectly water-tight, never want dressing, and, what is best of all, never get hard, and are always easy to pull on and off. They are certainly too heavy for walking much in, but for flight-shooting, boat-fishing, or any other work where the wearer is not constantly in motion, I will back them against any boots in the world. The American gutta-percha overalls are not worth anything for work. At all other times except flight-shooting, the best dress for the Australian duck-shooter is canvas or flannel trousers and low half-boots. The climate is so fine here, that a man may wade in the swamps with impunity at all seasons of the year, and the best clothes the shooter can wear are those which dry the quickest.

I do not believe any country in the world is better fitted by nature as a home for waterfowl than Australia. Dreary swamps, miles in extent, lagoons of immense size, where the bulrush and reed vegetate in rank luxuriance, creeks and water-holes completely hidden from view by dense masses of the tea-tree plant, afford unmolested shelter and breeding-places for the birds; and there must be thousands of places up-country, in the solitude of whose morasses and fens a gun is never heard, which literally swarm with wildfowl. I shall say nothing here with regard to the practical part of the shooting: all I have the space for is to inform the reader what sport he can meet with, and if he has been a sportsman at home, the tackle and experience that he brings out from the old country will suffice for him in the new one.

Duck-shooting is perhaps the most profitable kind of shooting out here, if there is a market for the game; and even on any station or at any public-house up-country (but it is quite as well not to be camped too near the latter), a pair or two of black ducks can always be exchanged for provisions or sold outright. Of course times have now altered, but when I first came into this country the palmy days of the duck-shooting were in their zenith—the fowls and buyers plentiful, the shooters scarce. The year previous there was not a float or big gun in this part of the colony, and the first punt that ever floated on Melbourne swamps was built in Melbourne Street, where the market now stands, in the morning launched, in the afternoon fitted up with an old musket, and the birds shot and sold in Melbourne before night. In this winter 1000*l.* was cleared off that swamp alone by the two men who launched this punt. The duck season begins about February, when the old birds bring their young down to the creeks; and should end in August, when the swamps begin to dry up, and the birds pair off and retire to their breeding haunts. After they have bred they keep about the creeks and water-holes in small flocks or families, till the rains fill the large swamps, when they congregate and frequent the open places on the swamps and plains, where there is shallow water and good feeding-ground. There is little to be done by day in the winter with a shoulder gun out here in these large swamps; but a punt-gun is the thing at this time of year, if the shooter can handle it well. If, however, there is any feeding-ground near the tent, and this the shooter will soon find out, he will do better by flight-shooting in the evening when the birds come down to feed, than by anything else. I know eight species of Australian wild duck: the black duck is the commonest and most valuable duck for the market. The black swan is hardly worth shooting save for its skin.

Snipe swarm in certain districts, but, like the snipe at home, they are very local. The Australian snipe is nearly double as large as the British snipe. The snipe season begins with September, and although of course the flush comes down first, you may find them on most good grounds till December. In the early part of the season some rattling sport may be had on good ground. I have bagged thirteen and a half couple myself in the day, and although I have heard of some most extraordinary days' snipe-shooting, I never myself saw twenty couples of Australian snipe fall to one gun in the day.

In many unfrequented places, especially on the edges of the

smaller scrub up towards the Murray, the bronze-winged pigeons swarm in hundreds, I may say thousands. I suppose in different districts the pigeons appear at different seasons. Their breeding season is from October till the end of January, when the young birds will be strong flyers. At all other times they may be killed whenever they can be met with.

I take it that the quail, like the pigeons, appear in different districts at different seasons; but I fancy their breeding season is the same everywhere, and they should be spared from about the beginning of November till the middle of January. The quail is the Australian partridge, and quail-shooting is certainly the pleasantest of all field sports out here. It reminds the sportsman of September at home, for it is fair open work, and in quail-shooting a man can, if he pleases, have the pleasure of seeing his dogs work in the old style. Moreover, they are generally pretty thickly dispersed over the whole country, and in a few hours' shooting a tolerable shot can always make a nice little bag. I used to consider from fifteen to twenty couple a good day's bag. I once killed thirty-seven couple, and I rarely bagged more than fifteen out of twenty. Taking in misses and lost birds I recovered, every couple of birds cost me 3*d.* to kill, and they averaged 1*s.* per couple throughout the year.

I may mention that a code of game laws for the protection of the game in Victoria during the breeding season has been framed since my day, but as I have never yet seen it I am unable to say during which months the birds are preserved.

Besides the game birds above mentioned, these swamps swarm with bitterns, rails, blue coots, herons, cranes, and many other waders. The wild turkey is met with on all the large plains in the interior, and the emu in many places even within the civilized districts.

Although the list of game birds indigenous to the Australian bush may be meagre when compared with that of many other lands, still the different species are met with in such vast quantities that there is a wide field open for the sportsman who is content with the smaller game, and a good living to be obtained by an industrious man in any district a little distance from town, where there is a sale for the birds. Prices run tolerably high for all kinds of game in Melbourne, and although the days are gone by when we could sell a couple of black ducks for 12s. or 15s., a couple of snipe for a crown (which I have done), or a couple of pigeons for 3s. 6d., there is still a good living to be made by the gun if a man works hard and is camped in a tolerable district, especially if he can skin and preserve pretty parrots and other showy birds' skins for sale.

To the regular fur-hunter the Australian bush offers few attractions, the kangaroo, the wallabee, the native bear, the opossum, the dingo, the native cats and squirrels, being about all I know in the bush worth hunting. The duck-billed platypus is abundant in many of the creeks and water-holes up the country, and this skin is always worth preserving.

But the very security with which one can live in these forests, safe from the attacks of any wild animals, is one of the greatest charms of bush life in Australia. There is not a single wild animal to fear (although at times a half-wild ox is dangerous); and were it not for the snakes which abound in all parts, there is little or nothing to be afraid of while wandering in this wild country. Always have a couple of bullets ready patched, to slip into your gun in case one of these cattle looks dangerous. It won't burst the gun even if you ram the bullet down on to the charge of shot, for I have tried it. Be cool; and if you must shoot, don't fire till he lowers his head. Aim, if possible, at the curl of the hair on the forehead. In case you have to shoot a bullock, go directly to the station and report it, or you may get into trouble. You may have to pay for the bullock, but better this than lose your life. The blacks are sometimes troublesome, and I can't say I ever liked them as neighbours; but there is little to be feared from them in the settled districts, and little presents of tea, sugar, and tobacco will go a long way to gain their favour. I have heard the Murray blacks spoken of as excellent fellows.

Considering the abundance of venomous snakes one meets with in all parts of the bush, it is very rarely that one hears of a bushman being bitten, and a black fellow never. I never was bitten by a snake. If such a casualty had occurred I should have cut the place with my knife, bound up my limb tight about the bite, flashed off a charge of powder in the wound, and gone up to Melbourne as soon as I could. I fancy a snake here is always more anxious to avoid than to commence the attack; and unless you actually tread on one, or pick it up by mistake, there is little to fear. It appears that by constant practice the eye becomes so accustomed to range over the ground, that in most instances one sees the snake, let it be coiled up ever so snugly. The snakes here all retire to their winter quarters in March, and do not appear again till September. There is no danger to be apprehended either from snakes or black fellows at night, for at this time these latter gentlemen are afraid to leave their camp-fire.

Of the minor bush annoyances I may mention scorpions and centipedes, principally met with in dry, stony places, the bites of both which are dangerous, but never fatal; large spiders, or, as we used to call them, " triantulopes," as large as penny-pieces; bulldog ants an inch long, and thousands of blowflies, musquitoes, and little sand-flies—the latter, so small as scarcely to be perceptible to the naked eye, are constantly invading the tent. But these annoyances need deter no one from taking the bush.

The list of fresh-water fish peculiar to these waters is very meagre, and I fancy the eel is about the most useful one to the bushman. Any one who is going to camp out should be provided with an eel-spear, hooks and twine of different sizes, and a long fine trammel or two, for most of these water-holes and creeks abound in fish of some kind or another, which at times may prove a very useful and agreeable addition to the bushman's larder. If, however, these waters did afford first-rate sport, and even when they have succeeded in acclimatizing our salmon (I hope my head will never ache till I see a salmon caught in the Yarra), I do not think angling is ever likely to become a favourite amusement with the present race of

Victorians. Unless he can make good wages at it, neither the regular colonial shooter nor fisherman deems the sport worth following, and angling in this country hardly affords excitement enough for the amateur sportsman. Of all field sports angling is without doubt the least mercenary, and peculiarly the sport of youth and declining years and a happy and contented mind. As long as the gold fever rages out here, there is not likely to be much quiet or content among the people. No one in this country, as long as he can earn a shilling, is considered old enough to knock off work; and as for the young " currency lads," they are far more precocious than the youth at home, and cracking a stock-whip is far more to their taste than throwing a fly.

If a shooting party attend to their business, and especially if they are collecting as well, there need scarcely be an idle day throughout the year in the bush-tent. Of course the shooter will never, if he can help it, shoot any animal whilst the young are dependent on the mother for food, and during the breeding season all should be spared. I never could find out, nor, I believe, does any one rightly know, when the Australian snipe breed, but I fancy very early. I think, however, that all game birds may be shot with impunity in every month save November, December, and January.

All the parrots, and, in fact, all the bush birds, are in the handsomest and best plumage in the winter and spring, and, I take it, must breed between September and February. No one but he who has spent a season in the Australian forest can picture to his mind the gorgeous plumage of some of the parrots and other bush birds, nor the immense flocks which visit particular districts at particular seasons; and did my space allow it, I could go deeper into this subject. But I will only add that, as in Europe, each district of this wide-stretched land has its peculiar avifauna; and in whatever part of the bush he is camped, the collector should make a general collection of every species of bird which frequents that district—bearing in mind that the most gaudy-coloured birds are the most saleable, but also that a very sombre-plumaged bird may often be very rare and valuable. Through the indefatigable exertions of

Mr. Gould, the ornithology of Australia is now pretty well known. I believe in 1848 he had figured and described above six hundred species as indigenous to the land, and doubtless, since then he has added many more to the list.

As a guide to a party of three men about to spend a year in the bush, I will just give an idea of what rations they will require. I will suppose they buy them in Melbourne to take up, and then the expense of carriage up will be probably less than the profits the country-storekeeper will demand. However, stores, as I have said, are to be obtained in most places within the settled districts, either on stations or of the country storekeepers—of course, at bush prices.

The monthly allowance for every man—and it will be easy to calculate the price and weight for a year's rations in the bush—of real necessaries, will be about 40lb. of flour (more than sufficient), 8lb. sugar (brown), salt and pepper *ad libitum*, 1lb. tea, 1lb. tobacco. As the party will live on the game they shoot, I allow no meat; a side or two of American bacon will be very useful for frying the dry kangaroo venison in. A few pounds of stearine candles (a photogen lamp is better) and matches must not be forgotten; and a tinder-box should always be kept in the tent.

Galton's "Art of Travel" will be the most useful book that a man can study who is going into the bush. A man who works hard will not have much time for reading, but it is wonderful what a treat a few books of light reading will be found for a rainy day or a leisure hour.

Of course the tent must be taken up. Let it be a good one, and not a round one, and it will probably stand about two years. An extra sheet of canvas or fly, to cover the whole top, placed at a distance of six inches above it, will render it perfectly watertight.

The less stores that are laid in at one time the better, always providing the party is camped where tea, sugar, flour, and tobacco are to be bought. As we rarely see a petticoat in a bush-tent, thrift is not the order of the day. The bushman is generally an extravagant housekeeper; and by far the best plan is never to have more than a month's provisions in the tent at a time.

Be careful, in pitching the tent, to choose a spot where by no possibility a branch from a gum-tree can fall on it. Huge branches from these trees are continually splitting off and falling in a most unaccountable manner, without a moment's notice. Pitch the tent on a slight rise, if possible, among heather, which, however, burn clear away, leaving a wide, open space all round the tent. If you see the slightest appearance of a rush growing, however small, be sure that spot will be flooded in the winter. The heavy rains are generally in May, June, and July. It rains principally at night, and if the tent is properly pitched and trenched, and has a good fly over it, the inmates will suffer no inconvenience.

The camp-fire can, if it be wished, be kept up day and night by banking up; and for a tent-stove, which will be often very comfortable in the winter, nothing answers better than an empty paint can of block-tin, with holes punched in it, filled with charcoal from the camp-fire.

Never sleep on the ground, but build up a bunk with forked sticks and cross-poles, over which sacking can be secured, so that you lie at least six inches from the ground. Recollect that in the bush, as well as on the diggings, a good night's rest is worth a meal of meat.

The bush outfit must include a good axe or two, a spoke-shave and gimlets, a spade, cross-cut saw, hammer and nails; a long-handled frying-pan, a tin bucket, and a dark-lantern; a camp-oven, and a couple of pots for boiling water. Every man must provide his own clothes, bedding, knives, plates, and pannikins, and see after them himself in the bush.

One of the party will be cook for the week, turn and turn about. He will also have to keep the tent neat, and always bear in mind this golden motto—"a place for everything, and everything in its place."

Recollect one thing, that a party who are neat in their tent, will live twice as comfortable, quite as cheap, and have far less trouble than a slovenly party.

It will save a deal of trouble if, instead of flour, the party took up a few hundredweight of good sea-biscuits. I should fancy less than a pound a day of good biscuit would suffice for any man.

As to ammunition, we may reckon that, with care (and the greatest care must be bestowed upon this all-important item), 1lb. of powder will furnish about eighty shots, and 1lb. of shot, sixteen; so the party may easily calculate how much they must take up. Be very careful, and buy the powder fresh; and the strongest and best will be the cheapest, for you lose so many wounded birds with bad powder.

Many other little items may be added which will conduce much to the comfort of the party; but I have, I think, omitted nothing that is really necessary. A revolver may prove useful, and will take up but little room, and a long spare single gun, to carry 4 oz., will be very serviceable in duck-shooting.

It would be quite as well, at starting, if the party made an irrefragable law that a bottle of spirits should never enter the tent, and of course every man finds his own "baccy" and soap.

A man going into the bush, no matter in what country, will do well to provide himself before starting with a tin canteen, such as our rifle volunteers have to carry their sandwiches and sherry in, only have it large enough to hold a quart of water at least. This he will fill with cold tea every morning before he leaves his tent, and the sandwich end will contain a small tin box of the best wax lucifer matches, a small compass, a knife, six spare bullets ready patched, two four-ounce steel charges filled with powder, ditto with large shot, a needle and strong thread, some spare caps, a couple of strong leather boot-laces, a cake of cavendish tobacco, and a little salt. Before leaving the tent in the morning, let him be sure that not one of these articles is forgotten, for he never knows how far he may wander or how soon he may lose himself in the bush; and this little canteen, which he can sling round his back without inconvenience, may save his life. It will be quite impossible that he can starve, even if he is bushed for a month, for I presume he will never leave his tent without his gun and his regular ammunition; and as it is very rarely that he can wander for thirty-six hours in any part of the bush without falling in with a creek or water-hole of some kind, and a quart of water, with care, will last a man a day, there is little fear, if he always has his canteen to fall back upon, of his suffering inconvenience from the most bitter of all pangs, that of thirst. This canteen is never to be resorted to except in cases of real emergency, for it contains what may keep a man alive for many days in case his ordinary ammunition has run out. I may here remark that water is often scarce in the bush, and the Australian creeks and water-holes are often so hidden in the scrub, that a man may easily pass by one. If, however, he sees a little patch of tea-tree scrub standing alone on a wide plain, he may be sure there is a water-hole in it; or a cattle-track through the scrub will almost always lead to water; and the cheery "ching-ching" of the little bell-bird, which may be heard at an immense distance in the pure clear air of this country, cries "water water," as plain as the bird's language can speak.

To sum up all, there is little danger or trouble attendant upon a bush life in Australia; and, with a couple of good mates, I know no life in the colony which I would prefer to it.

With a good mate, as long as his health stands, I do consider the shooter's life one of the happiest and most independent in the colony. A good waterproof tent, properly put up, with a fly on the roof and a turf chimney, is by no means a bad residence, and quite as as warm and comfortable as half the weather-boarded houses that are knocked up here. The shooter is generally camped amongst the most beautiful scenery, close to a good water-hole or creek, with plenty of wood at hand. He has few artificial wants, and the real necessaries of life are easily and cheaply obtained. His meat, of course, he procures by his own gun; and a bag of flour, a little tea sugar, salt, and tobacco, fill his larder. His cooking is simple, his furniture home-made, his time is fully occupied, and not an hour hangs heavily on his hands. His method of life is laid down by no

rule. He eats when he is hungry, sleeps when he is tired, and
works just when it pleases him. The laughing jackass calls him up
in the morning, and the flute-like note of the magpie is his vesper
bell. Content and health go hand in hand, and although he may
have a small share in the world's troubles—and what class is entirely
exempt from them ?—he has also the inward satisfaction of feeling
that he is leading a happy, healthy, and independent life, and has
no one to thank but himself for his daily bread.

I have lived at times quite by myself in the bush, and then, perhaps, it was a lonely, laborious life. Often have I toiled from sunrise to sunset, come home dead-beat to my lonely tent, and after
ten hours' fasting had to light my fire and cook my solitary
supper; and often have I turned in fairly "baked," and put my
supper off till morning. But with a good mate the case is
different. It is true I have spent many a rough day in the forest,
and many a night, when lost, have lit my pipe and thrown myself
down to sleep before a log fire—no companions but my dogs,
no covering save the sky, and no supper but an opossum or
bandicote thrown upon the ashes to roast. But I can also truly
say that some of the happiest hours in a life which certainly has
had its bright as well as its gloomy passages, have been passed in
my bush tent; when, after a good day's sport, supper finished, and
pipe lit, I have thrown myself upon my opossum-rug, and, the toils
of the day fairly over, have spent the hour just before turning-in
yarning with my old mate over "the past, the present, and the
future." At such a moment I would hardly exchange the rough
freedom of the shooter's life for the best situation in the colony.

Nowhere do we meet with more real friendship and true kindness of heart than in the bush. Rough in aspect, careless in dress,
off-hand in his manners, there is a vein of simple and warm-hearted
kindness running through the character of the real bushman which
we rarely, if ever, find among men whose better feelings have become insensibly deadened by a continual intercourse with the
world. Isolated, as it were, from his fellow-men, solely dependent
upon his own exertions for his daily bread, he feels himself under

no obligation to any one, cares little to form new acquaintances, and always appears shy and reserved before strangers, especially "new chums." But let him fall in with an old mate, or man of his own stamp, and the meeting is often of a boisterous character. No one more readily sympathizes with the reverses of a mate, and so little selfishness is there in his nature that he willingly shares his all with him, whether it be his last shilling or his last "fig" of tobacco. His rude hospitality is proverbial, and the benighted traveller always finds shelter and food at the bushman's tent as a matter of course; and, unlike the way of the world in general, the more "hard up" the stranger is, the more he is welcome. This is all done too without the slightest ostentation, as a duty he owes to his fellow-man, and upon the principle that any day or night he may require the same assistance himself. I am here only alluding to what I call the true bushmen, men who knock about the bush on their own resources, living by shooting, wood-splitting, &c.; and not to the regular settlers on stations, who—valuing a man as they do a working bullock, for just the work they can get out of him—will scarcely condescend to notice (other than as a parish beadle does a vagrant in the old country) a vagabond shooter who camps upon his run; although, for my part, I can say that there were but few stations which I called at where I was not welcome to such accommodation as the man's hut afforded—and this I believe they cannot deny you, but by law every settler at a certain distance from a public-house is obliged to furnish a supper and a night's lodging to any wayfarer who calls after sunset.

It is now some years since I left "my home a vagabond to be," and, during that period, have wandered over many lands, my gun and my fishing-rod my only companions, a free citizen of the world.

In the prime of years, in the full flush of youth and strength, such a life offers charms of wild independence, which can never be realized by that man who is of necessity tied to one spot, no matter with what comforts he may be surrounded, or what sports he may enjoy, ready-made to hand. But as years creep on, and one begins to feel that the "old gentleman with the scythe" is pressing hard upon his heels, his enthusiasm will in a measure abate, and the more he has buffeted with the rude waves of the world, the greater will be his desire to cast anchor in some quiet haven, which he may regard as a permanent home in declining years. For how truly has Sam Slick described the dark side of the wanderer's life in the following words:—" Here to-day, gone to-morrow, to know folks but to forget them, to love folks but to part with them—to come without pleasure, to go without pain—and at last—for a last will come to every story —still no home." Never, perhaps, was the history of a life written in so short a sentence.

THE END.

www.ingramcontent.com/pod-product-compliance
Lightning Source LLC
Chambersburg PA
CBHW022135300426
44115CB00006B/188